LIVING BONE

THE OTHER DAY I GOT AN X-RAY
AND SAW MY OWN BONES. IT WAS
A PRETTY SHOCKING IMAGE TO
ME. AM I ALWAYS TALKING ABOUT
BONES HERE BECAUSE OF ALL
THOSE SHINIGAMI I'M DRAWING?
- TAKESHI OBATA

Tsugumi Ohba
Born in Tokyo.
Hobby: Collecting teacups.
Day and night, develops manga plots
while holding knees on a chair.

Takeshi Obata was born in 1969 in Niigata, Japan, and
is the artist of the wildly popular SHONEN JUMP title
Hikaru no Go, which won the 2003 Tezuka Shinsei
"New Hope" award and the Shogakukan Manga award.
Obata is also the artist of **Arabian Majin Bokentan
Lamp Lamp**, **Ayatsuri Sakon**, and **Cyborg Jichan G.**

DEATH NOTE VOL 6
SHONEN JUMP ADVANCED Manga Edition

STORY BY TSUGUMI OHBA
ART BY TAKESHI OBATA

Translation & Adaptation/Alexis Kirsch
Touch-up Art & Lettering/Gia Cam Luc
Design/Sean Lee
Editor/Pancha Diaz

Printed in the U.S.A.

Published by VIZ Media, LLC
P.O. Box 77010
San Francisco, CA 94107

13
First printing, July 2006
Thirteenth printing, January 2012

RATED T+ FOR OLDER TEEN

PARENTAL ADVISORY
DEATH NOTE is rated T+ for Older Teen and is recommended for ages 16 and up. It contains fantasy violence.

ratings.viz.com

www.viz.com

THE WORLD'S MOST CUTTING-EDGE MANGA
SHONEN JUMP ADVANCED
www.shonenjump.com

SHONEN JUMP ADVANCED MANGA

DEATH NOTE

デスノート

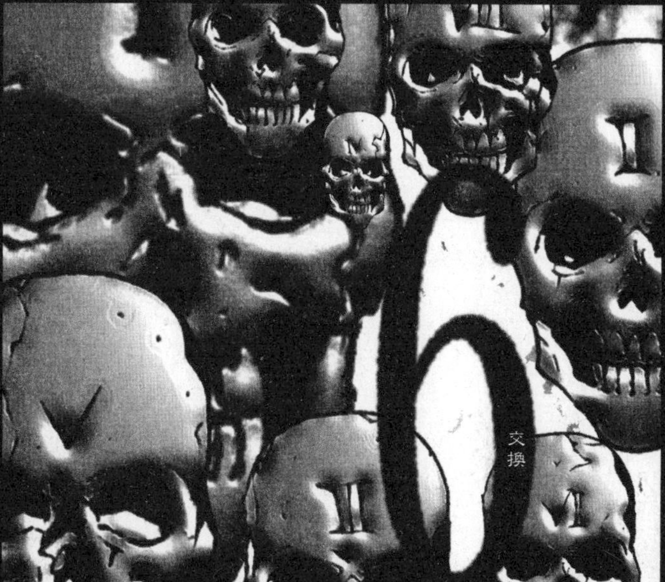
6
交換

Vol. 6
Give-and-Take

Story by Tsugumi Ohba
Art by Takeshi Obata

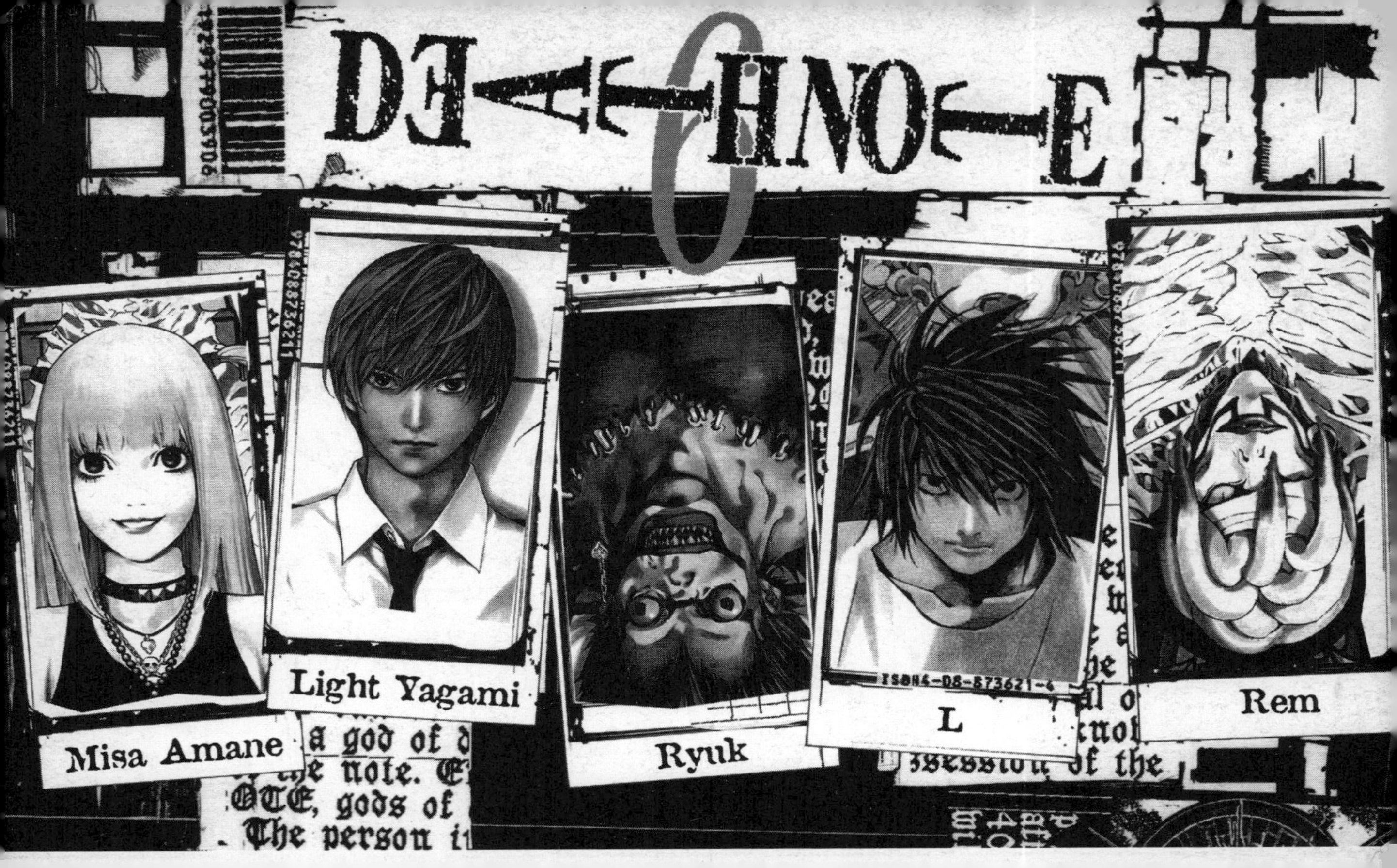
DEATH NOTE
6
Misa Amane
Light Yagami
Ryuk
L
Rem

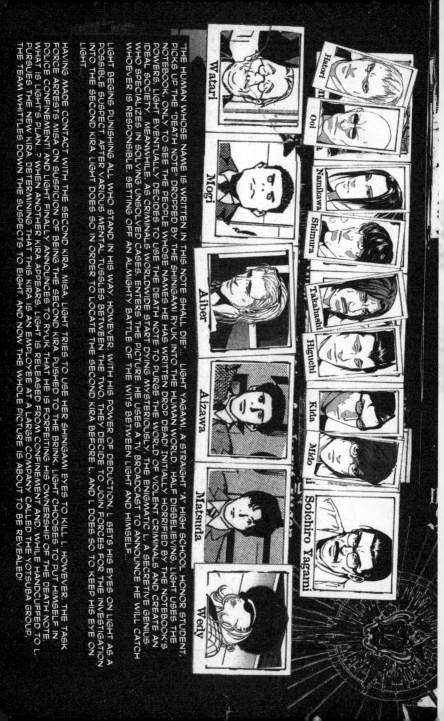

Hatori

Ooi

Watari

Namikawa

Shimura

Mogi

Takahashi

Higuchi

Aiber

Kida

Mido

Aizawa

Soichiro Yagami

Matsuda

Wedy

"THE HUMAN WHOSE NAME IS WRITTEN IN THIS NOTE SHALL DIE"... LIGHT YAGAMI, A STRAIGHT "A" HIGH SCHOOL HONOR STUDENT, PICKS UP THE 'DEATH NOTE' DROPPED BY THE SHINIGAMI RYUK INTO THE HUMAN WORLD. HALF DISBELIEVING, LIGHT USES THE NOTEBOOK, ONLY TO SEE THE PEOPLE WHOSE NAMES HE HAS WRITTEN DROP DEAD! INITIALLY HORRIFIED BY THE NOTEBOOK'S POWERS, LIGHT EVENTUALLY DECIDES TO USE THE DEATH NOTE TO PURGE THE WORLD OF VIOLENT CRIMINALS AND CREATE AN IDEAL SOCIETY. MEANWHILE, AS CRIMINALS WORLDWIDE START DYING MYSTERIOUSLY, THE ENIGMATIC L, A SECRETIVE GENIUS WHO SPECIALIZES IN SOLVING UNSOLVED CASES, ENTERS THE PICTURE. HE USES A TV BROADCAST TO ANNOUNCE HE WILL CATCH WHOEVER IS RESPONSIBLE, SETTING OFF AN ALMIGHTY BATTLE OF THE WITS BETWEEN LIGHT AND HIMSELF...

LIGHT BEGINS PUNISHING ALL WHO STAND IN HIS WAY. HOWEVER, WITH HIS POWER OF DEDUCTION, L SETS HIS EYES ON LIGHT AS A POSSIBLE SUSPECT. AFTER VARIOUS MENTAL TUSSLES BETWEEN THE TWO, THEY DECIDE TO JOIN FORCES FOR THE INVESTIGATION INTO THE SECOND KIRA. LIGHT DOES SO IN ORDER TO LOCATE THE SECOND KIRA BEFORE L, AND L DOES SO TO KEEP HIS EYE ON LIGHT...

HAVING MADE CONTACT WITH THE SECOND KIRA, MISA, LIGHT TRIES TO USE HER SHINIGAMI EYES TO KILL L. HOWEVER, THE TASK FORCE ARRESTS MISA ON SUSPICION OF BEING THE SECOND KIRA. PUSHED TO THE BRINK, LIGHT CHOOSES TO PUT HIMSELF IN POLICE CONFINEMENT! AND LIGHT FINALLY ANNOUNCES TO RYUK THAT HE IS FORFEITING HIS OWNERSHIP OF THE DEATH NOTE. WHAT IS LIGHT'S PLAN...? WHEN ANOTHER KIRA APPEARS, LIGHT IS RELEASED FROM CONFINEMENT AND, WHILE HANDCUFFED TO L, PURSUES THE NEW KIRA. DETERMINING THAT THIS KIRA IS AN EMPLOYEE AT A LARGE COMPANY CALLED THE YOTSUBA GROUP, THE TEAM WHITTLES DOWN THE SUSPECTS TO EIGHT. AND NOW THE WHOLE PICTURE IS ABOUT TO BE REVEALED!

DEATH NOTE
Vol. 6

CONTENTS

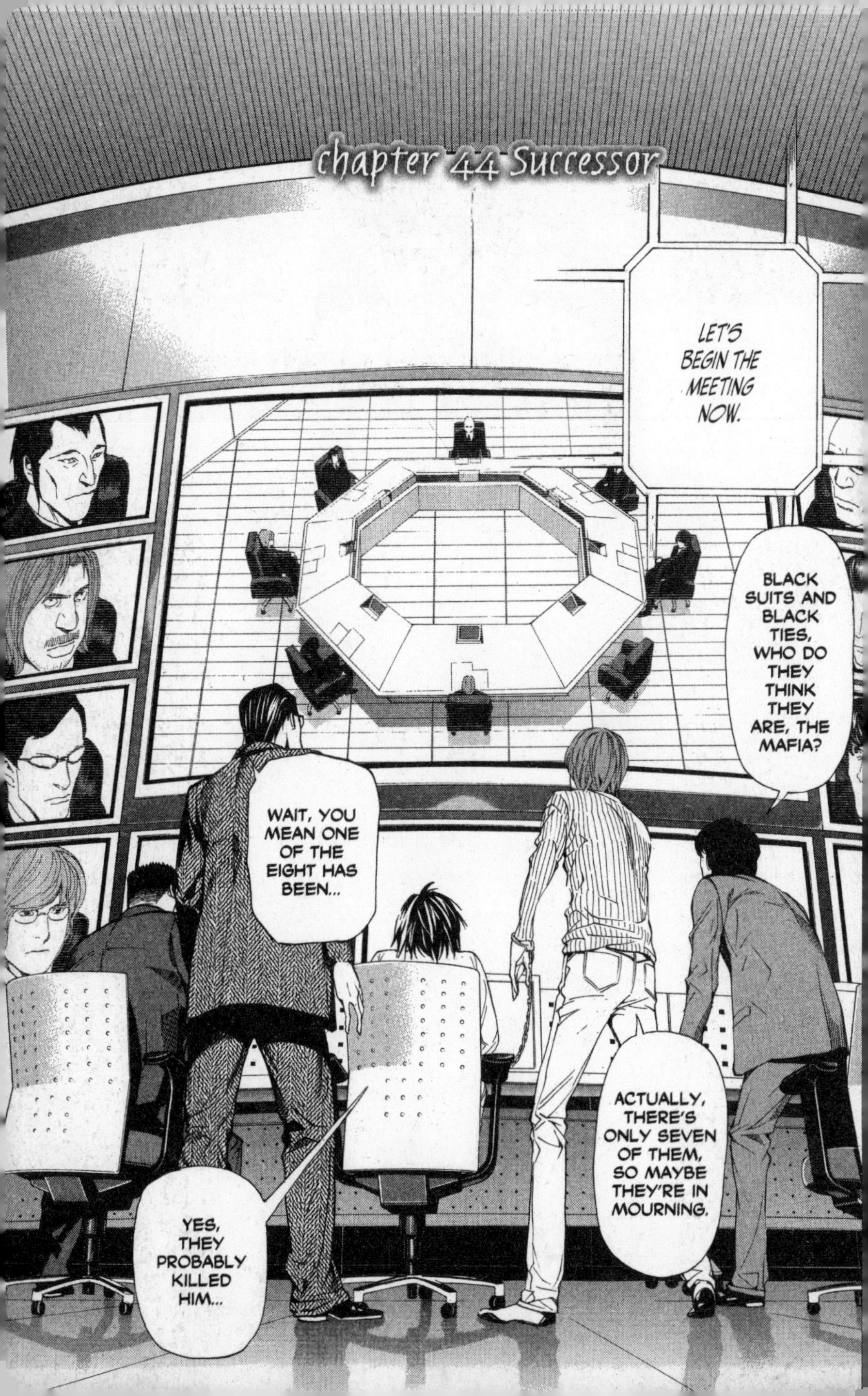
chapter 44 Successor
LET'S BEGIN THE MEETING NOW.
BLACK SUITS AND BLACK TIES, WHO DO THEY THINK THEY ARE, THE MAFIA?
ACTUALLY, THERE'S ONLY SEVEN OF THEM, SO MAYBE THEY'RE IN MOURNING.
WAIT, YOU MEAN ONE OF THE EIGHT HAS BEEN...
YES, THEY PROBABLY KILLED HIM...

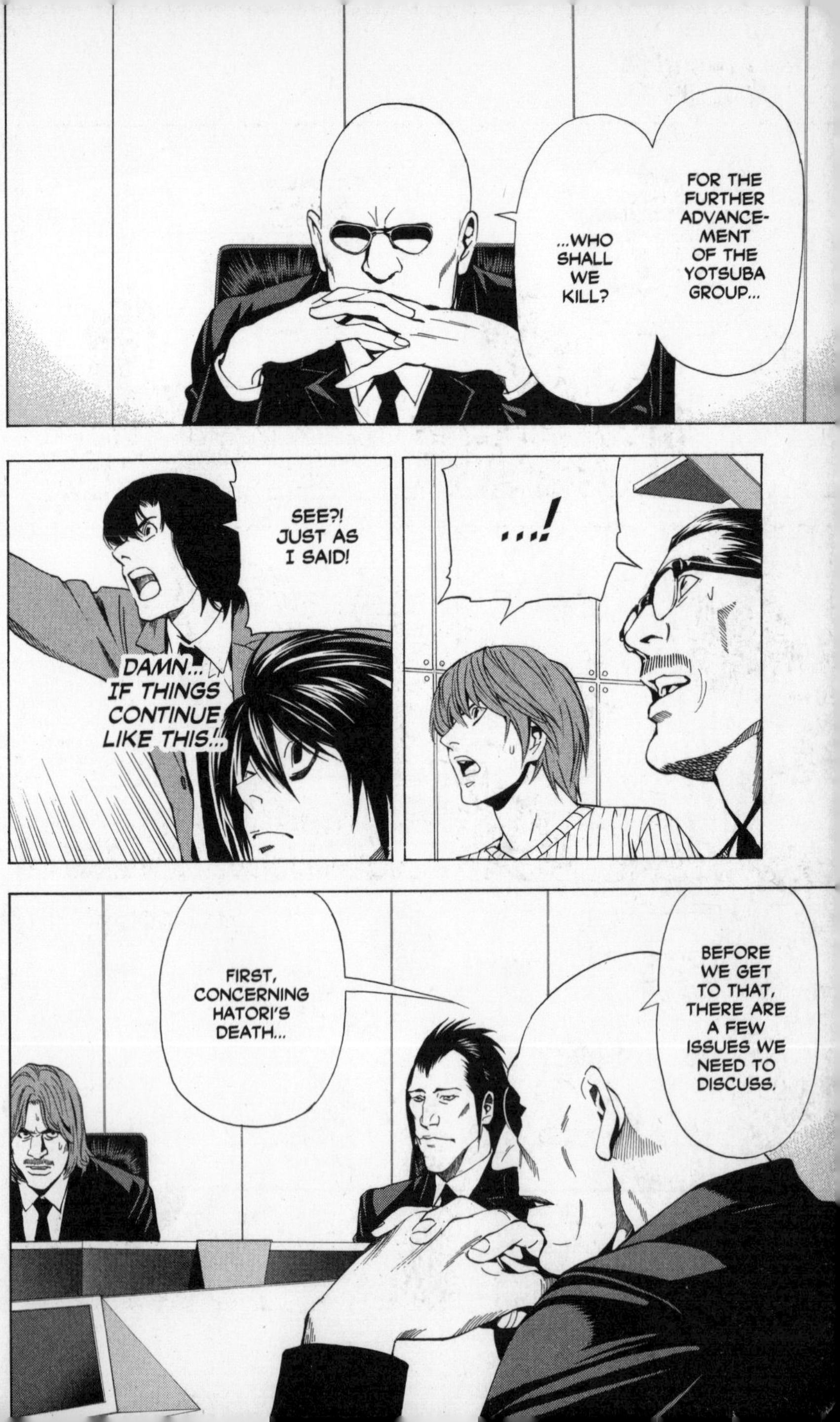
FOR THE FURTHER ADVANCEMENT OF THE YOTSUBA GROUP...
...WHO SHALL WE KILL?
...!
SEE?! JUST AS I SAID!
DAMN... IF THINGS CONTINUE LIKE THIS...
BEFORE WE GET TO THAT, THERE ARE A FEW ISSUES WE NEED TO DISCUSS.
FIRST, CONCERNING HATORI'S DEATH...

READ THIS WAY

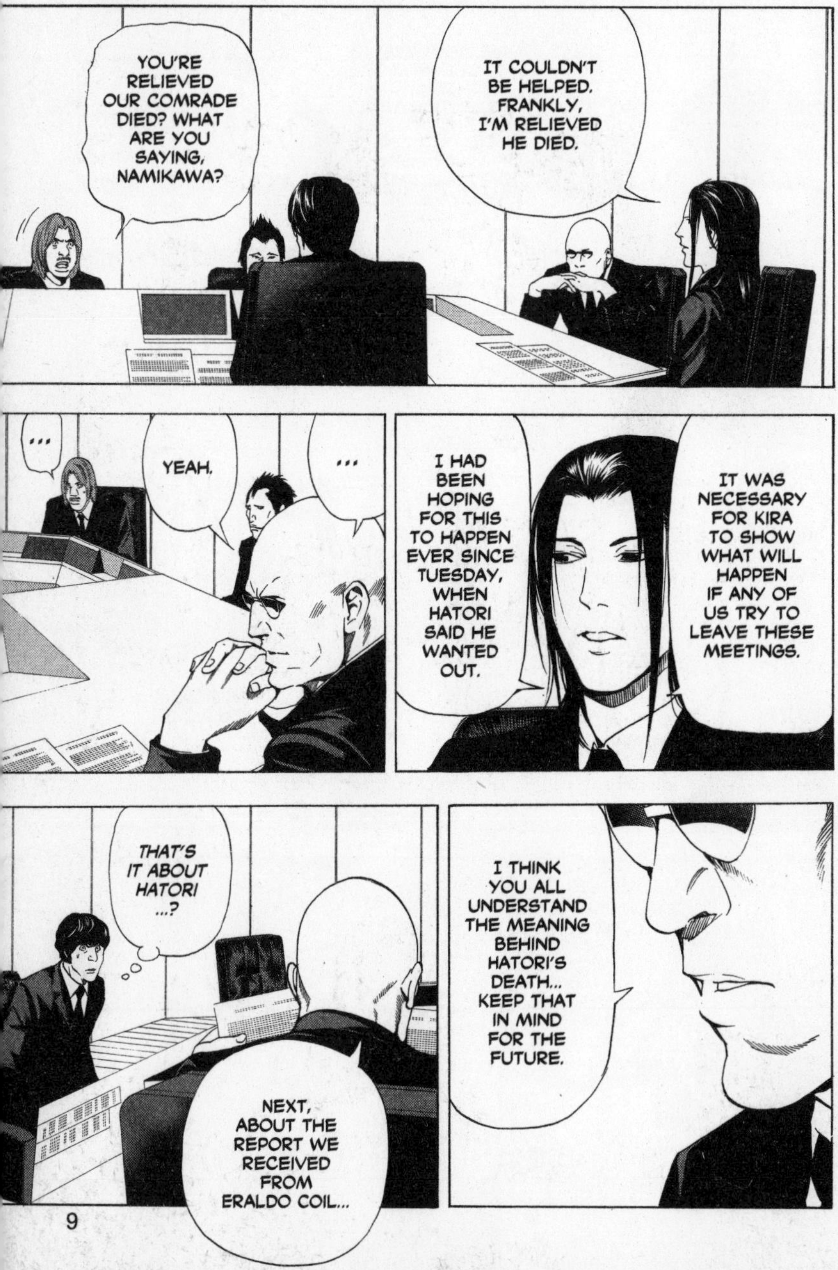
IT COULDN'T BE HELPED. FRANKLY, I'M RELIEVED HE DIED.
YOU'RE RELIEVED OUR COMRADE DIED? WHAT ARE YOU SAYING, NAMIKAWA?
IT WAS NECESSARY FOR KIRA TO SHOW WHAT WILL HAPPEN IF ANY OF US TRY TO LEAVE THESE MEETINGS.
I HAD BEEN HOPING FOR THIS TO HAPPEN EVER SINCE TUESDAY, WHEN HATORI SAID HE WANTED OUT.
...
YEAH.
...
I THINK YOU ALL UNDERSTAND THE MEANING BEHIND HATORI'S DEATH... KEEP THAT IN MIND FOR THE FUTURE.
THAT'S IT ABOUT HATORI ...?
NEXT, ABOUT THE REPORT WE RECEIVED FROM ERALDO COIL...

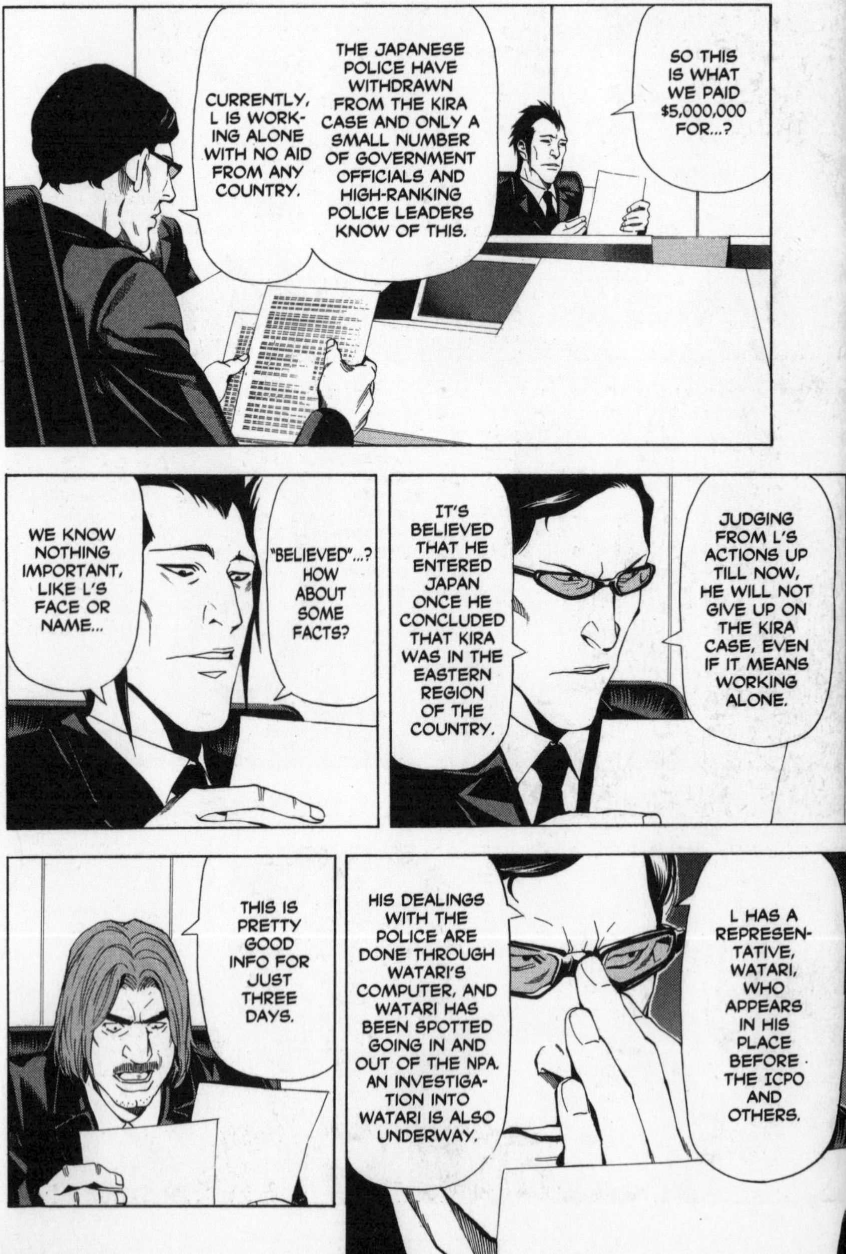
SO THIS IS WHAT WE PAID $5,000,000 FOR...?
THE JAPANESE POLICE HAVE WITHDRAWN FROM THE KIRA CASE AND ONLY A SMALL NUMBER OF GOVERNMENT OFFICIALS AND HIGH-RANKING POLICE LEADERS KNOW OF THIS.
CURRENTLY, L IS WORKING ALONE WITH NO AID FROM ANY COUNTRY.
JUDGING FROM L'S ACTIONS UP TILL NOW, HE WILL NOT GIVE UP ON THE KIRA CASE, EVEN IF IT MEANS WORKING ALONE.
IT'S BELIEVED THAT HE ENTERED JAPAN ONCE HE CONCLUDED THAT KIRA WAS IN THE EASTERN REGION OF THE COUNTRY.
"BELIEVED"...? HOW ABOUT SOME FACTS?
WE KNOW NOTHING IMPORTANT, LIKE L'S FACE OR NAME...
L HAS A REPRESENTATIVE, WATARI, WHO APPEARS IN HIS PLACE BEFORE THE ICPO AND OTHERS.
HIS DEALINGS WITH THE POLICE ARE DONE THROUGH WATARI'S COMPUTER, AND WATARI HAS BEEN SPOTTED GOING IN AND OUT OF THE NPA. AN INVESTIGATION INTO WATARI IS ALSO UNDERWAY.
THIS IS PRETTY GOOD INFO FOR JUST THREE DAYS.

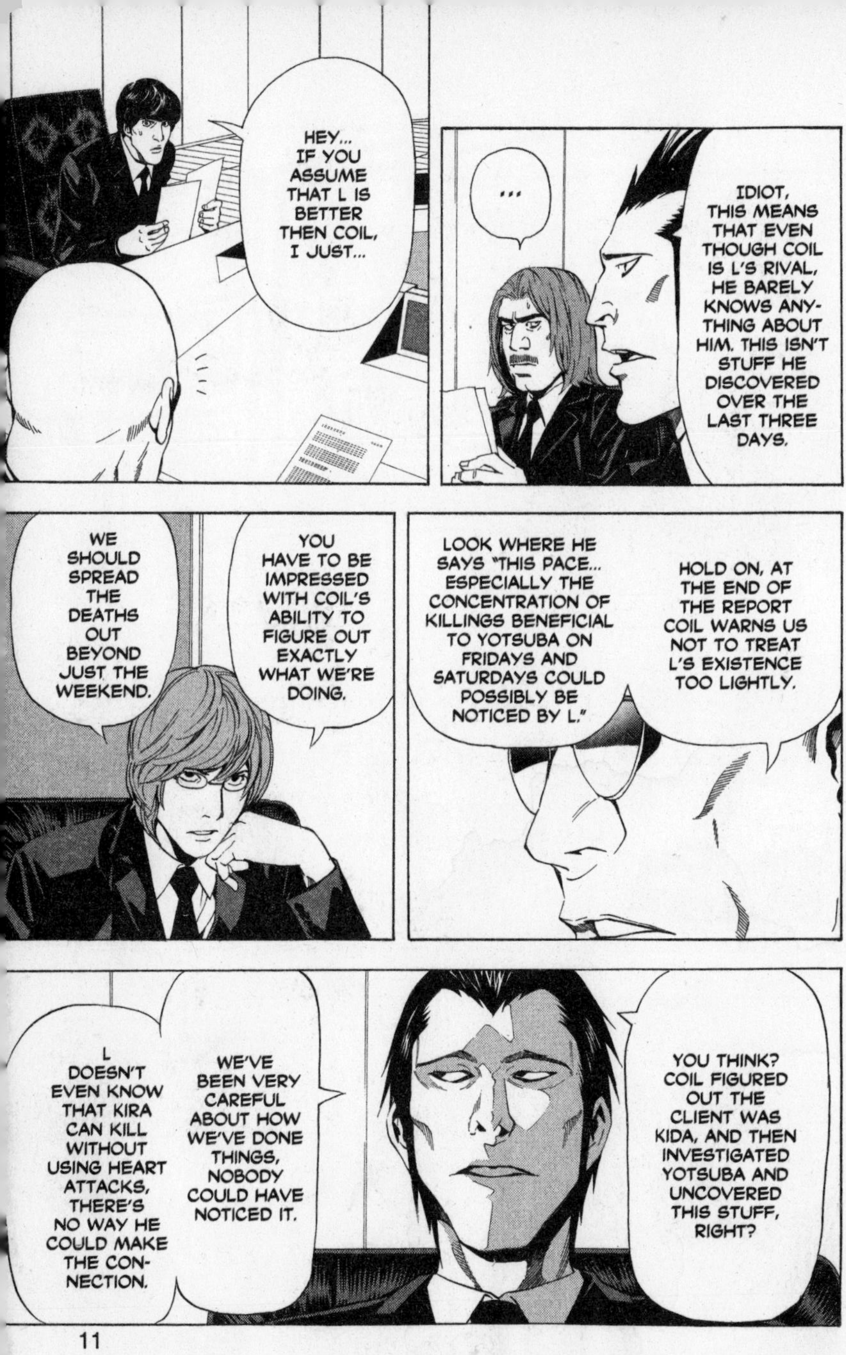
IDIOT, THIS MEANS THAT EVEN THOUGH COIL IS L'S RIVAL, HE BARELY KNOWS ANY-THING ABOUT HIM. THIS ISN'T STUFF HE DISCOVERED OVER THE LAST THREE DAYS.
...
HEY... IF YOU ASSUME THAT L IS BETTER THEN COIL, I JUST...
HOLD ON, AT THE END OF THE REPORT COIL WARNS US NOT TO TREAT L'S EXISTENCE TOO LIGHTLY.
LOOK WHERE HE SAYS "THIS PACE... ESPECIALLY THE CONCENTRATION OF KILLINGS BENEFICIAL TO YOTSUBA ON FRIDAYS AND SATURDAYS COULD POSSIBLY BE NOTICED BY L."
YOU HAVE TO BE IMPRESSED WITH COIL'S ABILITY TO FIGURE OUT EXACTLY WHAT WE'RE DOING.
WE SHOULD SPREAD THE DEATHS OUT BEYOND JUST THE WEEKEND.
YOU THINK? COIL FIGURED OUT THE CLIENT WAS KIDA, AND THEN INVESTIGATED YOTSUBA AND UNCOVERED THIS STUFF, RIGHT?
WE'VE BEEN VERY CAREFUL ABOUT HOW WE'VE DONE THINGS, NOBODY COULD HAVE NOTICED IT.
L DOESN'T EVEN KNOW THAT KIRA CAN KILL WITHOUT USING HEART ATTACKS, THERE'S NO WAY HE COULD MAKE THE CON-NECTION.

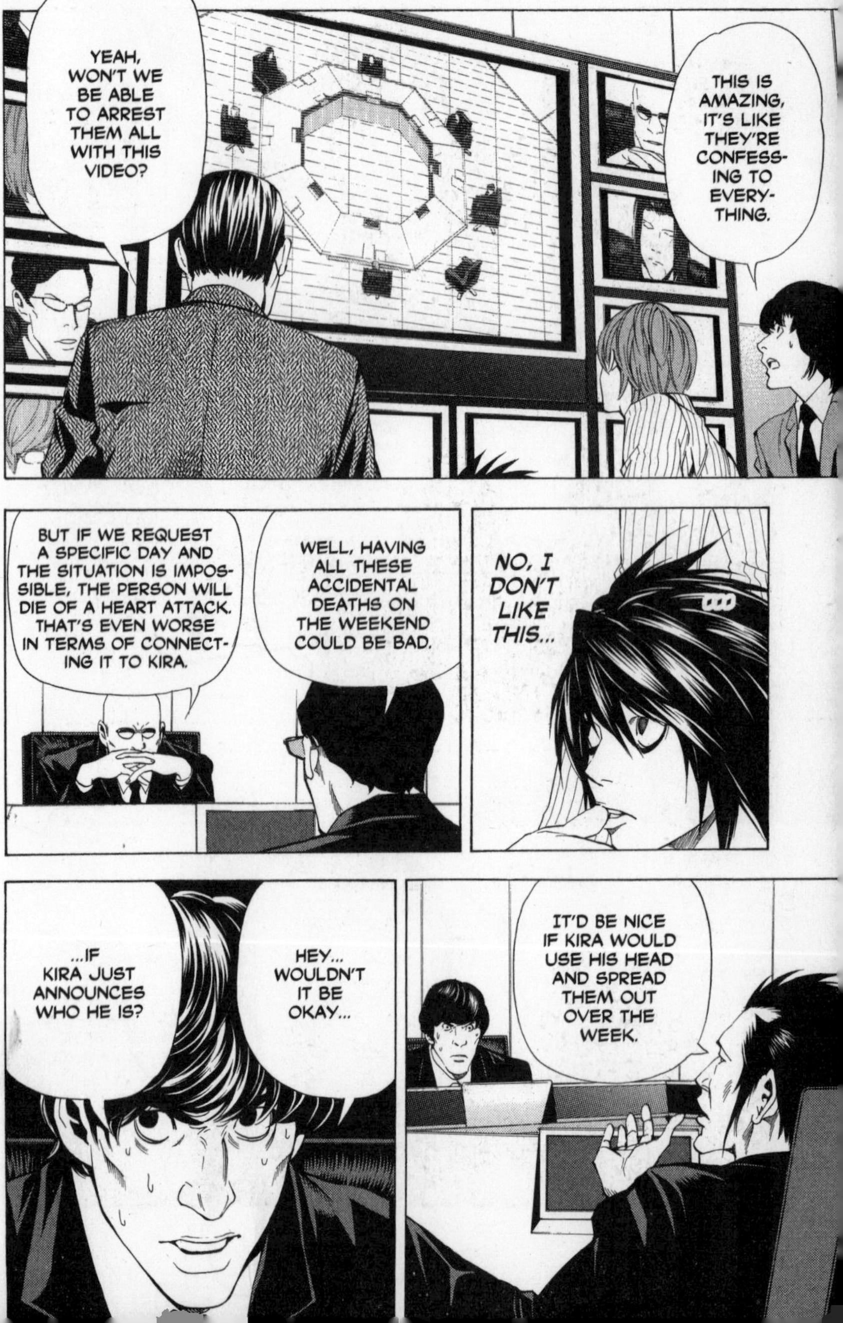
THIS IS AMAZING, IT'S LIKE THEY'RE CONFESSING TO EVERYTHING.
YEAH, WON'T WE BE ABLE TO ARREST THEM ALL WITH THIS VIDEO?
NO, I DON'T LIKE THIS...
WELL, HAVING ALL THESE ACCIDENTAL DEATHS ON THE WEEKEND COULD BE BAD.
BUT IF WE REQUEST A SPECIFIC DAY AND THE SITUATION IS IMPOSSIBLE, THE PERSON WILL DIE OF A HEART ATTACK. THAT'S EVEN WORSE IN TERMS OF CONNECTING IT TO KIRA.
IT'D BE NICE IF KIRA WOULD USE HIS HEAD AND SPREAD THEM OUT OVER THE WEEK.
HEY... WOULDN'T IT BE OKAY...
...IF KIRA JUST ANNOUNCES WHO HE IS?

READ THIS WAY

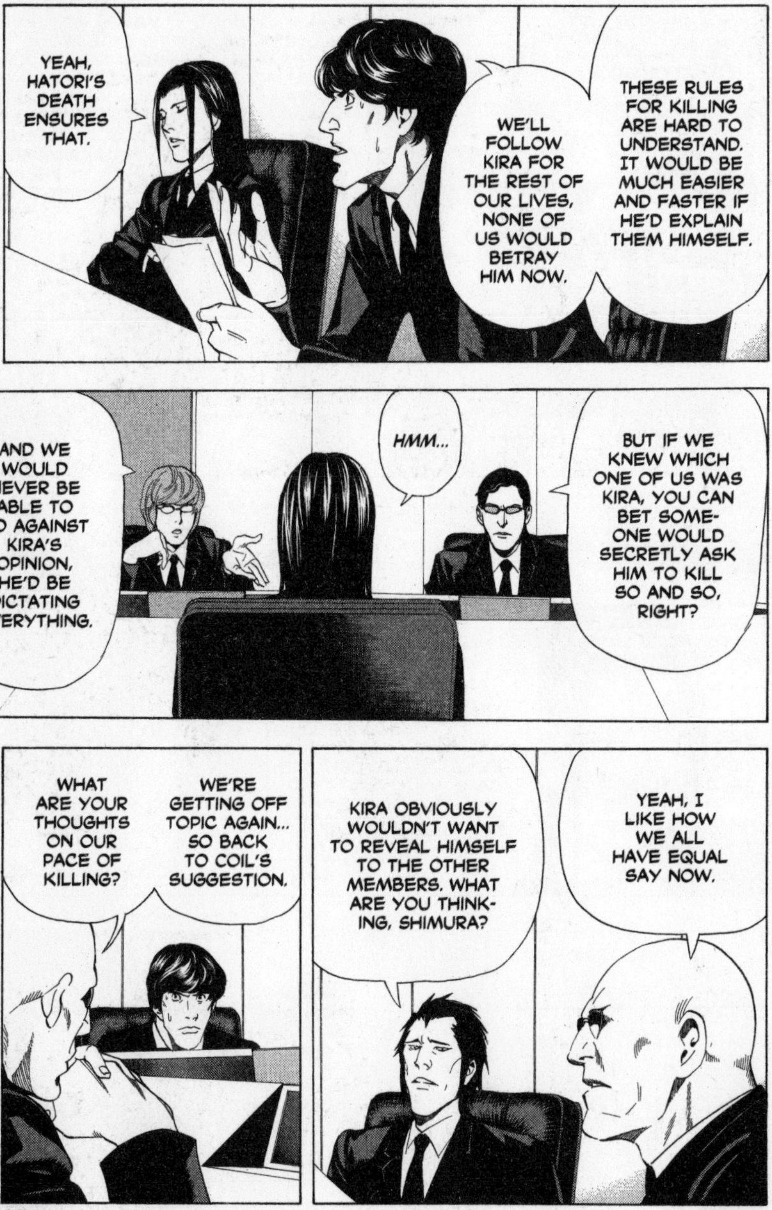
THESE RULES FOR KILLING ARE HARD TO UNDERSTAND. IT WOULD BE MUCH EASIER AND FASTER IF HE'D EXPLAIN THEM HIMSELF.
WE'LL FOLLOW KIRA FOR THE REST OF OUR LIVES, NONE OF US WOULD BETRAY HIM NOW.
YEAH, HATORI'S DEATH ENSURES THAT.
BUT IF WE KNEW WHICH ONE OF US WAS KIRA, YOU CAN BET SOME-ONE WOULD SECRETLY ASK HIM TO KILL SO AND SO, RIGHT?
HMM...
AND WE WOULD NEVER BE ABLE TO GO AGAINST KIRA'S OPINION, HE'D BE DICTATING EVERYTHING.
YEAH, I LIKE HOW WE ALL HAVE EQUAL SAY NOW.
KIRA OBVIOUSLY WOULDN'T WANT TO REVEAL HIMSELF TO THE OTHER MEMBERS. WHAT ARE YOU THINK-ING, SHIMURA?
WE'RE GETTING OFF TOPIC AGAIN... SO BACK TO COIL'S SUGGESTION.
WHAT ARE YOUR THOUGHTS ON OUR PACE OF KILLING?

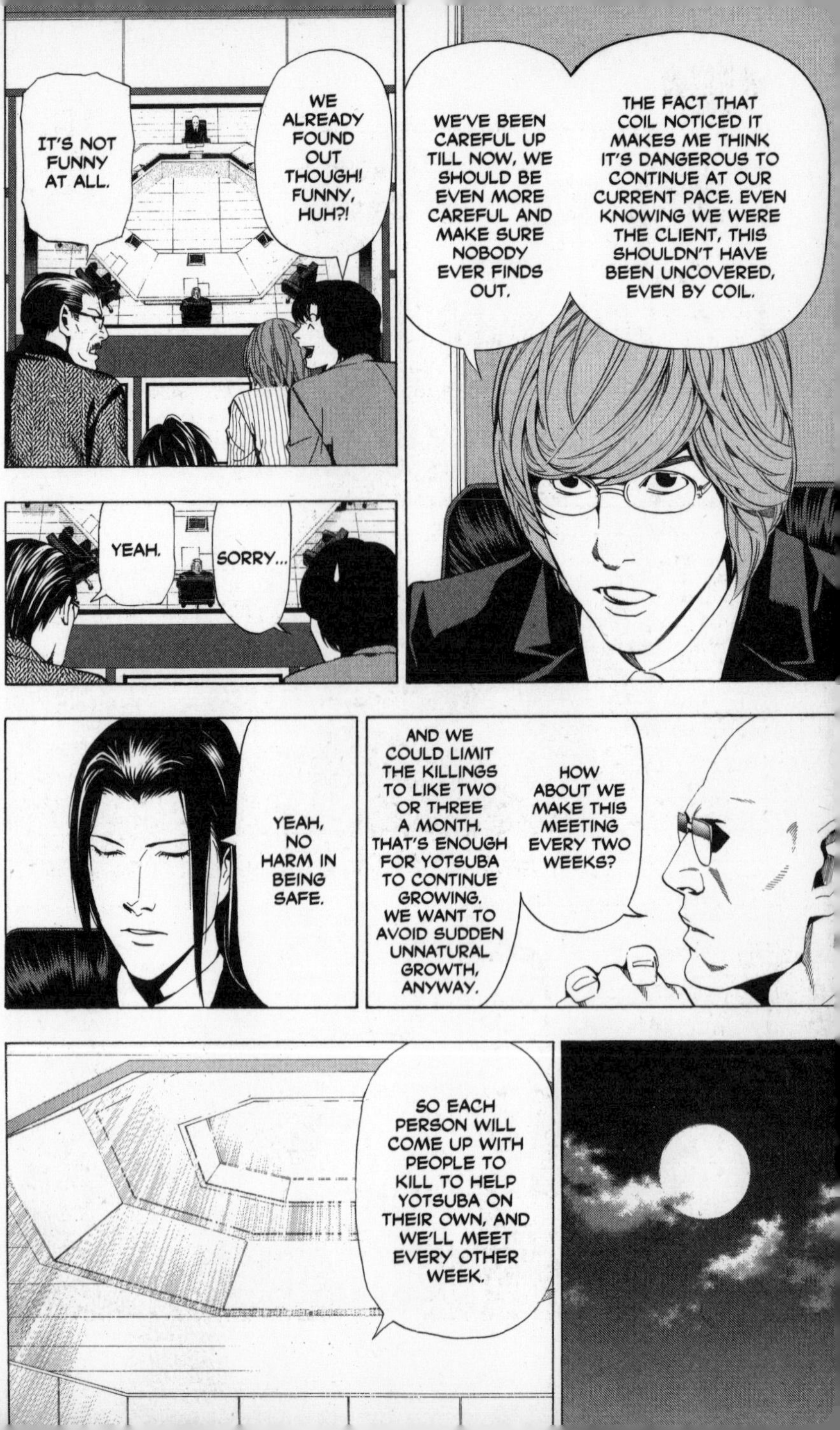
THE FACT THAT COIL NOTICED IT MAKES ME THINK IT'S DANGEROUS TO CONTINUE AT OUR CURRENT PACE. EVEN KNOWING WE WERE THE CLIENT, THIS SHOULDN'T HAVE BEEN UNCOVERED, EVEN BY COIL.
WE'VE BEEN CAREFUL UP TILL NOW, WE SHOULD BE EVEN MORE CAREFUL AND MAKE SURE NOBODY EVER FINDS OUT.
WE ALREADY FOUND OUT THOUGH! FUNNY, HUH?!
IT'S NOT FUNNY AT ALL.
SORRY...
YEAH.
HOW ABOUT WE MAKE THIS MEETING EVERY TWO WEEKS?
AND WE COULD LIMIT THE KILLINGS TO LIKE TWO OR THREE A MONTH. THAT'S ENOUGH FOR YOTSUBA TO CONTINUE GROWING. WE WANT TO AVOID SUDDEN UNNATURAL GROWTH, ANYWAY.
YEAH, NO HARM IN BEING SAFE.
SO EACH PERSON WILL COME UP WITH PEOPLE TO KILL TO HELP YOTSUBA ON THEIR OWN, AND WE'LL MEET EVERY OTHER WEEK.

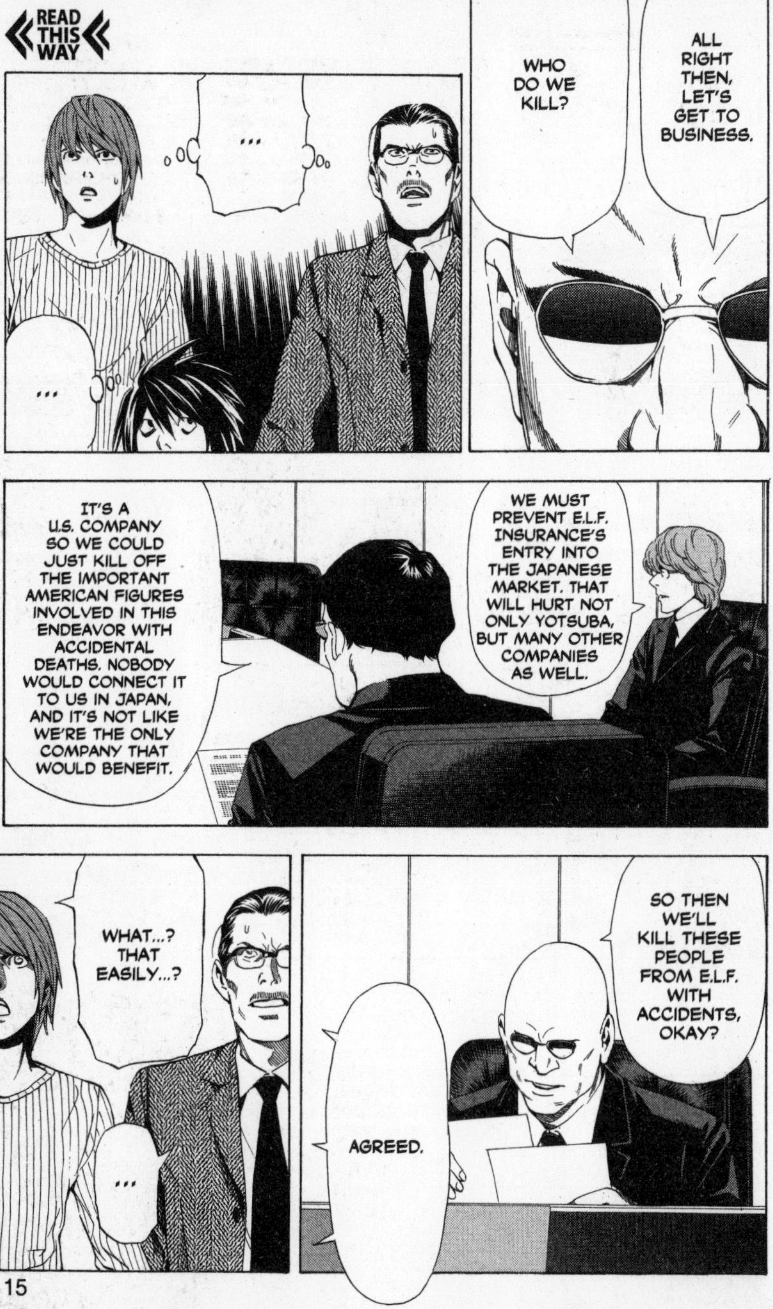
READ THIS WAY
ALL RIGHT THEN, LET'S GET TO BUSINESS.
WHO DO WE KILL?
...
...
WE MUST PREVENT E.L.F. INSURANCE'S ENTRY INTO THE JAPANESE MARKET. THAT WILL HURT NOT ONLY YOTSUBA, BUT MANY OTHER COMPANIES AS WELL.
IT'S A U.S. COMPANY SO WE COULD JUST KILL OFF THE IMPORTANT AMERICAN FIGURES INVOLVED IN THIS ENDEAVOR WITH ACCIDENTAL DEATHS. NOBODY WOULD CONNECT IT TO US IN JAPAN, AND IT'S NOT LIKE WE'RE THE ONLY COMPANY THAT WOULD BENEFIT.
SO THEN WE'LL KILL THESE PEOPLE FROM E.L.F. WITH ACCIDENTS, OKAY?
AGREED.
WHAT...? THAT EASILY...?
...

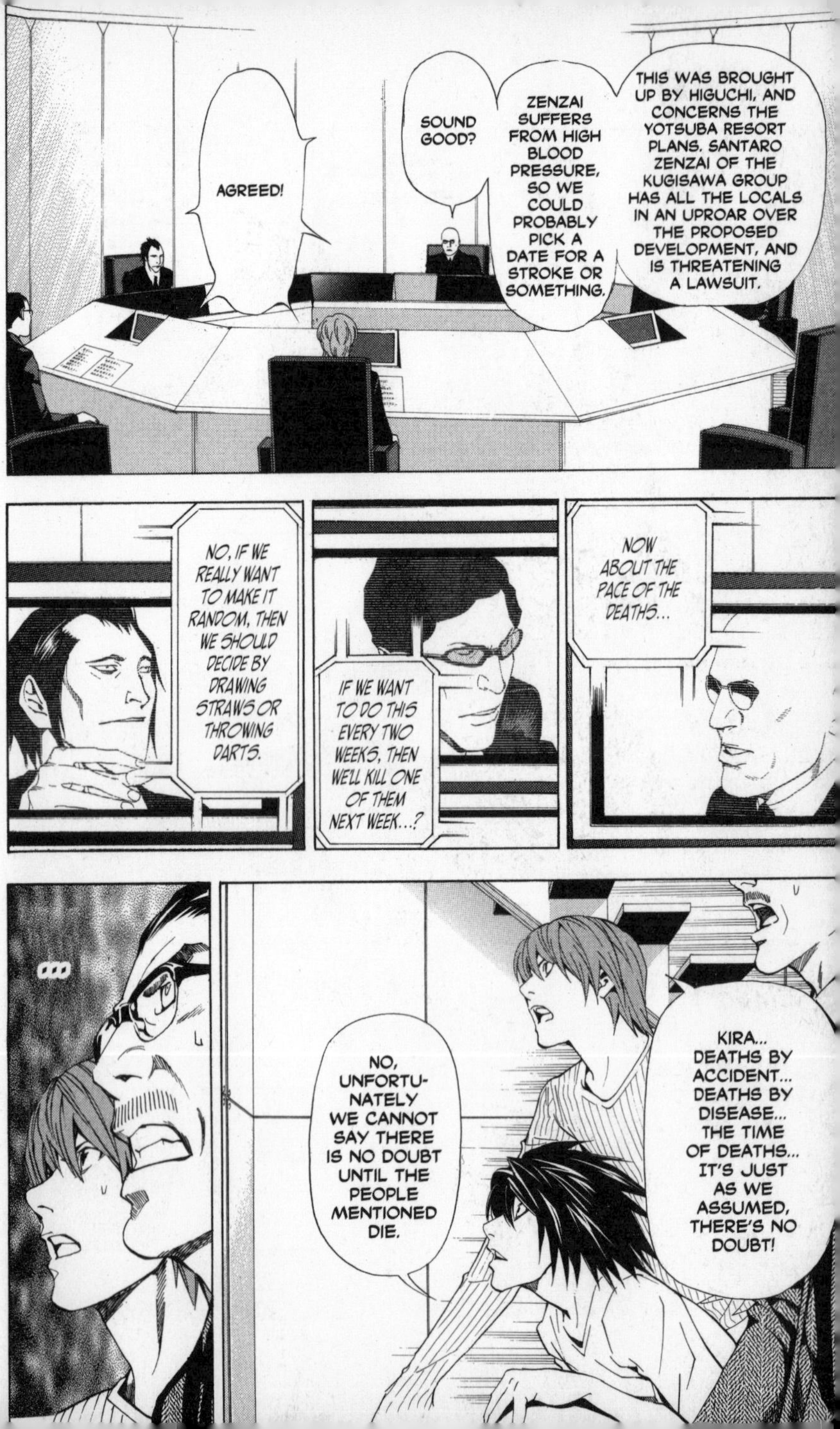
THIS WAS BROUGHT UP BY HIGUCHI, AND CONCERNS THE YOTSUBA RESORT PLANS. SANTARO ZENZAI OF THE KUGISAWA GROUP HAS ALL THE LOCALS IN AN UPROAR OVER THE PROPOSED DEVELOPMENT, AND IS THREATENING A LAWSUIT.
ZENZAI SUFFERS FROM HIGH BLOOD PRESSURE, SO WE COULD PROBABLY PICK A DATE FOR A STROKE OR SOMETHING.
SOUND GOOD?
AGREED!
NOW ABOUT THE PACE OF THE DEATHS...
IF WE WANT TO DO THIS EVERY TWO WEEKS, THEN WE'LL KILL ONE OF THEM NEXT WEEK...?
NO, IF WE REALLY WANT TO MAKE IT RANDOM, THEN WE SHOULD DECIDE BY DRAWING STRAWS OR THROWING DARTS.
KIRA... DEATHS BY ACCIDENT... DEATHS BY DISEASE... THE TIME OF DEATHS... IT'S JUST AS WE ASSUMED, THERE'S NO DOUBT!
NO, UNFORTUNATELY WE CANNOT SAY THERE IS NO DOUBT UNTIL THE PEOPLE MENTIONED DIE.
...

READ THIS WAY

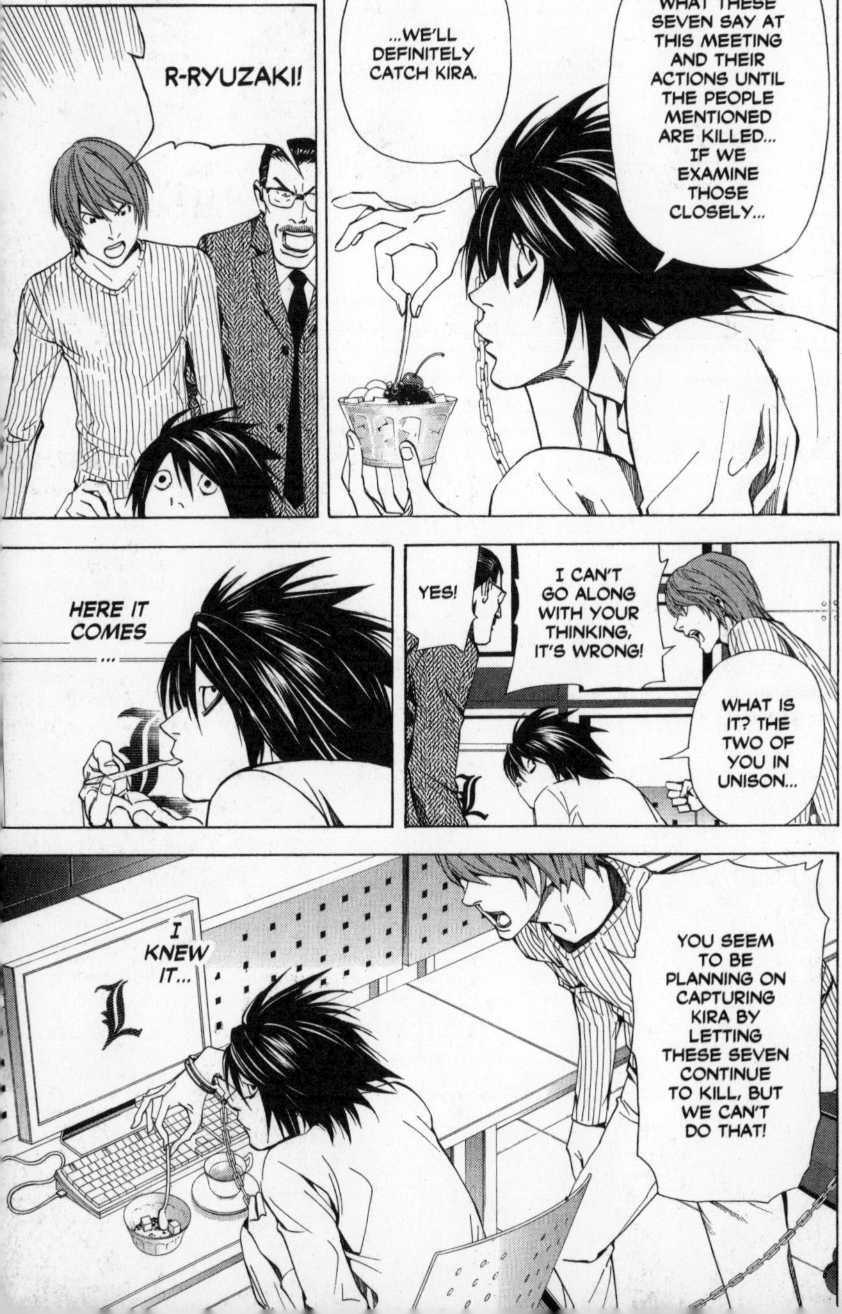

WHAT THESE SEVEN SAY AT THIS MEETING AND THEIR ACTIONS UNTIL THE PEOPLE MENTIONED ARE KILLED... IF WE EXAMINE THOSE CLOSELY...
...WE'LL DEFINITELY CATCH KIRA.
R-RYUZAKI!
I CAN'T GO ALONG WITH YOUR THINKING, IT'S WRONG!
YES!
WHAT IS IT? THE TWO OF YOU IN UNISON...
HERE IT COMES
...
YOU SEEM TO BE PLANNING ON CAPTURING KIRA BY LETTING THESE SEVEN CONTINUE TO KILL, BUT WE CAN'T DO THAT!
I KNEW IT...

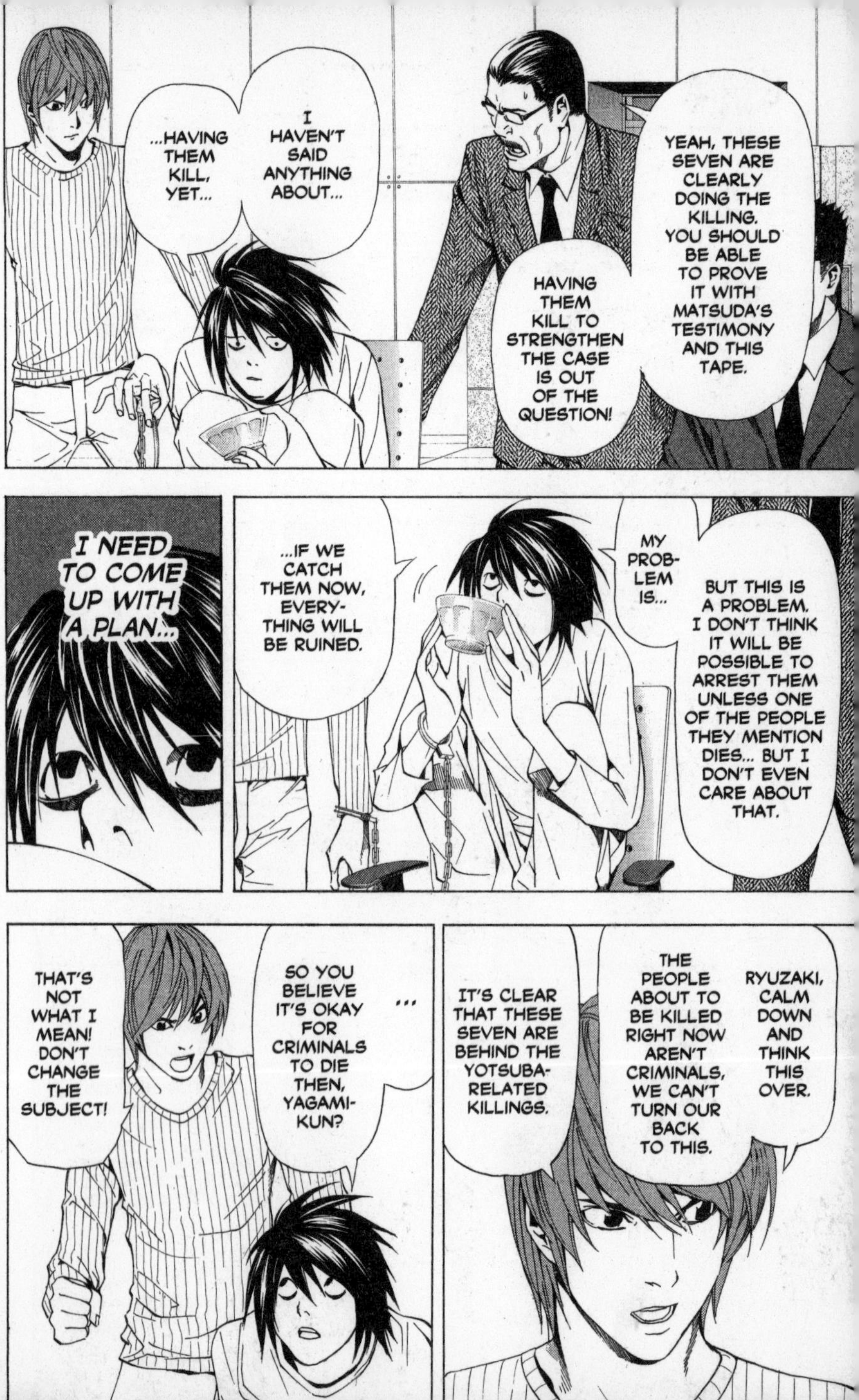
YEAH, THESE SEVEN ARE CLEARLY DOING THE KILLING. YOU SHOULD BE ABLE TO PROVE IT WITH MATSUDA'S TESTIMONY AND THIS TAPE.
HAVING THEM KILL TO STRENGTHEN THE CASE IS OUT OF THE QUESTION!
I HAVEN'T SAID ANYTHING ABOUT...
...HAVING THEM KILL, YET...
BUT THIS IS A PROBLEM. I DON'T THINK IT WILL BE POSSIBLE TO ARREST THEM UNLESS ONE OF THE PEOPLE THEY MENTION DIES... BUT I DON'T EVEN CARE ABOUT THAT.
MY PROB-LEM IS...
...IF WE CATCH THEM NOW, EVERY-THING WILL BE RUINED.
I NEED TO COME UP WITH A PLAN...
RYUZAKI, CALM DOWN AND THINK THIS OVER.
THE PEOPLE ABOUT TO BE KILLED RIGHT NOW AREN'T CRIMINALS, WE CAN'T TURN OUR BACK TO THIS.
IT'S CLEAR THAT THESE SEVEN ARE BEHIND THE YOTSUBA-RELATED KILLINGS.
...
SO YOU BELIEVE IT'S OKAY FOR CRIMINALS TO DIE THEN, YAGAMI-KUN?
THAT'S NOT WHAT I MEAN! DON'T CHANGE THE SUBJECT!

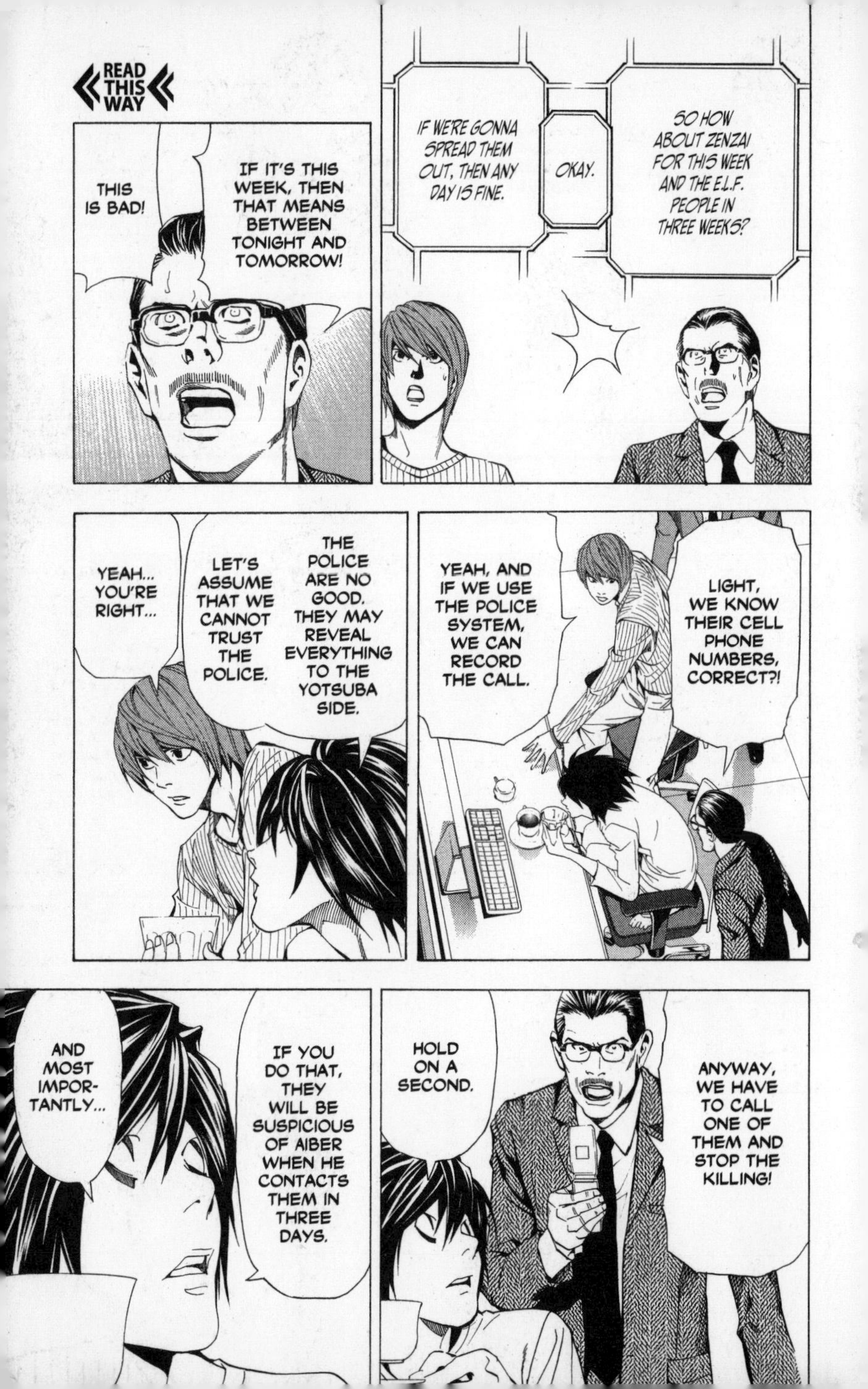
READ THIS WAY
SO HOW ABOUT ZENZAI FOR THIS WEEK AND THE E.L.F. PEOPLE IN THREE WEEKS?
OKAY.
IF WE'RE GONNA SPREAD THEM OUT, THEN ANY DAY IS FINE.
IF IT'S THIS WEEK, THEN THAT MEANS BETWEEN TONIGHT AND TOMORROW!
THIS IS BAD!
LIGHT, WE KNOW THEIR CELL PHONE NUMBERS, CORRECT?!
YEAH, AND IF WE USE THE POLICE SYSTEM, WE CAN RECORD THE CALL.
THE POLICE ARE NO GOOD. THEY MAY REVEAL EVERYTHING TO THE YOTSUBA SIDE.
LET'S ASSUME THAT WE CANNOT TRUST THE POLICE.
YEAH... YOU'RE RIGHT...
ANYWAY, WE HAVE TO CALL ONE OF THEM AND STOP THE KILLING!
HOLD ON A SECOND.
IF YOU DO THAT, THEY WILL BE SUSPICIOUS OF AIBER WHEN HE CONTACTS THEM IN THREE DAYS.
AND MOST IMPOR-TANTLY...

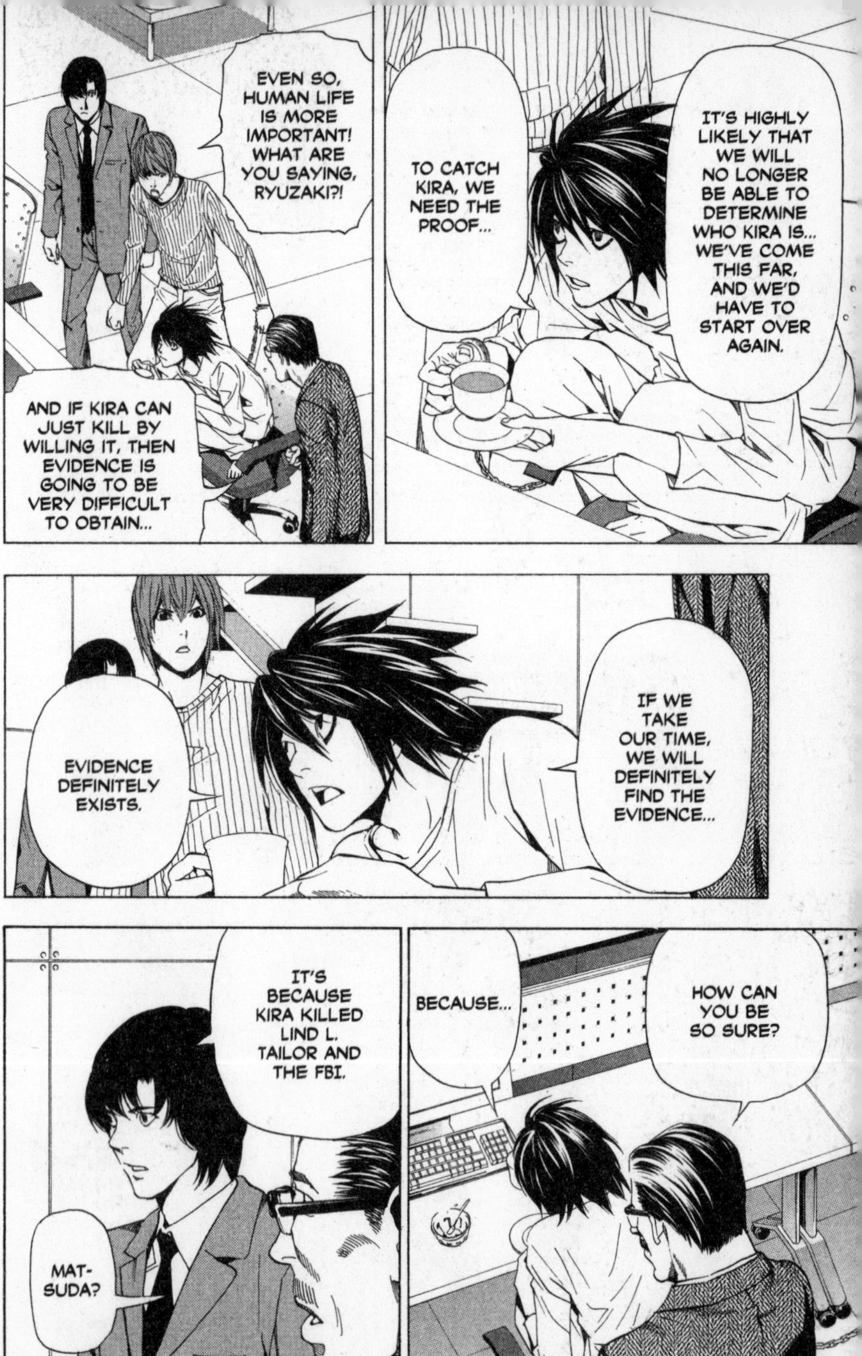
IT'S HIGHLY LIKELY THAT WE WILL NO LONGER BE ABLE TO DETERMINE WHO KIRA IS... WE'VE COME THIS FAR, AND WE'D HAVE TO START OVER AGAIN.
TO CATCH KIRA, WE NEED THE PROOF...
EVEN SO, HUMAN LIFE IS MORE IMPORTANT! WHAT ARE YOU SAYING, RYUZAKI?!
AND IF KIRA CAN JUST KILL BY WILLING IT, THEN EVIDENCE IS GOING TO BE VERY DIFFICULT TO OBTAIN...
IF WE TAKE OUR TIME, WE WILL DEFINITELY FIND THE EVIDENCE...
EVIDENCE DEFINITELY EXISTS.
HOW CAN YOU BE SO SURE?
BECAUSE...
IT'S BECAUSE KIRA KILLED LIND L. TAILOR AND THE FBI.
MAT-SUDA?

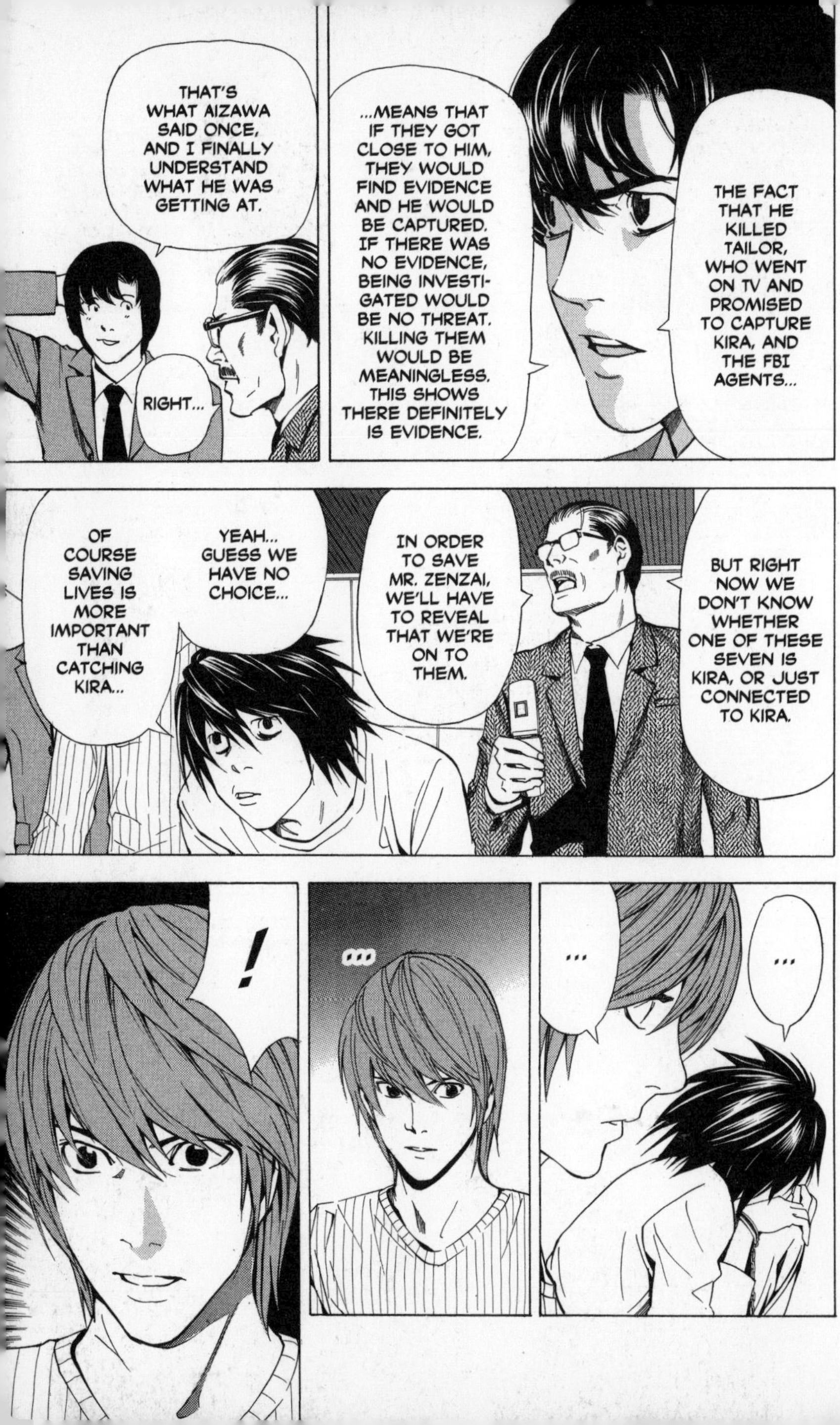
THE FACT THAT HE KILLED TAILOR, WHO WENT ON TV AND PROMISED TO CAPTURE KIRA, AND THE FBI AGENTS...
...MEANS THAT IF THEY GOT CLOSE TO HIM, THEY WOULD FIND EVIDENCE AND HE WOULD BE CAPTURED. IF THERE WAS NO EVIDENCE, BEING INVESTI-GATED WOULD BE NO THREAT. KILLING THEM WOULD BE MEANINGLESS. THIS SHOWS THERE DEFINITELY IS EVIDENCE.
THAT'S WHAT AIZAWA SAID ONCE, AND I FINALLY UNDERSTAND WHAT HE WAS GETTING AT.
RIGHT...
BUT RIGHT NOW WE DON'T KNOW WHETHER ONE OF THESE SEVEN IS KIRA, OR JUST CONNECTED TO KIRA.
IN ORDER TO SAVE MR. ZENZAI, WE'LL HAVE TO REVEAL THAT WE'RE ON TO THEM.
YEAH... GUESS WE HAVE NO CHOICE...
OF COURSE SAVING LIVES IS MORE IMPORTANT THAN CATCHING KIRA...
...
...
...
!

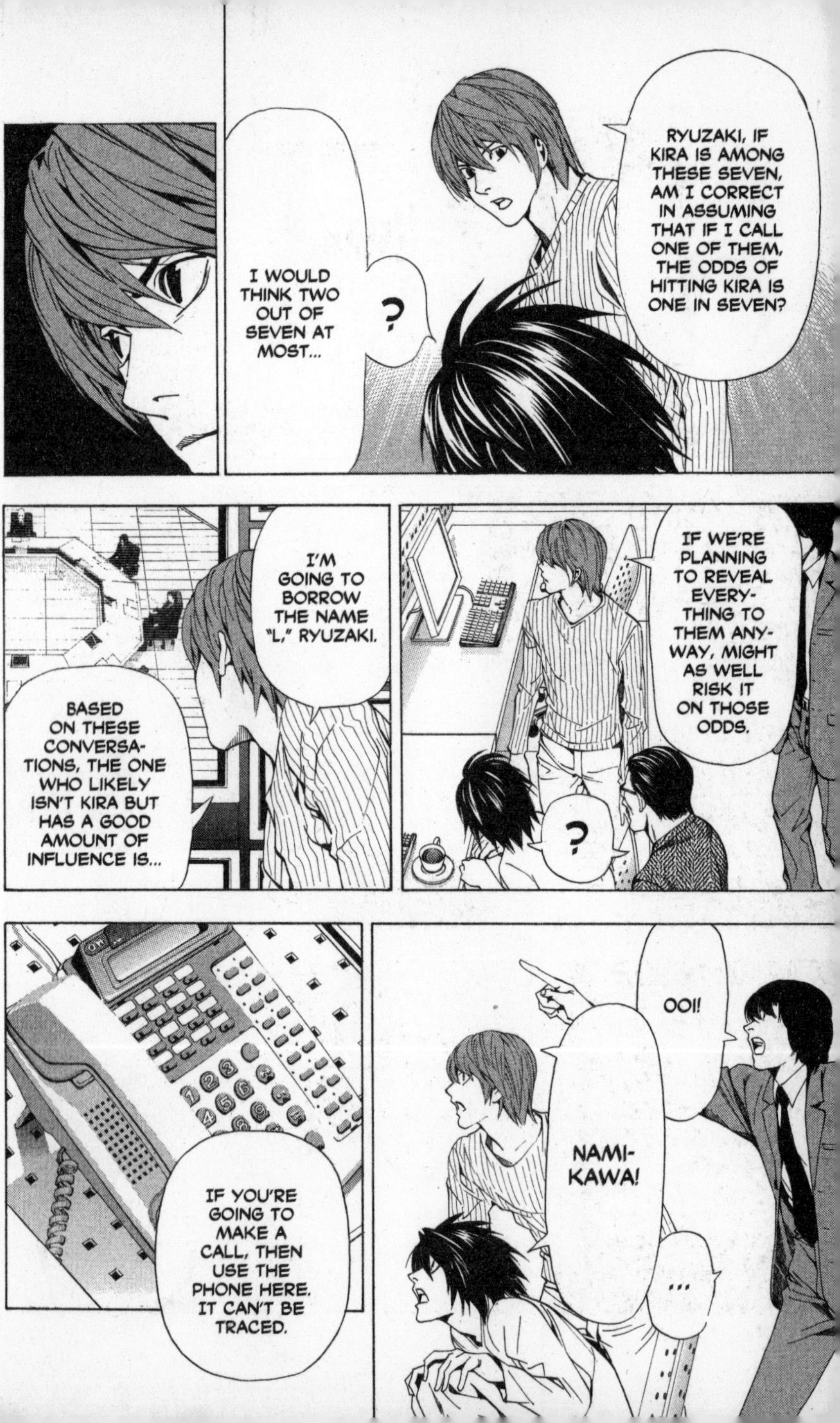
RYUZAKI, IF KIRA IS AMONG THESE SEVEN, AM I CORRECT IN ASSUMING THAT IF I CALL ONE OF THEM, THE ODDS OF HITTING KIRA IS ONE IN SEVEN?
?
I WOULD THINK TWO OUT OF SEVEN AT MOST...
IF WE'RE PLANNING TO REVEAL EVERY-THING TO THEM ANY-WAY, MIGHT AS WELL RISK IT ON THOSE ODDS.
?
I'M GOING TO BORROW THE NAME "L," RYUZAKI.
BASED ON THESE CONVERSA-TIONS, THE ONE WHO LIKELY ISN'T KIRA BUT HAS A GOOD AMOUNT OF INFLUENCE IS...
OOI!
NAMI-KAWA!
...
IF YOU'RE GOING TO MAKE A CALL, THEN USE THE PHONE HERE. IT CAN'T BE TRACED.

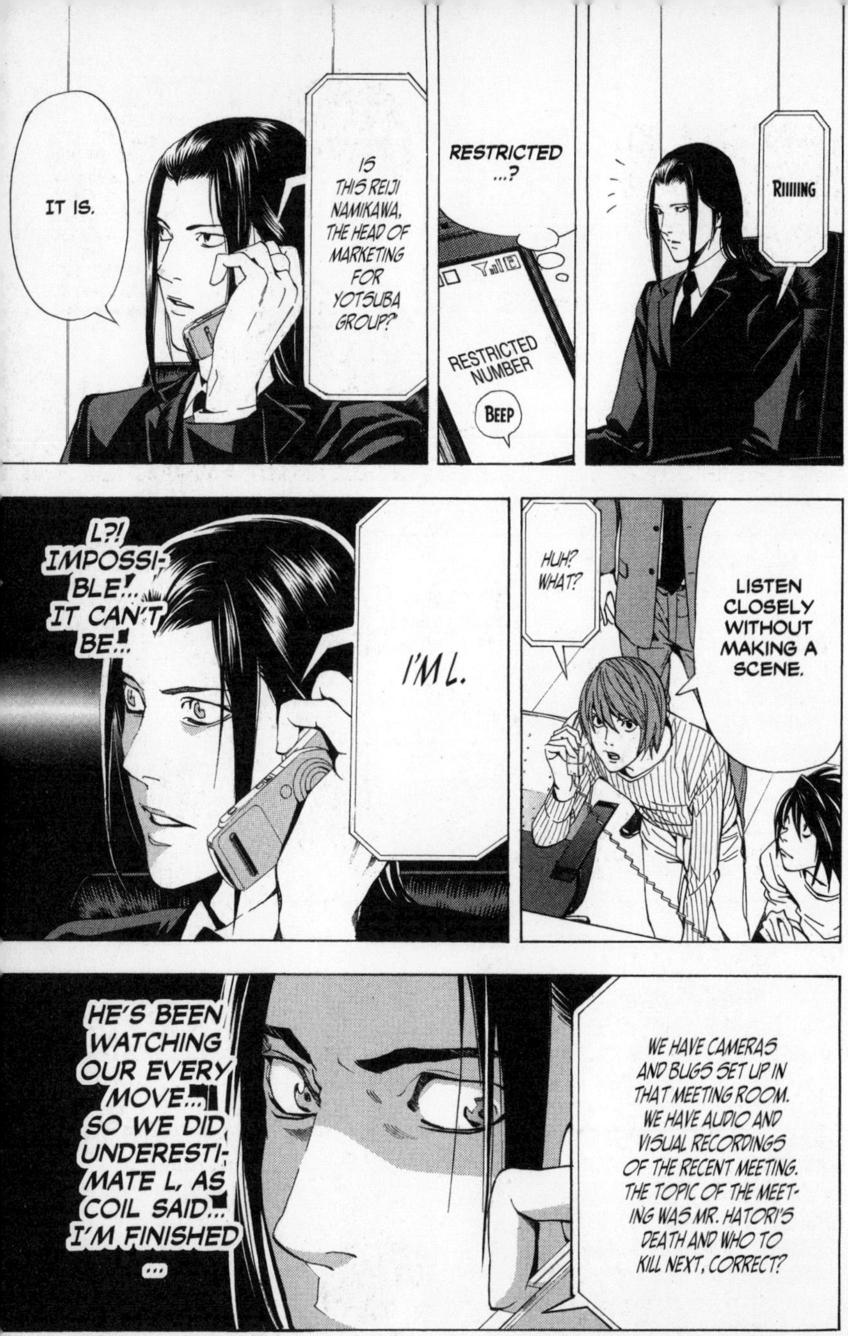
RIIIING
RESTRICTED ...?
RESTRICTED NUMBER
BEEP
IS THIS REIJI NAMIKAWA, THE HEAD OF MARKETING FOR YOTSUBA GROUP?
IT IS.
LISTEN CLOSELY WITHOUT MAKING A SCENE.
HUH? WHAT?
I'M L.
L?! IMPOSSI-BLE... IT CAN'T BE...
WE HAVE CAMERAS AND BUGS SET UP IN THAT MEETING ROOM. WE HAVE AUDIO AND VISUAL RECORDINGS OF THE RECENT MEETING. THE TOPIC OF THE MEET-ING WAS MR. HATORI'S DEATH AND WHO TO KILL NEXT, CORRECT?
HE'S BEEN WATCHING OUR EVERY MOVE... SO WE DID UNDERESTI-MATE L, AS COIL SAID... I'M FINISHED ...

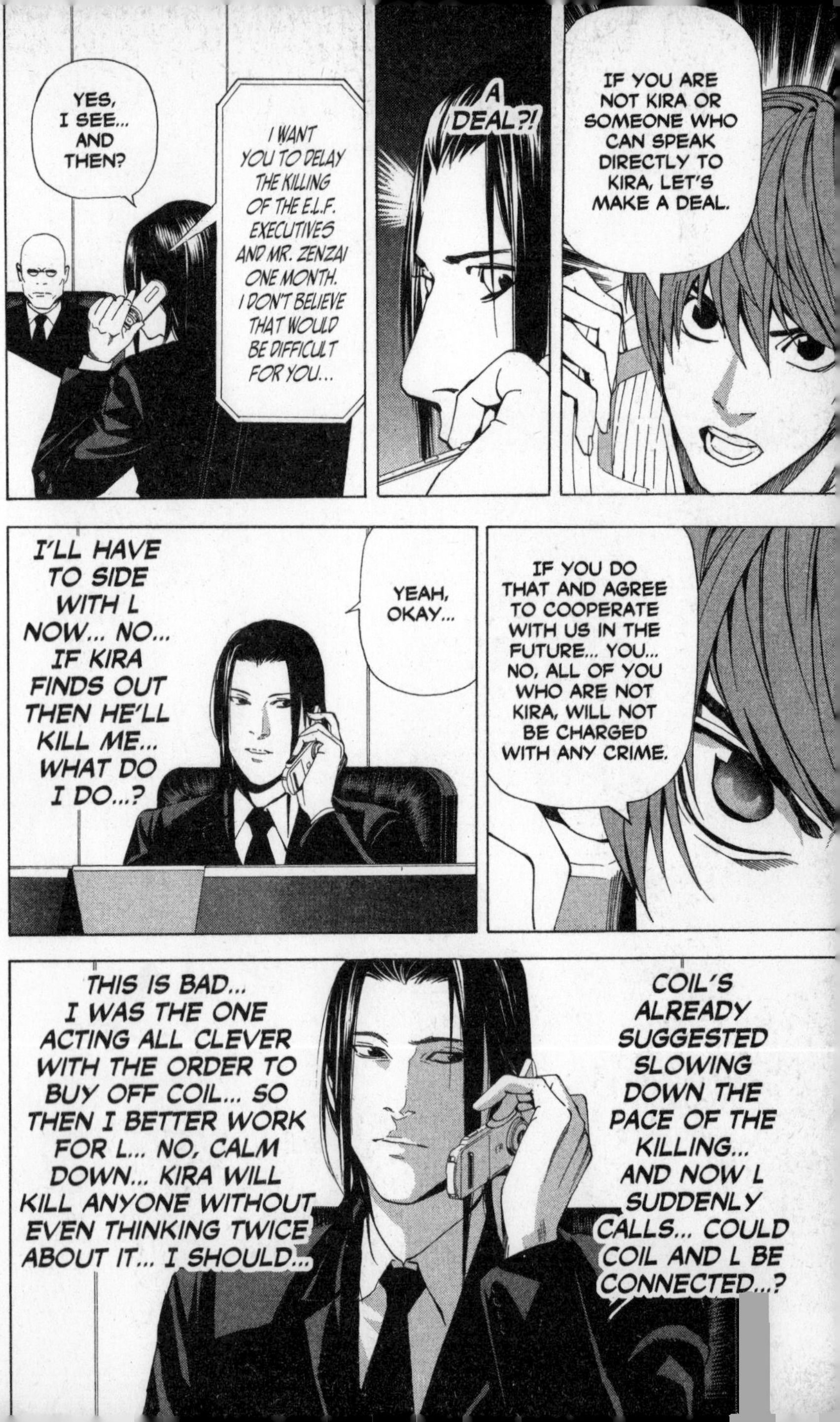
IF YOU ARE NOT KIRA OR SOMEONE WHO CAN SPEAK DIRECTLY TO KIRA, LET'S MAKE A DEAL.
A DEAL?!
I WANT YOU TO DELAY THE KILLING OF THE E.L.F. EXECUTIVES AND MR. ZENZAI ONE MONTH. I DON'T BELIEVE THAT WOULD BE DIFFICULT FOR YOU...
YES, I SEE... AND THEN?
IF YOU DO THAT AND AGREE TO COOPERATE WITH US IN THE FUTURE... YOU... NO, ALL OF YOU WHO ARE NOT KIRA, WILL NOT BE CHARGED WITH ANY CRIME.
YEAH, OKAY...
I'LL HAVE TO SIDE WITH L NOW... NO... IF KIRA FINDS OUT THEN HE'LL KILL ME... WHAT DO I DO...?
COIL'S ALREADY SUGGESTED SLOWING DOWN THE PACE OF THE KILLING... AND NOW L SUDDENLY CALLS... COULD COIL AND L BE CONNECTED...?
THIS IS BAD... I WAS THE ONE ACTING ALL CLEVER WITH THE ORDER TO BUY OFF COIL... SO THEN I BETTER WORK FOR L... NO, CALM DOWN... KIRA WILL KILL ANYONE WITHOUT EVEN THINKING TWICE ABOUT IT... I SHOULD...

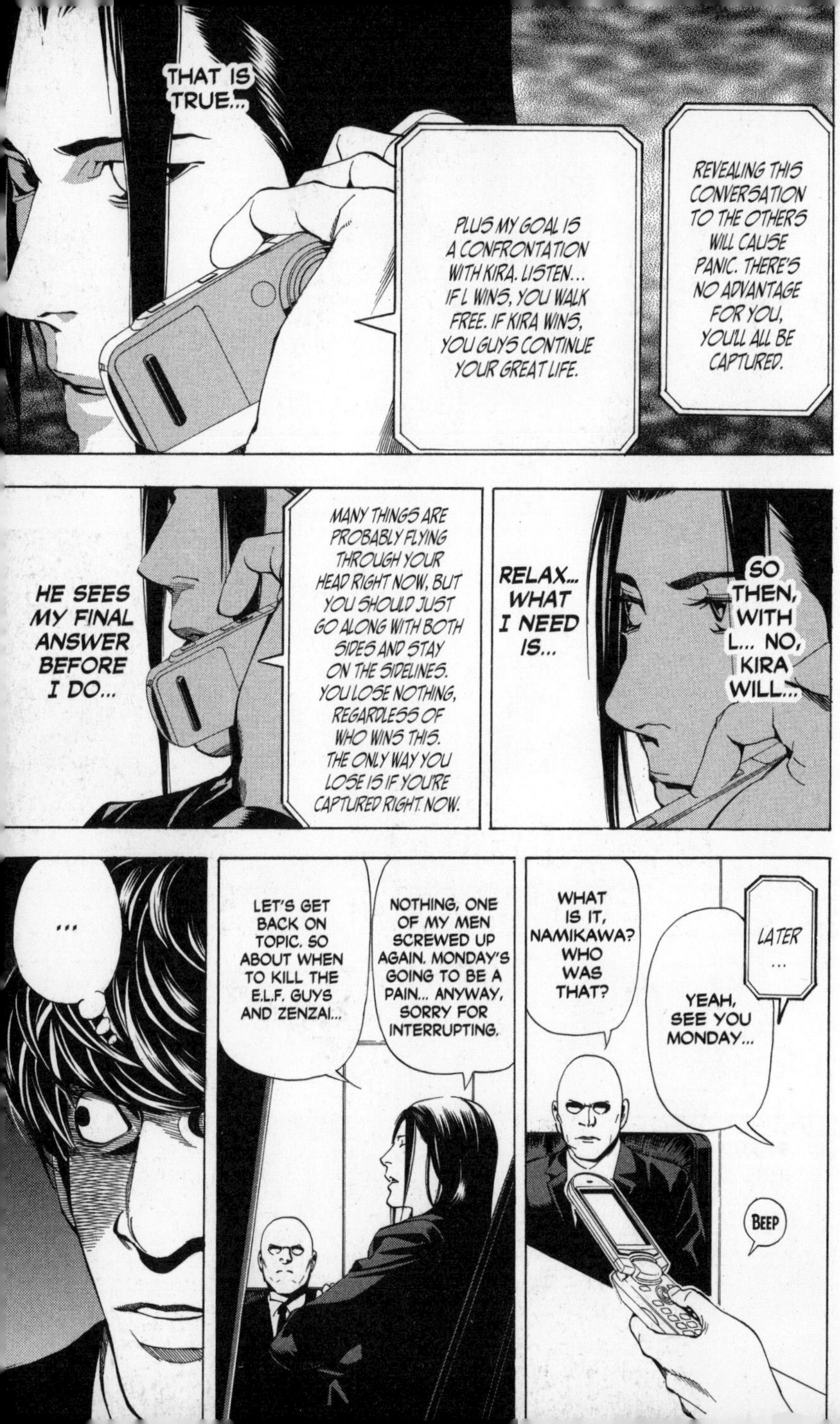
REVEALING THIS CONVERSATION TO THE OTHERS WILL CAUSE PANIC. THERE'S NO ADVANTAGE FOR YOU, YOU'LL ALL BE CAPTURED.
PLUS MY GOAL IS A CONFRONTATION WITH KIRA. LISTEN... IF L WINS, YOU WALK FREE. IF KIRA WINS, YOU GUYS CONTINUE YOUR GREAT LIFE.
THAT IS TRUE...
SO THEN, WITH L... NO, KIRA WILL...
RELAX... WHAT I NEED IS...
MANY THINGS ARE PROBABLY FLYING THROUGH YOUR HEAD RIGHT NOW, BUT YOU SHOULD JUST GO ALONG WITH BOTH SIDES AND STAY ON THE SIDELINES. YOU LOSE NOTHING, REGARDLESS OF WHO WINS THIS. THE ONLY WAY YOU LOSE IS IF YOU'RE CAPTURED RIGHT NOW.
HE SEES MY FINAL ANSWER BEFORE I DO...
LATER ...
YEAH, SEE YOU MONDAY...
BEEP
WHAT IS IT, NAMIKAWA? WHO WAS THAT?
NOTHING, ONE OF MY MEN SCREWED UP AGAIN. MONDAY'S GOING TO BE A PAIN... ANYWAY, SORRY FOR INTERRUPTING.
LET'S GET BACK ON TOPIC. SO ABOUT WHEN TO KILL THE E.L.F. GUYS AND ZENZAI...
...

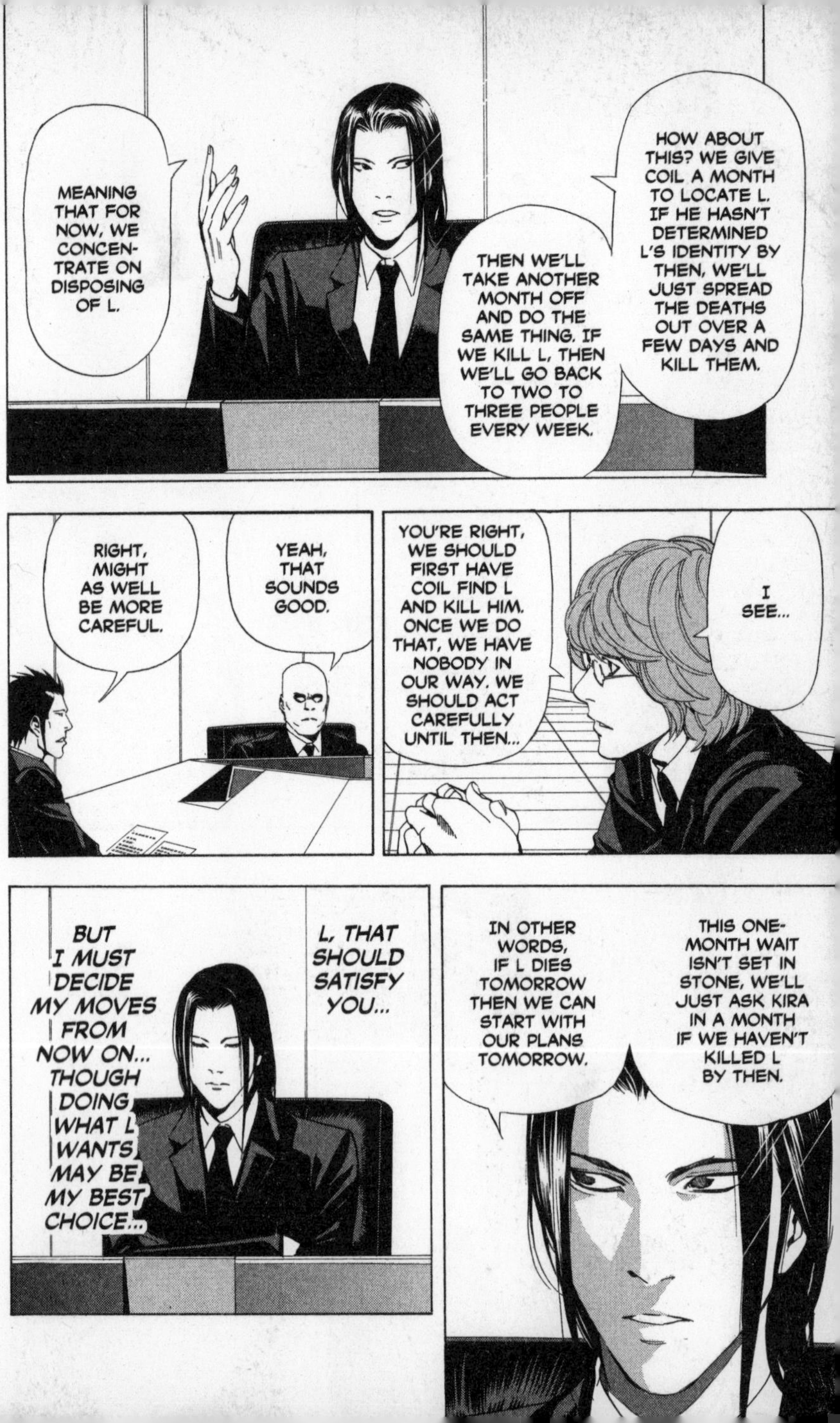
HOW ABOUT THIS? WE GIVE COIL A MONTH TO LOCATE L. IF HE HASN'T DETERMINED L'S IDENTITY BY THEN, WE'LL JUST SPREAD THE DEATHS OUT OVER A FEW DAYS AND KILL THEM.
THEN WE'LL TAKE ANOTHER MONTH OFF AND DO THE SAME THING. IF WE KILL L, THEN WE'LL GO BACK TO TWO TO THREE PEOPLE EVERY WEEK.
MEANING THAT FOR NOW, WE CONCEN-TRATE ON DISPOSING OF L.
I SEE...
YOU'RE RIGHT, WE SHOULD FIRST HAVE COIL FIND L AND KILL HIM. ONCE WE DO THAT, WE HAVE NOBODY IN OUR WAY. WE SHOULD ACT CAREFULLY UNTIL THEN...
YEAH, THAT SOUNDS GOOD.
RIGHT, MIGHT AS WELL BE MORE CAREFUL.
THIS ONE-MONTH WAIT ISN'T SET IN STONE, WE'LL JUST ASK KIRA IN A MONTH IF WE HAVEN'T KILLED L BY THEN.
IN OTHER WORDS, IF L DIES TOMORROW THEN WE CAN START WITH OUR PLANS TOMORROW.
L, THAT SHOULD SATISFY YOU...
BUT I MUST DECIDE MY MOVES FROM NOW ON... THOUGH DOING WHAT L WANTS MAY BE MY BEST CHOICE...

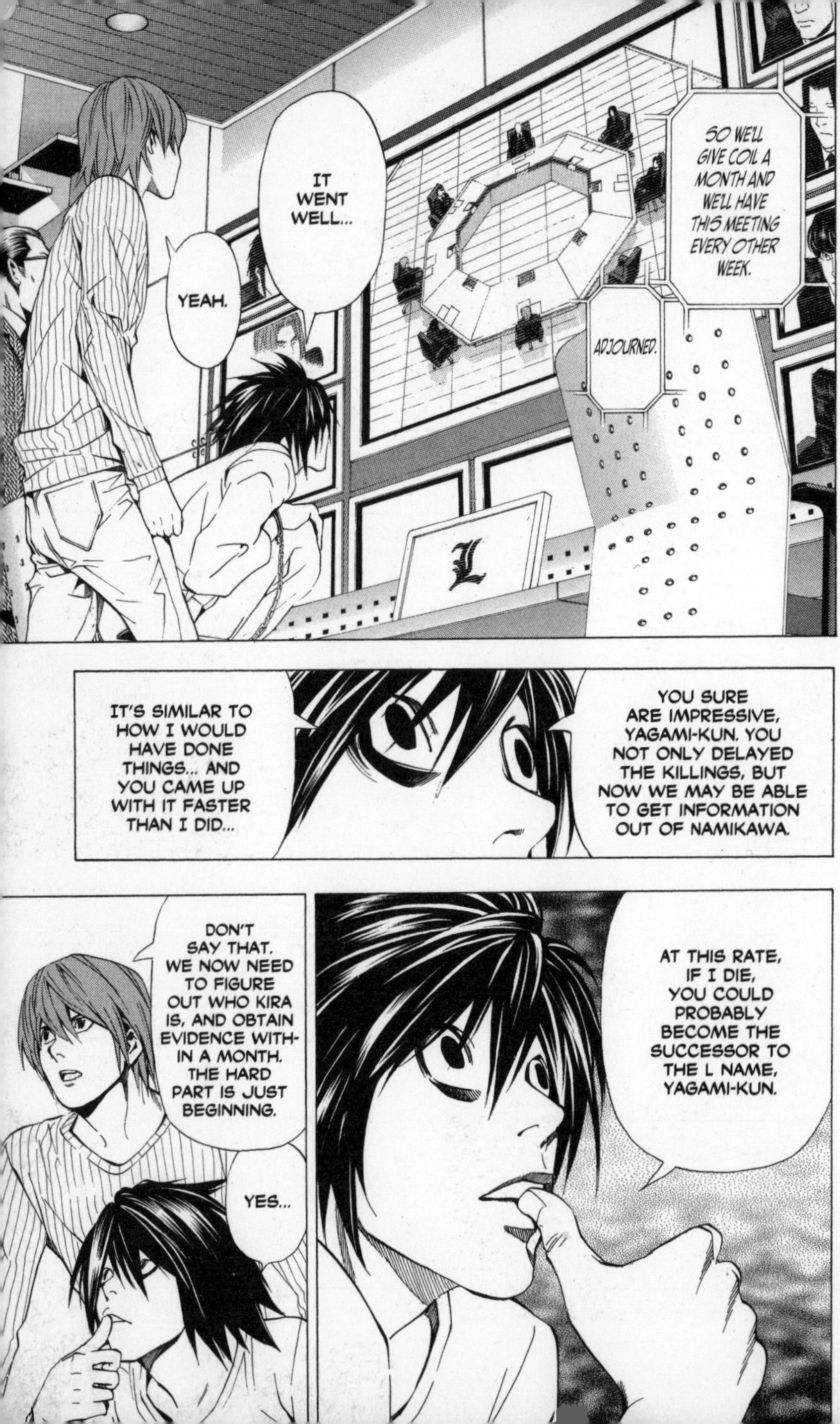
SO WE'LL GIVE COIL A MONTH AND WE'LL HAVE THIS MEETING EVERY OTHER WEEK.
ADJOURNED.
IT WENT WELL...
YEAH.
YOU SURE ARE IMPRESSIVE, YAGAMI-KUN. YOU NOT ONLY DELAYED THE KILLINGS, BUT NOW WE MAY BE ABLE TO GET INFORMATION OUT OF NAMIKAWA.
IT'S SIMILAR TO HOW I WOULD HAVE DONE THINGS... AND YOU CAME UP WITH IT FASTER THAN I DID...
AT THIS RATE, IF I DIE, YOU COULD PROBABLY BECOME THE SUCCESSOR TO THE L NAME, YAGAMI-KUN.
DON'T SAY THAT. WE NOW NEED TO FIGURE OUT WHO KIRA IS, AND OBTAIN EVIDENCE WITH-IN A MONTH. THE HARD PART IS JUST BEGINNING.
YES...

DEATH NOTE
How to use it
XXXII

○ If someone possesses more than one DEATH NOTE, by visualizing the victim, then writing down the name in one of the DEATH NOTES and the cause of death in the other, it will take effect.

The order however, is unimportant, if you write down the cause of death in one DEATH NOTE and afterwards, write the name in the other, it will still take effect.

二冊以上のデスノートを所有した場合、
同じ人間の顔を思い浮かべて書き込めば、一冊に名前、
もう一冊に死因・死の状況を書いても、その通りになる。
ゆえに、一冊に死因・死の状況を書き、後からもう一冊に名前というのも有効。

○ This can also be accomplished by two DEATH NOTE owners working together. In this case, it's necessary that the two touch each other's DEATH NOTES.

上記を所有権の異なる二人の人間が共同でする事も、
互いのノートに触れ合っていれば可能である。

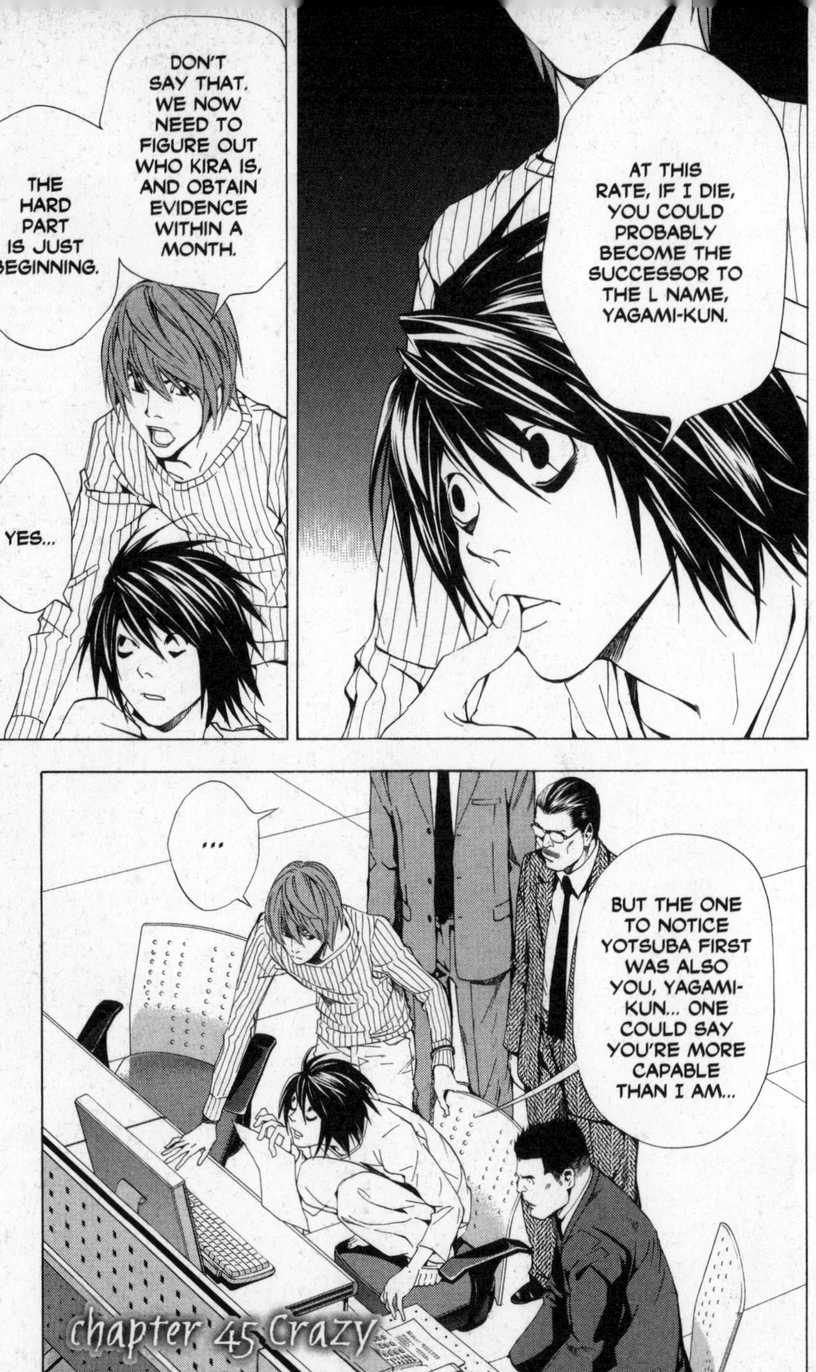
AT THIS RATE, IF I DIE, YOU COULD PROBABLY BECOME THE SUCCESSOR TO THE L NAME, YAGAMI-KUN.
DON'T SAY THAT. WE NOW NEED TO FIGURE OUT WHO KIRA IS, AND OBTAIN EVIDENCE WITHIN A MONTH.
THE HARD PART IS JUST BEGINNING.
YES...
BUT THE ONE TO NOTICE YOTSUBA FIRST WAS ALSO YOU, YAGAMI-KUN... ONE COULD SAY YOU'RE MORE CAPABLE THAN I AM...
...
chapter 45 Crazy

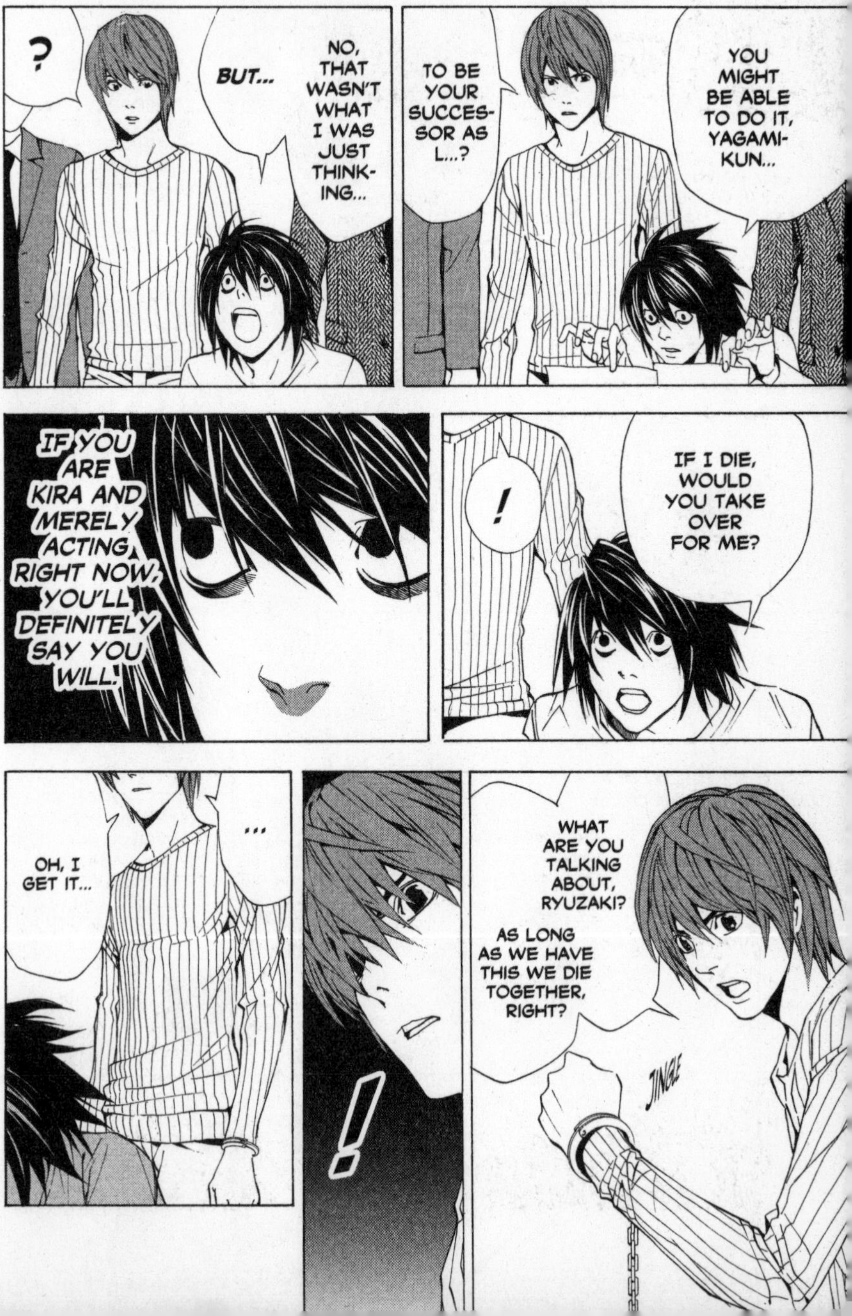
YOU MIGHT BE ABLE TO DO IT, YAGAMI-KUN...
TO BE YOUR SUCCESSOR AS L...?
NO, THAT WASN'T WHAT I WAS JUST THINKING...
BUT...
?
IF I DIE, WOULD YOU TAKE OVER FOR ME?
!
IF YOU ARE KIRA AND MERELY ACTING RIGHT NOW, YOU'LL DEFINITELY SAY YOU WILL.
WHAT ARE YOU TALKING ABOUT, RYUZAKI?
AS LONG AS WE HAVE THIS WE DIE TOGETHER, RIGHT?
JINGLE
!
...
OH, I GET IT...

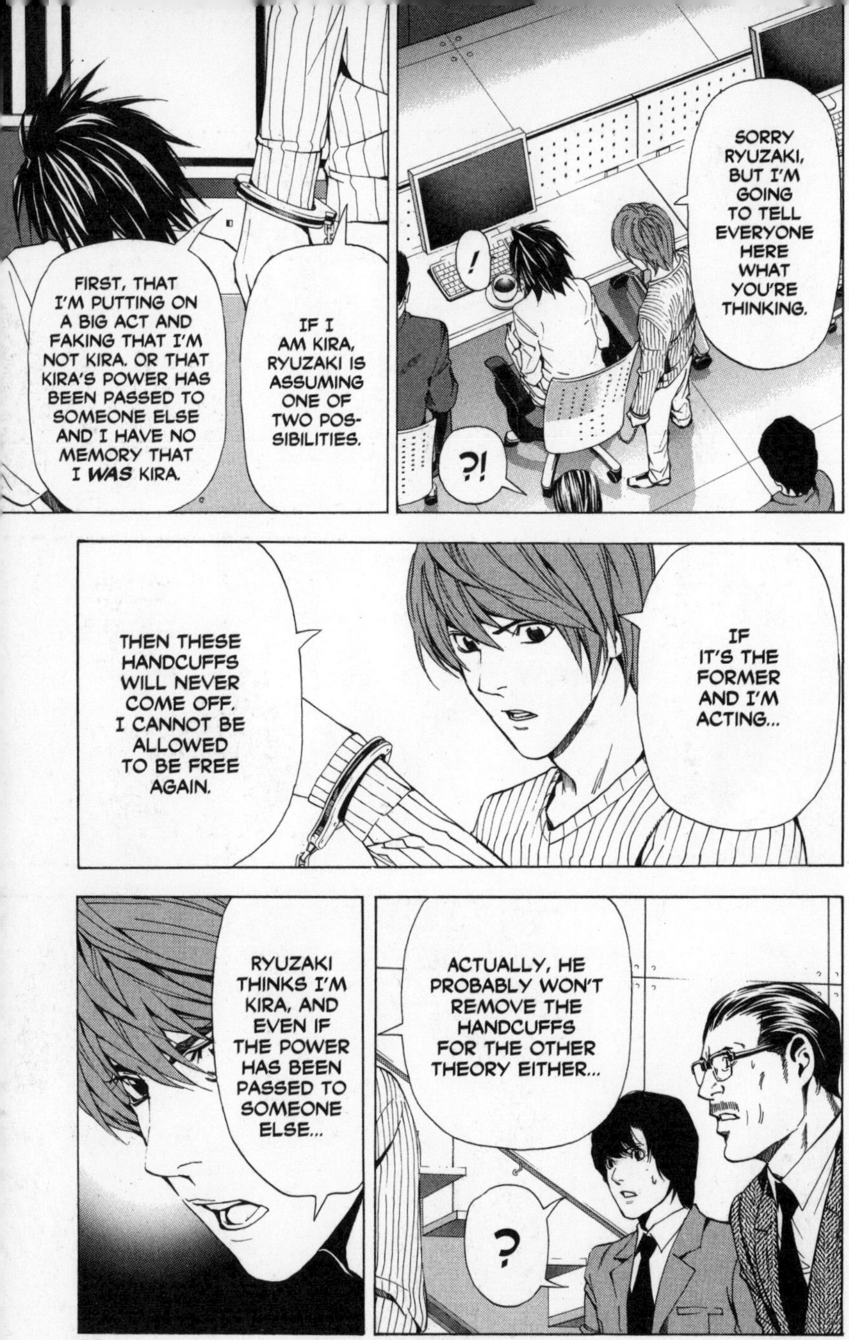
SORRY RYUZAKI, BUT I'M GOING TO TELL EVERYONE HERE WHAT YOU'RE THINKING.
!
?!
IF I AM KIRA, RYUZAKI IS ASSUMING ONE OF TWO POS-SIBILITIES.
FIRST, THAT I'M PUTTING ON A BIG ACT AND FAKING THAT I'M NOT KIRA. OR THAT KIRA'S POWER HAS BEEN PASSED TO SOMEONE ELSE AND I HAVE NO MEMORY THAT I *WAS* KIRA.
IF IT'S THE FORMER AND I'M ACTING...
THEN THESE HANDCUFFS WILL NEVER COME OFF. I CANNOT BE ALLOWED TO BE FREE AGAIN.
ACTUALLY, HE PROBABLY WON'T REMOVE THE HANDCUFFS FOR THE OTHER THEORY EITHER...
?
RYUZAKI THINKS I'M KIRA, AND EVEN IF THE POWER HAS BEEN PASSED TO SOMEONE ELSE...

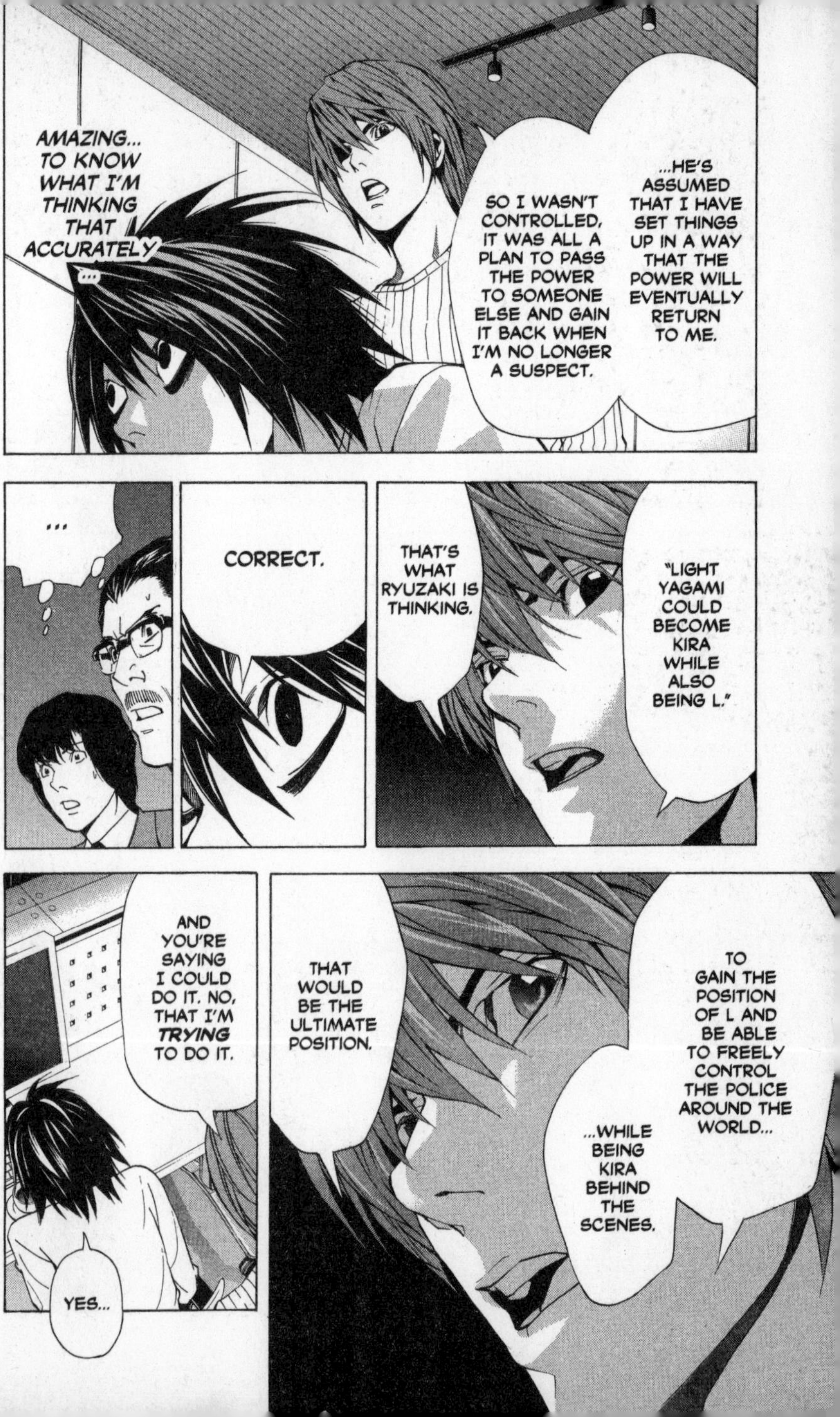
...HE'S ASSUMED THAT I HAVE SET THINGS UP IN A WAY THAT THE POWER WILL EVENTUALLY RETURN TO ME.
SO I WASN'T CONTROLLED, IT WAS ALL A PLAN TO PASS THE POWER TO SOMEONE ELSE AND GAIN IT BACK WHEN I'M NO LONGER A SUSPECT.
AMAZING... TO KNOW WHAT I'M THINKING THAT ACCURATELY...
"LIGHT YAGAMI COULD BECOME KIRA WHILE ALSO BEING L."
THAT'S WHAT RYUZAKI IS THINKING.
CORRECT.
...
TO GAIN THE POSITION OF L AND BE ABLE TO FREELY CONTROL THE POLICE AROUND THE WORLD...
...WHILE BEING KIRA BEHIND THE SCENES.
THAT WOULD BE THE ULTIMATE POSITION.
AND YOU'RE SAYING I COULD DO IT. NO, THAT I'M *TRYING* TO DO IT.
YES...

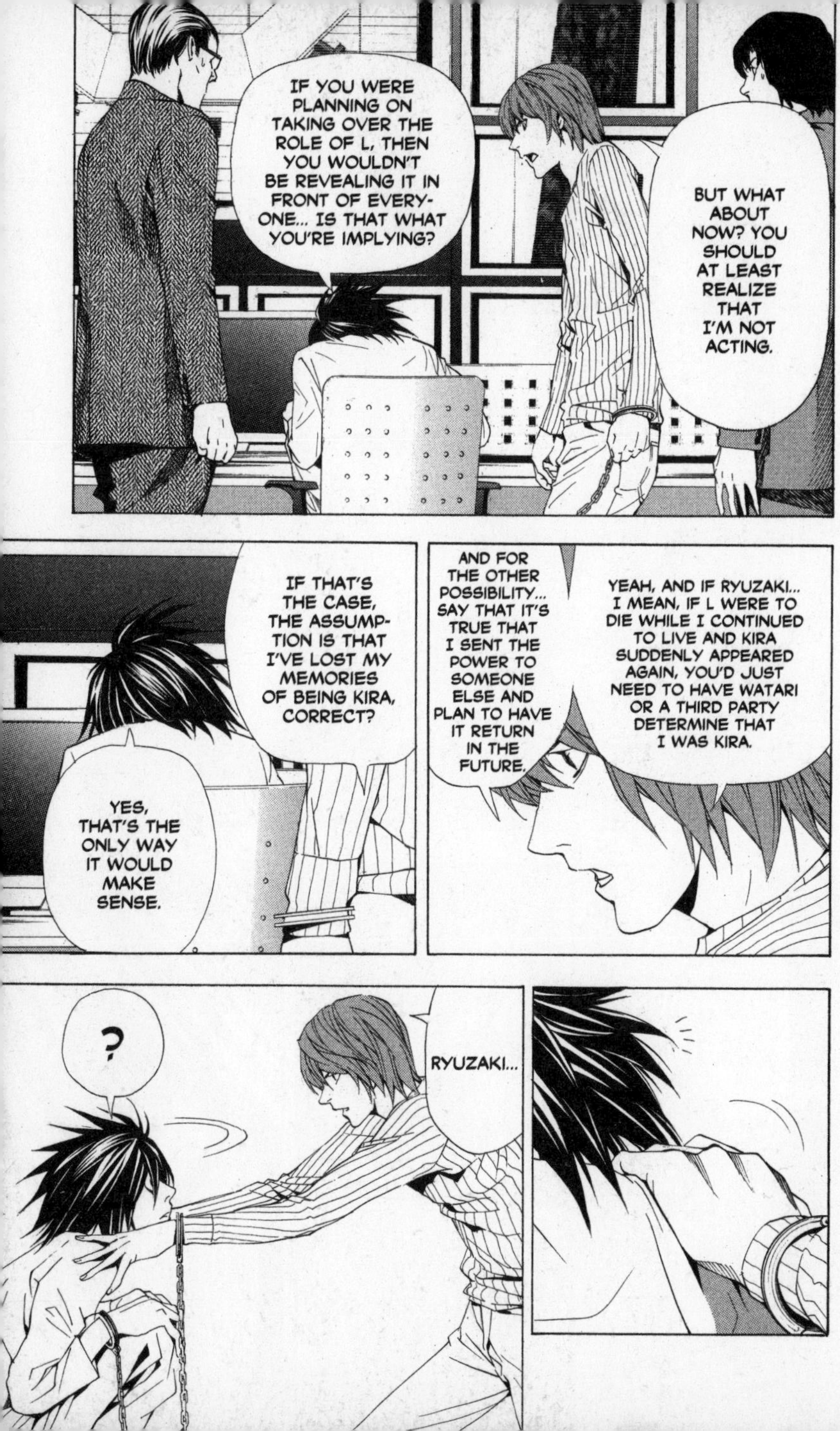
BUT WHAT ABOUT NOW? YOU SHOULD AT LEAST REALIZE THAT I'M NOT ACTING.
IF YOU WERE PLANNING ON TAKING OVER THE ROLE OF L, THEN YOU WOULDN'T BE REVEALING IT IN FRONT OF EVERY-ONE... IS THAT WHAT YOU'RE IMPLYING?
YEAH, AND IF RYUZAKI... I MEAN, IF L WERE TO DIE WHILE I CONTINUED TO LIVE AND KIRA SUDDENLY APPEARED AGAIN, YOU'D JUST NEED TO HAVE WATARI OR A THIRD PARTY DETERMINE THAT I WAS KIRA.
AND FOR THE OTHER POSSIBILITY... SAY THAT IT'S TRUE THAT I SENT THE POWER TO SOMEONE ELSE AND PLAN TO HAVE IT RETURN IN THE FUTURE.
IF THAT'S THE CASE, THE ASSUMP-TION IS THAT I'VE LOST MY MEMORIES OF BEING KIRA, CORRECT?
YES, THAT'S THE ONLY WAY IT WOULD MAKE SENSE.
RYUZAKI...
?

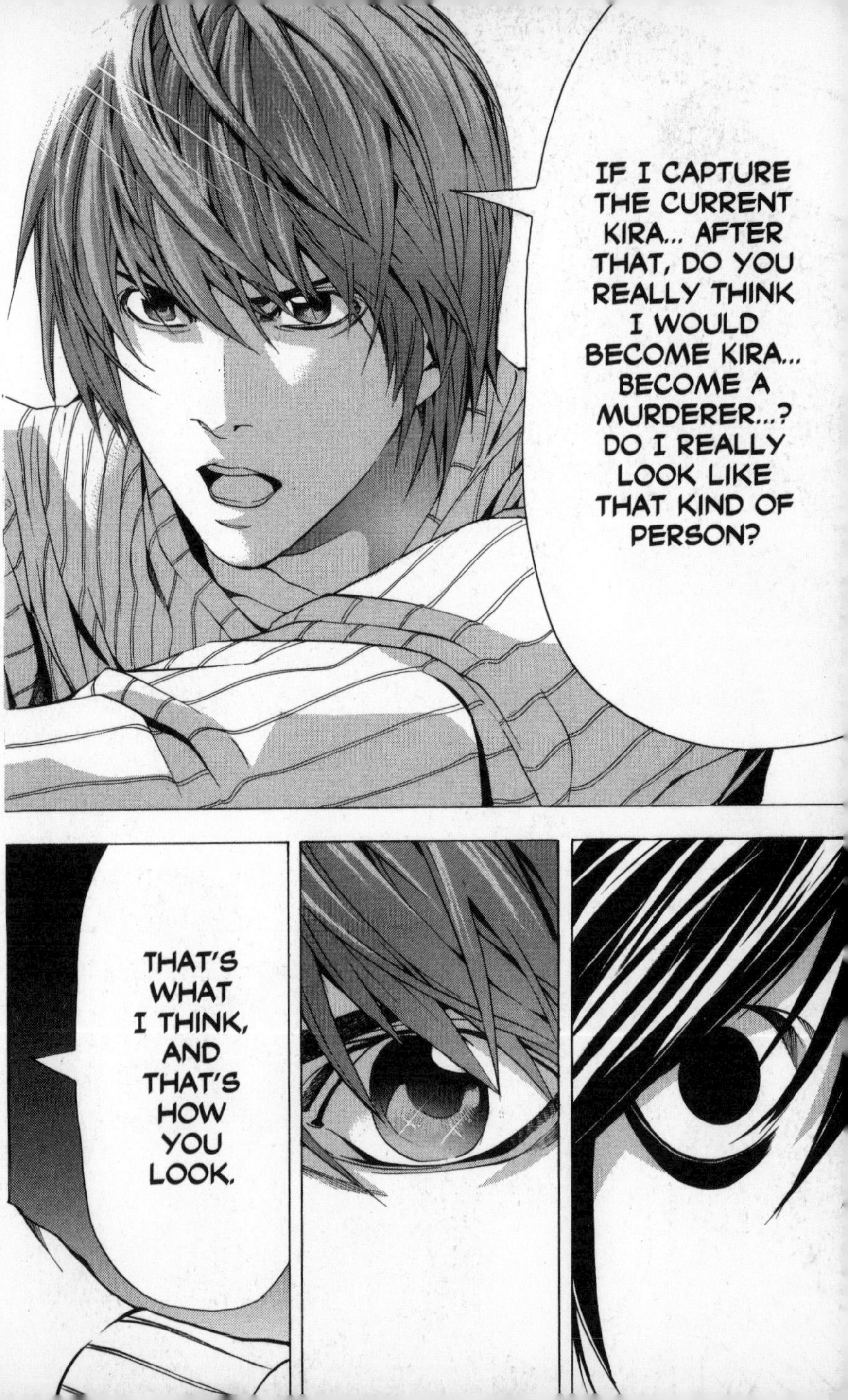
IF I CAPTURE THE CURRENT KIRA... AFTER THAT, DO YOU REALLY THINK I WOULD BECOME KIRA... BECOME A MURDERER...? DO I REALLY LOOK LIKE THAT KIND OF PERSON?
THAT'S WHAT I THINK, AND THAT'S HOW YOU LOOK.

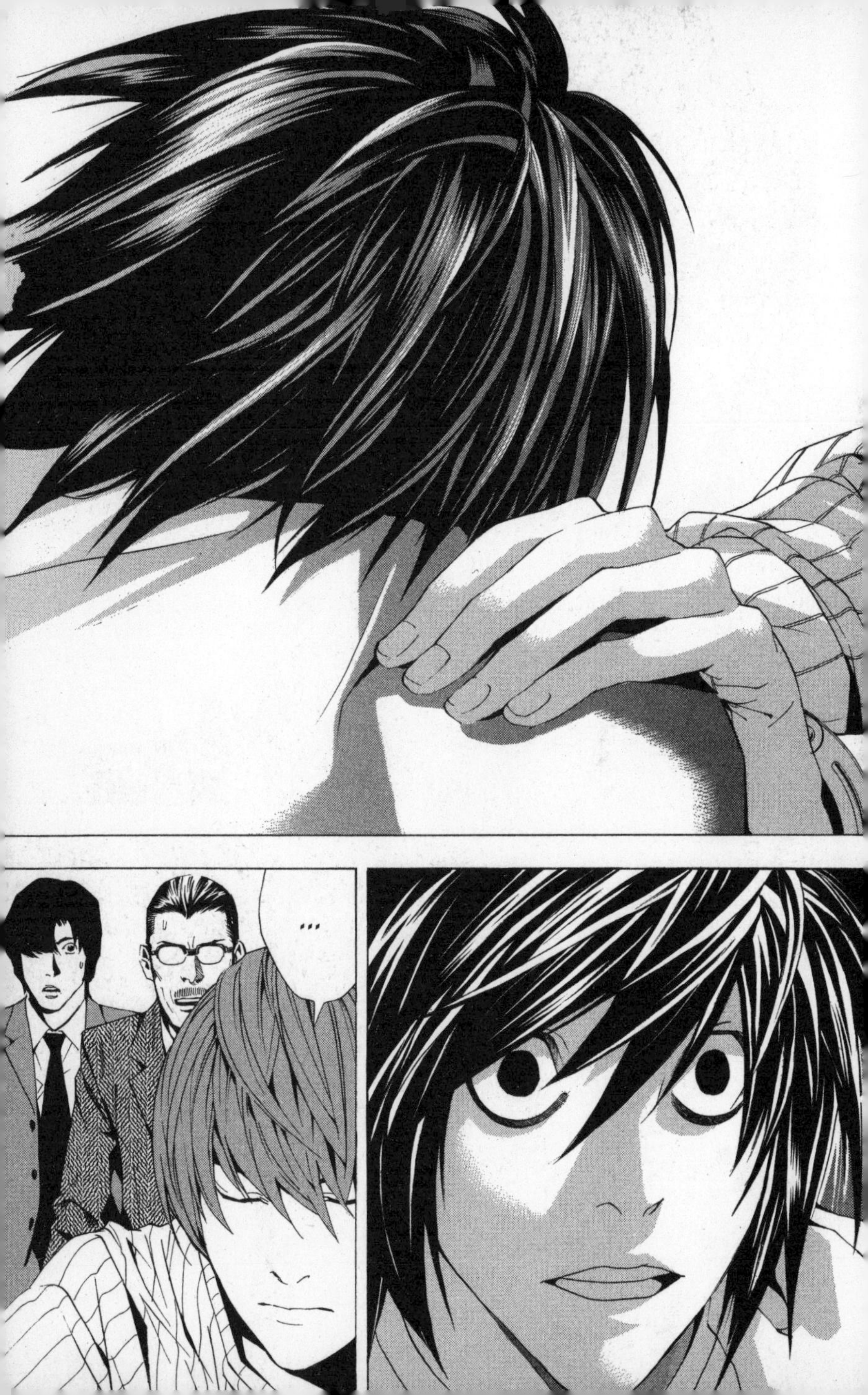
...

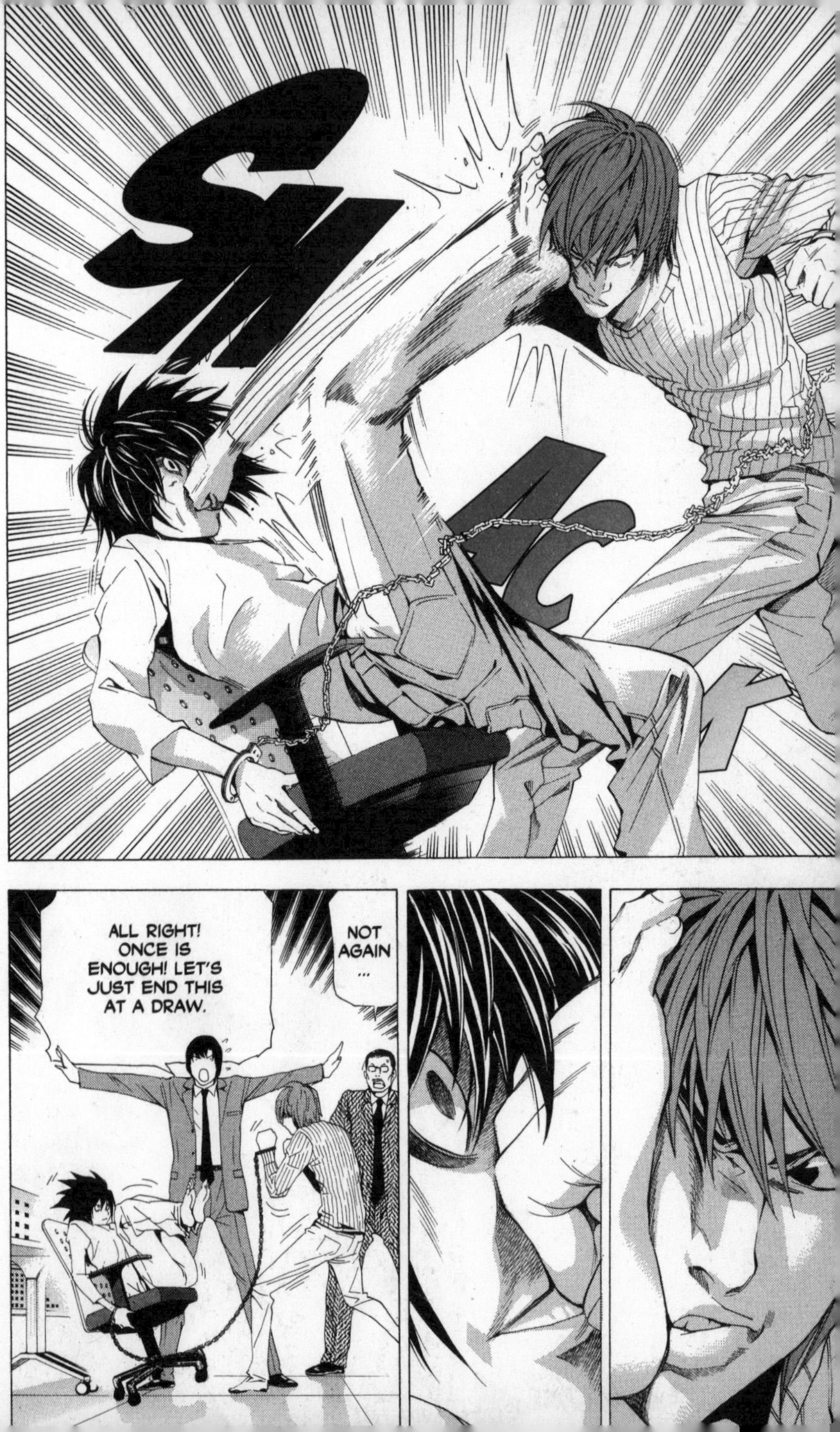
SMACK
NOT AGAIN ...
ALL RIGHT! ONCE IS ENOUGH! LET'S JUST END THIS AT A DRAW.

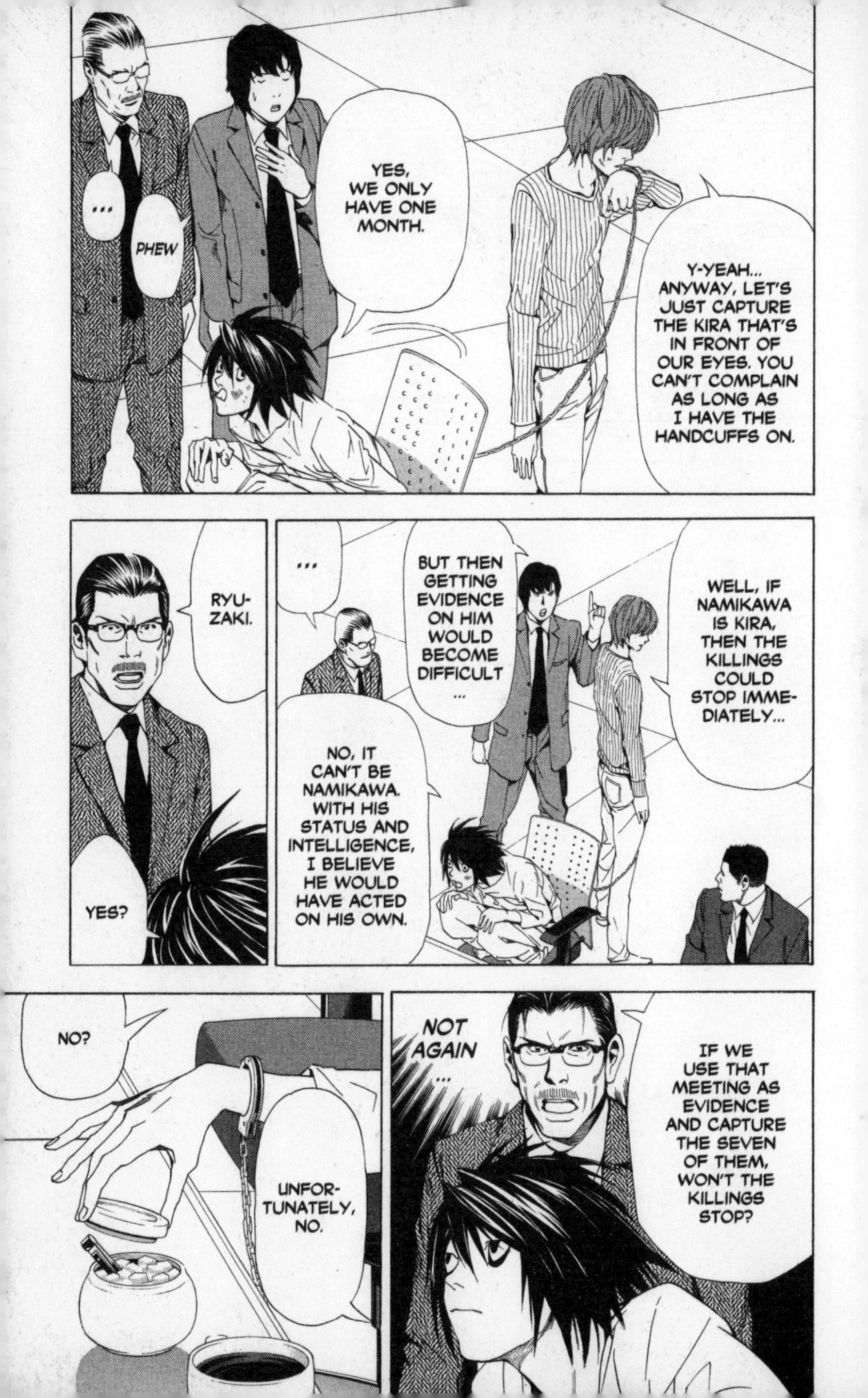
Y-YEAH... ANYWAY, LET'S JUST CAPTURE THE KIRA THAT'S IN FRONT OF OUR EYES. YOU CAN'T COMPLAIN AS LONG AS I HAVE THE HANDCUFFS ON.
YES, WE ONLY HAVE ONE MONTH.
PHEW
...
WELL, IF NAMIKAWA IS KIRA, THEN THE KILLINGS COULD STOP IMMEDIATELY...
BUT THEN GETTING EVIDENCE ON HIM WOULD BECOME DIFFICULT ...
...
NO, IT CAN'T BE NAMIKAWA. WITH HIS STATUS AND INTELLIGENCE, I BELIEVE HE WOULD HAVE ACTED ON HIS OWN.
RYU-ZAKI.
YES?
IF WE USE THAT MEETING AS EVIDENCE AND CAPTURE THE SEVEN OF THEM, WON'T THE KILLINGS STOP?
NOT AGAIN ...
NO?
UNFORTUNATELY, NO.

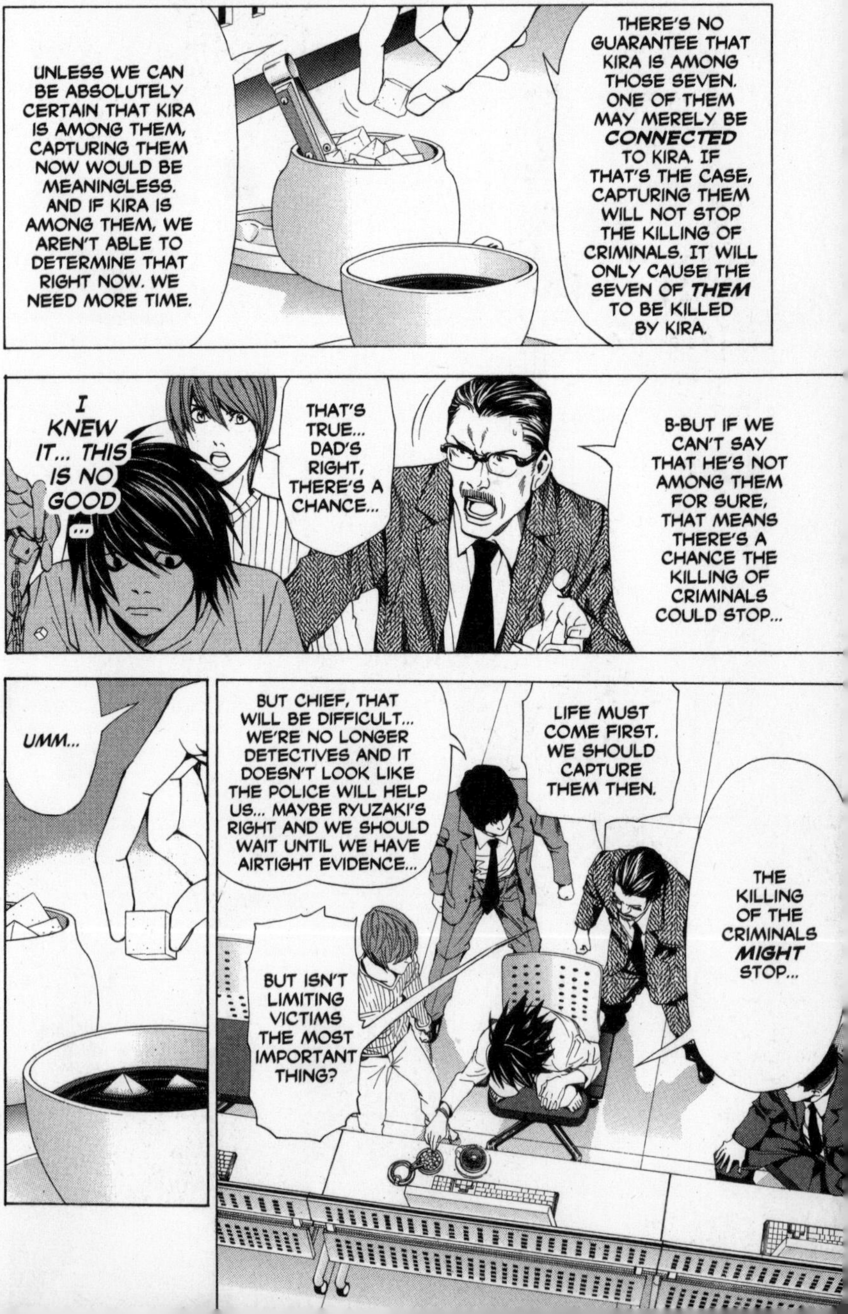
THERE'S NO GUARANTEE THAT KIRA IS AMONG THOSE SEVEN. ONE OF THEM MAY MERELY BE *CONNECTED* TO KIRA. IF THAT'S THE CASE, CAPTURING THEM WILL NOT STOP THE KILLING OF CRIMINALS. IT WILL ONLY CAUSE THE SEVEN OF *THEM* TO BE KILLED BY KIRA.
UNLESS WE CAN BE ABSOLUTELY CERTAIN THAT KIRA IS AMONG THEM, CAPTURING THEM NOW WOULD BE MEANINGLESS. AND IF KIRA IS AMONG THEM, WE AREN'T ABLE TO DETERMINE THAT RIGHT NOW. WE NEED MORE TIME.
B-BUT IF WE CAN'T SAY THAT HE'S NOT AMONG THEM FOR SURE, THAT MEANS THERE'S A CHANCE THE KILLING OF CRIMINALS COULD STOP...
THAT'S TRUE... DAD'S RIGHT, THERE'S A CHANCE...
I KNEW IT... THIS IS NO GOOD...
THE KILLING OF THE CRIMINALS *MIGHT* STOP...
LIFE MUST COME FIRST. WE SHOULD CAPTURE THEM THEN.
BUT CHIEF, THAT WILL BE DIFFICULT... WE'RE NO LONGER DETECTIVES AND IT DOESN'T LOOK LIKE THE POLICE WILL HELP US... MAYBE RYUZAKI'S RIGHT AND WE SHOULD WAIT UNTIL WE HAVE AIRTIGHT EVIDENCE...
BUT ISN'T LIMITING VICTIMS THE MOST IMPORTANT THING?
UMM...

READ THIS WAY

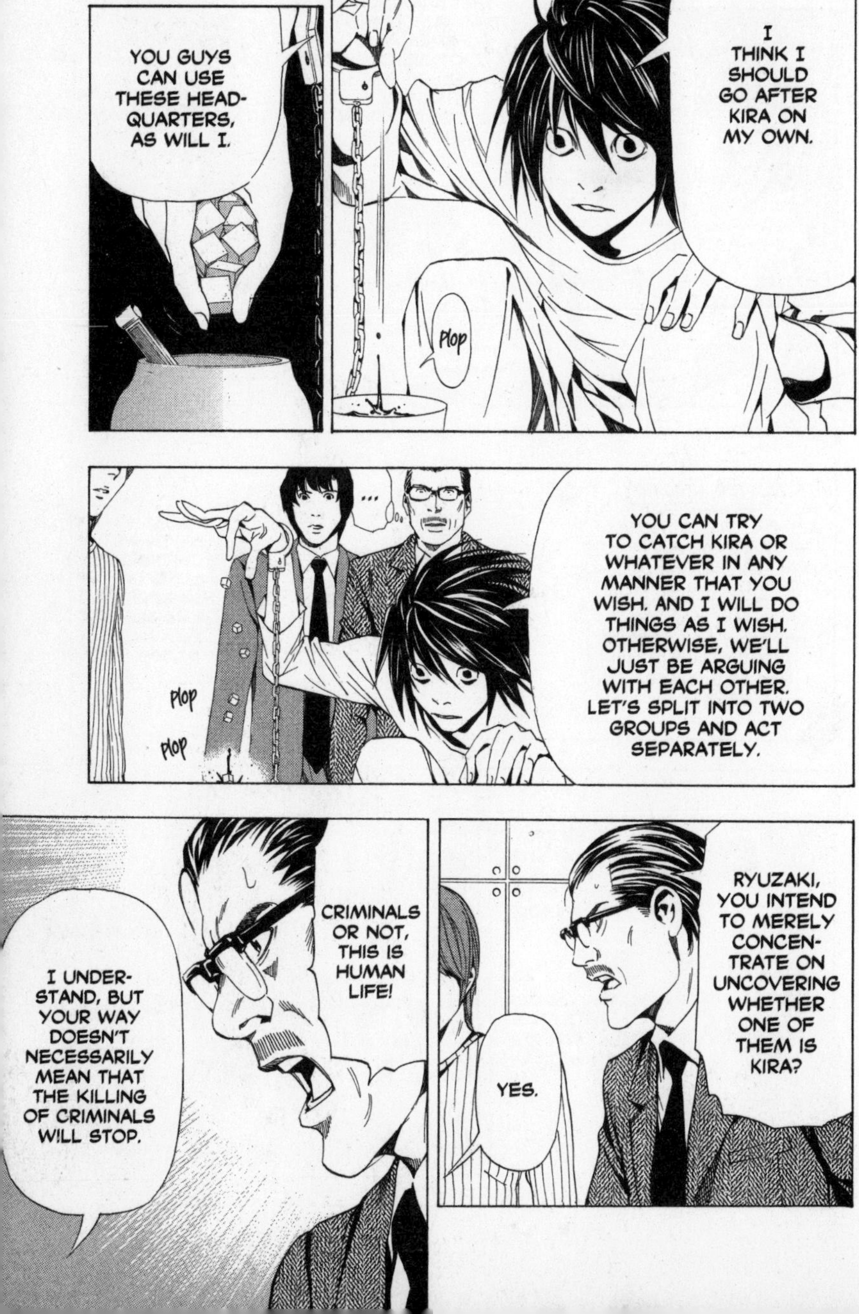
I THINK I SHOULD GO AFTER KIRA ON MY OWN.
Plop
YOU GUYS CAN USE THESE HEAD-QUARTERS, AS WILL I.
YOU CAN TRY TO CATCH KIRA OR WHATEVER IN ANY MANNER THAT YOU WISH. AND I WILL DO THINGS AS I WISH. OTHERWISE, WE'LL JUST BE ARGUING WITH EACH OTHER. LET'S SPLIT INTO TWO GROUPS AND ACT SEPARATELY.
...
Plop
Plop
RYUZAKI, YOU INTEND TO MERELY CONCEN-TRATE ON UNCOVERING WHETHER ONE OF THEM IS KIRA?
YES.
CRIMINALS OR NOT, THIS IS HUMAN LIFE!
I UNDER-STAND, BUT YOUR WAY DOESN'T NECESSARILY MEAN THAT THE KILLING OF CRIMINALS WILL STOP.

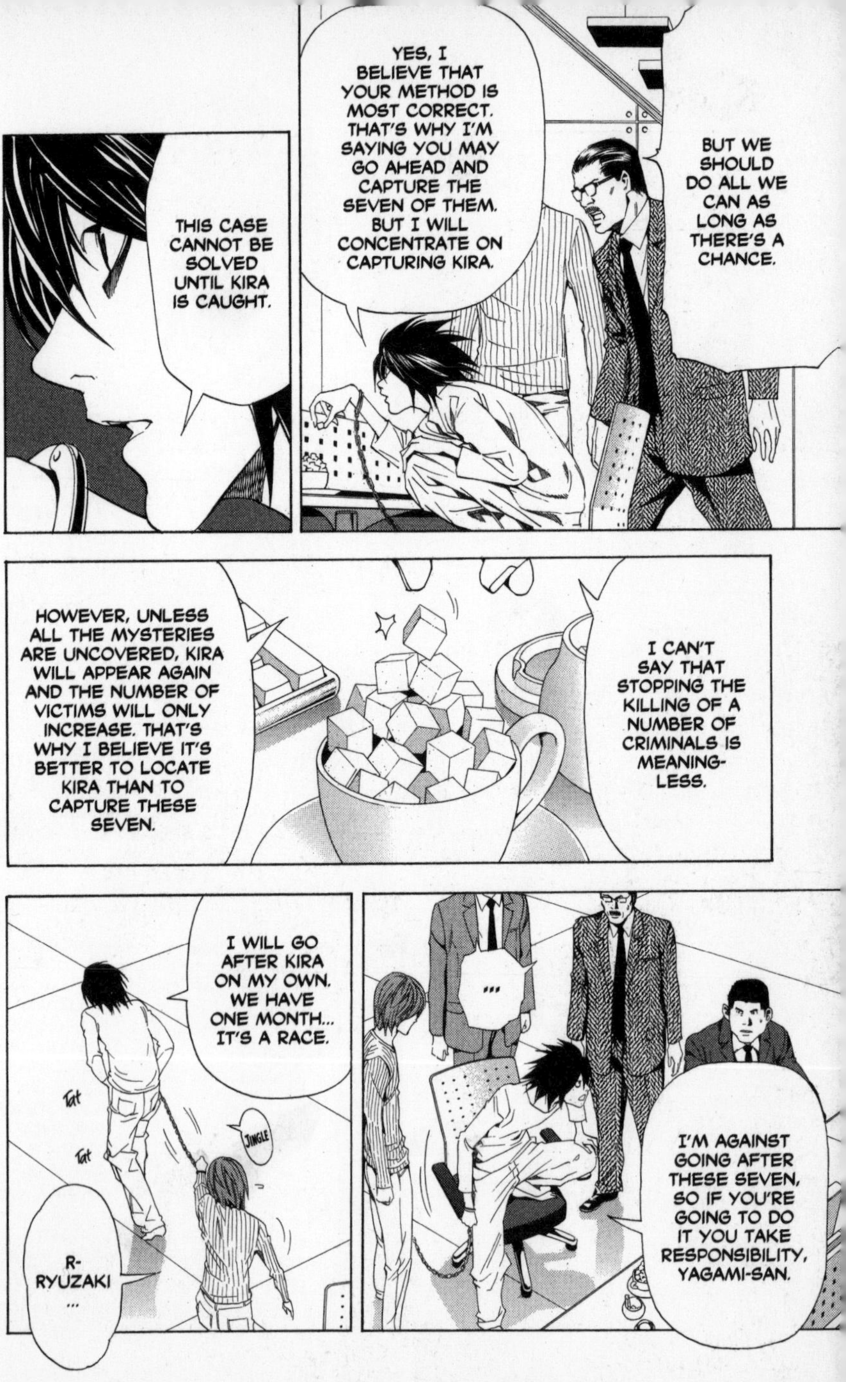
BUT WE SHOULD DO ALL WE CAN AS LONG AS THERE'S A CHANCE.
YES, I BELIEVE THAT YOUR METHOD IS MOST CORRECT. THAT'S WHY I'M SAYING YOU MAY GO AHEAD AND CAPTURE THE SEVEN OF THEM. BUT I WILL CONCENTRATE ON CAPTURING KIRA.
THIS CASE CANNOT BE SOLVED UNTIL KIRA IS CAUGHT.
I CAN'T SAY THAT STOPPING THE KILLING OF A NUMBER OF CRIMINALS IS MEANING-LESS.
HOWEVER, UNLESS ALL THE MYSTERIES ARE UNCOVERED, KIRA WILL APPEAR AGAIN AND THE NUMBER OF VICTIMS WILL ONLY INCREASE. THAT'S WHY I BELIEVE IT'S BETTER TO LOCATE KIRA THAN TO CAPTURE THESE SEVEN.
...
I'M AGAINST GOING AFTER THESE SEVEN, SO IF YOU'RE GOING TO DO IT YOU TAKE RESPONSIBILITY, YAGAMI-SAN.
I WILL GO AFTER KIRA ON MY OWN. WE HAVE ONE MONTH... IT'S A RACE.
Tat
Tat
JINGLE
R-RYUZAKI ...

READ THIS WAY

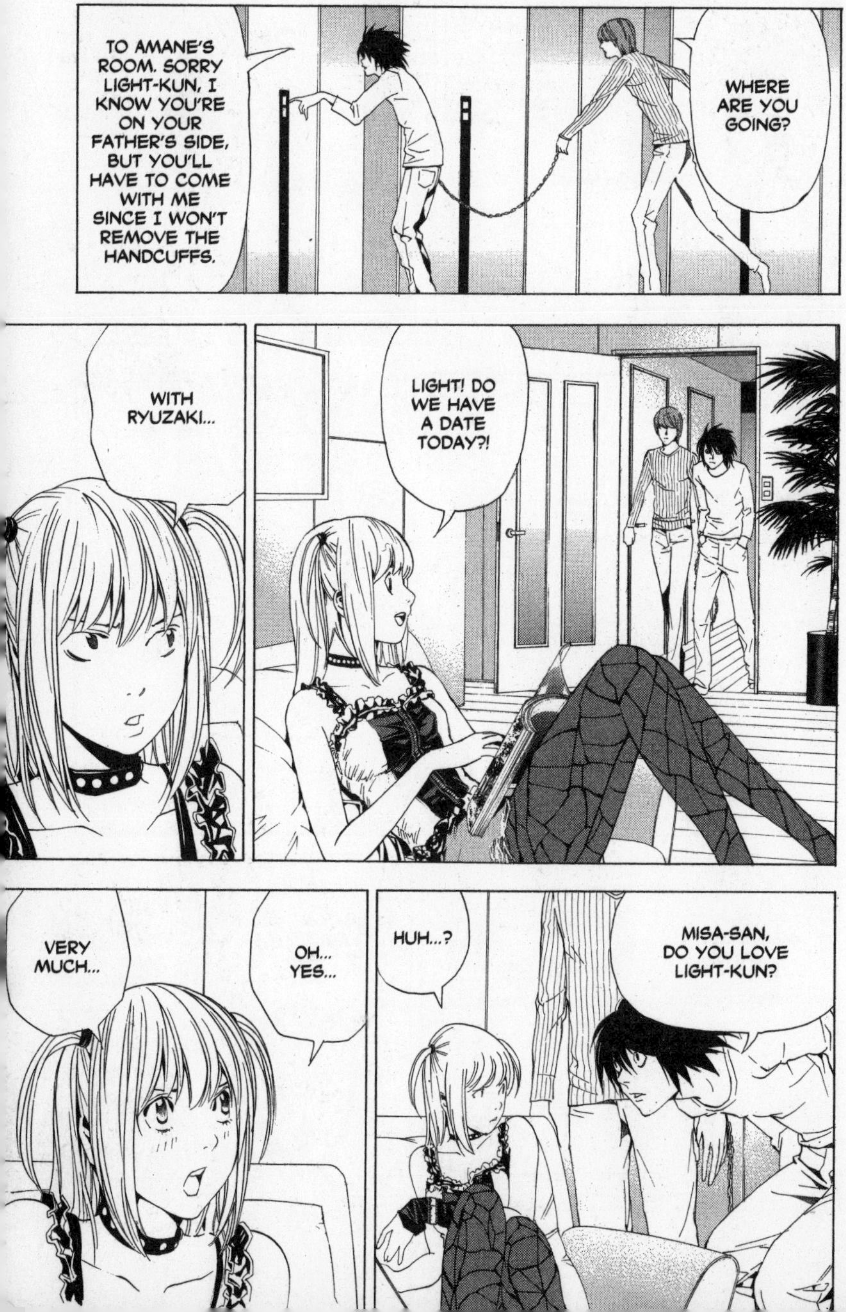
WHERE ARE YOU GOING?
TO AMANE'S ROOM. SORRY LIGHT-KUN, I KNOW YOU'RE ON YOUR FATHER'S SIDE, BUT YOU'LL HAVE TO COME WITH ME SINCE I WON'T REMOVE THE HANDCUFFS.
LIGHT! DO WE HAVE A DATE TODAY?!
WITH RYUZAKI...
MISA-SAN, DO YOU LOVE LIGHT-KUN?
HUH...?
OH... YES...
VERY MUCH...

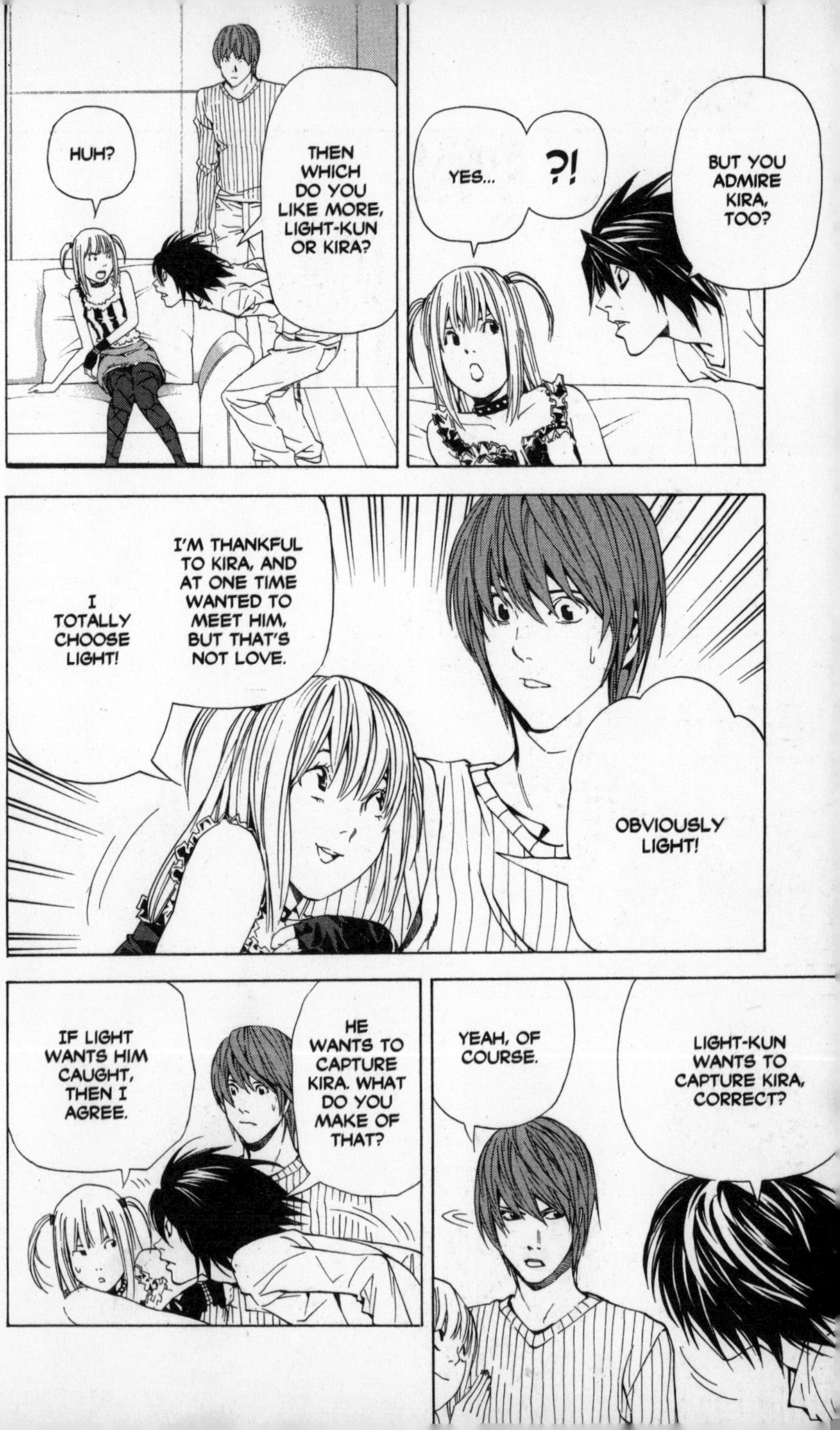
BUT YOU ADMIRE KIRA, TOO?
YES... ?!
THEN WHICH DO YOU LIKE MORE, LIGHT-KUN OR KIRA?
HUH?
OBVIOUSLY LIGHT!
I'M THANKFUL TO KIRA, AND AT ONE TIME WANTED TO MEET HIM, BUT THAT'S NOT LOVE.
I TOTALLY CHOOSE LIGHT!
LIGHT-KUN WANTS TO CAPTURE KIRA, CORRECT?
YEAH, OF COURSE.
HE WANTS TO CAPTURE KIRA. WHAT DO YOU MAKE OF THAT?
IF LIGHT WANTS HIM CAUGHT, THEN I AGREE.

READ THIS WAY

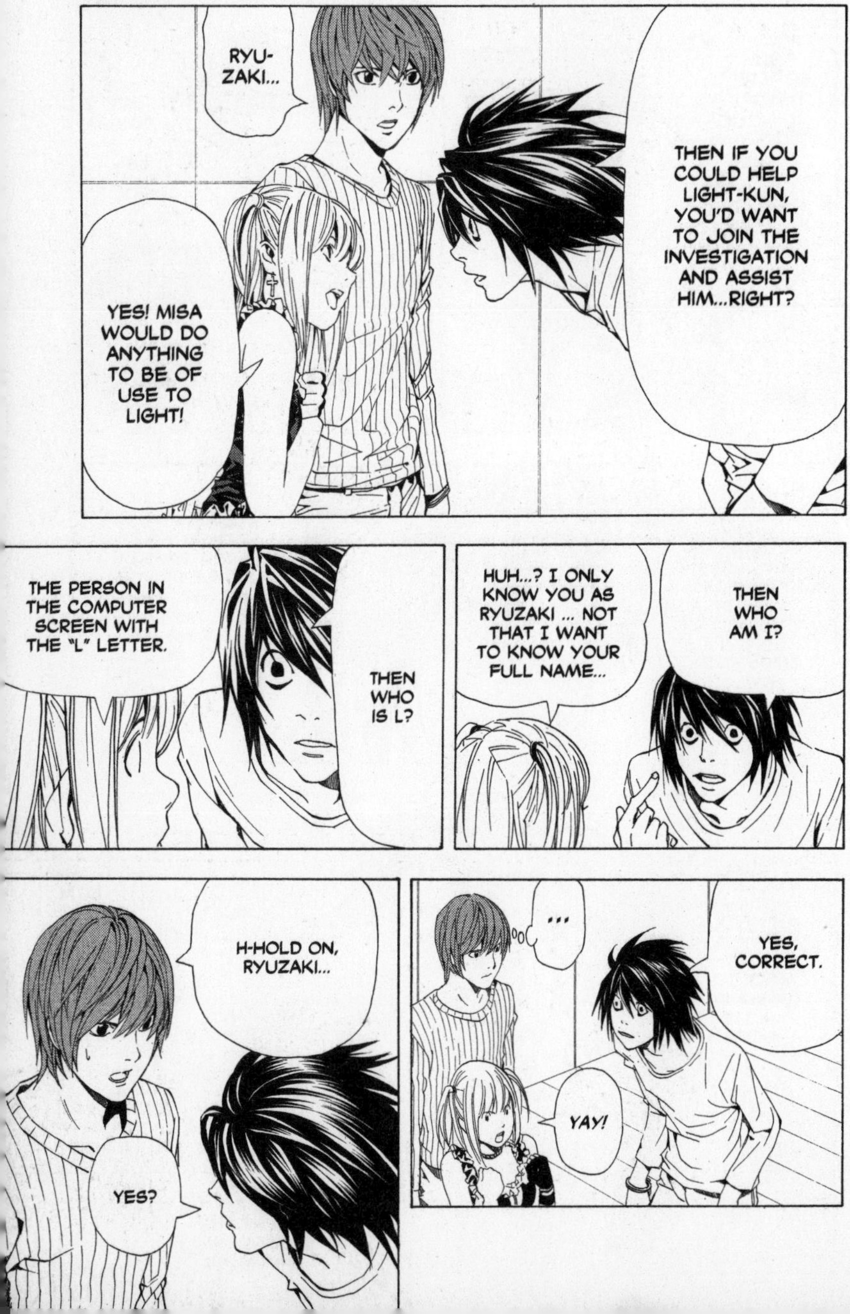
THEN IF YOU COULD HELP LIGHT-KUN, YOU'D WANT TO JOIN THE INVESTIGATION AND ASSIST HIM...RIGHT?
YES! MISA WOULD DO ANYTHING TO BE OF USE TO LIGHT!
RYU-ZAKI...
THEN WHO AM I?
HUH...? I ONLY KNOW YOU AS RYUZAKI ... NOT THAT I WANT TO KNOW YOUR FULL NAME...
THEN WHO IS L?
THE PERSON IN THE COMPUTER SCREEN WITH THE "L" LETTER.
YES, CORRECT.
...
YAY!
H-HOLD ON, RYUZAKI...
YES?

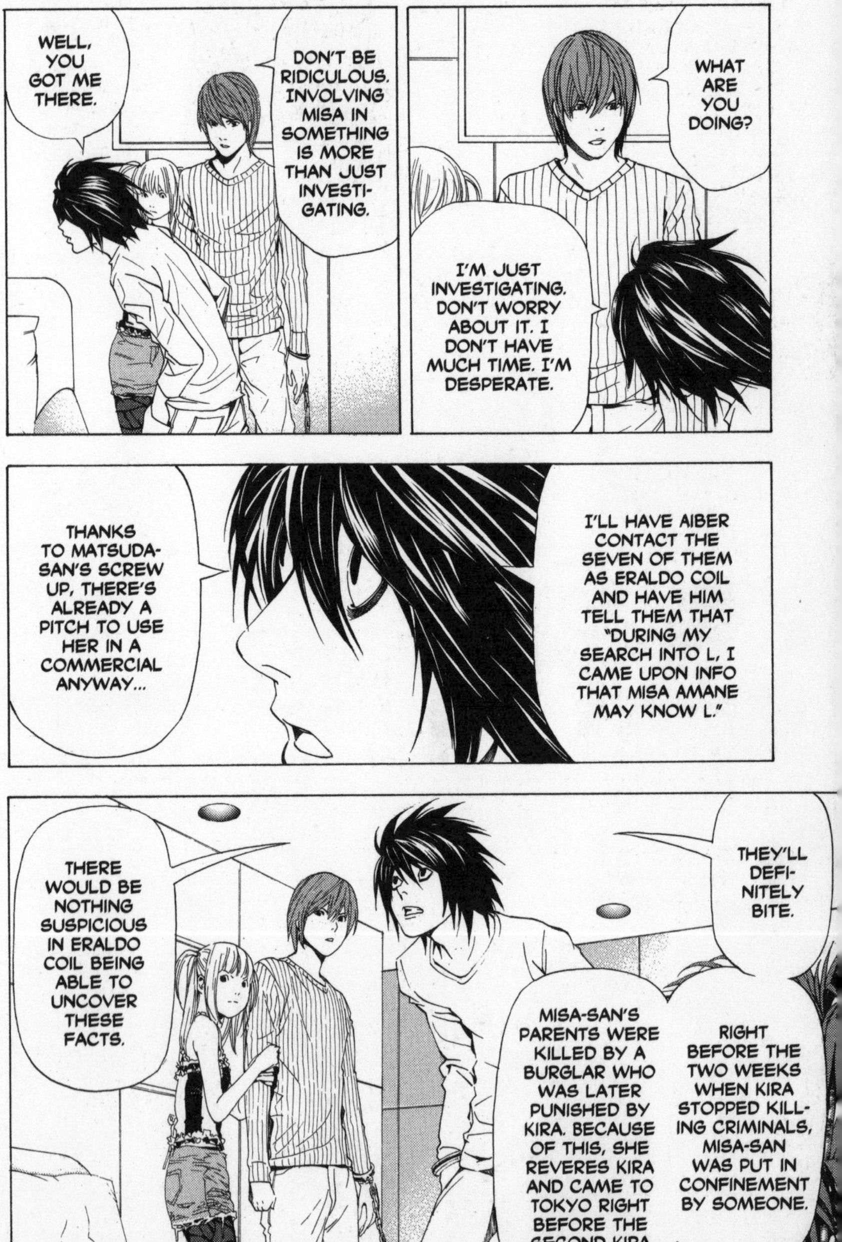
WHAT ARE YOU DOING?
I'M JUST INVESTIGATING. DON'T WORRY ABOUT IT. I DON'T HAVE MUCH TIME. I'M DESPERATE.
DON'T BE RIDICULOUS. INVOLVING MISA IN SOMETHING IS MORE THAN JUST INVESTIGATING.
WELL, YOU GOT ME THERE.
I'LL HAVE AIBER CONTACT THE SEVEN OF THEM AS ERALDO COIL AND HAVE HIM TELL THEM THAT "DURING MY SEARCH INTO L, I CAME UPON INFO THAT MISA AMANE MAY KNOW L."
THANKS TO MATSUDA-SAN'S SCREW UP, THERE'S ALREADY A PITCH TO USE HER IN A COMMERCIAL ANYWAY...
THEY'LL DEFINITELY BITE.
RIGHT BEFORE THE TWO WEEKS WHEN KIRA STOPPED KILLING CRIMINALS, MISA-SAN WAS PUT IN CONFINEMENT BY SOMEONE.
MISA-SAN'S PARENTS WERE KILLED BY A BURGLAR WHO WAS LATER PUNISHED BY KIRA. BECAUSE OF THIS, SHE REVERES KIRA AND CAME TO TOKYO RIGHT BEFORE THE SECOND KIRA APPEARED.
THERE WOULD BE NOTHING SUSPICIOUS IN ERALDO COIL BEING ABLE TO UNCOVER THESE FACTS.

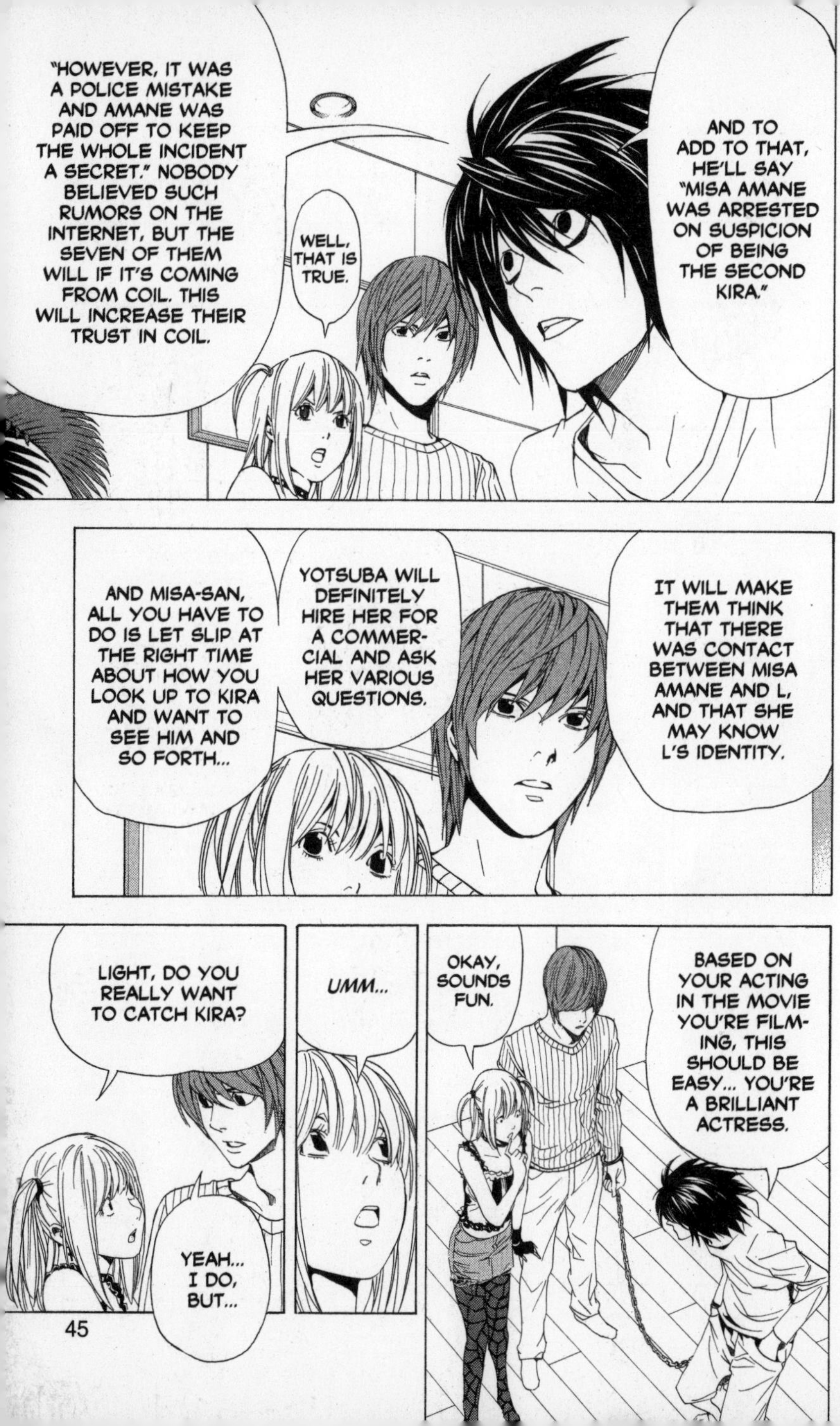
AND TO ADD TO THAT, HE'LL SAY "MISA AMANE WAS ARRESTED ON SUSPICION OF BEING THE SECOND KIRA."
"HOWEVER, IT WAS A POLICE MISTAKE AND AMANE WAS PAID OFF TO KEEP THE WHOLE INCIDENT A SECRET." NOBODY BELIEVED SUCH RUMORS ON THE INTERNET, BUT THE SEVEN OF THEM WILL IF IT'S COMING FROM COIL. THIS WILL INCREASE THEIR TRUST IN COIL.
WELL, THAT IS TRUE.
IT WILL MAKE THEM THINK THAT THERE WAS CONTACT BETWEEN MISA AMANE AND L, AND THAT SHE MAY KNOW L'S IDENTITY.
YOTSUBA WILL DEFINITELY HIRE HER FOR A COMMERCIAL AND ASK HER VARIOUS QUESTIONS.
AND MISA-SAN, ALL YOU HAVE TO DO IS LET SLIP AT THE RIGHT TIME ABOUT HOW YOU LOOK UP TO KIRA AND WANT TO SEE HIM AND SO FORTH...
BASED ON YOUR ACTING IN THE MOVIE YOU'RE FILMING, THIS SHOULD BE EASY... YOU'RE A BRILLIANT ACTRESS.
OKAY, SOUNDS FUN.
UMM...
LIGHT, DO YOU REALLY WANT TO CATCH KIRA?
YEAH... I DO, BUT...

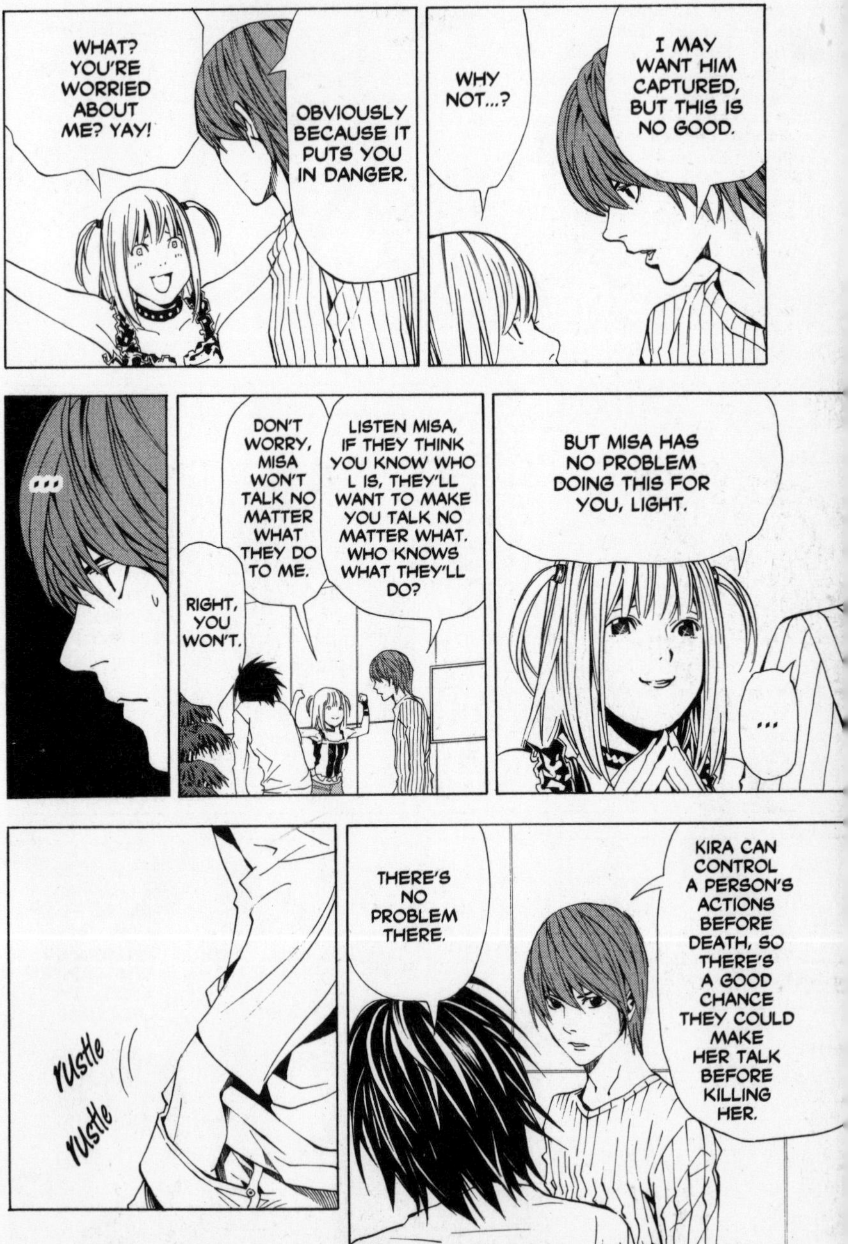
I MAY WANT HIM CAPTURED, BUT THIS IS NO GOOD.
WHY NOT...?
OBVIOUSLY BECAUSE IT PUTS YOU IN DANGER.
WHAT? YOU'RE WORRIED ABOUT ME? YAY!
BUT MISA HAS NO PROBLEM DOING THIS FOR YOU, LIGHT.
...
LISTEN MISA, IF THEY THINK YOU KNOW WHO L IS, THEY'LL WANT TO MAKE YOU TALK NO MATTER WHAT. WHO KNOWS WHAT THEY'LL DO?
DON'T WORRY, MISA WON'T TALK NO MATTER WHAT THEY DO TO ME.
RIGHT, YOU WON'T.
...
KIRA CAN CONTROL A PERSON'S ACTIONS BEFORE DEATH, SO THERE'S A GOOD CHANCE THEY COULD MAKE HER TALK BEFORE KILLING HER.
THERE'S NO PROBLEM THERE.
rustle
rustle

READ THIS WAY

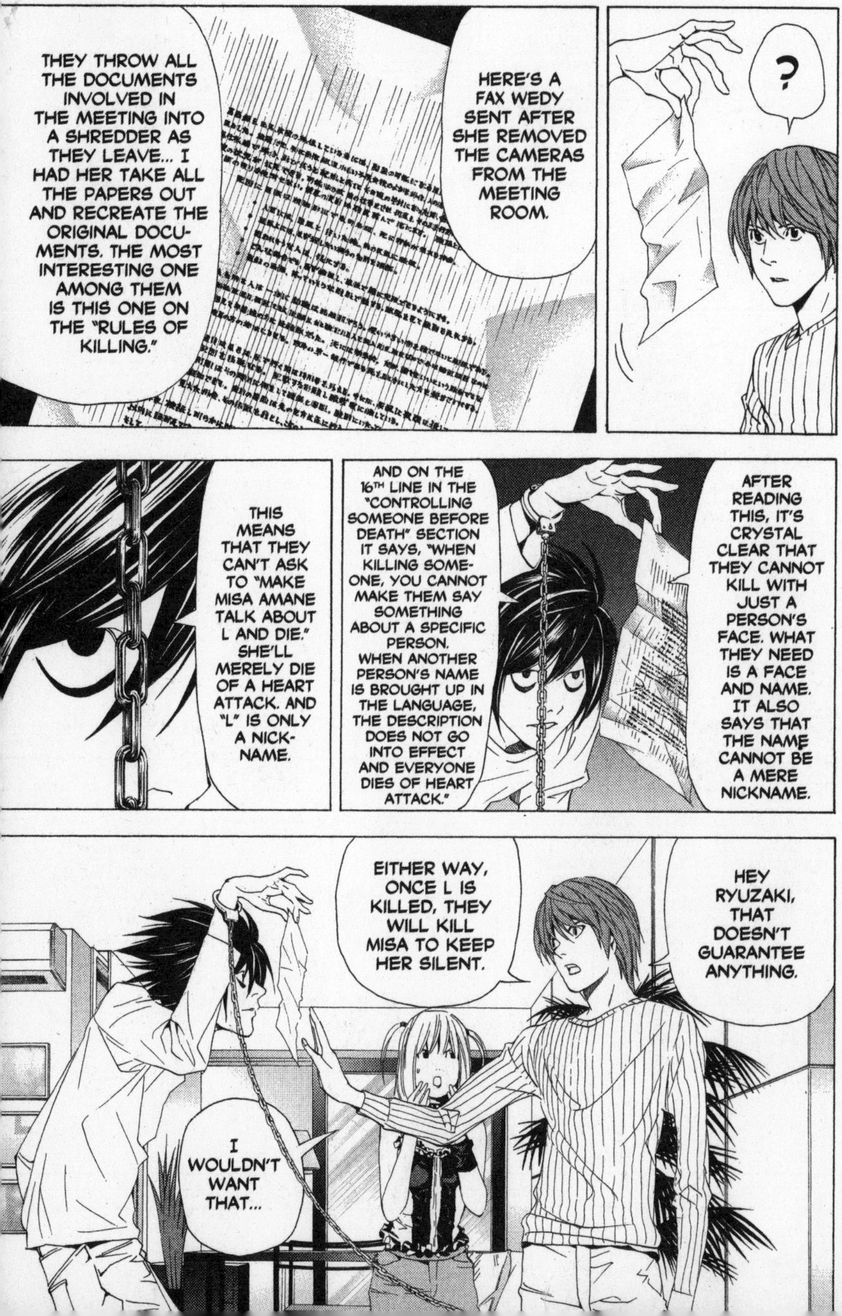
?
HERE'S A FAX WEDY SENT AFTER SHE REMOVED THE CAMERAS FROM THE MEETING ROOM.
THEY THROW ALL THE DOCUMENTS INVOLVED IN THE MEETING INTO A SHREDDER AS THEY LEAVE... I HAD HER TAKE ALL THE PAPERS OUT AND RECREATE THE ORIGINAL DOCU-MENTS. THE MOST INTERESTING ONE AMONG THEM IS THIS ONE ON THE "RULES OF KILLING."
AFTER READING THIS, IT'S CRYSTAL CLEAR THAT THEY CANNOT KILL WITH JUST A PERSON'S FACE. WHAT THEY NEED IS A FACE AND NAME. IT ALSO SAYS THAT THE NAME CANNOT BE A MERE NICKNAME.
AND ON THE 16TH LINE IN THE "CONTROLLING SOMEONE BEFORE DEATH" SECTION IT SAYS, "WHEN KILLING SOME-ONE, YOU CANNOT MAKE THEM SAY SOMETHING ABOUT A SPECIFIC PERSON. WHEN ANOTHER PERSON'S NAME IS BROUGHT UP IN THE LANGUAGE, THE DESCRIPTION DOES NOT GO INTO EFFECT AND EVERYONE DIES OF HEART ATTACK."
THIS MEANS THAT THEY CAN'T ASK TO "MAKE MISA AMANE TALK ABOUT L AND DIE." SHE'LL MERELY DIE OF A HEART ATTACK. AND "L" IS ONLY A NICK-NAME.
HEY RYUZAKI, THAT DOESN'T GUARANTEE ANYTHING.
EITHER WAY, ONCE L IS KILLED, THEY WILL KILL MISA TO KEEP HER SILENT.
I WOULDN'T WANT THAT...

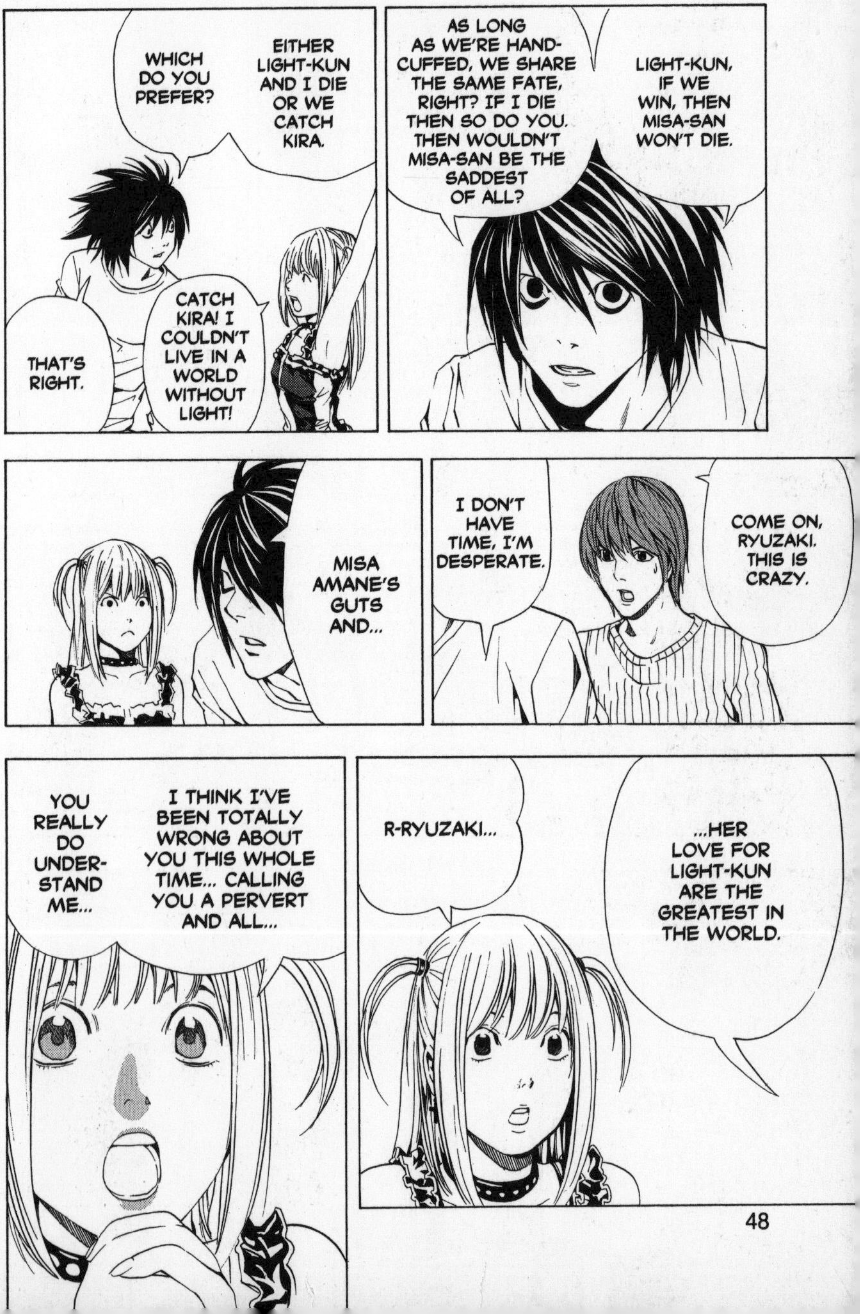
LIGHT-KUN, IF WE WIN, THEN MISA-SAN WON'T DIE.
AS LONG AS WE'RE HAND-CUFFED, WE SHARE THE SAME FATE, RIGHT? IF I DIE THEN SO DO YOU. THEN WOULDN'T MISA-SAN BE THE SADDEST OF ALL?
EITHER LIGHT-KUN AND I DIE OR WE CATCH KIRA.
WHICH DO YOU PREFER?
CATCH KIRA! I COULDN'T LIVE IN A WORLD WITHOUT LIGHT!
THAT'S RIGHT.
COME ON, RYUZAKI. THIS IS CRAZY.
I DON'T HAVE TIME, I'M DESPERATE.
MISA AMANE'S GUTS AND...
...HER LOVE FOR LIGHT-KUN ARE THE GREATEST IN THE WORLD.
R-RYUZAKI...
I THINK I'VE BEEN TOTALLY WRONG ABOUT YOU THIS WHOLE TIME... CALLING YOU A PERVERT AND ALL...
YOU REALLY DO UNDERSTAND ME...

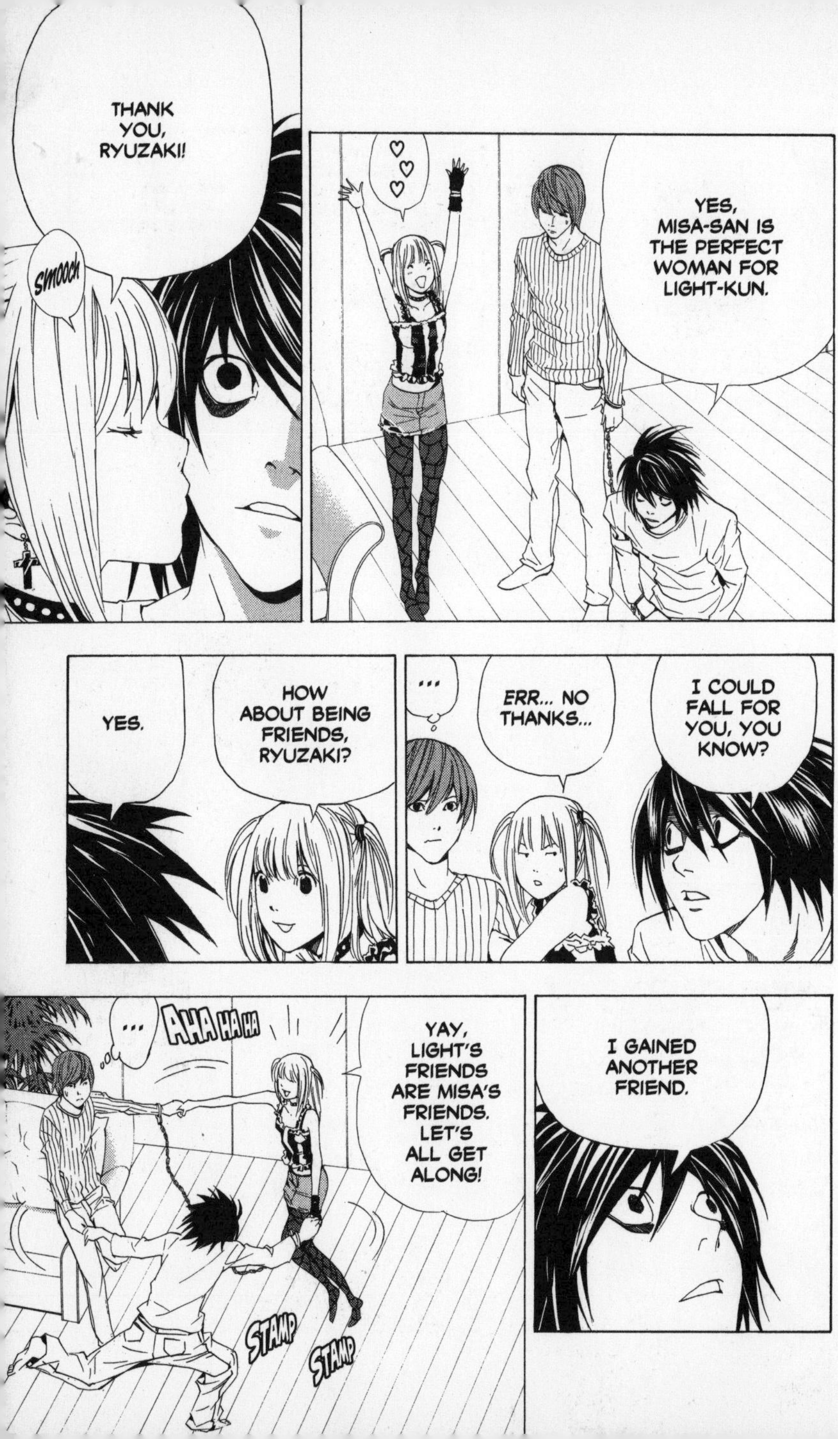
YES, MISA-SAN IS THE PERFECT WOMAN FOR LIGHT-KUN.
THANK YOU, RYUZAKI!
SMOOCH
I COULD FALL FOR YOU, YOU KNOW?
ERR... NO THANKS...
...
HOW ABOUT BEING FRIENDS, RYUZAKI?
YES.
I GAINED ANOTHER FRIEND.
YAY, LIGHT'S FRIENDS ARE MISA'S FRIENDS. LET'S ALL GET ALONG!
AHAHAHA
...
STAMP
STAMP

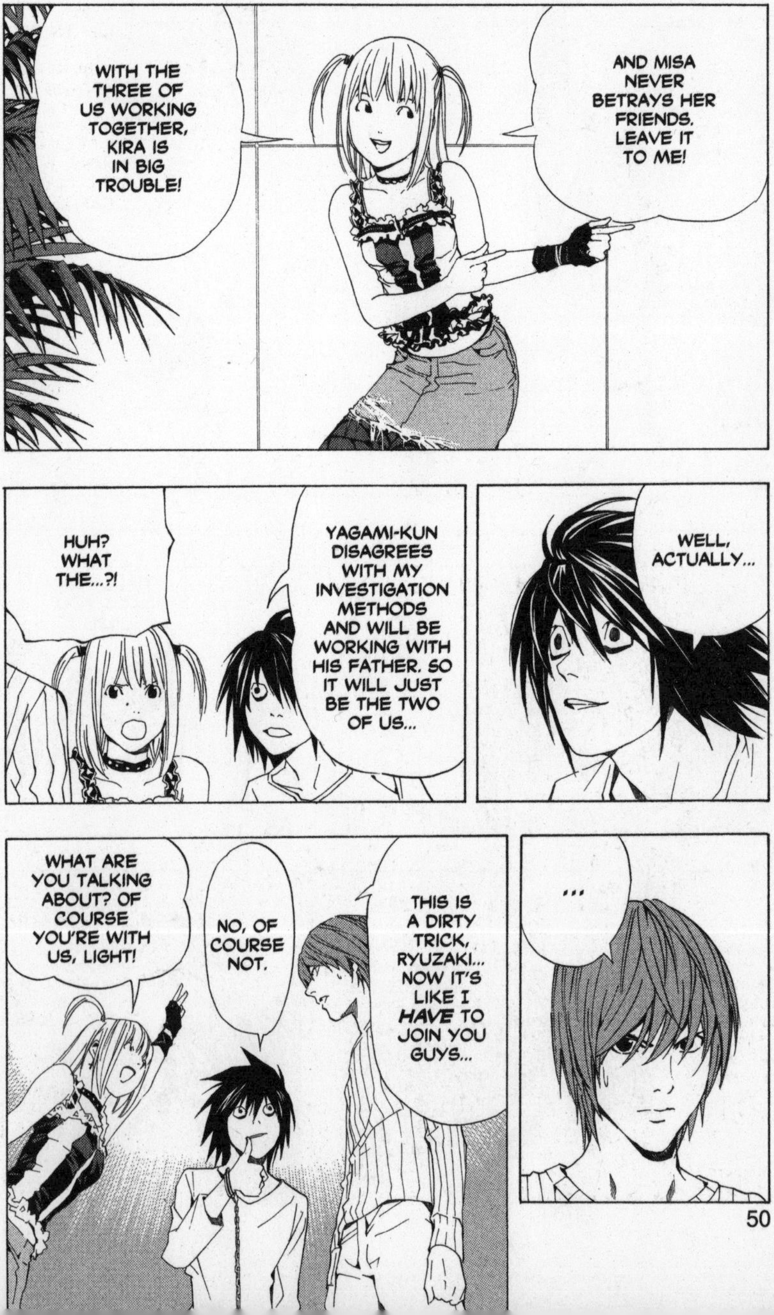
WITH THE THREE OF US WORKING TOGETHER, KIRA IS IN BIG TROUBLE!
AND MISA NEVER BETRAYS HER FRIENDS. LEAVE IT TO ME!
WELL, ACTUALLY...
YAGAMI-KUN DISAGREES WITH MY INVESTIGATION METHODS AND WILL BE WORKING WITH HIS FATHER. SO IT WILL JUST BE THE TWO OF US...
HUH? WHAT THE...?!
...
WHAT ARE YOU TALKING ABOUT? OF COURSE YOU'RE WITH US, LIGHT!
NO, OF COURSE NOT.
THIS IS A DIRTY TRICK, RYUZAKI... NOW IT'S LIKE I *HAVE* TO JOIN YOU GUYS...

READ THIS WAY

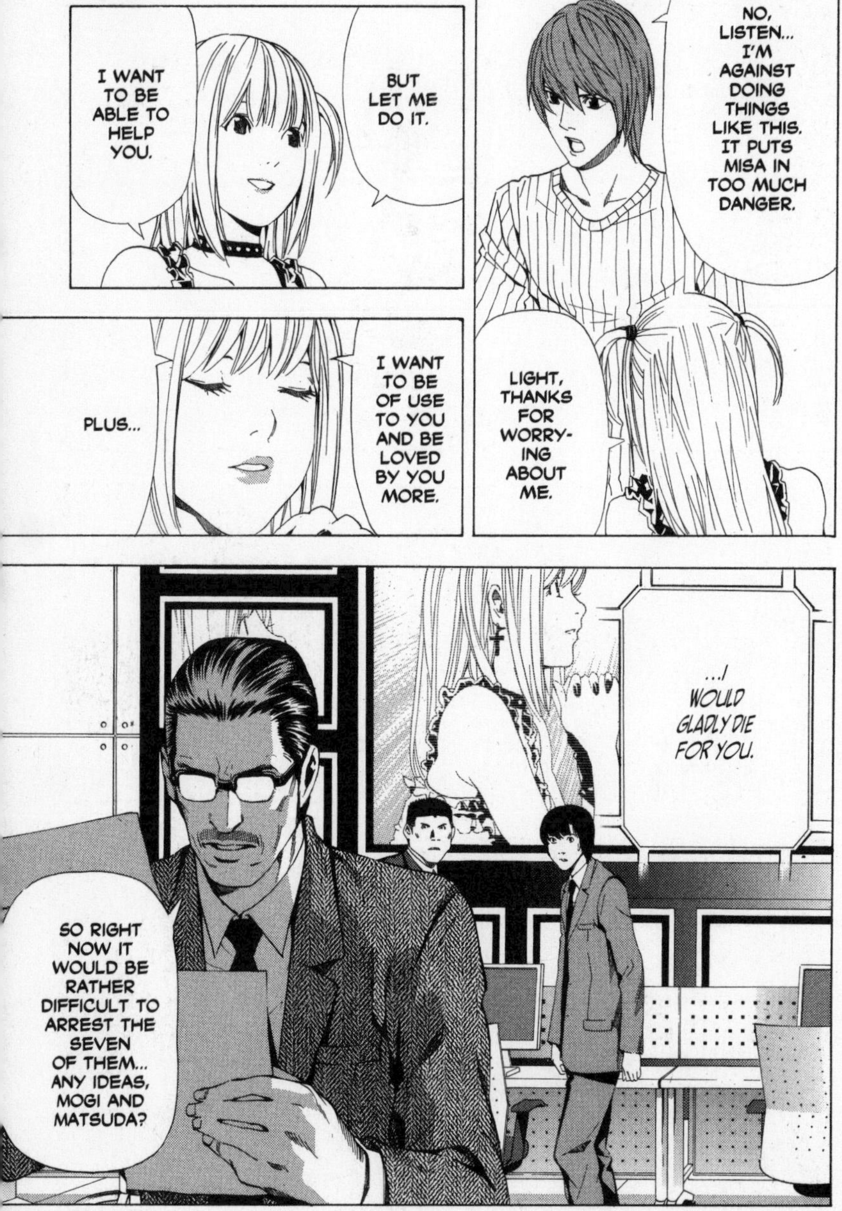

NO, LISTEN... I'M AGAINST DOING THINGS LIKE THIS. IT PUTS MISA IN TOO MUCH DANGER.
LIGHT, THANKS FOR WORRYING ABOUT ME.
BUT LET ME DO IT.
I WANT TO BE ABLE TO HELP YOU.
I WANT TO BE OF USE TO YOU AND BE LOVED BY YOU MORE.
PLUS...
...I WOULD GLADLY DIE FOR YOU.
SO RIGHT NOW IT WOULD BE RATHER DIFFICULT TO ARREST THE SEVEN OF THEM... ANY IDEAS, MOGI AND MATSUDA?

DEATH NOTE
How to use it

XXXII

○ If a person loses possession of a DEATH NOTE, they will not recognize the gods of death by sight or voice any more. If however, the owner lets someone else touch his DEATH NOTE, from that time on, that person will recognize the god of death.

デスノートの所有権を失うと、そのデスノートに憑いていた死神の姿や声は認知できなくなるが、所有者でないノートに触れた人間には、その持ち主の死神の姿や声が認知され続ける。

○ In accordance with the above, the human who touched the DEATH NOTE and began to recognize the gods of death's sight and voice, will continue to recognize it until that human actually owns the DEATH NOTE and subsequently looses possession of it.

よって、ノートの所有権のない人間がノートに触れる事で認知した死神は、そのノートの所有権を得て所有権を失わない限り、認知される事になる。

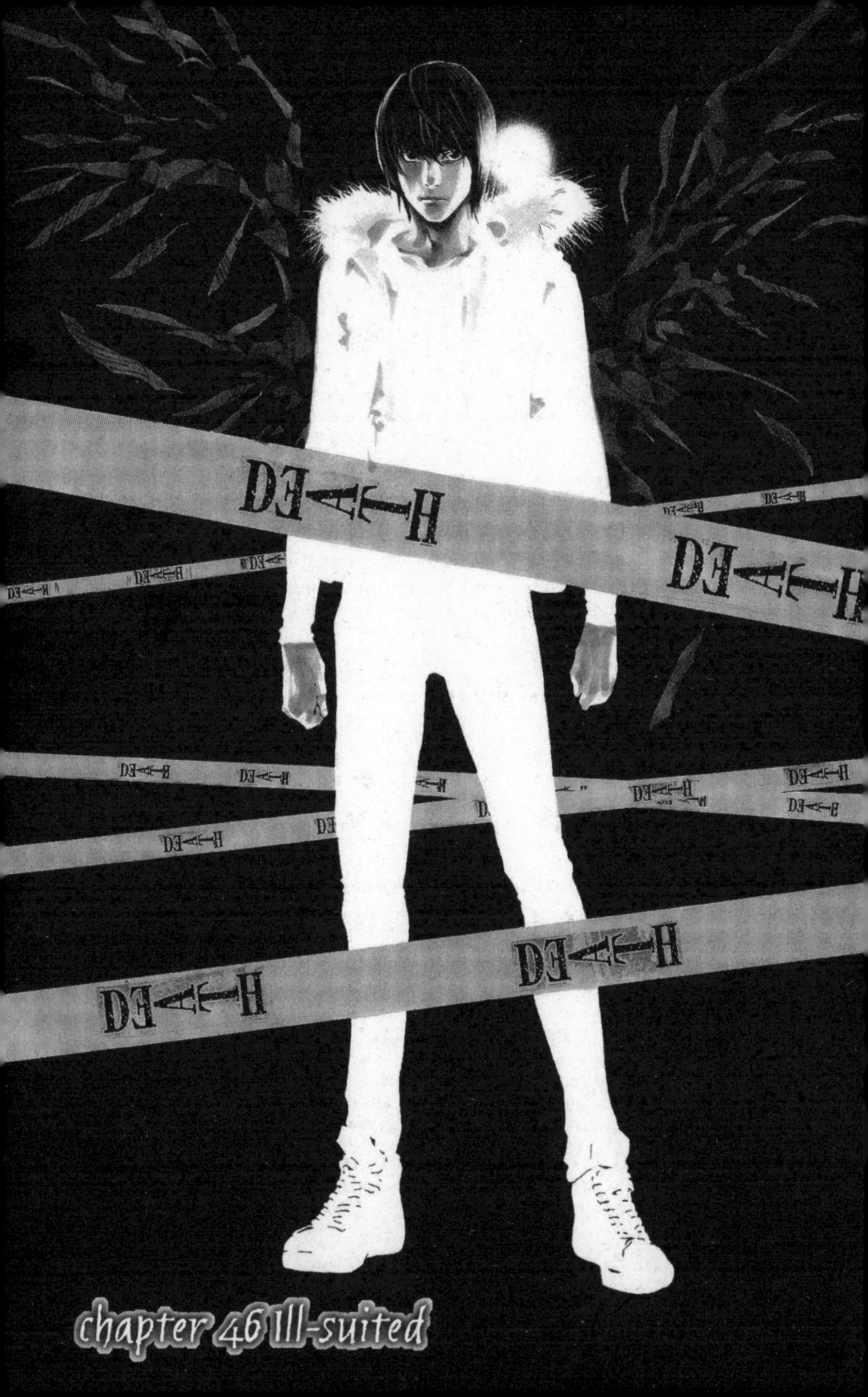
DEATH
DEATH
DEATH
DEATH

chapter 46 Ill-suited

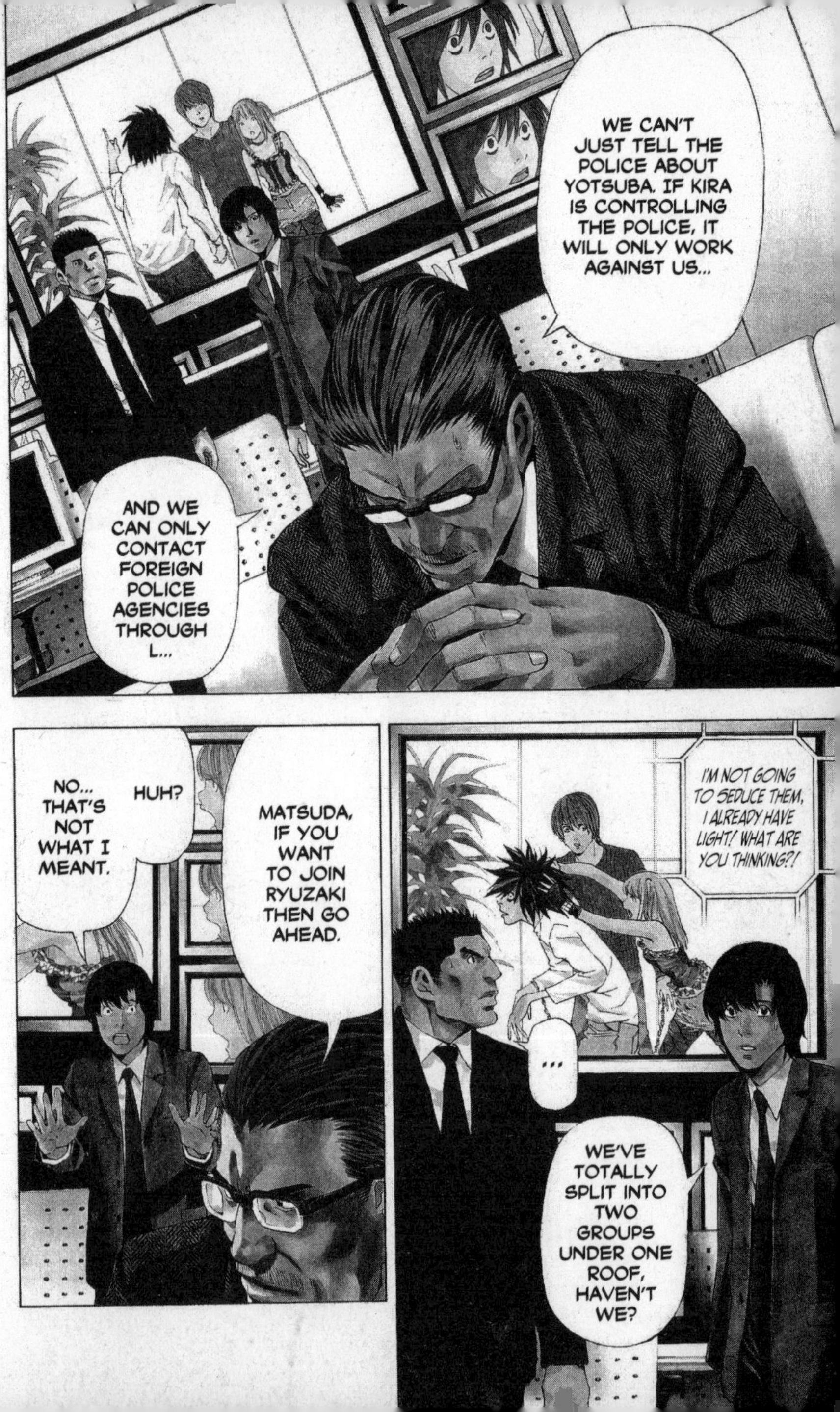
WE CAN'T JUST TELL THE POLICE ABOUT YOTSUBA. IF KIRA IS CONTROLLING THE POLICE, IT WILL ONLY WORK AGAINST US...
AND WE CAN ONLY CONTACT FOREIGN POLICE AGENCIES THROUGH L...
I'M NOT GOING TO SEDUCE THEM, I ALREADY HAVE LIGHT! WHAT ARE YOU THINKING?!
...
WE'VE TOTALLY SPLIT INTO TWO GROUPS UNDER ONE ROOF, HAVEN'T WE?
MATSUDA, IF YOU WANT TO JOIN RYUZAKI THEN GO AHEAD.
HUH?
NO... THAT'S NOT WHAT I MEANT.

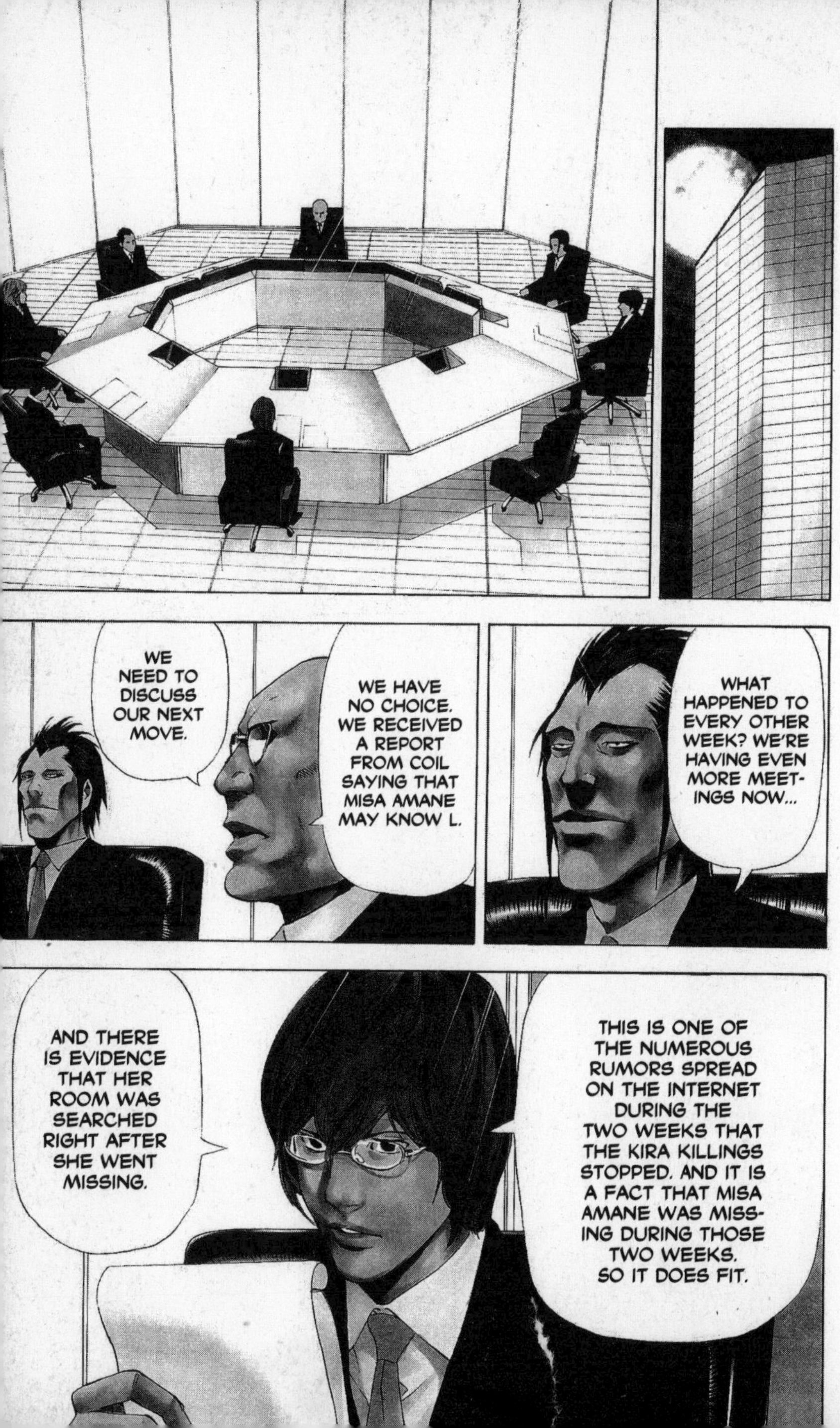
WHAT HAPPENED TO EVERY OTHER WEEK? WE'RE HAVING EVEN MORE MEET-INGS NOW...
WE HAVE NO CHOICE. WE RECEIVED A REPORT FROM COIL SAYING THAT MISA AMANE MAY KNOW L.
WE NEED TO DISCUSS OUR NEXT MOVE.
THIS IS ONE OF THE NUMEROUS RUMORS SPREAD ON THE INTERNET DURING THE TWO WEEKS THAT THE KIRA KILLINGS STOPPED. AND IT IS A FACT THAT MISA AMANE WAS MISS-ING DURING THOSE TWO WEEKS. SO IT DOES FIT.
AND THERE IS EVIDENCE THAT HER ROOM WAS SEARCHED RIGHT AFTER SHE WENT MISSING.

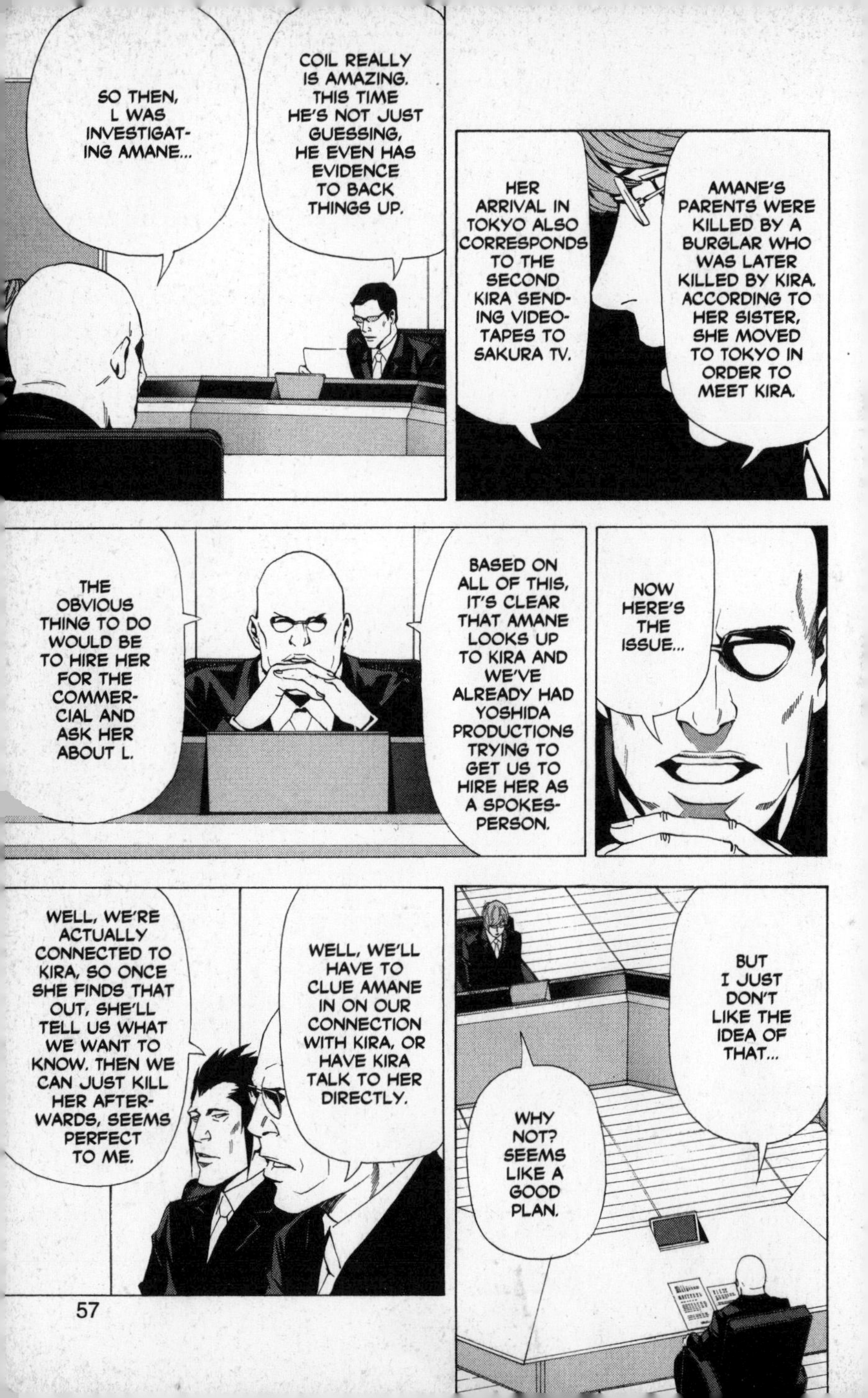
AMANE'S PARENTS WERE KILLED BY A BURGLAR WHO WAS LATER KILLED BY KIRA. ACCORDING TO HER SISTER, SHE MOVED TO TOKYO IN ORDER TO MEET KIRA.
HER ARRIVAL IN TOKYO ALSO CORRESPONDS TO THE SECOND KIRA SENDING VIDEOTAPES TO SAKURA TV.
COIL REALLY IS AMAZING. THIS TIME HE'S NOT JUST GUESSING, HE EVEN HAS EVIDENCE TO BACK THINGS UP.
SO THEN, L WAS INVESTIGATING AMANE...
NOW HERE'S THE ISSUE...
BASED ON ALL OF THIS, IT'S CLEAR THAT AMANE LOOKS UP TO KIRA AND WE'VE ALREADY HAD YOSHIDA PRODUCTIONS TRYING TO GET US TO HIRE HER AS A SPOKESPERSON.
THE OBVIOUS THING TO DO WOULD BE TO HIRE HER FOR THE COMMERCIAL AND ASK HER ABOUT L.
BUT I JUST DON'T LIKE THE IDEA OF THAT...
WHY NOT? SEEMS LIKE A GOOD PLAN.
WELL, WE'LL HAVE TO CLUE AMANE IN ON OUR CONNECTION WITH KIRA, OR HAVE KIRA TALK TO HER DIRECTLY.
WELL, WE'RE ACTUALLY CONNECTED TO KIRA, SO ONCE SHE FINDS THAT OUT, SHE'LL TELL US WHAT WE WANT TO KNOW. THEN WE CAN JUST KILL HER AFTERWARDS, SEEMS PERFECT TO ME.

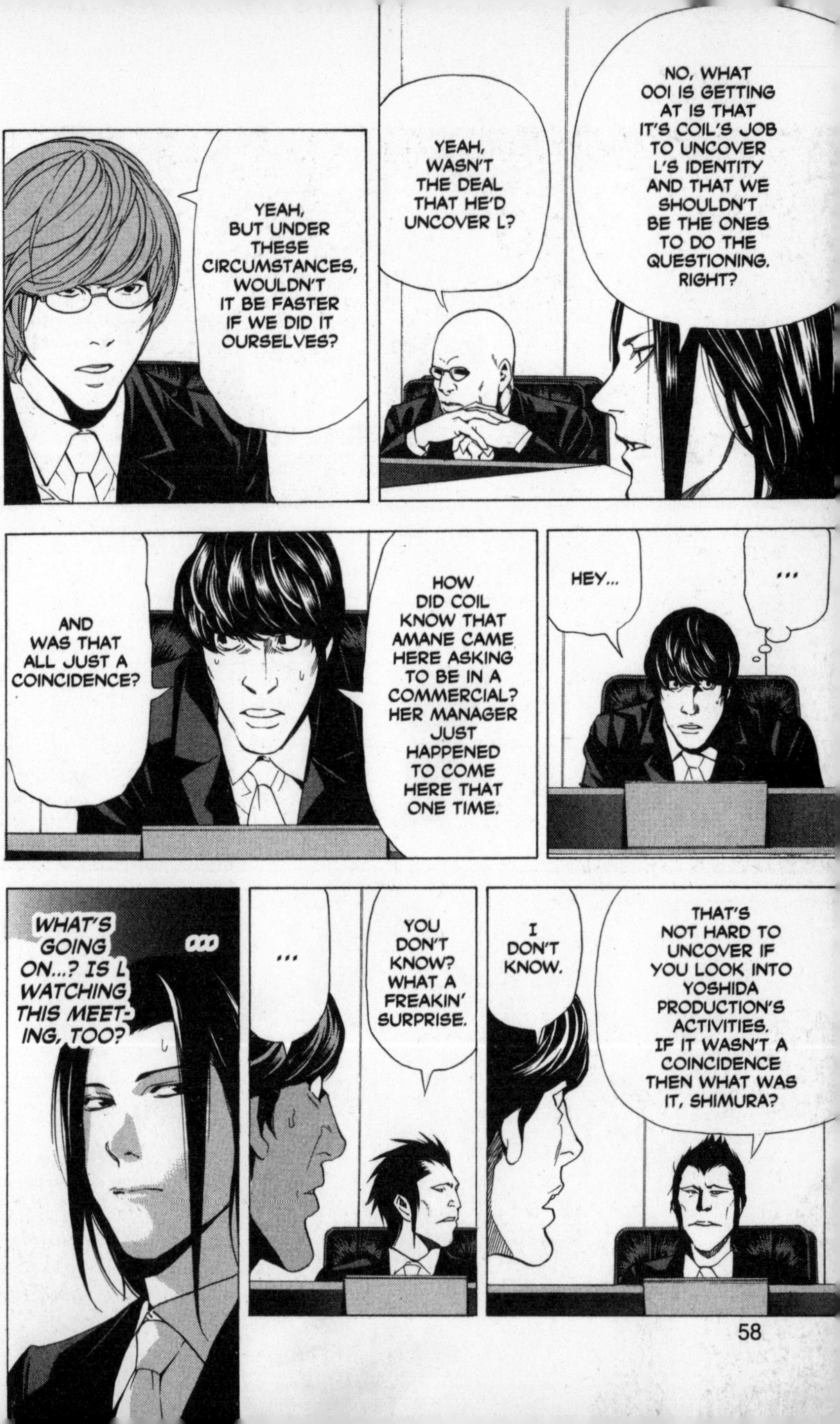
NO, WHAT OOI IS GETTING AT IS THAT IT'S COIL'S JOB TO UNCOVER L'S IDENTITY AND THAT WE SHOULDN'T BE THE ONES TO DO THE QUESTIONING. RIGHT?
YEAH, WASN'T THE DEAL THAT HE'D UNCOVER L?
YEAH, BUT UNDER THESE CIRCUMSTANCES, WOULDN'T IT BE FASTER IF WE DID IT OURSELVES?
...
HEY...
HOW DID COIL KNOW THAT AMANE CAME HERE ASKING TO BE IN A COMMERCIAL? HER MANAGER JUST HAPPENED TO COME HERE THAT ONE TIME.
AND WAS THAT ALL JUST A COINCIDENCE?
THAT'S NOT HARD TO UNCOVER IF YOU LOOK INTO YOSHIDA PRODUCTION'S ACTIVITIES. IF IT WASN'T A COINCIDENCE THEN WHAT WAS IT, SHIMURA?
I DON'T KNOW.
YOU DON'T KNOW? WHAT A FREAKIN' SURPRISE.
...
WHAT'S GOING ON...? IS L WATCHING THIS MEETING, TOO?

READ THIS WAY

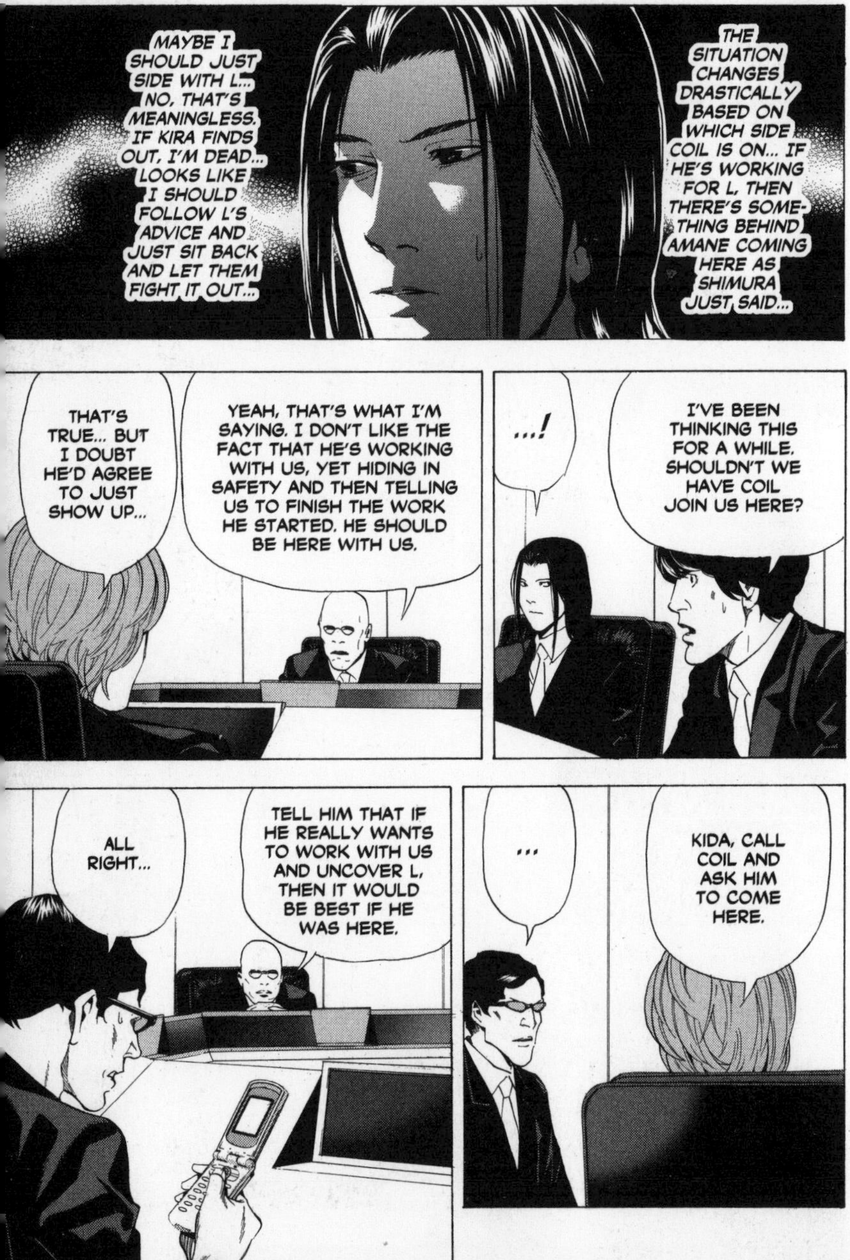
THE SITUATION CHANGES DRASTICALLY BASED ON WHICH SIDE COIL IS ON... IF HE'S WORKING FOR L, THEN THERE'S SOMETHING BEHIND AMANE COMING HERE AS SHIMURA JUST SAID...
MAYBE I SHOULD JUST SIDE WITH L... NO, THAT'S MEANINGLESS. IF KIRA FINDS OUT, I'M DEAD... LOOKS LIKE I SHOULD FOLLOW L'S ADVICE AND JUST SIT BACK AND LET THEM FIGHT IT OUT...
I'VE BEEN THINKING THIS FOR A WHILE. SHOULDN'T WE HAVE COIL JOIN US HERE?
...!
YEAH, THAT'S WHAT I'M SAYING. I DON'T LIKE THE FACT THAT HE'S WORKING WITH US, YET HIDING IN SAFETY AND THEN TELLING US TO FINISH THE WORK HE STARTED. HE SHOULD BE HERE WITH US.
THAT'S TRUE... BUT I DOUBT HE'D AGREE TO JUST SHOW UP...
KIDA, CALL COIL AND ASK HIM TO COME HERE.
...
TELL HIM THAT IF HE REALLY WANTS TO WORK WITH US AND UNCOVER L, THEN IT WOULD BE BEST IF HE WAS HERE.
ALL RIGHT...

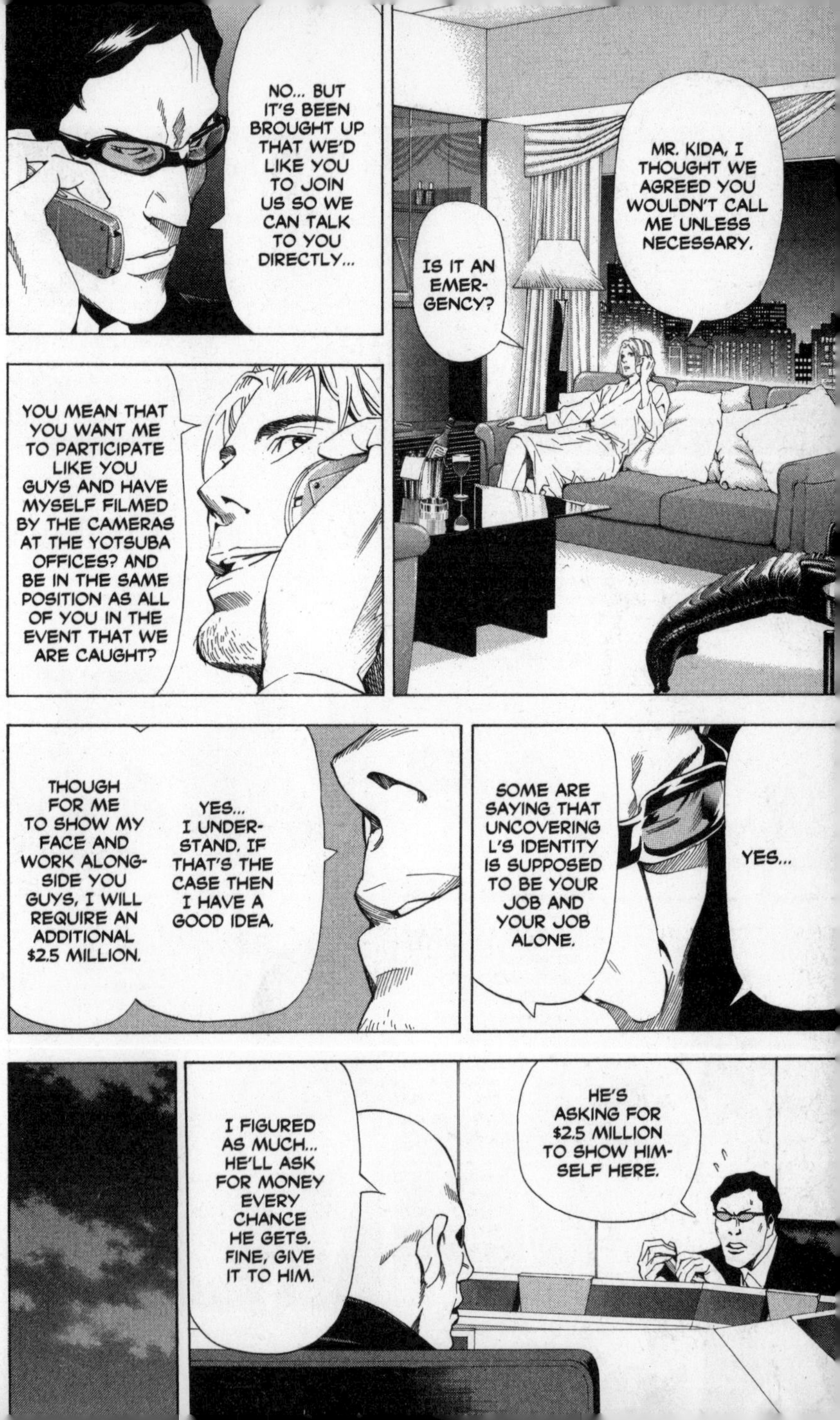

MR. KIDA, I THOUGHT WE AGREED YOU WOULDN'T CALL ME UNLESS NECESSARY.
IS IT AN EMERGENCY?
NO... BUT IT'S BEEN BROUGHT UP THAT WE'D LIKE YOU TO JOIN US SO WE CAN TALK TO YOU DIRECTLY...
YOU MEAN THAT YOU WANT ME TO PARTICIPATE LIKE YOU GUYS AND HAVE MYSELF FILMED BY THE CAMERAS AT THE YOTSUBA OFFICES? AND BE IN THE SAME POSITION AS ALL OF YOU IN THE EVENT THAT WE ARE CAUGHT?
YES...
SOME ARE SAYING THAT UNCOVERING L'S IDENTITY IS SUPPOSED TO BE YOUR JOB AND YOUR JOB ALONE.
YES... I UNDERSTAND. IF THAT'S THE CASE THEN I HAVE A GOOD IDEA.
THOUGH FOR ME TO SHOW MY FACE AND WORK ALONGSIDE YOU GUYS, I WILL REQUIRE AN ADDITIONAL $2.5 MILLION.
HE'S ASKING FOR $2.5 MILLION TO SHOW HIMSELF HERE.
I FIGURED AS MUCH... HE'LL ASK FOR MONEY EVERY CHANCE HE GETS. FINE, GIVE IT TO HIM.

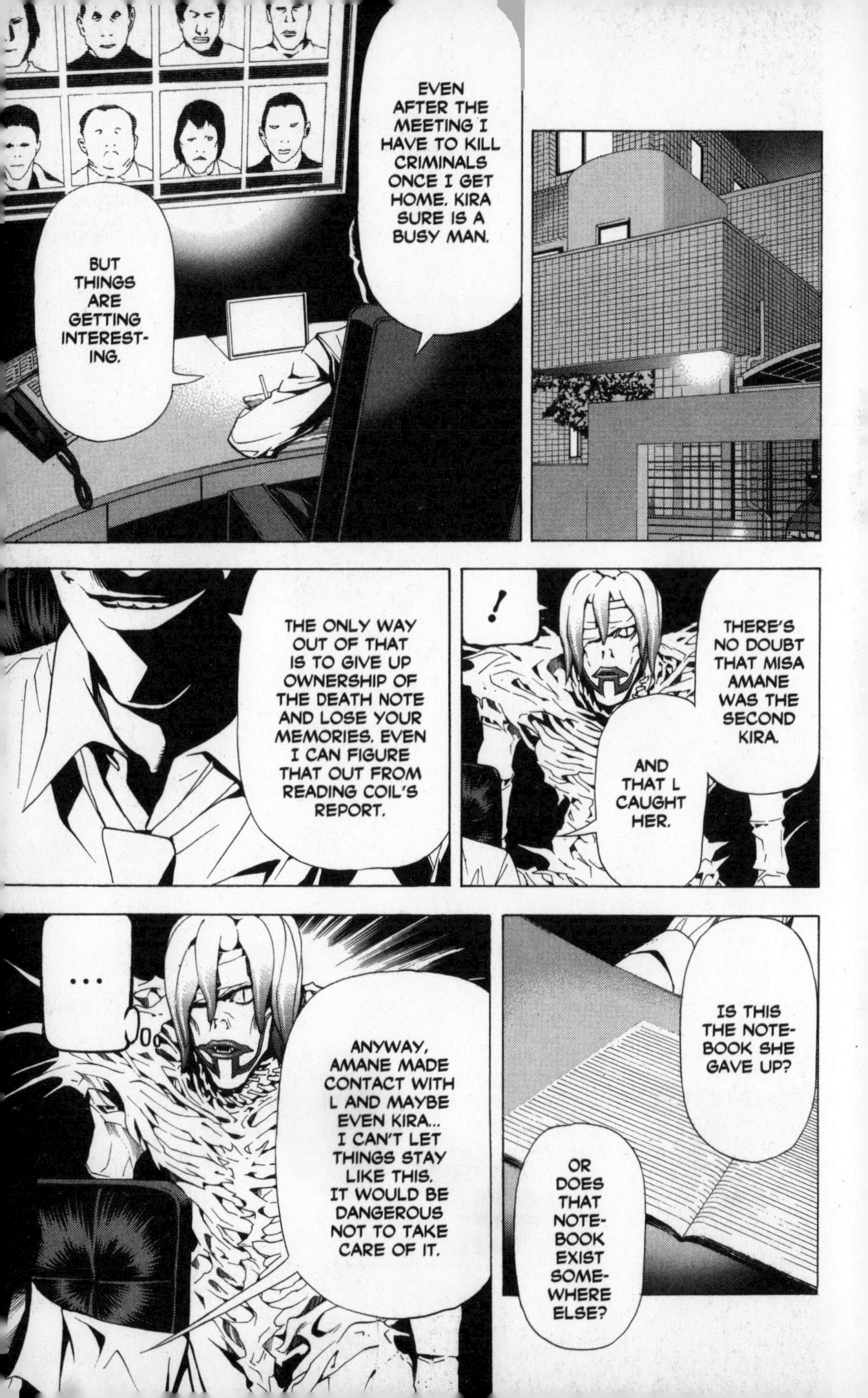
EVEN AFTER THE MEETING I HAVE TO KILL CRIMINALS ONCE I GET HOME. KIRA SURE IS A BUSY MAN.
BUT THINGS ARE GETTING INTEREST-ING.
!
THERE'S NO DOUBT THAT MISA AMANE WAS THE SECOND KIRA.
AND THAT L CAUGHT HER.
THE ONLY WAY OUT OF THAT IS TO GIVE UP OWNERSHIP OF THE DEATH NOTE AND LOSE YOUR MEMORIES. EVEN I CAN FIGURE THAT OUT FROM READING COIL'S REPORT.
IS THIS THE NOTE-BOOK SHE GAVE UP?
OR DOES THAT NOTE-BOOK EXIST SOME-WHERE ELSE?
...
ANYWAY, AMANE MADE CONTACT WITH L AND MAYBE EVEN KIRA... I CAN'T LET THINGS STAY LIKE THIS. IT WOULD BE DANGEROUS NOT TO TAKE CARE OF IT.

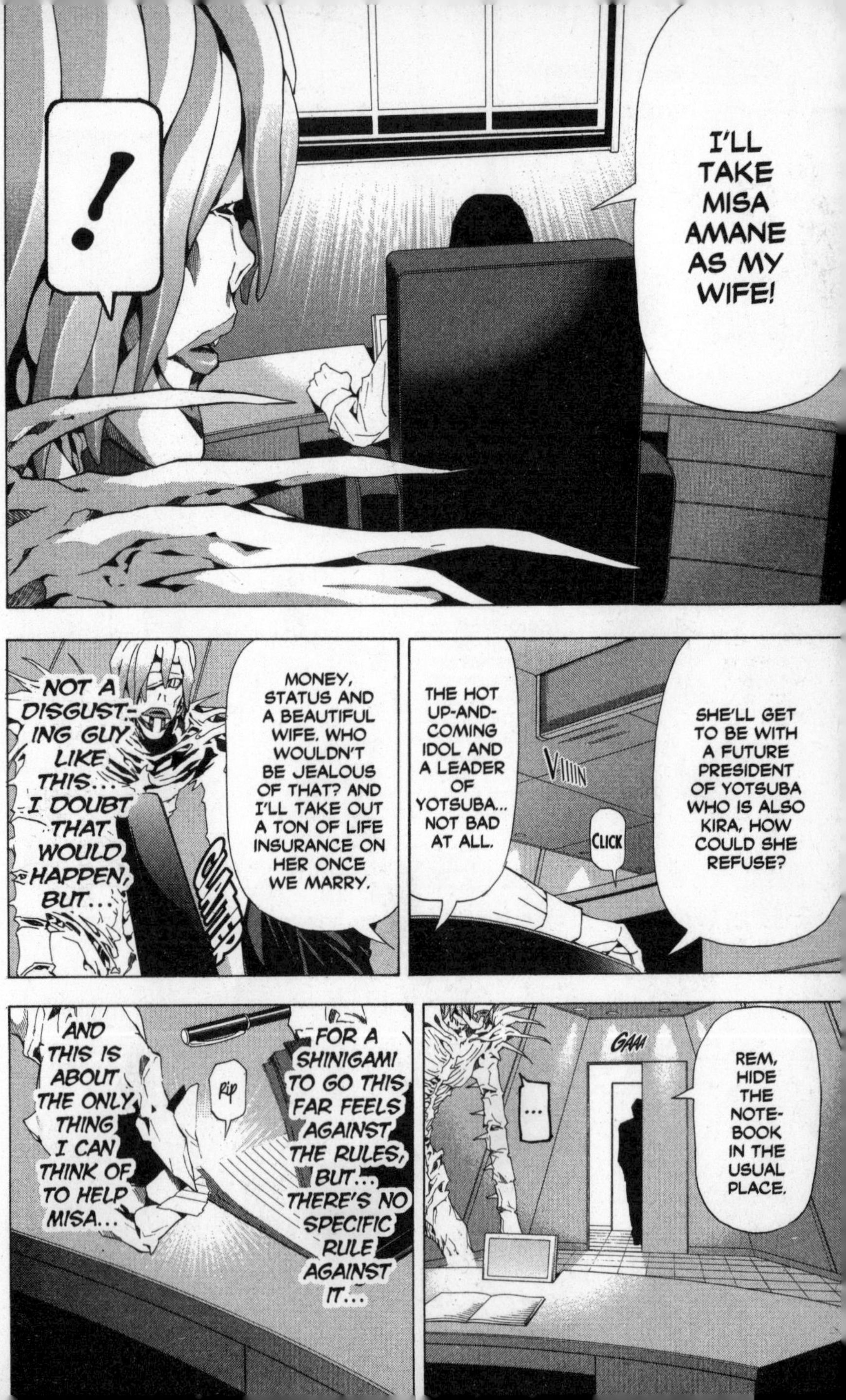
I'LL TAKE MISA AMANE AS MY WIFE!
!
SHE'LL GET TO BE WITH A FUTURE PRESIDENT OF YOTSUBA WHO IS ALSO KIRA, HOW COULD SHE REFUSE?
CLICK
VIIIN
THE HOT UP-AND-COMING IDOL AND A LEADER OF YOTSUBA... NOT BAD AT ALL.
MONEY, STATUS AND A BEAUTIFUL WIFE. WHO WOULDN'T BE JEALOUS OF THAT? AND I'LL TAKE OUT A TON OF LIFE INSURANCE ON HER ONCE WE MARRY.
NOT A DISGUSTING GUY LIKE THIS... I DOUBT THAT WOULD HAPPEN, BUT...
GAAA
REM, HIDE THE NOTEBOOK IN THE USUAL PLACE.
...
FOR A SHINIGAMI TO GO THIS FAR FEELS AGAINST THE RULES, BUT... THERE'S NO SPECIFIC RULE AGAINST IT...
Rip
AND THIS IS ABOUT THE ONLY THING I CAN THINK OF TO HELP MISA...

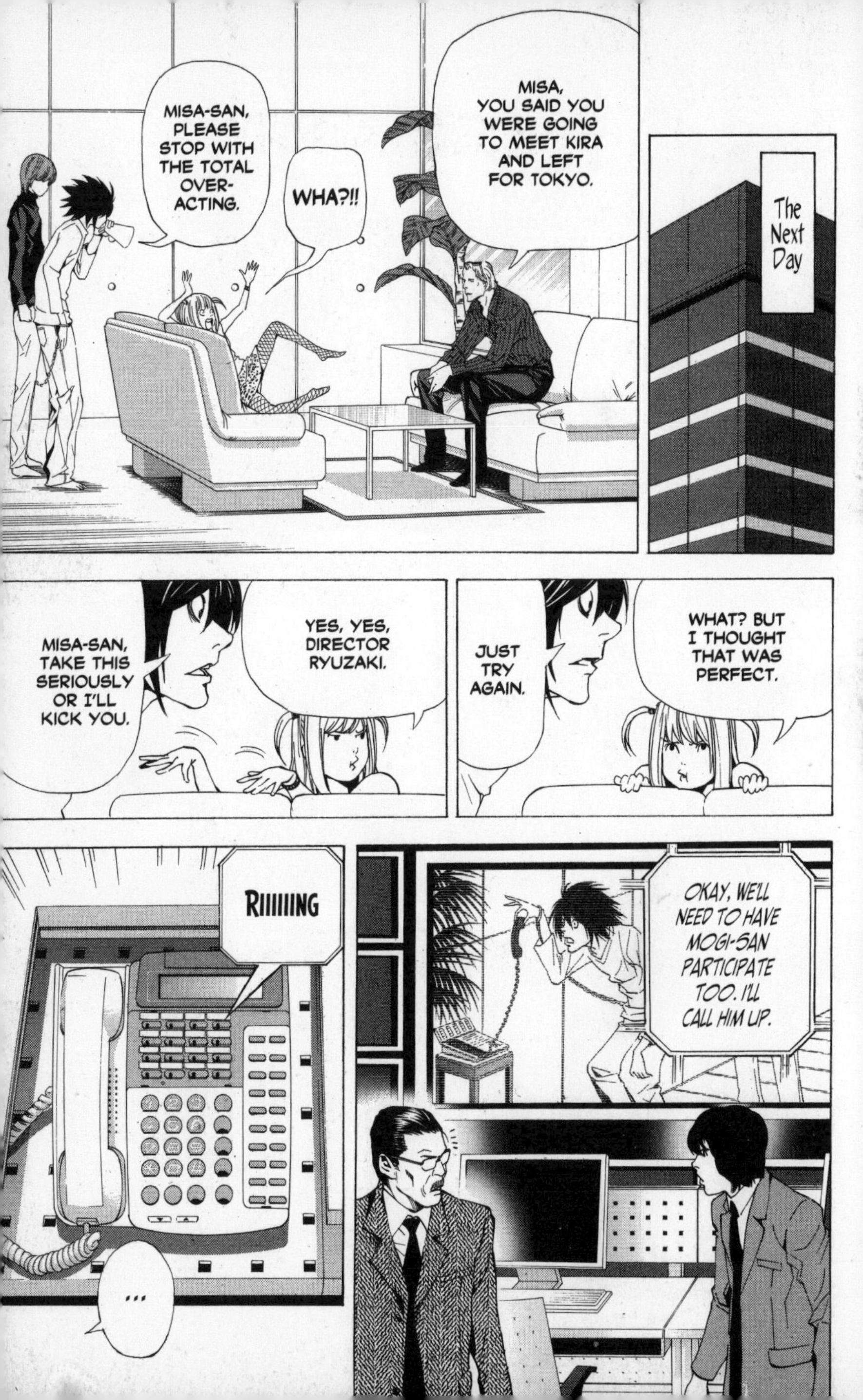
The Next Day
MISA, YOU SAID YOU WERE GOING TO MEET KIRA AND LEFT FOR TOKYO.
WHA?!!
MISA-SAN, PLEASE STOP WITH THE TOTAL OVER-ACTING.
WHAT? BUT I THOUGHT THAT WAS PERFECT.
JUST TRY AGAIN.
YES, YES, DIRECTOR RYUZAKI.
MISA-SAN, TAKE THIS SERIOUSLY OR I'LL KICK YOU.
OKAY, WE'LL NEED TO HAVE MOGI-SAN PARTICIPATE TOO. I'LL CALL HIM UP.
RIIIIIING
...

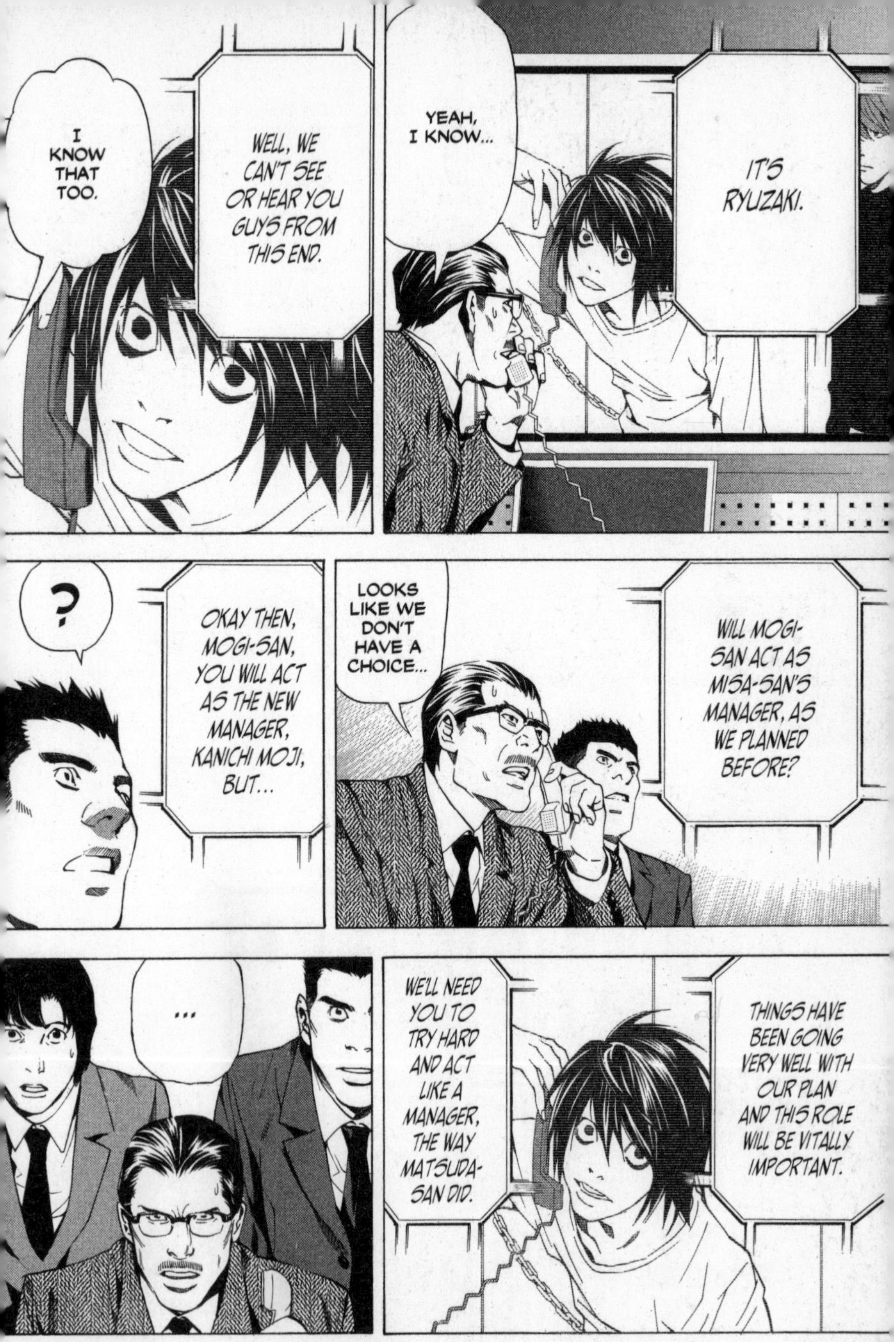
IT'S RYUZAKI.
YEAH, I KNOW...
WELL, WE CAN'T SEE OR HEAR YOU GUYS FROM THIS END.
I KNOW THAT TOO.
WILL MOGI-SAN ACT AS MISA-SAN'S MANAGER, AS WE PLANNED BEFORE?
LOOKS LIKE WE DON'T HAVE A CHOICE...
OKAY THEN, MOGI-SAN, YOU WILL ACT AS THE NEW MANAGER, KANICHI MOJI, BUT...
?
THINGS HAVE BEEN GOING VERY WELL WITH OUR PLAN AND THIS ROLE WILL BE VITALLY IMPORTANT.
WE'LL NEED YOU TO TRY HARD AND ACT LIKE A MANAGER, THE WAY MATSUDA-SAN DID.
...

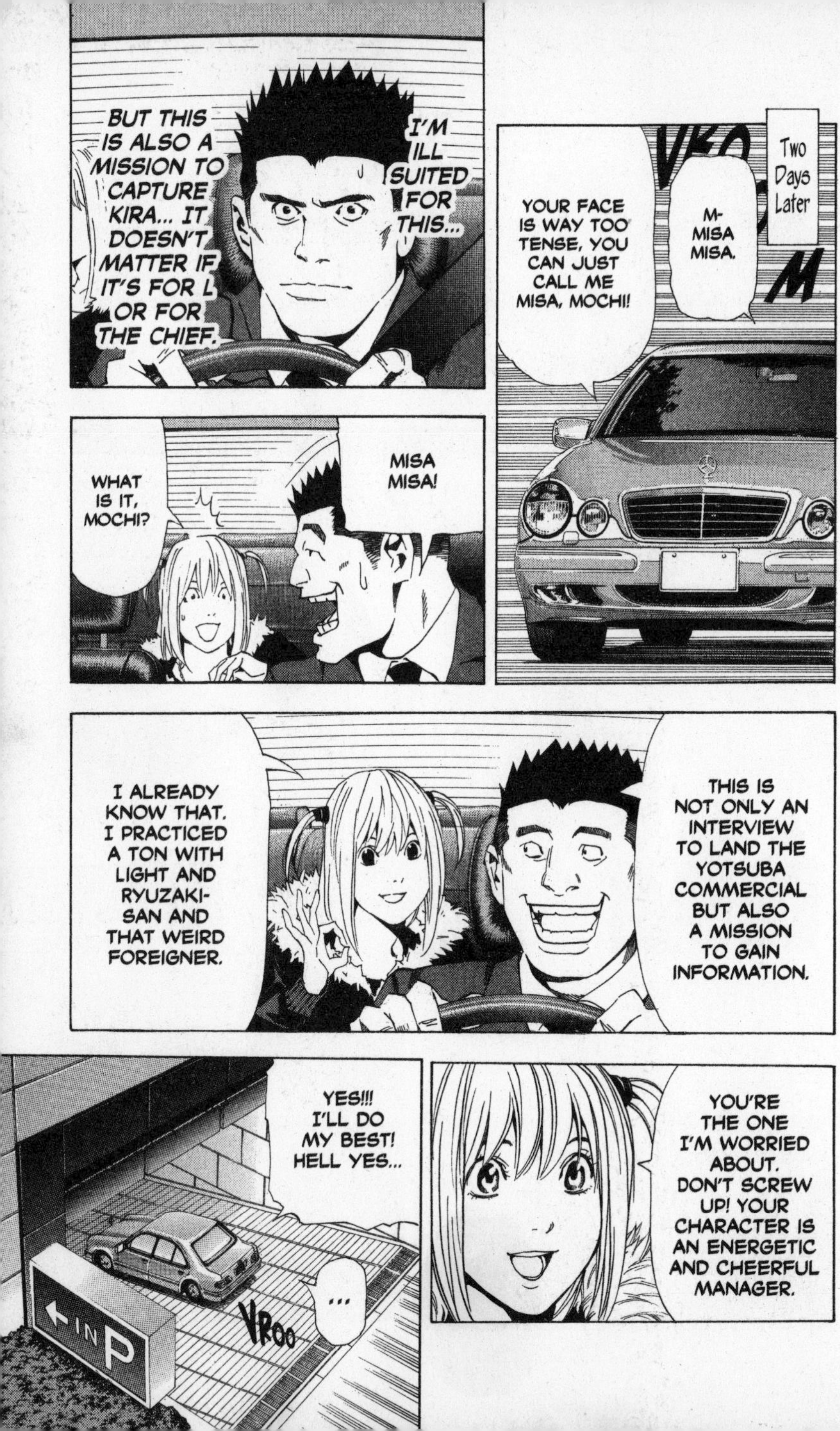
Two Days Later
M-MISA MISA.
YOUR FACE IS WAY TOO TENSE, YOU CAN JUST CALL ME MISA, MOCHI!
I'M ILL SUITED FOR THIS...
BUT THIS IS ALSO A MISSION TO CAPTURE KIRA... IT DOESN'T MATTER IF IT'S FOR L OR FOR THE CHIEF.
MISA MISA!
WHAT IS IT, MOCHI?
THIS IS NOT ONLY AN INTERVIEW TO LAND THE YOTSUBA COMMERCIAL BUT ALSO A MISSION TO GAIN INFORMATION.
I ALREADY KNOW THAT. I PRACTICED A TON WITH LIGHT AND RYUZAKI-SAN AND THAT WEIRD FOREIGNER.
YOU'RE THE ONE I'M WORRIED ABOUT. DON'T SCREW UP! YOUR CHARACTER IS AN ENERGETIC AND CHEERFUL MANAGER.
YES!!! I'LL DO MY BEST! HELL YES...
...
VROO
IN P

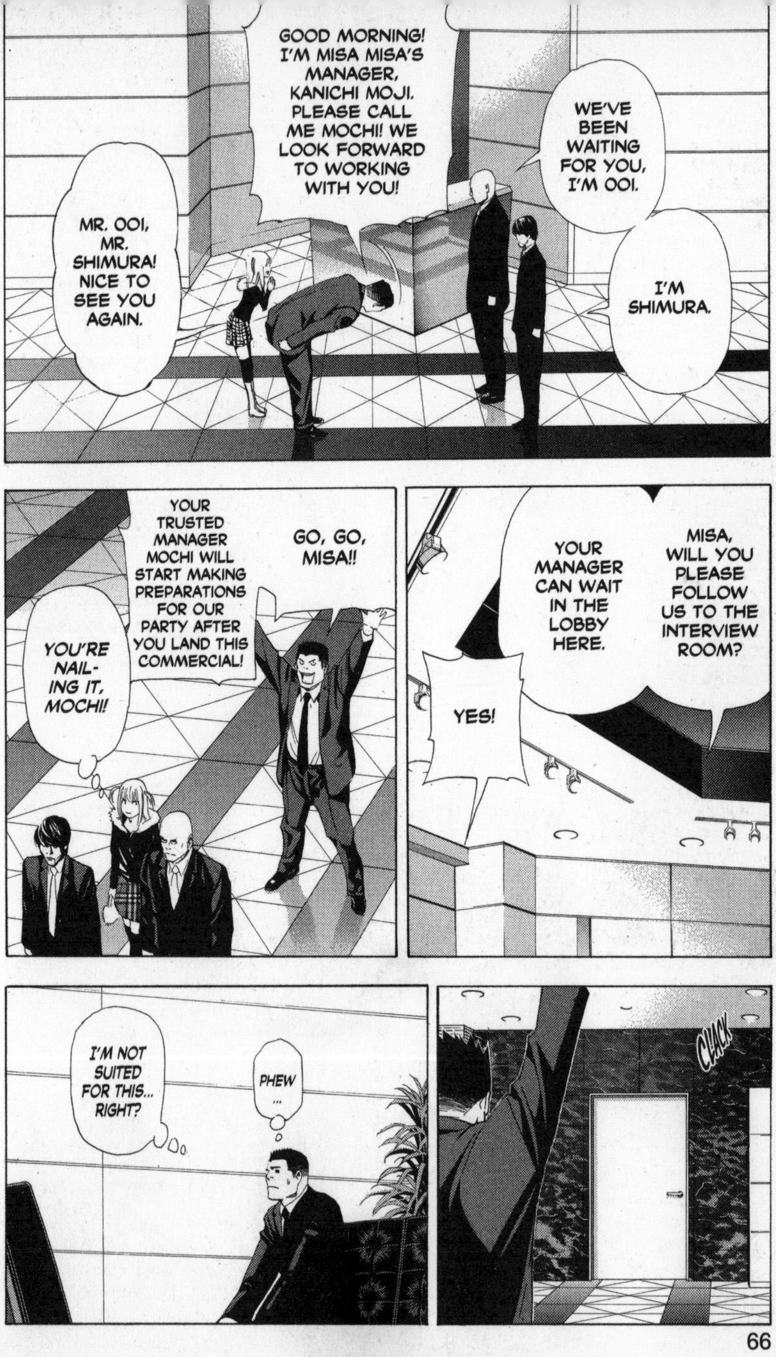
WE'VE BEEN WAITING FOR YOU, I'M OOI.
I'M SHIMURA.
GOOD MORNING! I'M MISA MISA'S MANAGER, KANICHI MOJI. PLEASE CALL ME MOCHI! WE LOOK FORWARD TO WORKING WITH YOU!
MR. OOI, MR. SHIMURA! NICE TO SEE YOU AGAIN.
MISA, WILL YOU PLEASE FOLLOW US TO THE INTERVIEW ROOM?
YOUR MANAGER CAN WAIT IN THE LOBBY HERE.
YES!
GO, GO, MISA!!
YOUR TRUSTED MANAGER MOCHI WILL START MAKING PREPARATIONS FOR OUR PARTY AFTER YOU LAND THIS COMMERCIAL!
YOU'RE NAIL-ING IT, MOCHI!
CLACK
PHEW ...
I'M NOT SUITED FOR THIS... RIGHT?

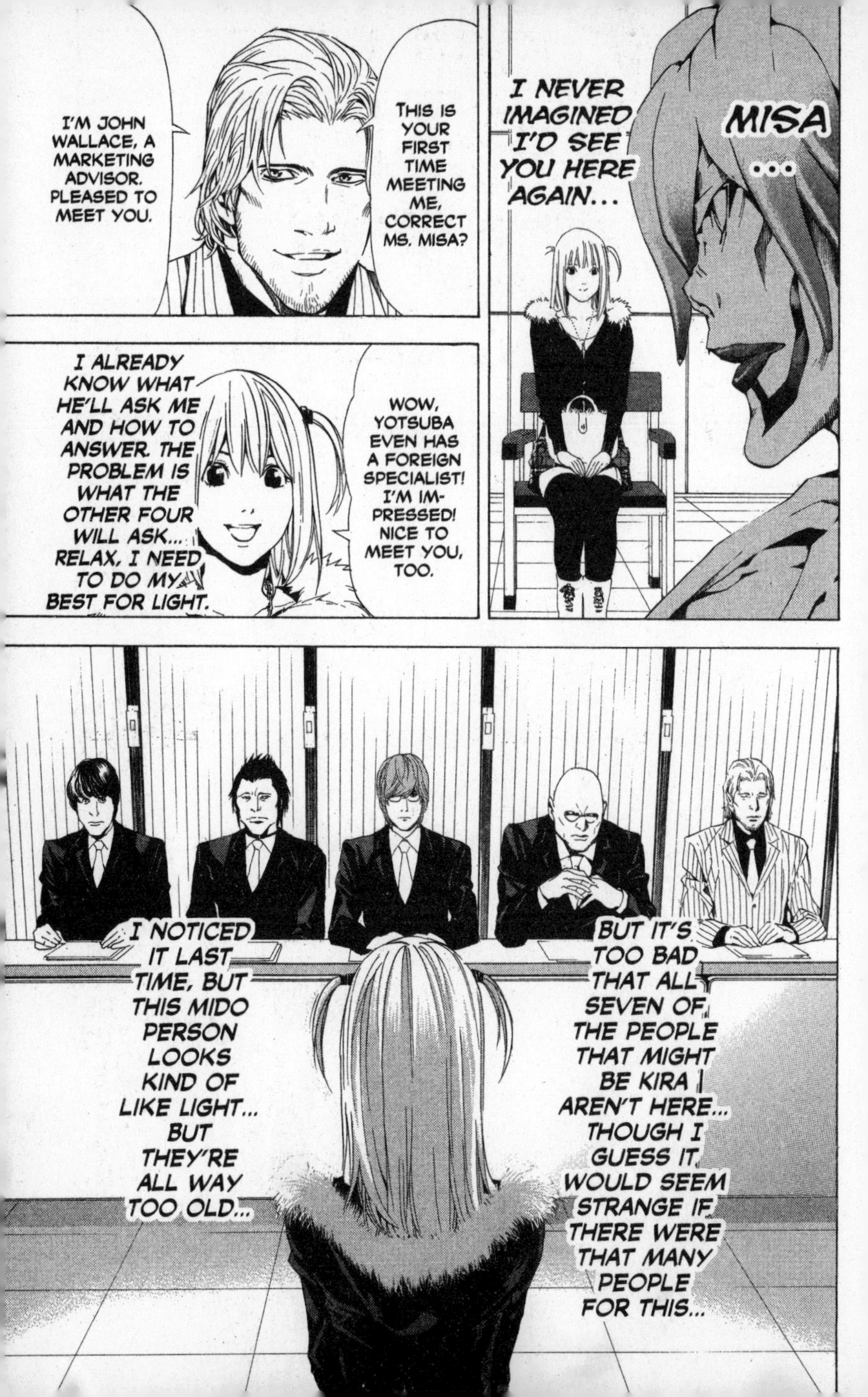
MISA ...
I NEVER IMAGINED I'D SEE YOU HERE AGAIN...
THIS IS YOUR FIRST TIME MEETING ME, CORRECT MS. MISA?
I'M JOHN WALLACE, A MARKETING ADVISOR. PLEASED TO MEET YOU.
WOW, YOTSUBA EVEN HAS A FOREIGN SPECIALIST! I'M IM-PRESSED! NICE TO MEET YOU, TOO.
I ALREADY KNOW WHAT HE'LL ASK ME AND HOW TO ANSWER. THE PROBLEM IS WHAT THE OTHER FOUR WILL ASK... RELAX, I NEED TO DO MY BEST FOR LIGHT.
BUT IT'S TOO BAD THAT ALL SEVEN OF THE PEOPLE THAT MIGHT BE KIRA AREN'T HERE... THOUGH I GUESS IT WOULD SEEM STRANGE IF THERE WERE THAT MANY PEOPLE FOR THIS...
I NOTICED IT LAST TIME, BUT THIS MIDO PERSON LOOKS KIND OF LIKE LIGHT... BUT THEY'RE ALL WAY TOO OLD...

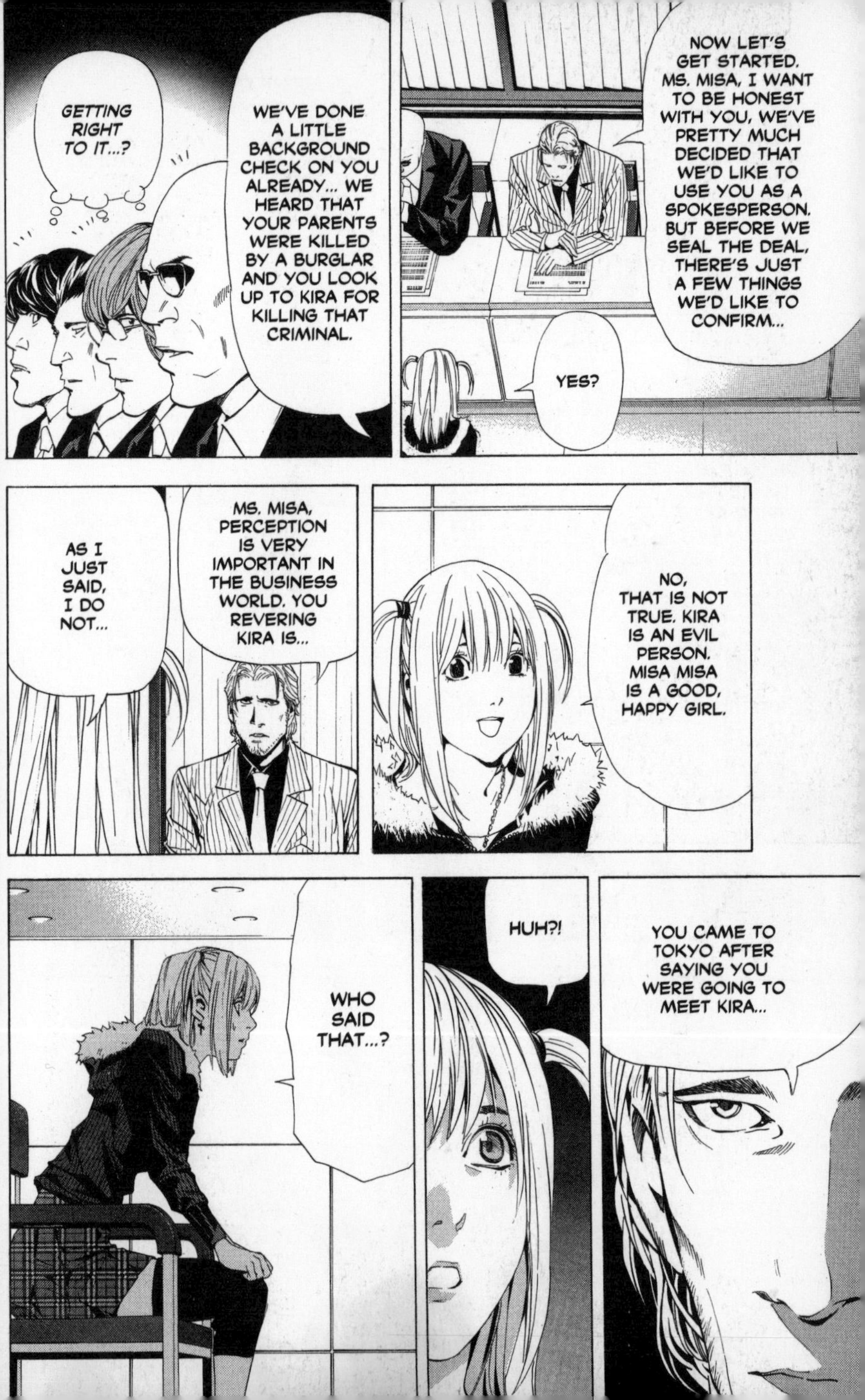
NOW LET'S GET STARTED. MS. MISA, I WANT TO BE HONEST WITH YOU, WE'VE PRETTY MUCH DECIDED THAT WE'D LIKE TO USE YOU AS A SPOKESPERSON. BUT BEFORE WE SEAL THE DEAL, THERE'S JUST A FEW THINGS WE'D LIKE TO CONFIRM...
YES?
WE'VE DONE A LITTLE BACKGROUND CHECK ON YOU ALREADY... WE HEARD THAT YOUR PARENTS WERE KILLED BY A BURGLAR AND YOU LOOK UP TO KIRA FOR KILLING THAT CRIMINAL.
GETTING RIGHT TO IT...?
NO, THAT IS NOT TRUE. KIRA IS AN EVIL PERSON. MISA MISA IS A GOOD, HAPPY GIRL.
MS. MISA, PERCEPTION IS VERY IMPORTANT IN THE BUSINESS WORLD. YOU REVERING KIRA IS...
AS I JUST SAID, I DO NOT...
YOU CAME TO TOKYO AFTER SAYING YOU WERE GOING TO MEET KIRA...
HUH?!
WHO SAID THAT...?

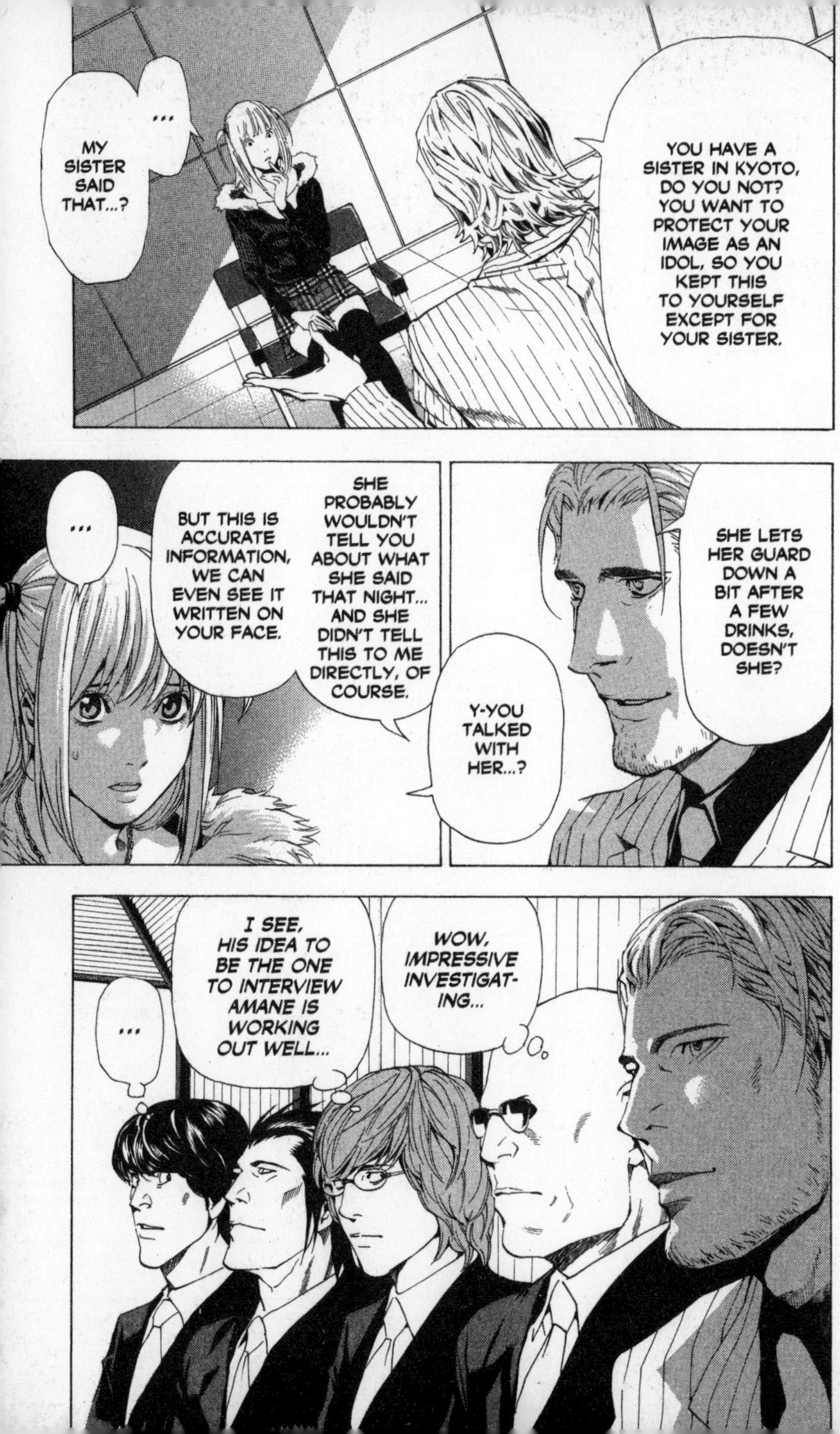
YOU HAVE A SISTER IN KYOTO, DO YOU NOT? YOU WANT TO PROTECT YOUR IMAGE AS AN IDOL, SO YOU KEPT THIS TO YOURSELF EXCEPT FOR YOUR SISTER.
...
MY SISTER SAID THAT...?
SHE LETS HER GUARD DOWN A BIT AFTER A FEW DRINKS, DOESN'T SHE?
Y-YOU TALKED WITH HER...?
SHE PROBABLY WOULDN'T TELL YOU ABOUT WHAT SHE SAID THAT NIGHT... AND SHE DIDN'T TELL THIS TO ME DIRECTLY, OF COURSE.
BUT THIS IS ACCURATE INFORMATION, WE CAN EVEN SEE IT WRITTEN ON YOUR FACE.
...
WOW, IMPRESSIVE INVESTIGAT-ING...
I SEE, HIS IDEA TO BE THE ONE TO INTERVIEW AMANE IS WORKING OUT WELL...
...

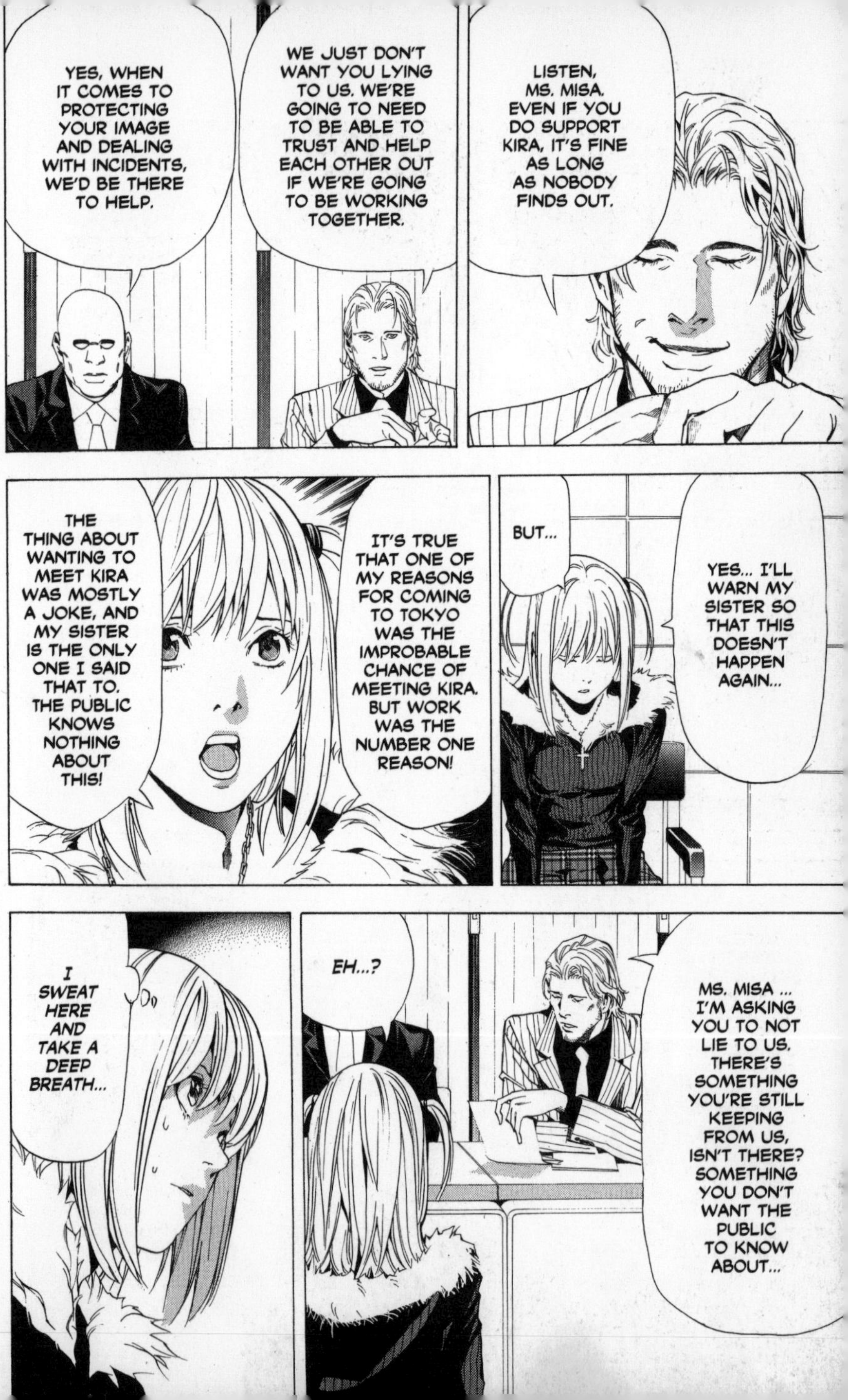
LISTEN, MS. MISA. EVEN IF YOU DO SUPPORT KIRA, IT'S FINE AS LONG AS NOBODY FINDS OUT.
WE JUST DON'T WANT YOU LYING TO US. WE'RE GOING TO NEED TO BE ABLE TO TRUST AND HELP EACH OTHER OUT IF WE'RE GOING TO BE WORKING TOGETHER.
YES, WHEN IT COMES TO PROTECTING YOUR IMAGE AND DEALING WITH INCIDENTS, WE'D BE THERE TO HELP.
YES... I'LL WARN MY SISTER SO THAT THIS DOESN'T HAPPEN AGAIN...
BUT...
IT'S TRUE THAT ONE OF MY REASONS FOR COMING TO TOKYO WAS THE IMPROBABLE CHANCE OF MEETING KIRA. BUT WORK WAS THE NUMBER ONE REASON!
THE THING ABOUT WANTING TO MEET KIRA WAS MOSTLY A JOKE, AND MY SISTER IS THE ONLY ONE I SAID THAT TO. THE PUBLIC KNOWS NOTHING ABOUT THIS!
MS. MISA ... I'M ASKING YOU TO NOT LIE TO US. THERE'S SOMETHING YOU'RE STILL KEEPING FROM US, ISN'T THERE? SOMETHING YOU DON'T WANT THE PUBLIC TO KNOW ABOUT...
EH...?
I SWEAT HERE AND TAKE A DEEP BREATH...

READ THIS WAY

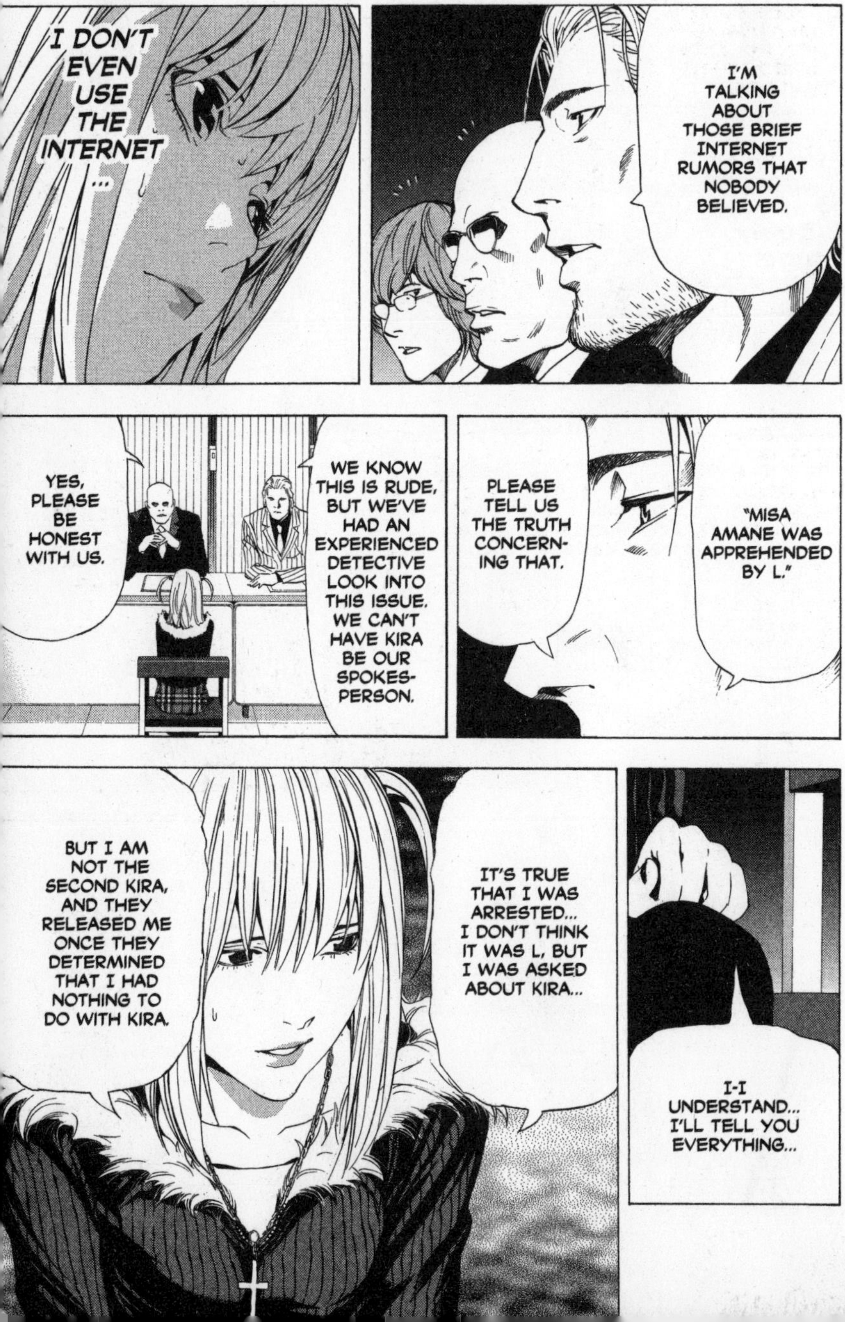
I'M TALKING ABOUT THOSE BRIEF INTERNET RUMORS THAT NOBODY BELIEVED.
I DON'T EVEN USE THE INTERNET...
"MISA AMANE WAS APPREHENDED BY L."
PLEASE TELL US THE TRUTH CONCERNING THAT.
WE KNOW THIS IS RUDE, BUT WE'VE HAD AN EXPERIENCED DETECTIVE LOOK INTO THIS ISSUE. WE CAN'T HAVE KIRA BE OUR SPOKES-PERSON.
YES, PLEASE BE HONEST WITH US.
I-I UNDERSTAND... I'LL TELL YOU EVERYTHING...
IT'S TRUE THAT I WAS ARRESTED... I DON'T THINK IT WAS L, BUT I WAS ASKED ABOUT KIRA...
BUT I AM NOT THE SECOND KIRA, AND THEY RELEASED ME ONCE THEY DETERMINED THAT I HAD NOTHING TO DO WITH KIRA.

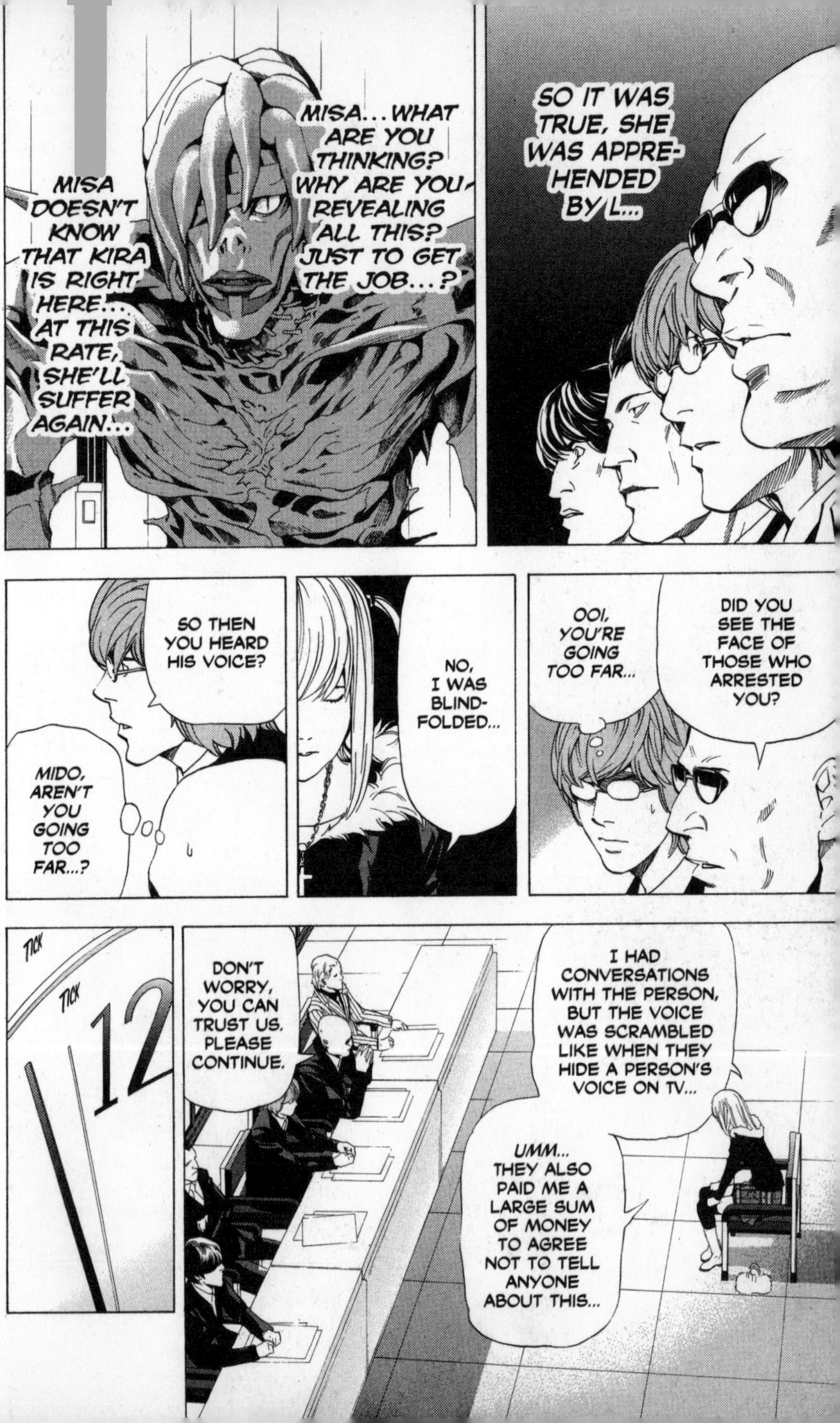
SO IT WAS TRUE, SHE WAS APPRE-HENDED BY L...
MISA...WHAT ARE YOU THINKING? WHY ARE YOU REVEALING ALL THIS? JUST TO GET THE JOB...?
MISA DOESN'T KNOW THAT KIRA IS RIGHT HERE... AT THIS RATE, SHE'LL SUFFER AGAIN...
DID YOU SEE THE FACE OF THOSE WHO ARRESTED YOU?
OOI, YOU'RE GOING TOO FAR...
NO, I WAS BLIND-FOLDED...
SO THEN YOU HEARD HIS VOICE?
MIDO, AREN'T YOU GOING TOO FAR...?
I HAD CONVERSATIONS WITH THE PERSON, BUT THE VOICE WAS SCRAMBLED LIKE WHEN THEY HIDE A PERSON'S VOICE ON TV...
UMM... THEY ALSO PAID ME A LARGE SUM OF MONEY TO AGREE NOT TO TELL ANYONE ABOUT THIS...
DON'T WORRY, YOU CAN TRUST US. PLEASE CONTINUE.
TICK
TICK

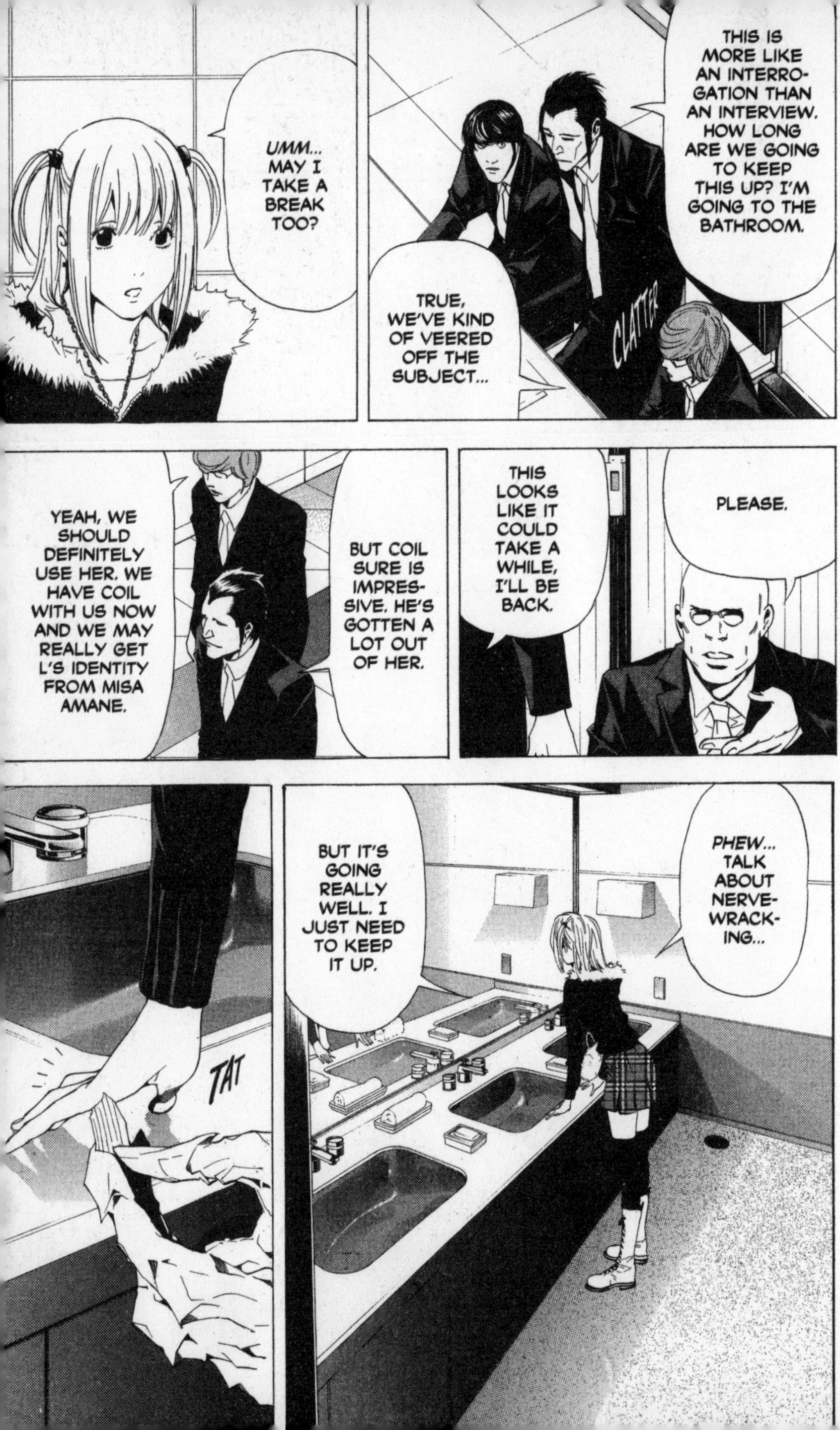
THIS IS MORE LIKE AN INTERROGATION THAN AN INTERVIEW. HOW LONG ARE WE GOING TO KEEP THIS UP? I'M GOING TO THE BATHROOM.
CLATTER
TRUE, WE'VE KIND OF VEERED OFF THE SUBJECT...
UMM... MAY I TAKE A BREAK TOO?
PLEASE.
THIS LOOKS LIKE IT COULD TAKE A WHILE, I'LL BE BACK.
BUT COIL SURE IS IMPRESSIVE. HE'S GOTTEN A LOT OUT OF HER.
YEAH, WE SHOULD DEFINITELY USE HER. WE HAVE COIL WITH US NOW AND WE MAY REALLY GET L'S IDENTITY FROM MISA AMANE.
PHEW... TALK ABOUT NERVE-WRACKING...
BUT IT'S GOING REALLY WELL. I JUST NEED TO KEEP IT UP.
TAT

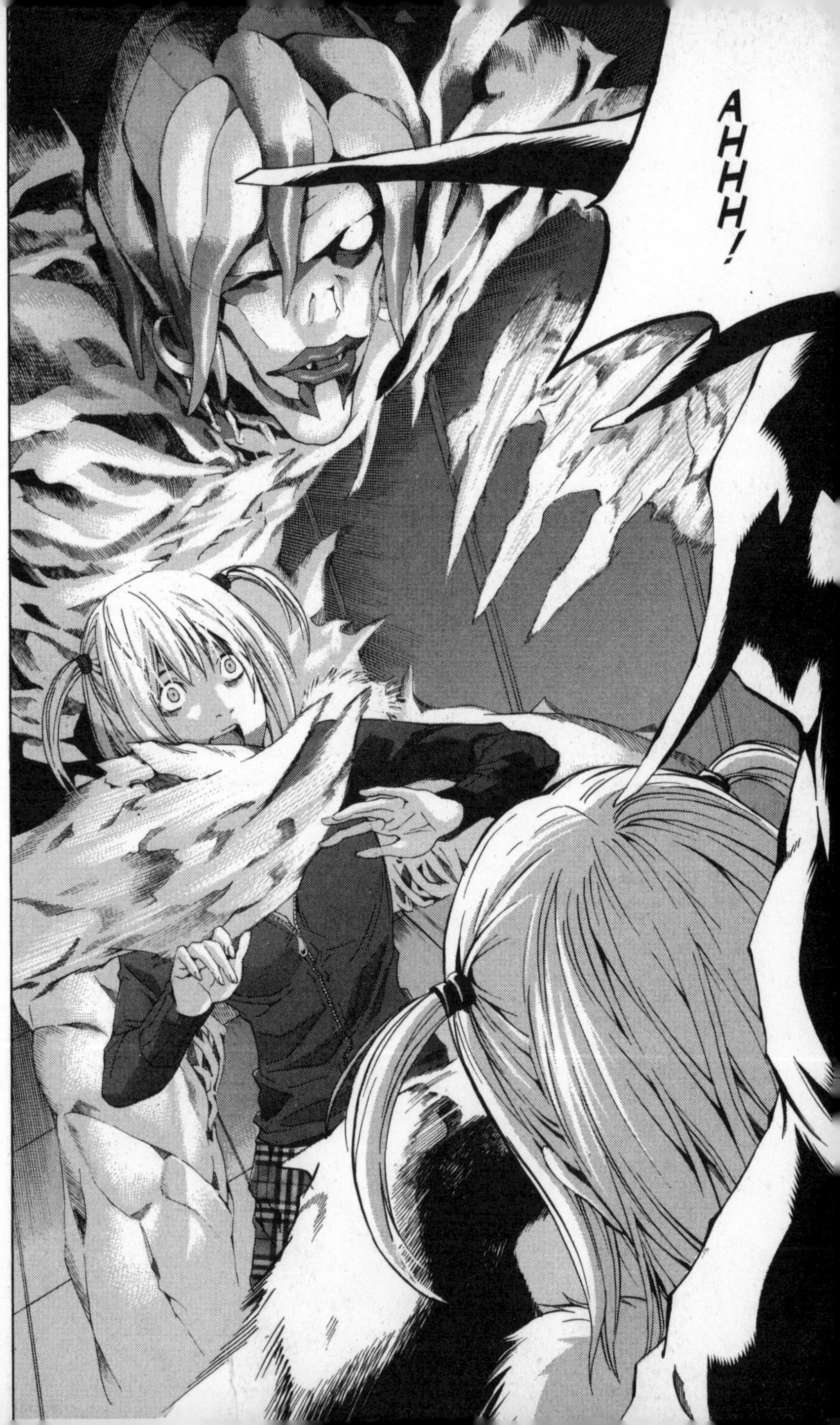
AHHH!

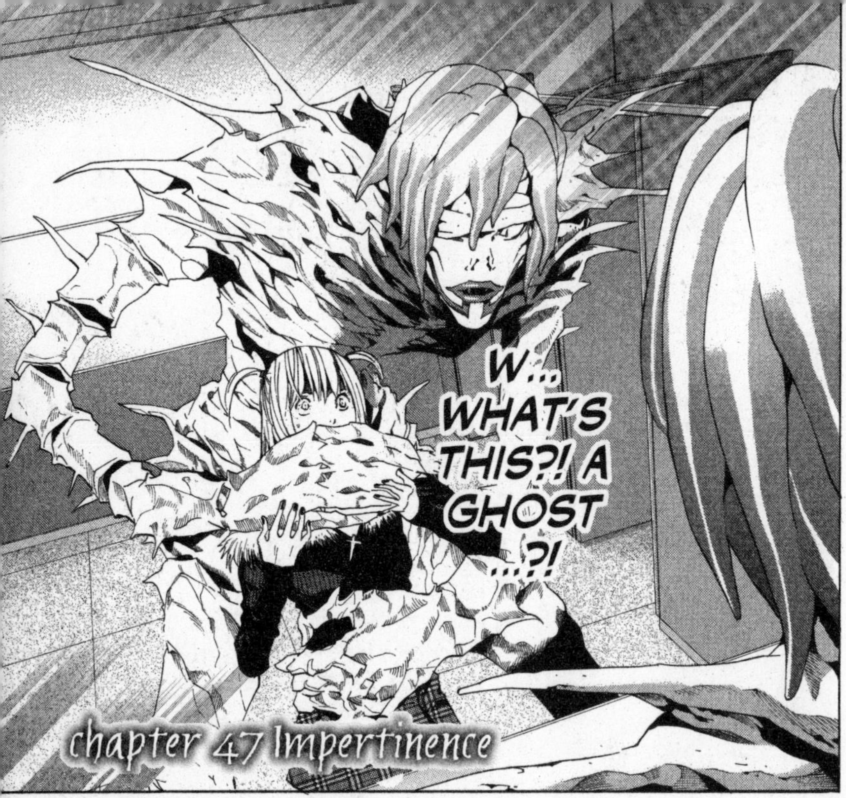
W... WHAT'S THIS?! A GHOST ...?!
chapter 47 Impertinence
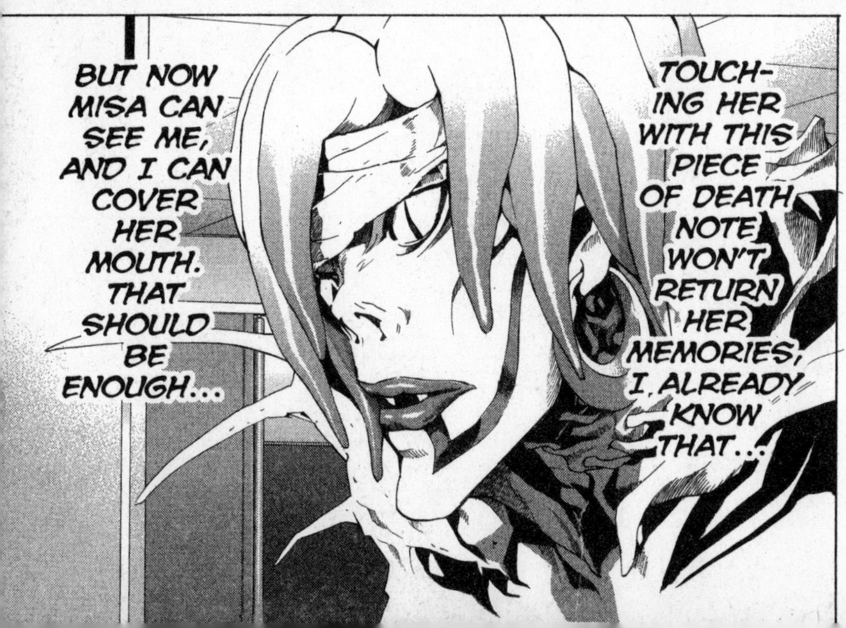
TOUCHING HER WITH THIS PIECE OF DEATH NOTE WON'T RETURN HER MEMORIES, I ALREADY KNOW THAT...
BUT NOW MISA CAN SEE ME, AND I CAN COVER HER MOUTH. THAT SHOULD BE ENOUGH...

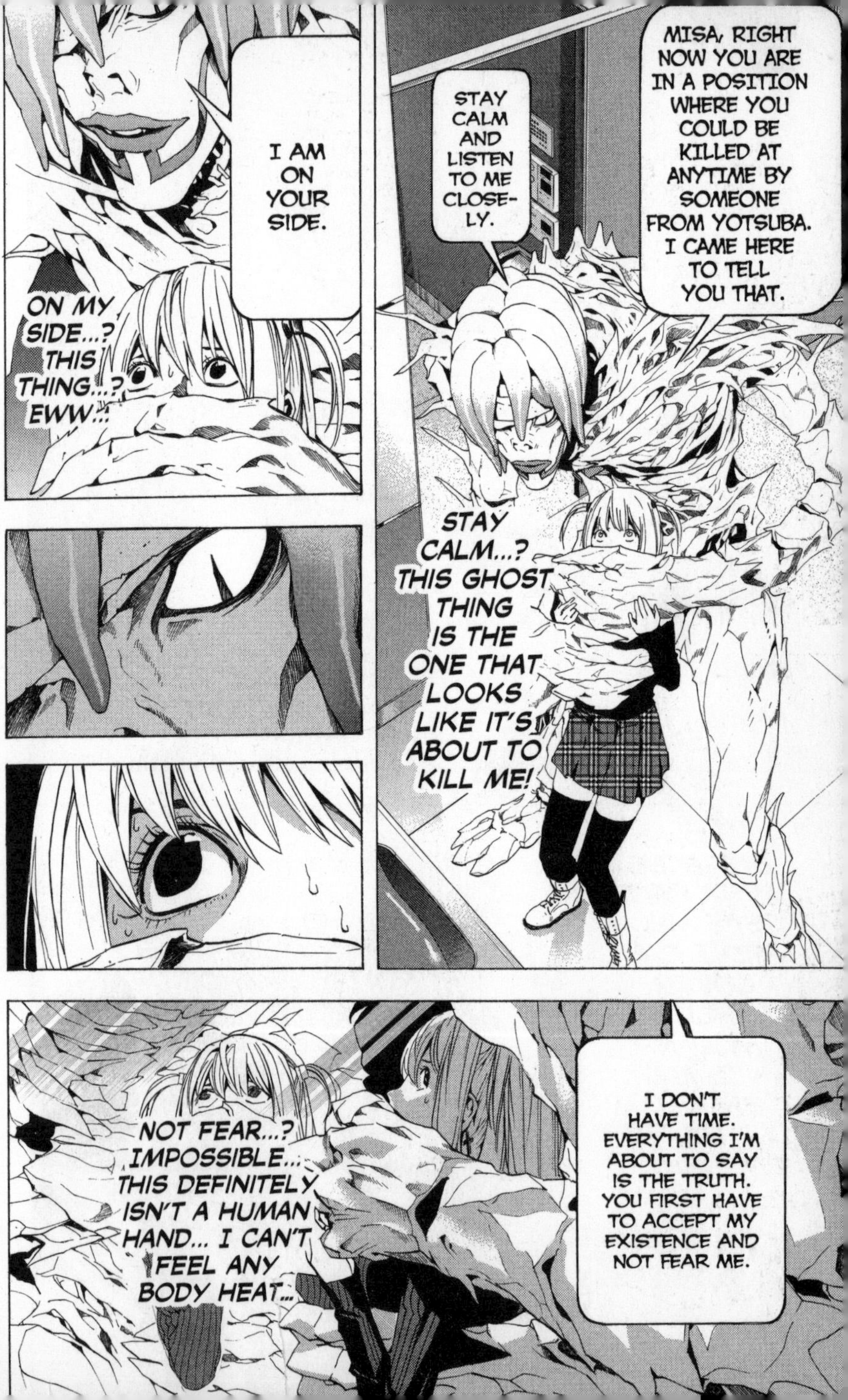
MISA, RIGHT NOW YOU ARE IN A POSITION WHERE YOU COULD BE KILLED AT ANYTIME BY SOMEONE FROM YOTSUBA. I CAME HERE TO TELL YOU THAT.
STAY CALM AND LISTEN TO ME CLOSE-LY.
STAY CALM...? THIS GHOST THING IS THE ONE THAT LOOKS LIKE IT'S ABOUT TO KILL ME!
I AM ON YOUR SIDE.
ON MY SIDE...? THIS THING...? EWW...
I DON'T HAVE TIME. EVERYTHING I'M ABOUT TO SAY IS THE TRUTH. YOU FIRST HAVE TO ACCEPT MY EXISTENCE AND NOT FEAR ME.
NOT FEAR...? IMPOSSIBLE... THIS DEFINITELY ISN'T A HUMAN HAND... I CAN'T FEEL ANY BODY HEAT...

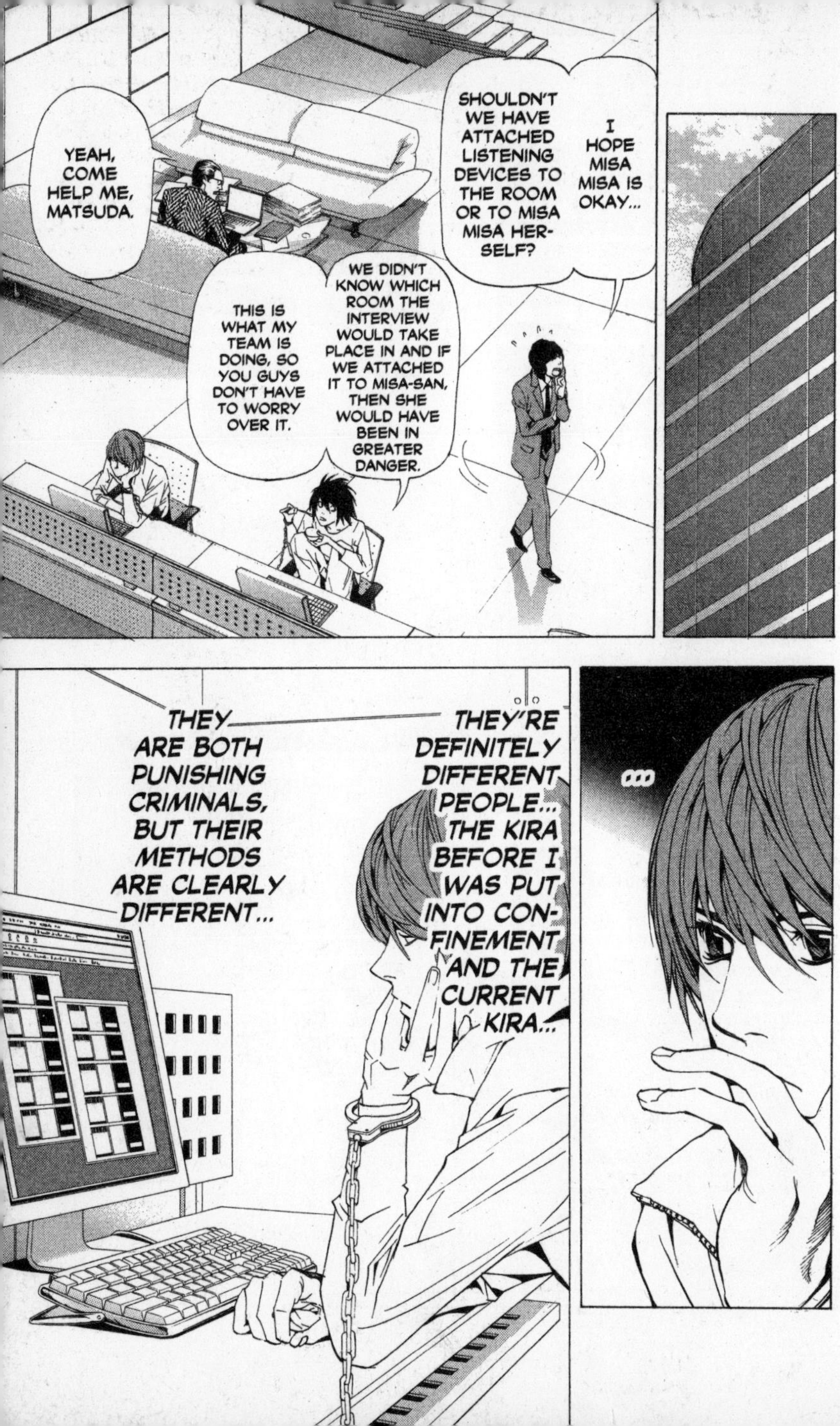
I HOPE MISA MISA IS OKAY...
SHOULDN'T WE HAVE ATTACHED LISTENING DEVICES TO THE ROOM OR TO MISA MISA HER-SELF?
WE DIDN'T KNOW WHICH ROOM THE INTERVIEW WOULD TAKE PLACE IN AND IF WE ATTACHED IT TO MISA-SAN, THEN SHE WOULD HAVE BEEN IN GREATER DANGER.
THIS IS WHAT MY TEAM IS DOING, SO YOU GUYS DON'T HAVE TO WORRY OVER IT.
YEAH, COME HELP ME, MATSUDA.
...
THEY'RE DEFINITELY DIFFERENT PEOPLE... THE KIRA BEFORE I WAS PUT INTO CON-FINEMENT AND THE CURRENT KIRA...
THEY ARE BOTH PUNISHING CRIMINALS, BUT THEIR METHODS ARE CLEARLY DIFFERENT...

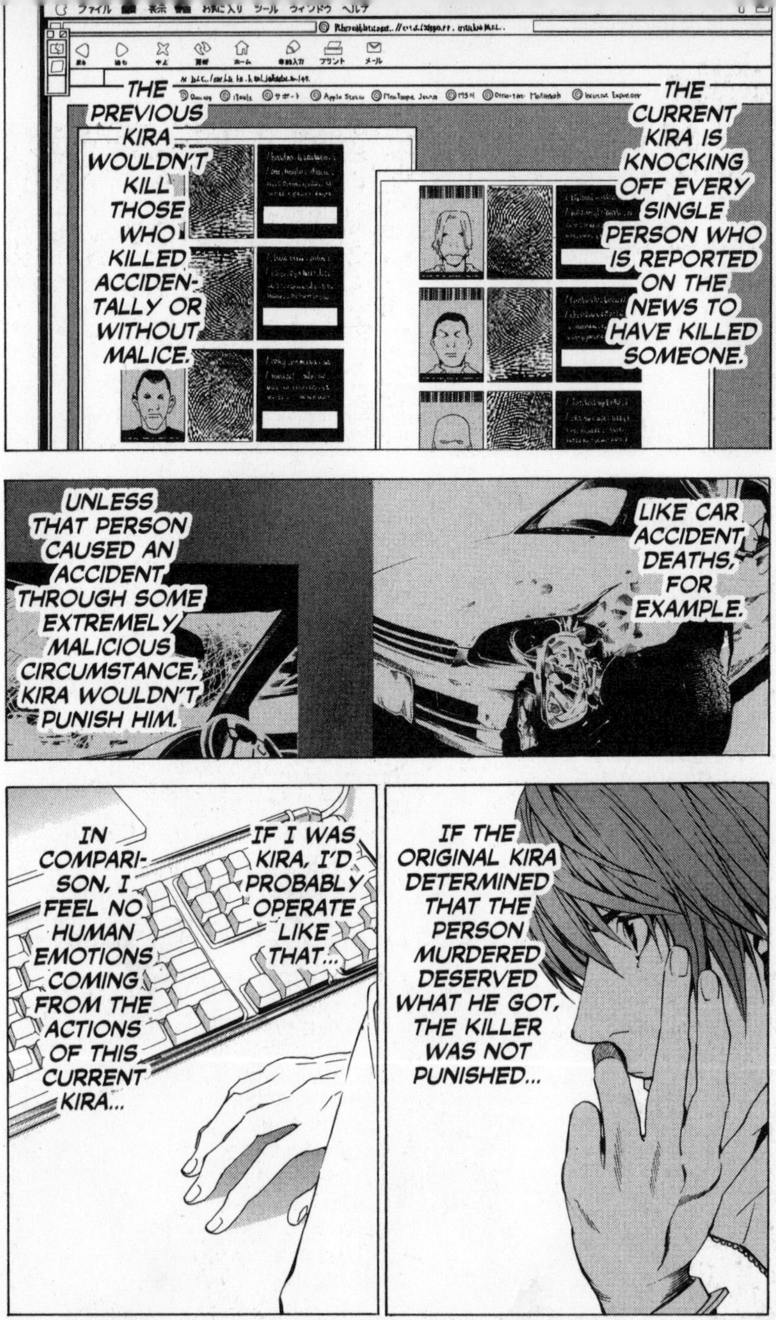
THE CURRENT KIRA IS KNOCKING OFF EVERY SINGLE PERSON WHO IS REPORTED ON THE NEWS TO HAVE KILLED SOMEONE.
THE PREVIOUS KIRA WOULDN'T KILL THOSE WHO KILLED ACCIDENTALLY OR WITHOUT MALICE.
LIKE CAR ACCIDENT DEATHS, FOR EXAMPLE.
UNLESS THAT PERSON CAUSED AN ACCIDENT THROUGH SOME EXTREMELY MALICIOUS CIRCUMSTANCE, KIRA WOULDN'T PUNISH HIM.
IF THE ORIGINAL KIRA DETERMINED THAT THE PERSON MURDERED DESERVED WHAT HE GOT, THE KILLER WAS NOT PUNISHED...
IF I WAS KIRA, I'D PROBABLY OPERATE LIKE THAT...
IN COMPARISON, I FEEL NO HUMAN EMOTIONS COMING FROM THE ACTIONS OF THIS CURRENT KIRA...

READ THIS WAY

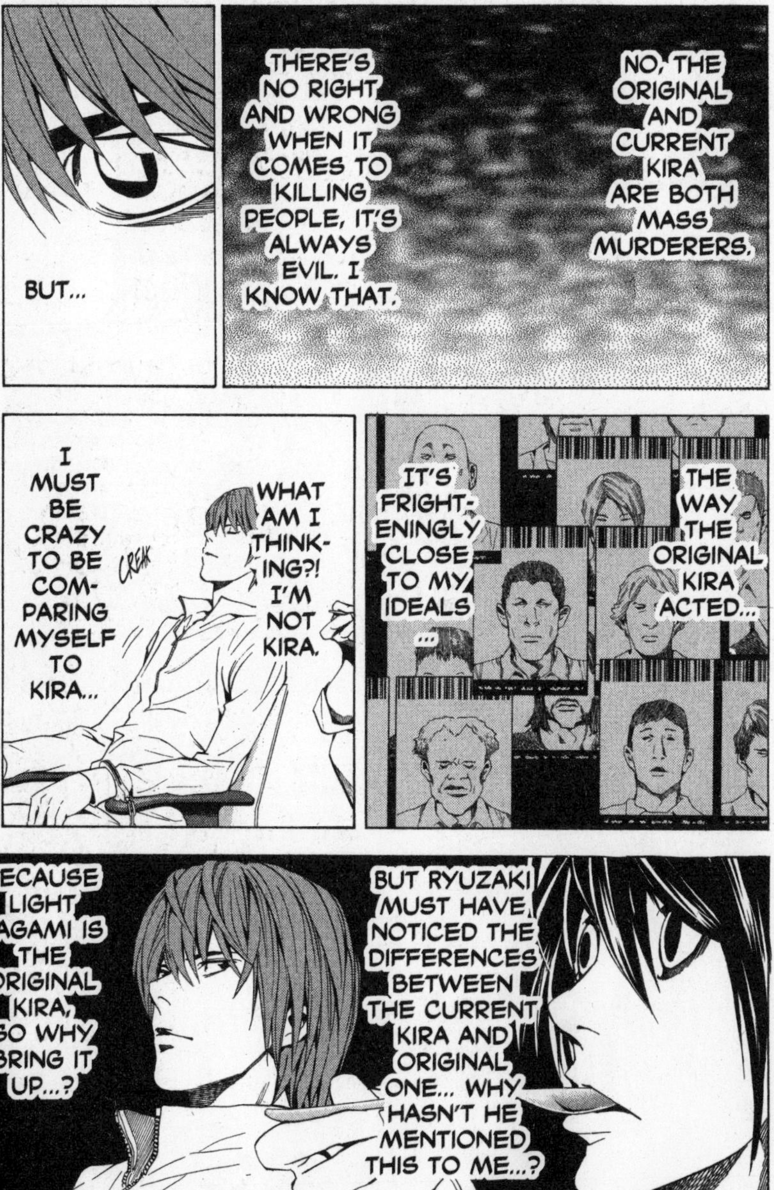
NO, THE ORIGINAL AND CURRENT KIRA ARE BOTH MASS MURDERERS.
THERE'S NO RIGHT AND WRONG WHEN IT COMES TO KILLING PEOPLE, IT'S ALWAYS EVIL. I KNOW THAT.
BUT...
THE WAY THE ORIGINAL KIRA ACTED...
IT'S FRIGHT-ENINGLY CLOSE TO MY IDEALS ...
WHAT AM I THINKING?! I'M NOT KIRA.
CREAK
I MUST BE CRAZY TO BE COM-PARING MYSELF TO KIRA...
BUT RYUZAKI MUST HAVE NOTICED THE DIFFERENCES BETWEEN THE CURRENT KIRA AND ORIGINAL ONE... WHY HASN'T HE MENTIONED THIS TO ME...?
BECAUSE LIGHT YAGAMI IS THE ORIGINAL KIRA, SO WHY BRING IT UP...?

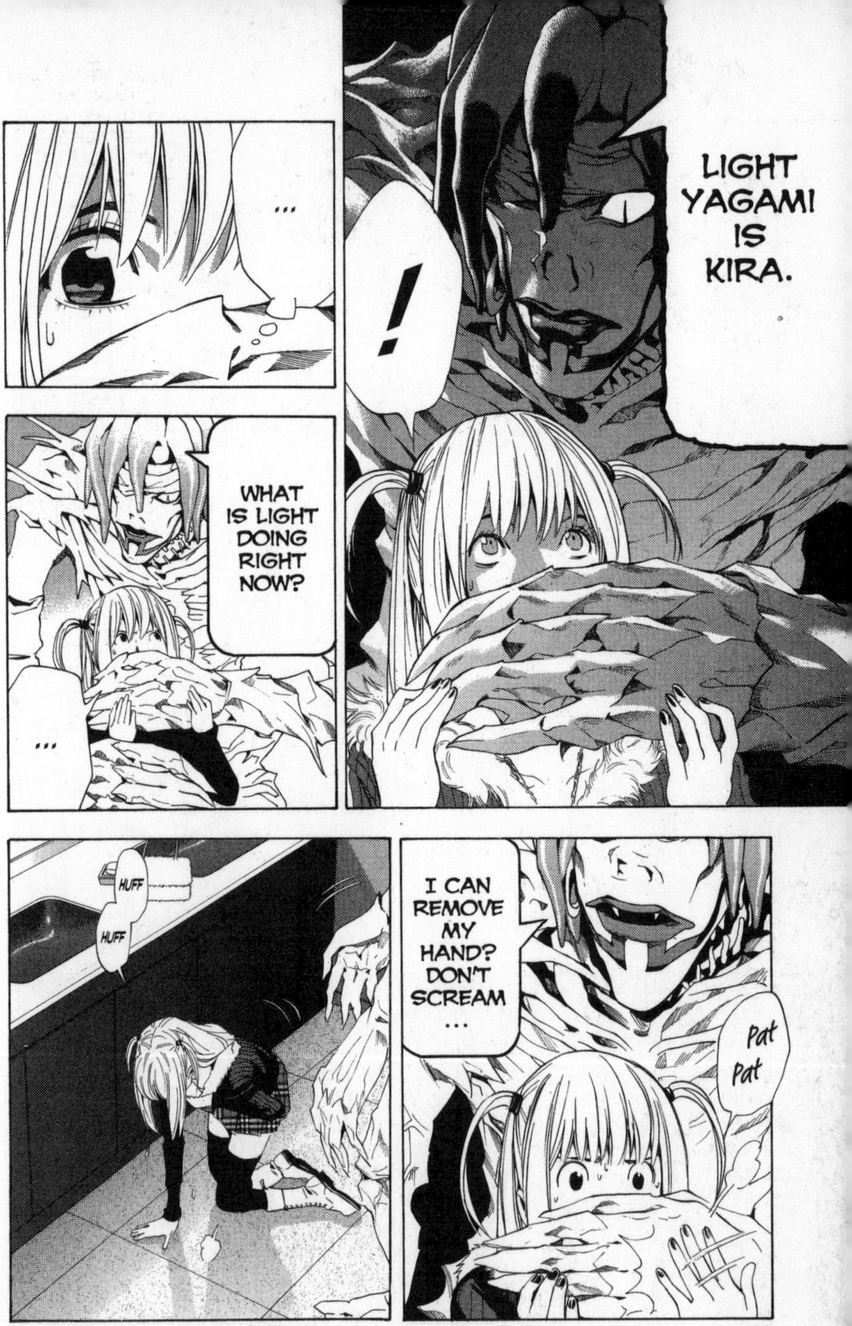
LIGHT YAGAMI IS KIRA.
!
...
WHAT IS LIGHT DOING RIGHT NOW?
...
I CAN REMOVE MY HAND? DON'T SCREAM ...
Pat Pat
HUFF
HUFF

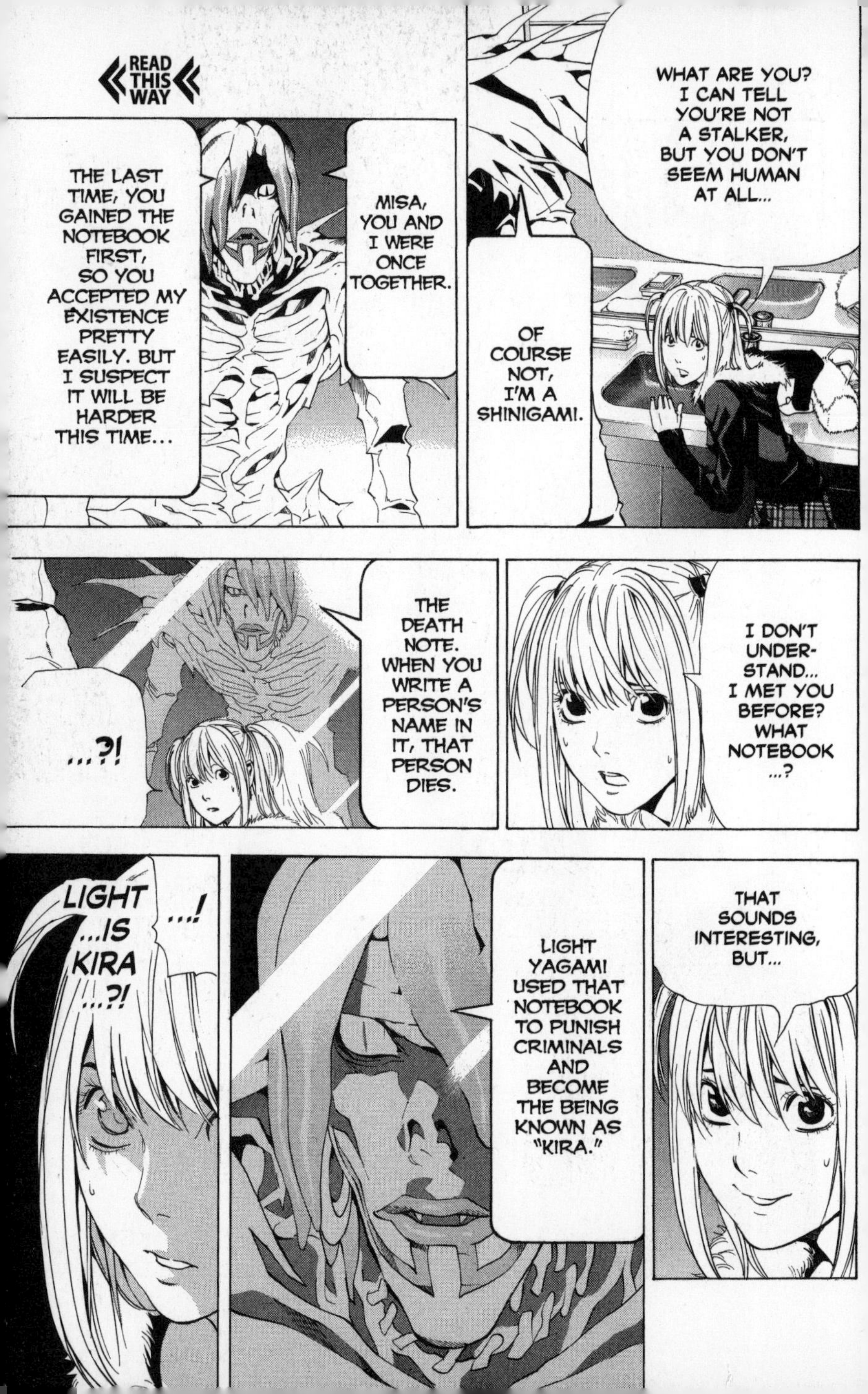
READ THIS WAY
WHAT ARE YOU? I CAN TELL YOU'RE NOT A STALKER, BUT YOU DON'T SEEM HUMAN AT ALL...
OF COURSE NOT, I'M A SHINIGAMI.
MISA, YOU AND I WERE ONCE TOGETHER.
THE LAST TIME, YOU GAINED THE NOTEBOOK FIRST, SO YOU ACCEPTED MY EXISTENCE PRETTY EASILY. BUT I SUSPECT IT WILL BE HARDER THIS TIME...
I DON'T UNDER-STAND... I MET YOU BEFORE? WHAT NOTEBOOK ...?
THE DEATH NOTE. WHEN YOU WRITE A PERSON'S NAME IN IT, THAT PERSON DIES.
...?!
THAT SOUNDS INTERESTING, BUT...
LIGHT YAGAMI USED THAT NOTEBOOK TO PUNISH CRIMINALS AND BECOME THE BEING KNOWN AS "KIRA."
...!
LIGHT ...IS KIRA ...?!

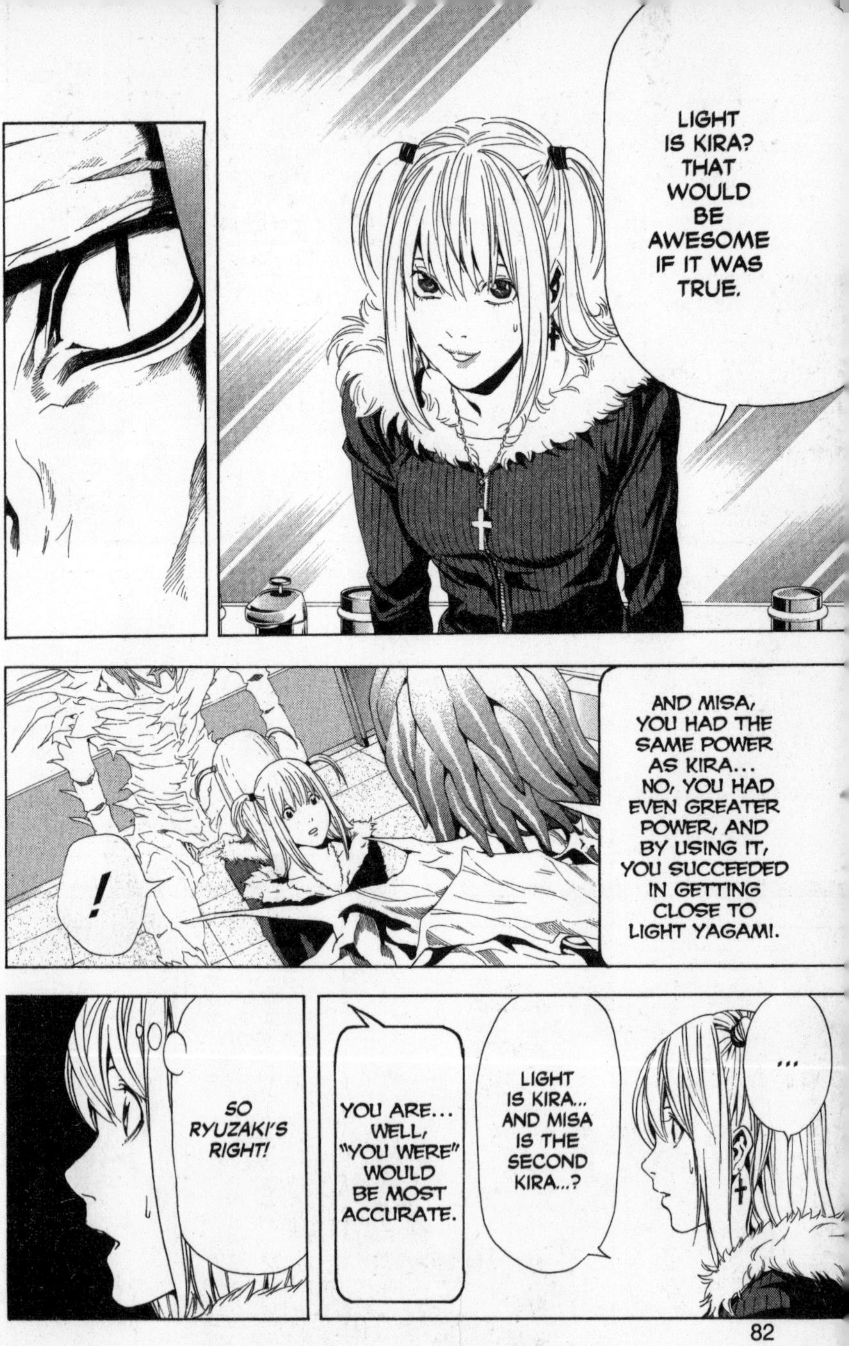
LIGHT IS KIRA? THAT WOULD BE AWESOME IF IT WAS TRUE.
AND MISA, YOU HAD THE SAME POWER AS KIRA... NO, YOU HAD EVEN GREATER POWER, AND BY USING IT, YOU SUCCEEDED IN GETTING CLOSE TO LIGHT YAGAMI.
!
...
LIGHT IS KIRA... AND MISA IS THE SECOND KIRA...?
YOU ARE... WELL, "YOU WERE" WOULD BE MOST ACCURATE.
SO RYUZAKI'S RIGHT!

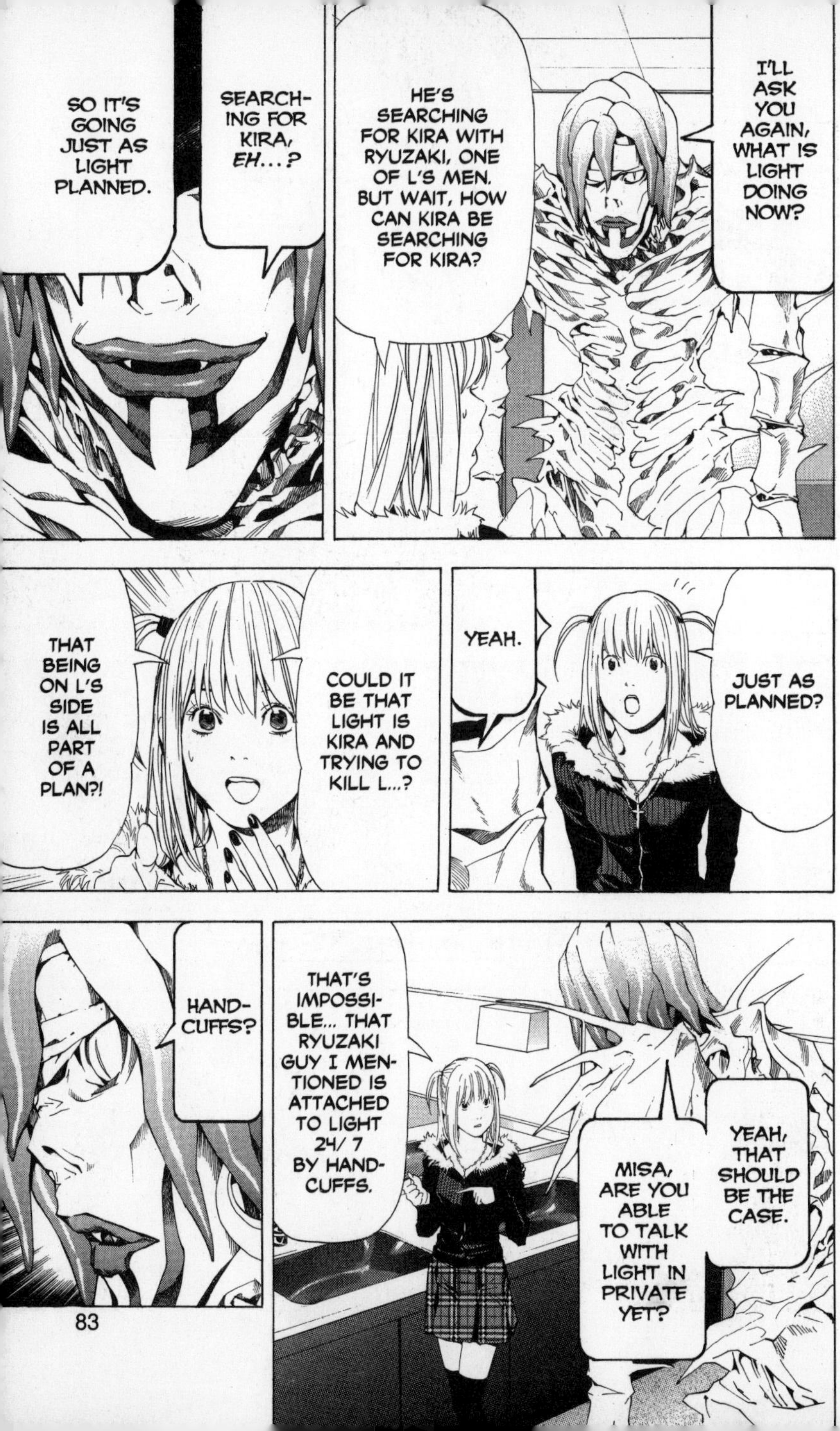

I'LL ASK YOU AGAIN, WHAT IS LIGHT DOING NOW?
HE'S SEARCHING FOR KIRA WITH RYUZAKI, ONE OF L'S MEN. BUT WAIT, HOW CAN KIRA BE SEARCHING FOR KIRA?
SEARCHING FOR KIRA, *EH...?*
SO IT'S GOING JUST AS LIGHT PLANNED.
JUST AS PLANNED?
YEAH.
COULD IT BE THAT LIGHT IS KIRA AND TRYING TO KILL L...?
THAT BEING ON L'S SIDE IS ALL PART OF A PLAN?!
YEAH, THAT SHOULD BE THE CASE.
MISA, ARE YOU ABLE TO TALK WITH LIGHT IN PRIVATE YET?
THAT'S IMPOSSIBLE... THAT RYUZAKI GUY I MENTIONED IS ATTACHED TO LIGHT 24/7 BY HANDCUFFS.
HANDCUFFS?

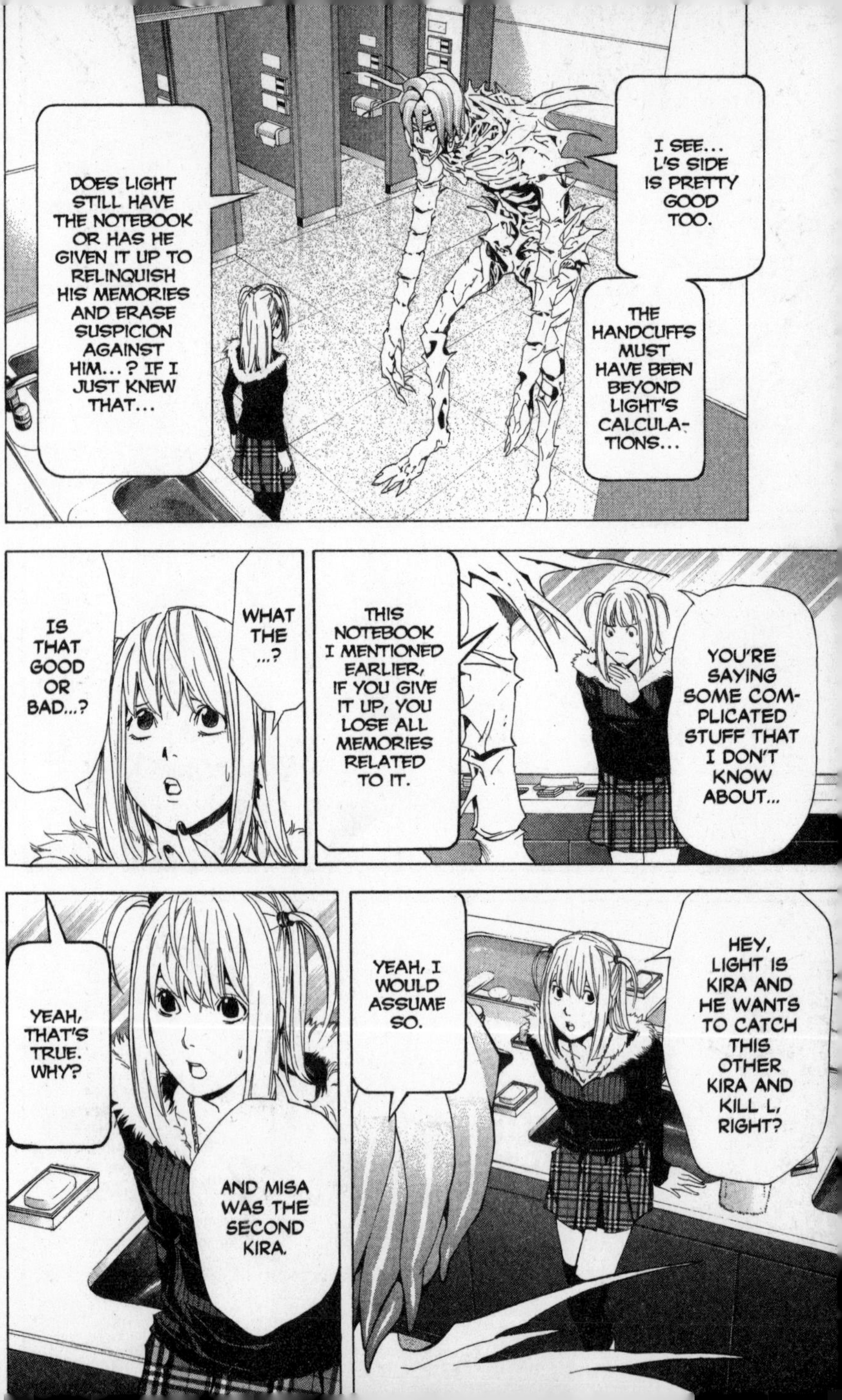
I SEE... L'S SIDE IS PRETTY GOOD TOO.
THE HANDCUFFS MUST HAVE BEEN BEYOND LIGHT'S CALCULA- TIONS...
DOES LIGHT STILL HAVE THE NOTEBOOK OR HAS HE GIVEN IT UP TO RELINQUISH HIS MEMORIES AND ERASE SUSPICION AGAINST HIM...? IF I JUST KNEW THAT...
YOU'RE SAYING SOME COM- PLICATED STUFF THAT I DON'T KNOW ABOUT...
THIS NOTEBOOK I MENTIONED EARLIER, IF YOU GIVE IT UP, YOU LOSE ALL MEMORIES RELATED TO IT.
WHAT THE ...?
IS THAT GOOD OR BAD...?
HEY, LIGHT IS KIRA AND HE WANTS TO CATCH THIS OTHER KIRA AND KILL L, RIGHT?
YEAH, I WOULD ASSUME SO.
AND MISA WAS THE SECOND KIRA.
YEAH, THAT'S TRUE. WHY?

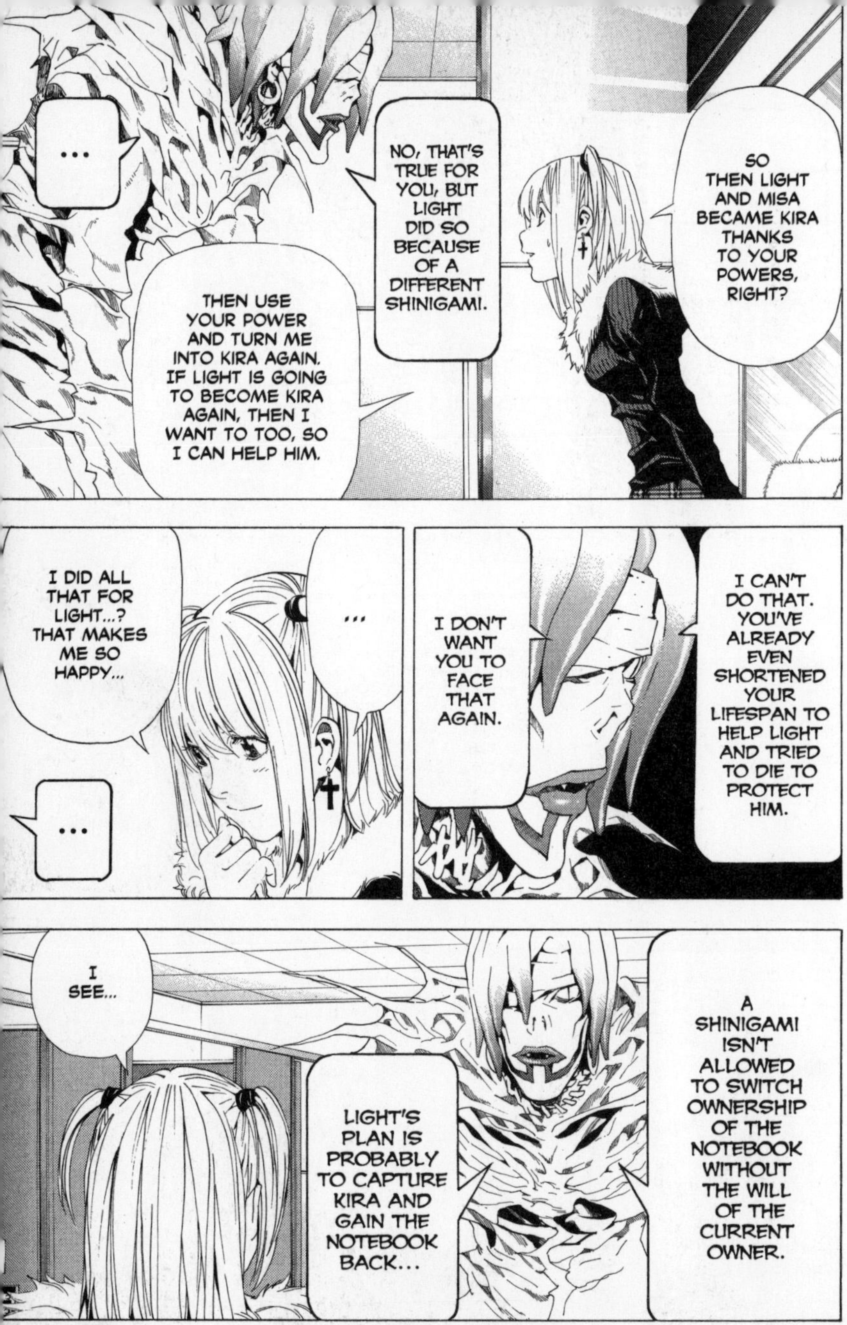
SO THEN LIGHT AND MISA BECAME KIRA THANKS TO YOUR POWERS, RIGHT?
NO, THAT'S TRUE FOR YOU, BUT LIGHT DID SO BECAUSE OF A DIFFERENT SHINIGAMI.
...
THEN USE YOUR POWER AND TURN ME INTO KIRA AGAIN. IF LIGHT IS GOING TO BECOME KIRA AGAIN, THEN I WANT TO TOO, SO I CAN HELP HIM.
I CAN'T DO THAT. YOU'VE ALREADY EVEN SHORTENED YOUR LIFESPAN TO HELP LIGHT AND TRIED TO DIE TO PROTECT HIM.
I DON'T WANT YOU TO FACE THAT AGAIN.
...
I DID ALL THAT FOR LIGHT...? THAT MAKES ME SO HAPPY...
...
A SHINIGAMI ISN'T ALLOWED TO SWITCH OWNERSHIP OF THE NOTEBOOK WITHOUT THE WILL OF THE CURRENT OWNER.
LIGHT'S PLAN IS PROBABLY TO CAPTURE KIRA AND GAIN THE NOTEBOOK BACK...
I SEE...

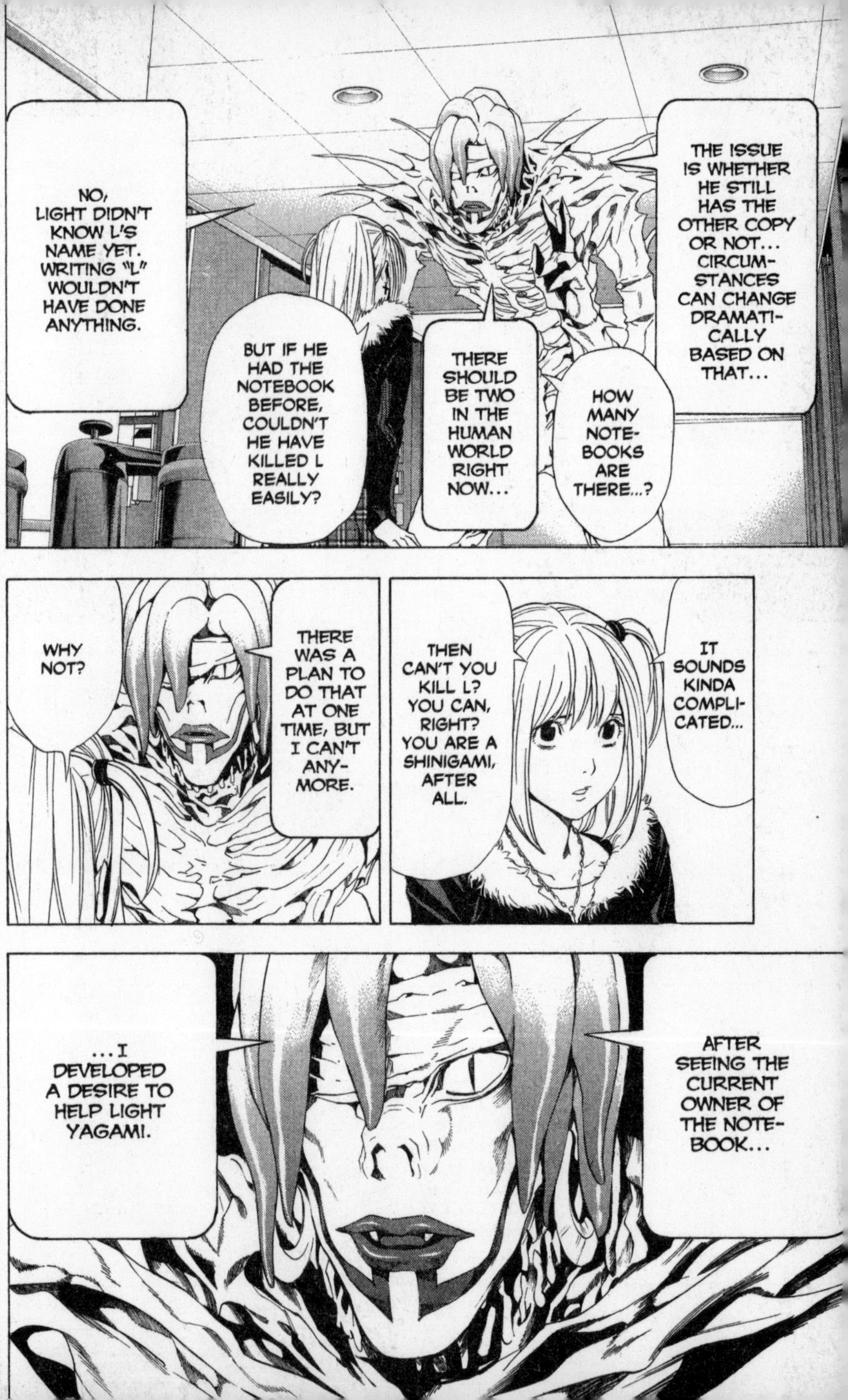
THE ISSUE IS WHETHER HE STILL HAS THE OTHER COPY OR NOT... CIRCUM-STANCES CAN CHANGE DRAMATI-CALLY BASED ON THAT...
HOW MANY NOTE-BOOKS ARE THERE...?
THERE SHOULD BE TWO IN THE HUMAN WORLD RIGHT NOW...
BUT IF HE HAD THE NOTEBOOK BEFORE, COULDN'T HE HAVE KILLED L REALLY EASILY?
NO, LIGHT DIDN'T KNOW L'S NAME YET. WRITING "L" WOULDN'T HAVE DONE ANYTHING.
IT SOUNDS KINDA COMPLI-CATED...
THEN CAN'T YOU KILL L? YOU CAN, RIGHT? YOU ARE A SHINIGAMI, AFTER ALL.
THERE WAS A PLAN TO DO THAT AT ONE TIME, BUT I CAN'T ANY-MORE.
WHY NOT?
AFTER SEEING THE CURRENT OWNER OF THE NOTE-BOOK...
...I DEVELOPED A DESIRE TO HELP LIGHT YAGAMI.

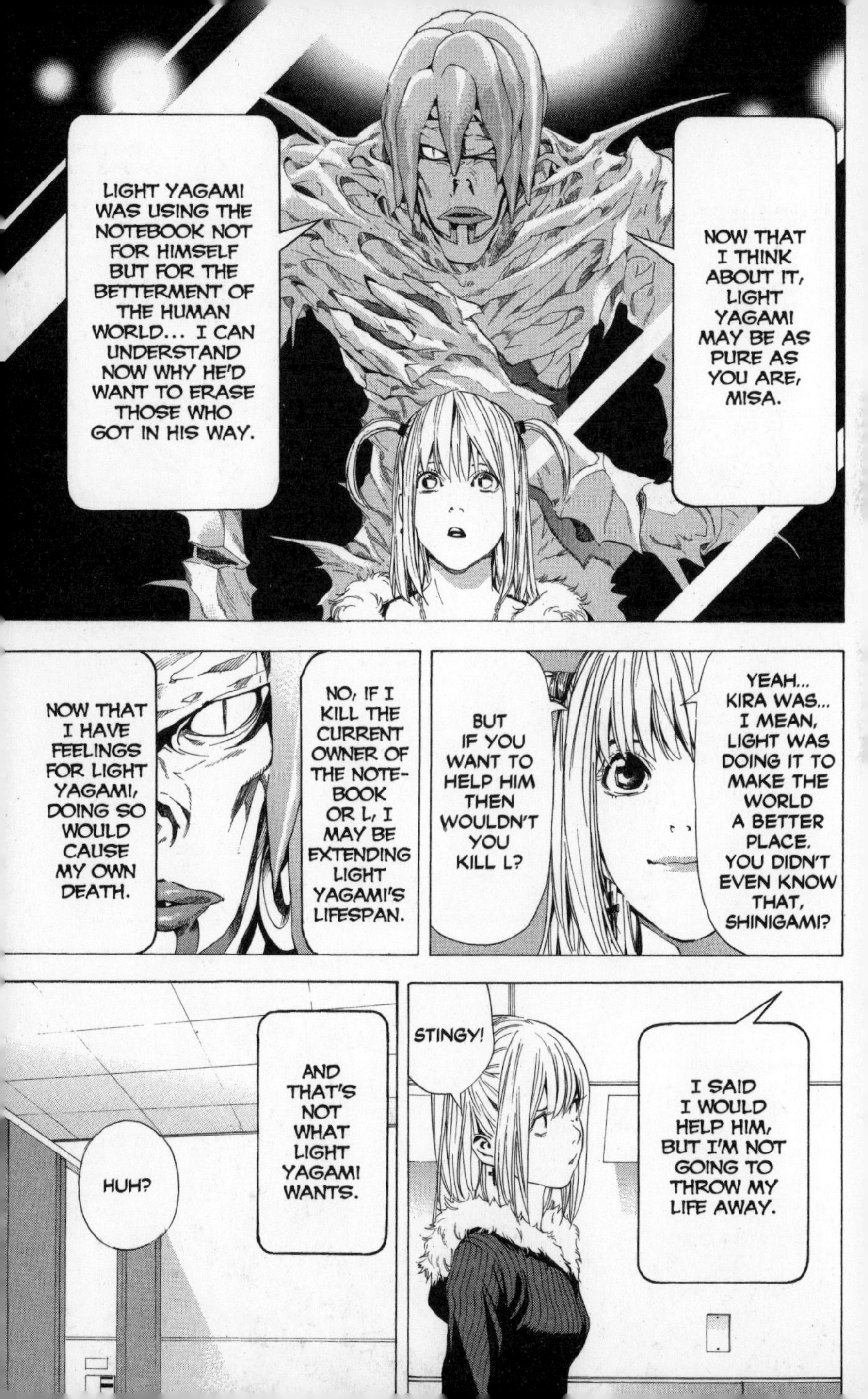
NOW THAT I THINK ABOUT IT, LIGHT YAGAMI MAY BE AS PURE AS YOU ARE, MISA.
LIGHT YAGAMI WAS USING THE NOTEBOOK NOT FOR HIMSELF BUT FOR THE BETTERMENT OF THE HUMAN WORLD... I CAN UNDERSTAND NOW WHY HE'D WANT TO ERASE THOSE WHO GOT IN HIS WAY.
YEAH... KIRA WAS... I MEAN, LIGHT WAS DOING IT TO MAKE THE WORLD A BETTER PLACE. YOU DIDN'T EVEN KNOW THAT, SHINIGAMI?
BUT IF YOU WANT TO HELP HIM THEN WOULDN'T YOU KILL L?
NO, IF I KILL THE CURRENT OWNER OF THE NOTE-BOOK OR L, I MAY BE EXTENDING LIGHT YAGAMI'S LIFESPAN.
NOW THAT I HAVE FEELINGS FOR LIGHT YAGAMI, DOING SO WOULD CAUSE MY OWN DEATH.
I SAID I WOULD HELP HIM, BUT I'M NOT GOING TO THROW MY LIFE AWAY.
STINGY!
AND THAT'S NOT WHAT LIGHT YAGAMI WANTS.
HUH?

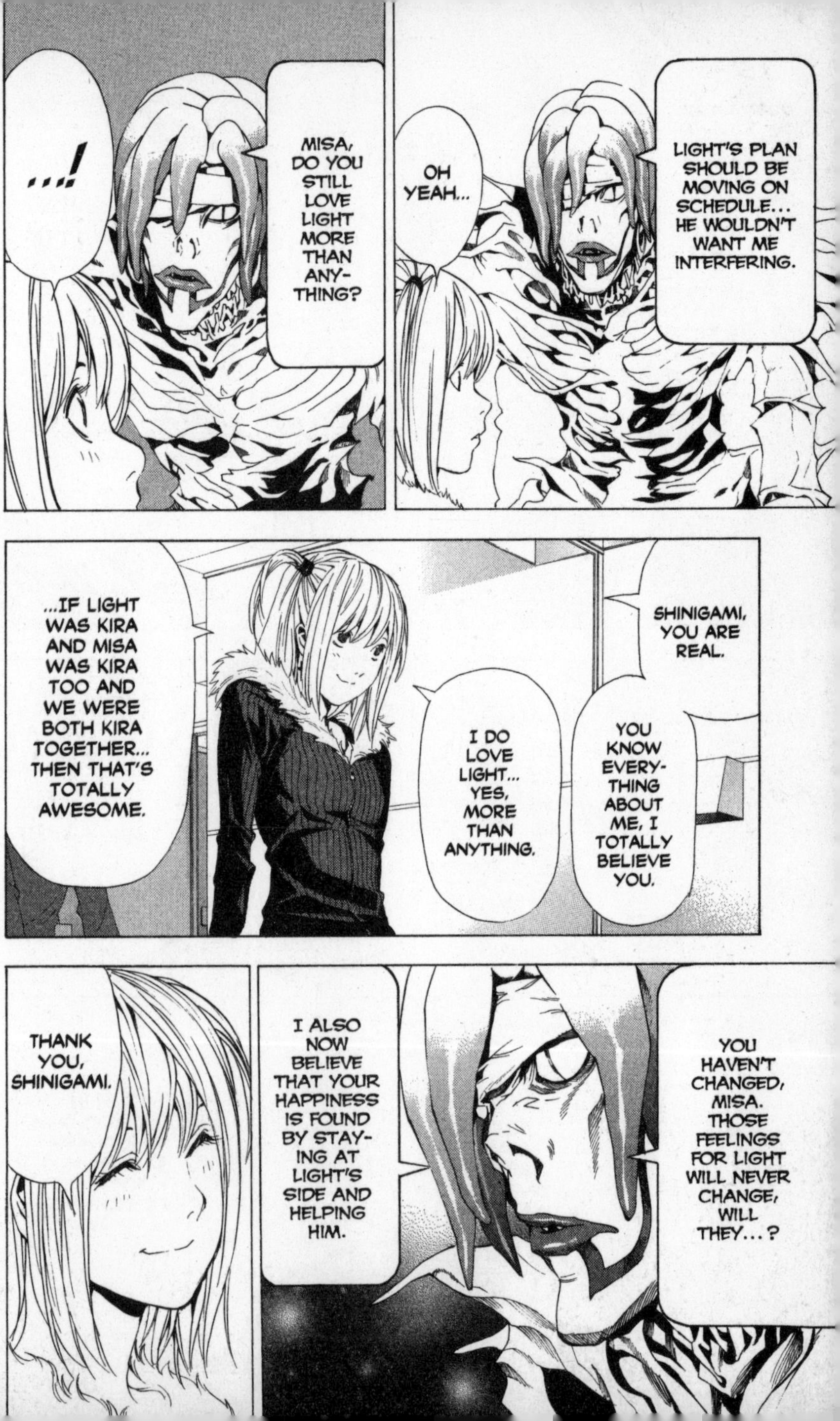
LIGHT'S PLAN SHOULD BE MOVING ON SCHEDULE... HE WOULDN'T WANT ME INTERFERING.
OH YEAH...
MISA, DO YOU STILL LOVE LIGHT MORE THAN ANY-THING?
...!
SHINIGAMI, YOU ARE REAL.
YOU KNOW EVERY-THING ABOUT ME, I TOTALLY BELIEVE YOU.
I DO LOVE LIGHT... YES, MORE THAN ANYTHING.
...IF LIGHT WAS KIRA AND MISA WAS KIRA TOO AND WE WERE BOTH KIRA TOGETHER... THEN THAT'S TOTALLY AWESOME.
YOU HAVEN'T CHANGED, MISA. THOSE FEELINGS FOR LIGHT WILL NEVER CHANGE, WILL THEY...?
I ALSO NOW BELIEVE THAT YOUR HAPPINESS IS FOUND BY STAY-ING AT LIGHT'S SIDE AND HELPING HIM.
THANK YOU, SHINIGAMI.

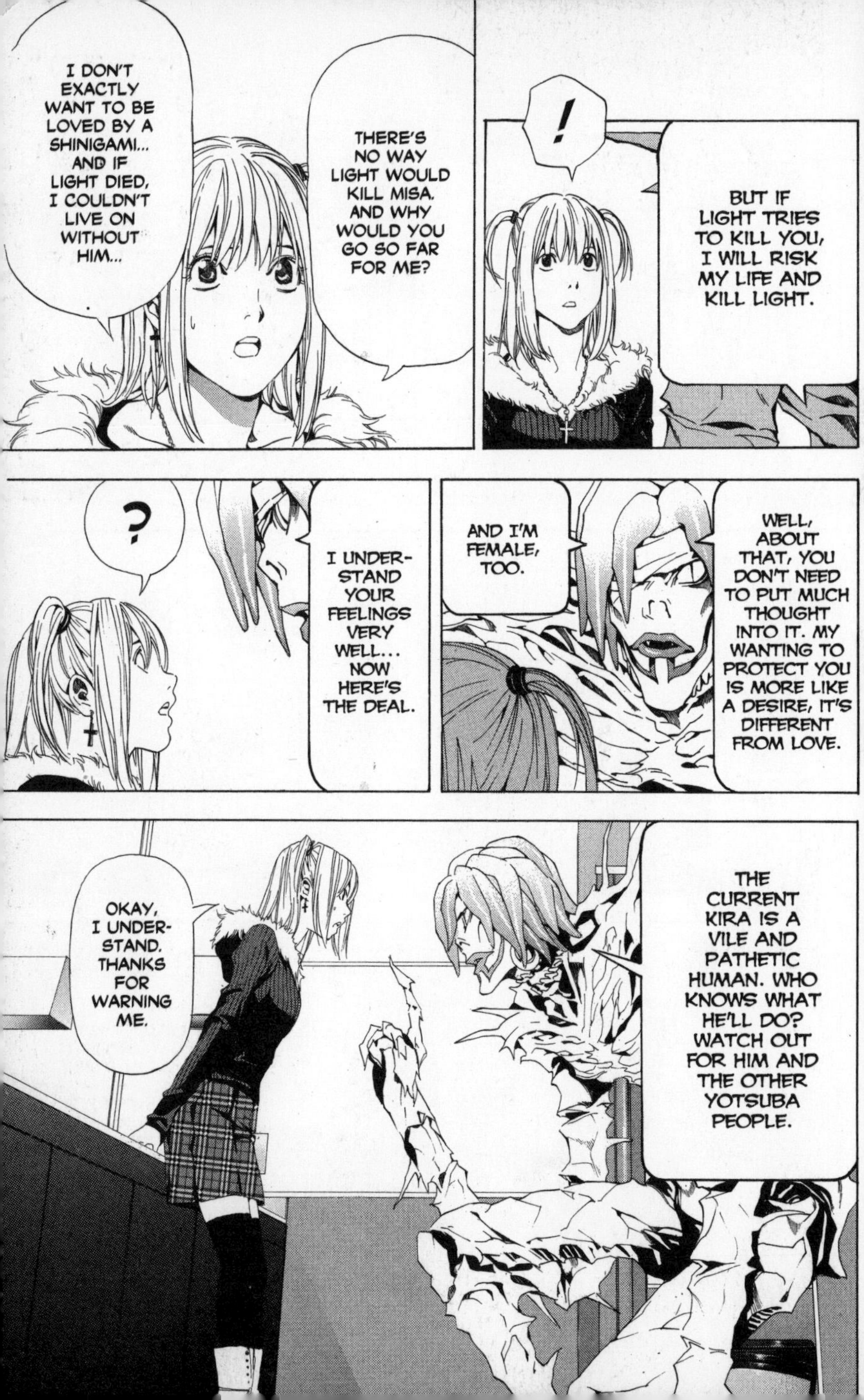
BUT IF LIGHT TRIES TO KILL YOU, I WILL RISK MY LIFE AND KILL LIGHT.
!
THERE'S NO WAY LIGHT WOULD KILL MISA. AND WHY WOULD YOU GO SO FAR FOR ME?
I DON'T EXACTLY WANT TO BE LOVED BY A SHINIGAMI... AND IF LIGHT DIED, I COULDN'T LIVE ON WITHOUT HIM...
WELL, ABOUT THAT, YOU DON'T NEED TO PUT MUCH THOUGHT INTO IT. MY WANTING TO PROTECT YOU IS MORE LIKE A DESIRE, IT'S DIFFERENT FROM LOVE.
AND I'M FEMALE, TOO.
I UNDER-STAND YOUR FEELINGS VERY WELL... NOW HERE'S THE DEAL.
?
THE CURRENT KIRA IS A VILE AND PATHETIC HUMAN. WHO KNOWS WHAT HE'LL DO? WATCH OUT FOR HIM AND THE OTHER YOTSUBA PEOPLE.
OKAY, I UNDER-STAND. THANKS FOR WARNING ME.

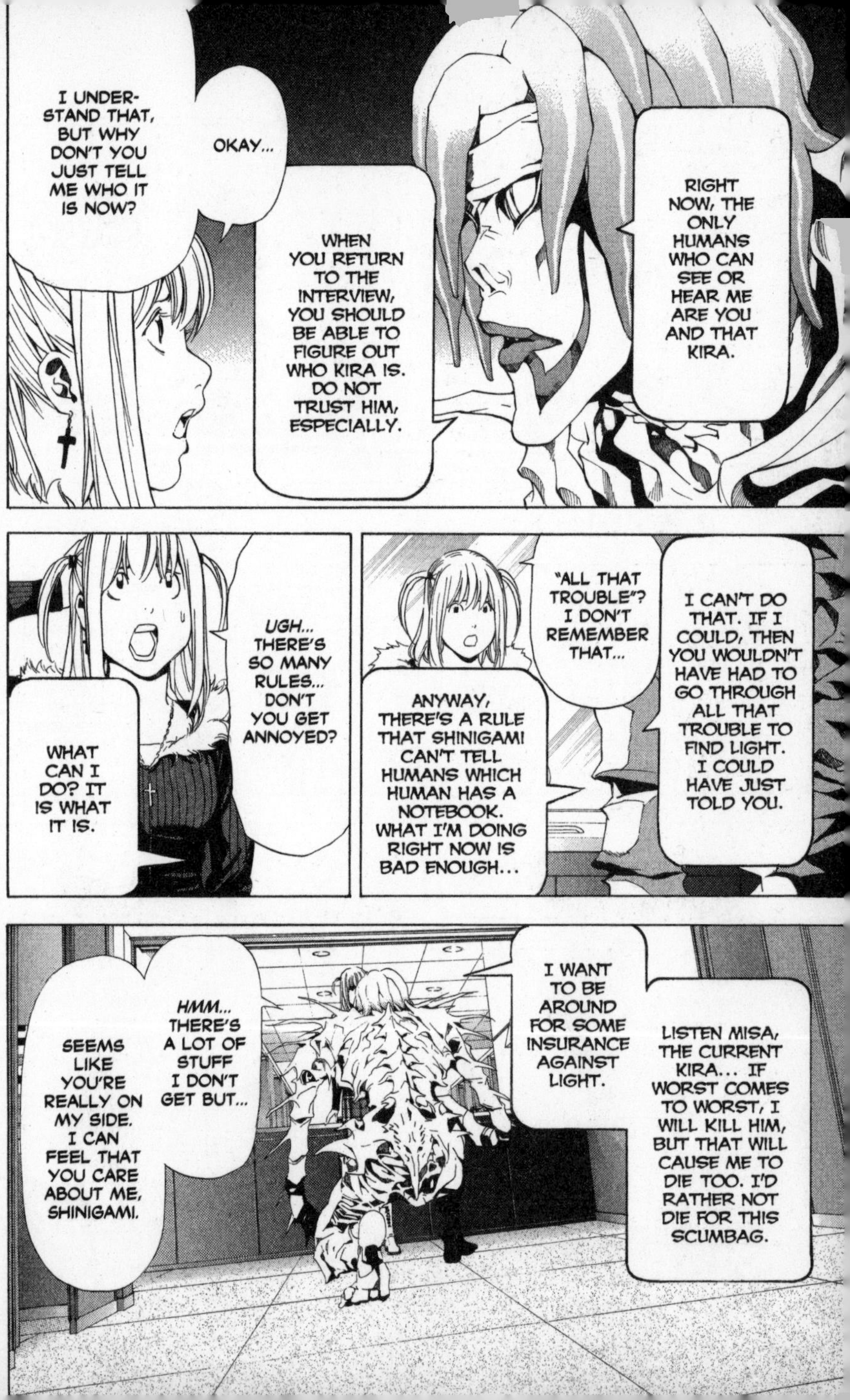
RIGHT NOW, THE ONLY HUMANS WHO CAN SEE OR HEAR ME ARE YOU AND THAT KIRA.
WHEN YOU RETURN TO THE INTERVIEW, YOU SHOULD BE ABLE TO FIGURE OUT WHO KIRA IS. DO NOT TRUST HIM, ESPECIALLY.
OKAY...
I UNDER-STAND THAT, BUT WHY DON'T YOU JUST TELL ME WHO IT IS NOW?
I CAN'T DO THAT. IF I COULD, THEN YOU WOULDN'T HAVE HAD TO GO THROUGH ALL THAT TROUBLE TO FIND LIGHT. I COULD HAVE JUST TOLD YOU.
"ALL THAT TROUBLE"? I DON'T REMEMBER THAT...
ANYWAY, THERE'S A RULE THAT SHINIGAMI CAN'T TELL HUMANS WHICH HUMAN HAS A NOTEBOOK. WHAT I'M DOING RIGHT NOW IS BAD ENOUGH...
UGH... THERE'S SO MANY RULES... DON'T YOU GET ANNOYED?
WHAT CAN I DO? IT IS WHAT IT IS.
LISTEN MISA, THE CURRENT KIRA... IF WORST COMES TO WORST, I WILL KILL HIM, BUT THAT WILL CAUSE ME TO DIE TOO. I'D RATHER NOT DIE FOR THIS SCUMBAG.
I WANT TO BE AROUND FOR SOME INSURANCE AGAINST LIGHT.
HMM... THERE'S A LOT OF STUFF I DON'T GET BUT...
SEEMS LIKE YOU'RE REALLY ON MY SIDE. I CAN FEEL THAT YOU CARE ABOUT ME, SHINIGAMI.

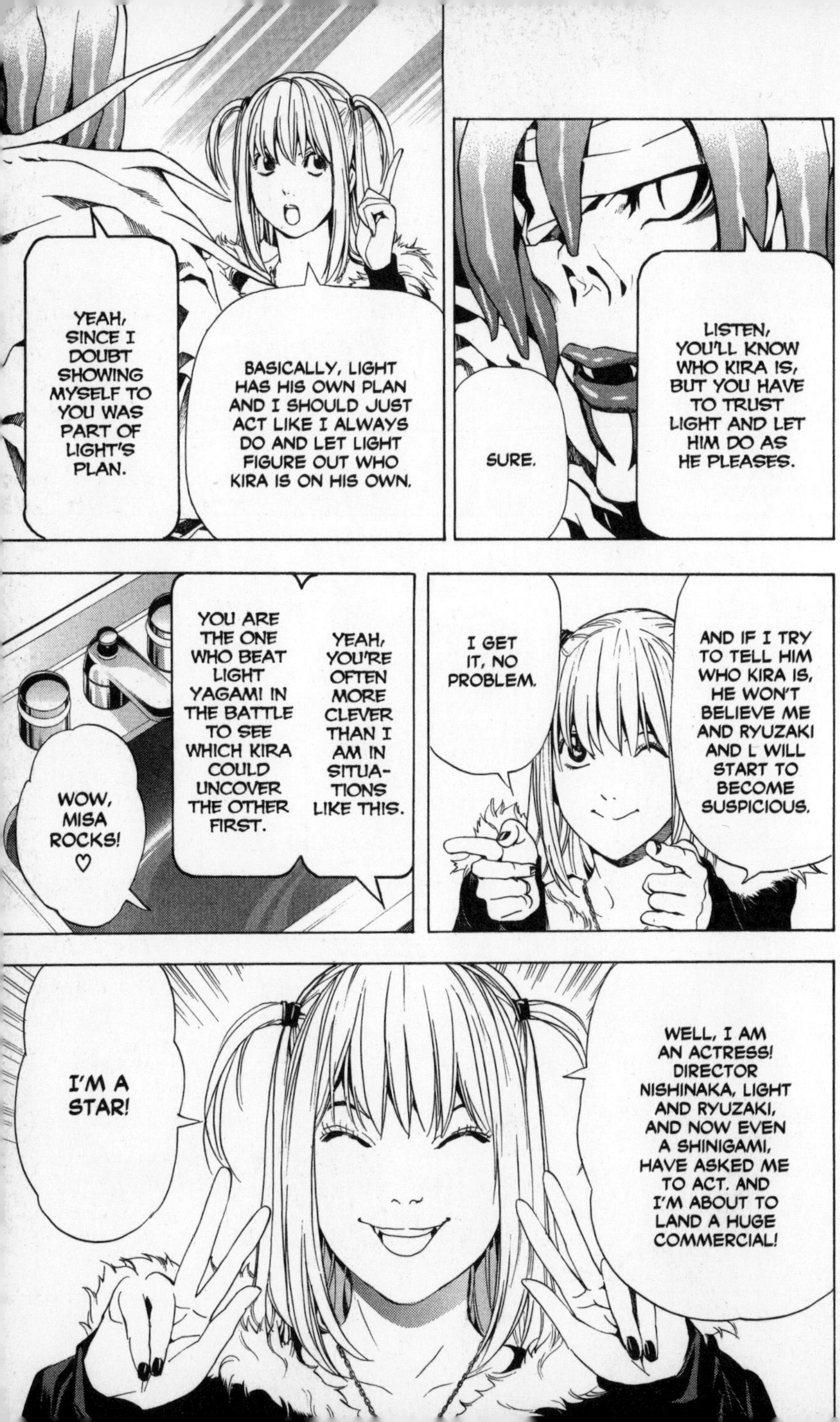
LISTEN, YOU'LL KNOW WHO KIRA IS, BUT YOU HAVE TO TRUST LIGHT AND LET HIM DO AS HE PLEASES.
SURE.
BASICALLY, LIGHT HAS HIS OWN PLAN AND I SHOULD JUST ACT LIKE I ALWAYS DO AND LET LIGHT FIGURE OUT WHO KIRA IS ON HIS OWN.
YEAH, SINCE I DOUBT SHOWING MYSELF TO YOU WAS PART OF LIGHT'S PLAN.
AND IF I TRY TO TELL HIM WHO KIRA IS, HE WON'T BELIEVE ME AND RYUZAKI AND L WILL START TO BECOME SUSPICIOUS.
I GET IT, NO PROBLEM.
YEAH, YOU'RE OFTEN MORE CLEVER THAN I AM IN SITUATIONS LIKE THIS.
YOU ARE THE ONE WHO BEAT LIGHT YAGAMI IN THE BATTLE TO SEE WHICH KIRA COULD UNCOVER THE OTHER FIRST.
WOW, MISA ROCKS! ♡
WELL, I AM AN ACTRESS! DIRECTOR NISHINAKA, LIGHT AND RYUZAKI, AND NOW EVEN A SHINIGAMI, HAVE ASKED ME TO ACT. AND I'M ABOUT TO LAND A HUGE COMMERCIAL!
I'M A STAR!

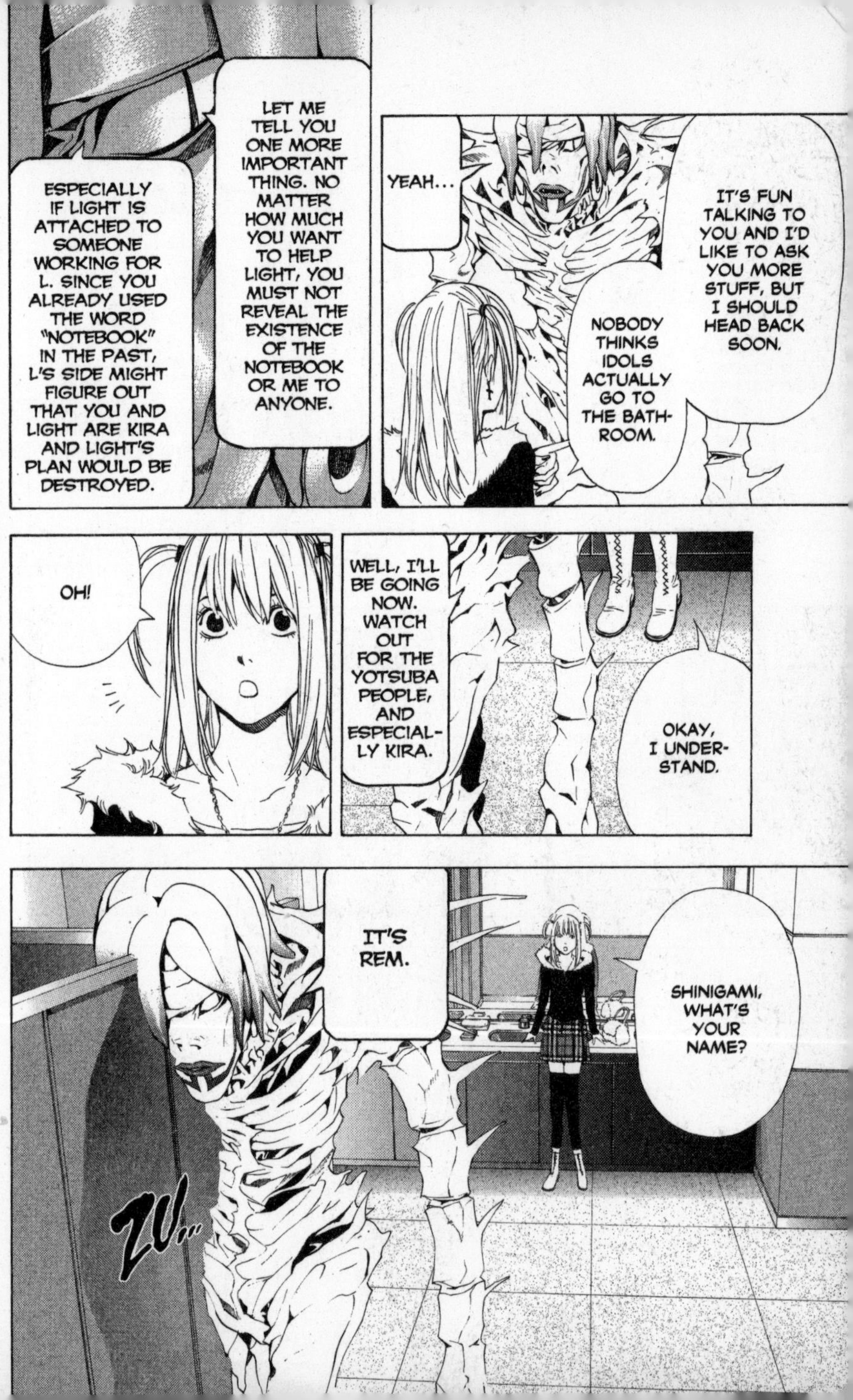
IT'S FUN TALKING TO YOU AND I'D LIKE TO ASK YOU MORE STUFF, BUT I SHOULD HEAD BACK SOON.
NOBODY THINKS IDOLS ACTUALLY GO TO THE BATH-ROOM.
YEAH...
LET ME TELL YOU ONE MORE IMPORTANT THING. NO MATTER HOW MUCH YOU WANT TO HELP LIGHT, YOU MUST NOT REVEAL THE EXISTENCE OF THE NOTEBOOK OR ME TO ANYONE.
ESPECIALLY IF LIGHT IS ATTACHED TO SOMEONE WORKING FOR L. SINCE YOU ALREADY USED THE WORD "NOTEBOOK" IN THE PAST, L'S SIDE MIGHT FIGURE OUT THAT YOU AND LIGHT ARE KIRA AND LIGHT'S PLAN WOULD BE DESTROYED.
WELL, I'LL BE GOING NOW. WATCH OUT FOR THE YOTSUBA PEOPLE, AND ESPECIAL-LY KIRA.
OKAY, I UNDER-STAND.
OH!
SHINIGAMI, WHAT'S YOUR NAME?
IT'S REM.
ZU...

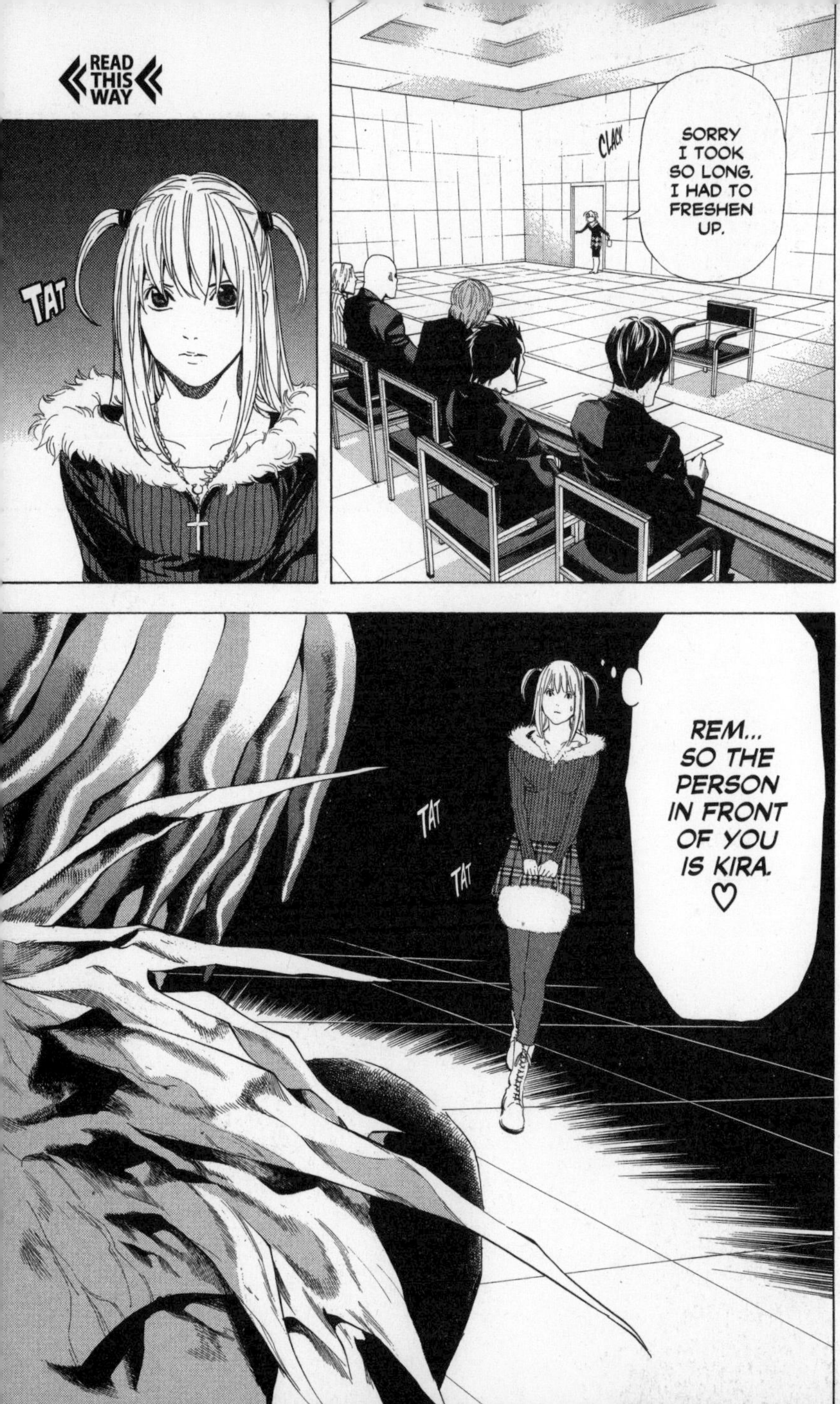
READ THIS WAY
CLACK
SORRY I TOOK SO LONG. I HAD TO FRESHEN UP.
TAT
REM... SO THE PERSON IN FRONT OF YOU IS KIRA. ♡
TAT
TAT

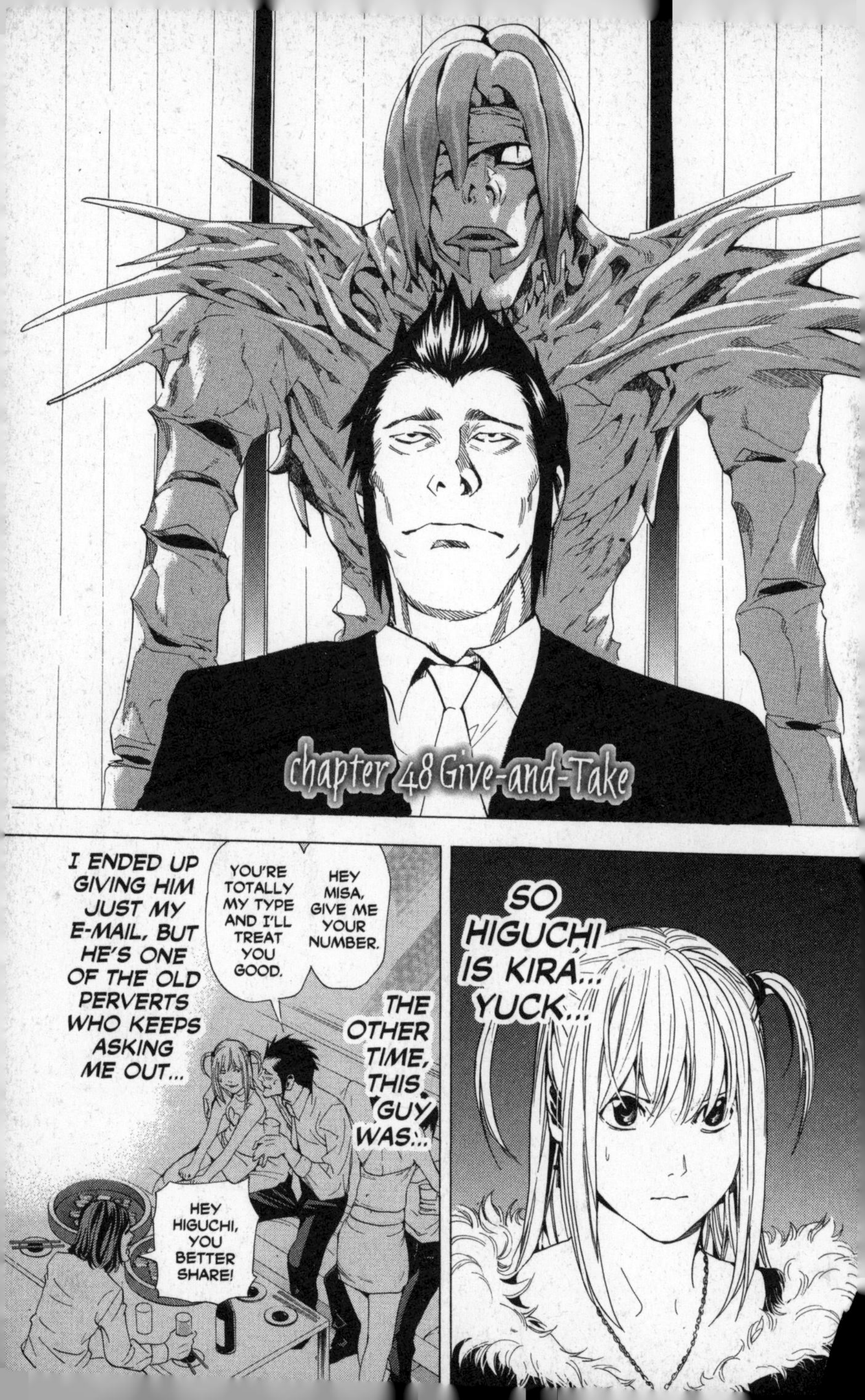
chapter 48 Give-and-Take
SO HIGUCHI IS KIRA... YUCK...
THE OTHER TIME, THIS GUY WAS...
HEY MISA, GIVE ME YOUR NUMBER.
YOU'RE TOTALLY MY TYPE AND I'LL TREAT YOU GOOD.
I ENDED UP GIVING HIM JUST MY E-MAIL, BUT HE'S ONE OF THE OLD PERVERTS WHO KEEPS ASKING ME OUT...
HEY HIGUCHI, YOU BETTER SHARE!

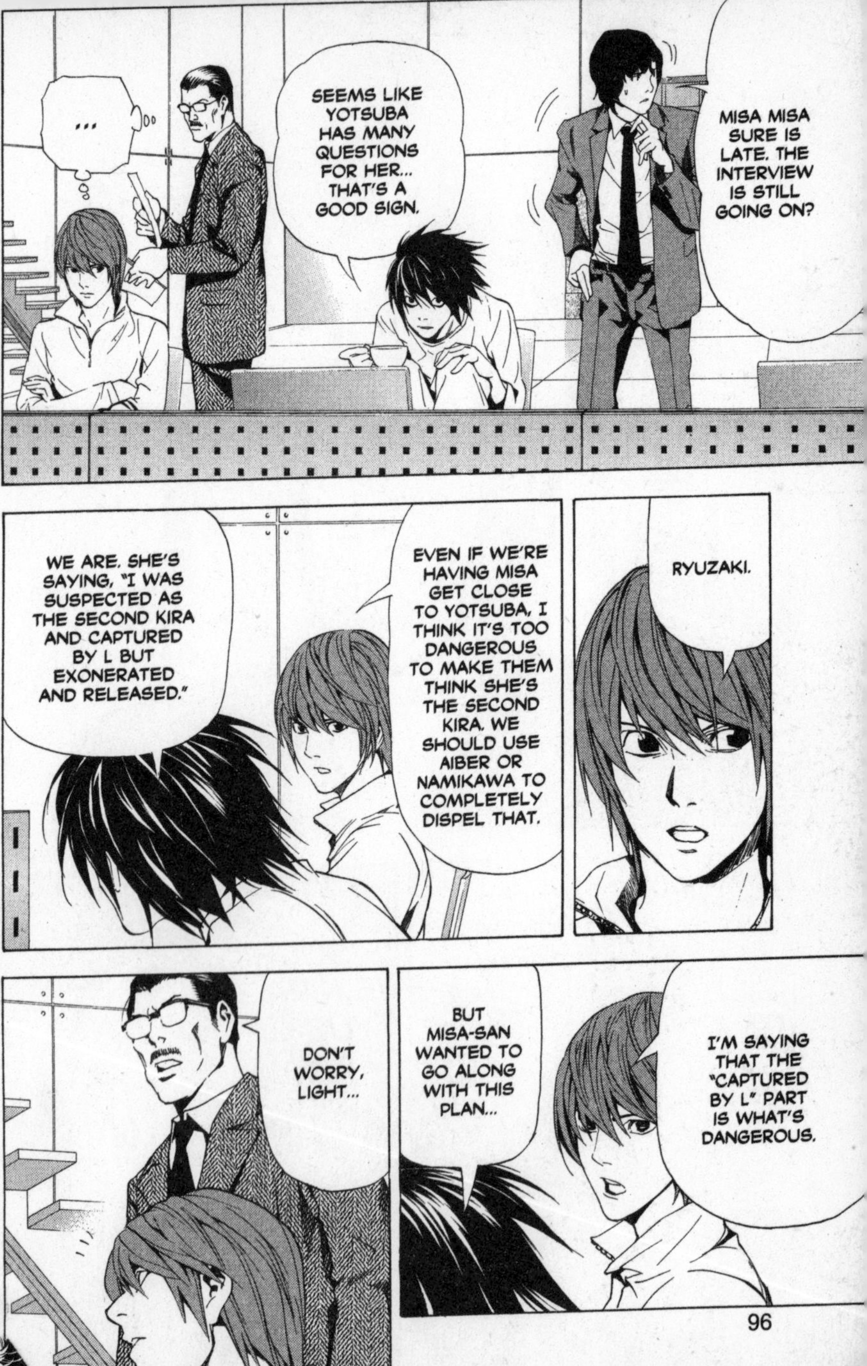
MISA MISA SURE IS LATE. THE INTERVIEW IS STILL GOING ON?
SEEMS LIKE YOTSUBA HAS MANY QUESTIONS FOR HER... THAT'S A GOOD SIGN.
...
RYUZAKI.
EVEN IF WE'RE HAVING MISA GET CLOSE TO YOTSUBA, I THINK IT'S TOO DANGEROUS TO MAKE THEM THINK SHE'S THE SECOND KIRA. WE SHOULD USE AIBER OR NAMIKAWA TO COMPLETELY DISPEL THAT.
WE ARE. SHE'S SAYING, "I WAS SUSPECTED AS THE SECOND KIRA AND CAPTURED BY L BUT EXONERATED AND RELEASED."
I'M SAYING THAT THE "CAPTURED BY L" PART IS WHAT'S DANGEROUS.
BUT MISA-SAN WANTED TO GO ALONG WITH THIS PLAN...
DON'T WORRY, LIGHT...

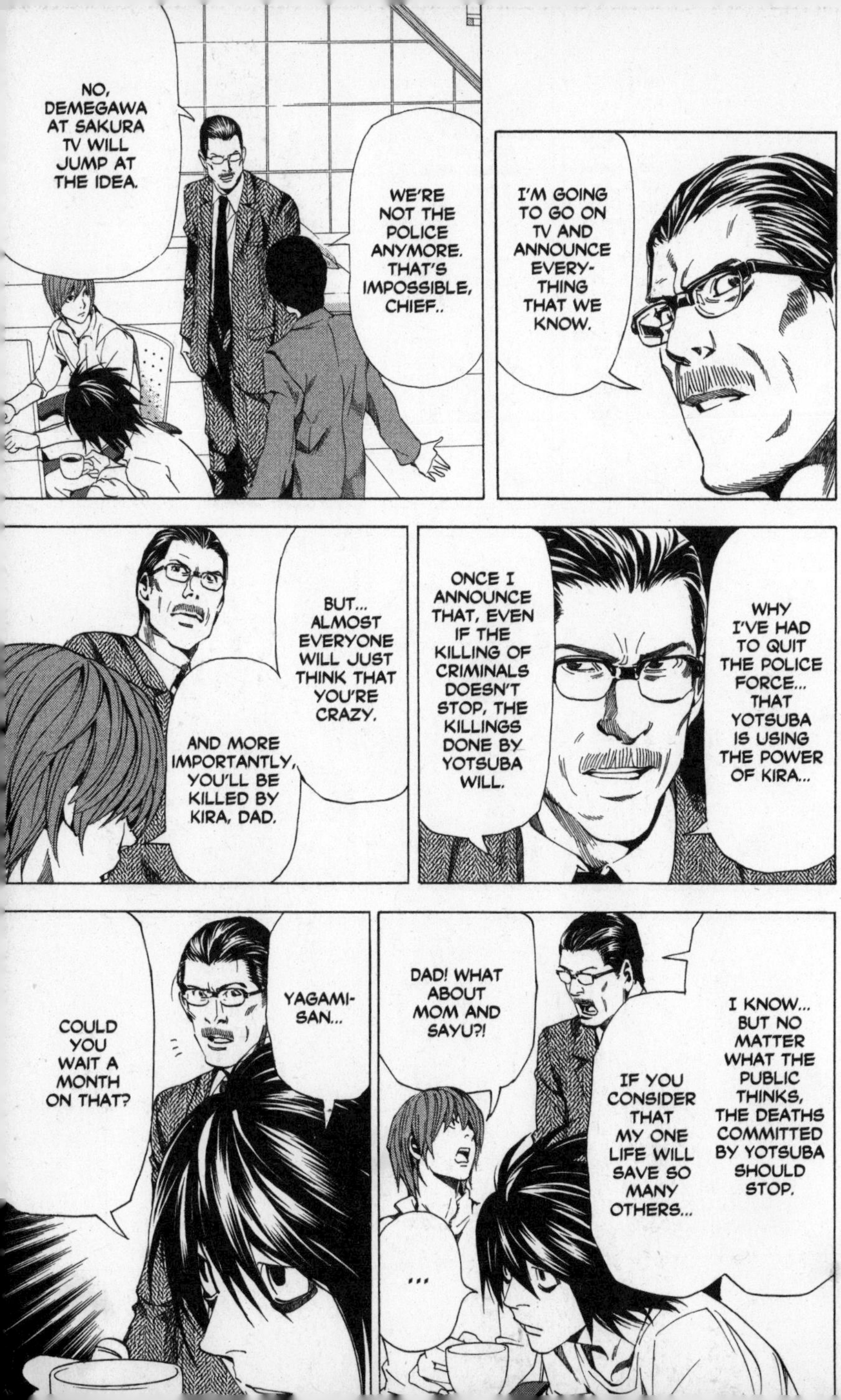
I'M GOING TO GO ON TV AND ANNOUNCE EVERY-THING THAT WE KNOW.
WE'RE NOT THE POLICE ANYMORE. THAT'S IMPOSSIBLE, CHIEF..
NO, DEMEGAWA AT SAKURA TV WILL JUMP AT THE IDEA.
WHY I'VE HAD TO QUIT THE POLICE FORCE... THAT YOTSUBA IS USING THE POWER OF KIRA...
ONCE I ANNOUNCE THAT, EVEN IF THE KILLING OF CRIMINALS DOESN'T STOP, THE KILLINGS DONE BY YOTSUBA WILL.
BUT... ALMOST EVERYONE WILL JUST THINK THAT YOU'RE CRAZY.
AND MORE IMPORTANTLY, YOU'LL BE KILLED BY KIRA, DAD.
I KNOW... BUT NO MATTER WHAT THE PUBLIC THINKS, THE DEATHS COMMITTED BY YOTSUBA SHOULD STOP.
IF YOU CONSIDER THAT MY ONE LIFE WILL SAVE SO MANY OTHERS...
DAD! WHAT ABOUT MOM AND SAYU?!
...
YAGAMI-SAN...
COULD YOU WAIT A MONTH ON THAT?

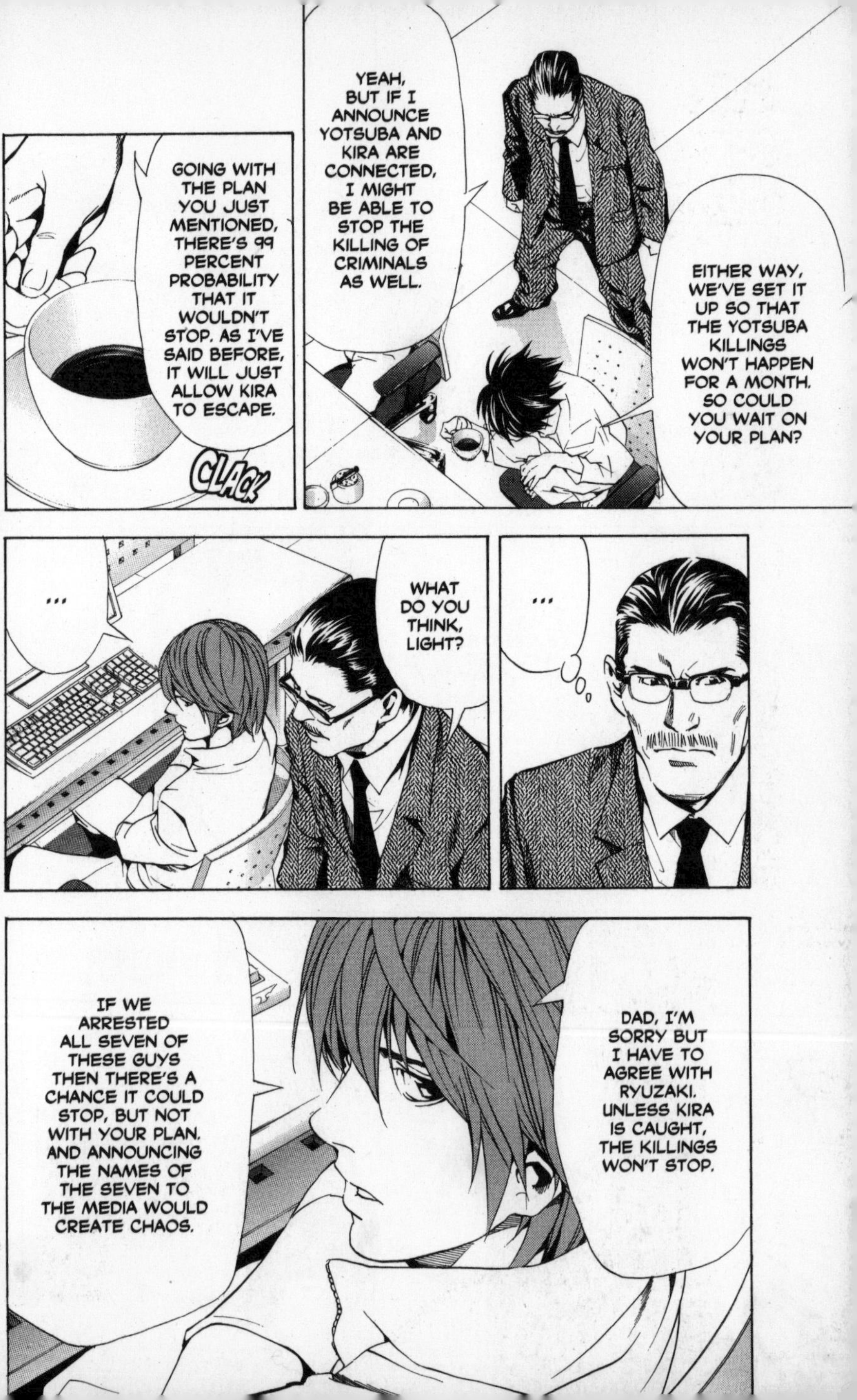
EITHER WAY, WE'VE SET IT UP SO THAT THE YOTSUBA KILLINGS WON'T HAPPEN FOR A MONTH. SO COULD YOU WAIT ON YOUR PLAN?
YEAH, BUT IF I ANNOUNCE YOTSUBA AND KIRA ARE CONNECTED, I MIGHT BE ABLE TO STOP THE KILLING OF CRIMINALS AS WELL.
GOING WITH THE PLAN YOU JUST MENTIONED, THERE'S 99 PERCENT PROBABILITY THAT IT WOULDN'T STOP. AS I'VE SAID BEFORE, IT WILL JUST ALLOW KIRA TO ESCAPE.
CLACK
...
WHAT DO YOU THINK, LIGHT?
...
DAD, I'M SORRY BUT I HAVE TO AGREE WITH RYUZAKI. UNLESS KIRA IS CAUGHT, THE KILLINGS WON'T STOP.
IF WE ARRESTED ALL SEVEN OF THESE GUYS THEN THERE'S A CHANCE IT COULD STOP, BUT NOT WITH YOUR PLAN. AND ANNOUNCING THE NAMES OF THE SEVEN TO THE MEDIA WOULD CREATE CHAOS.

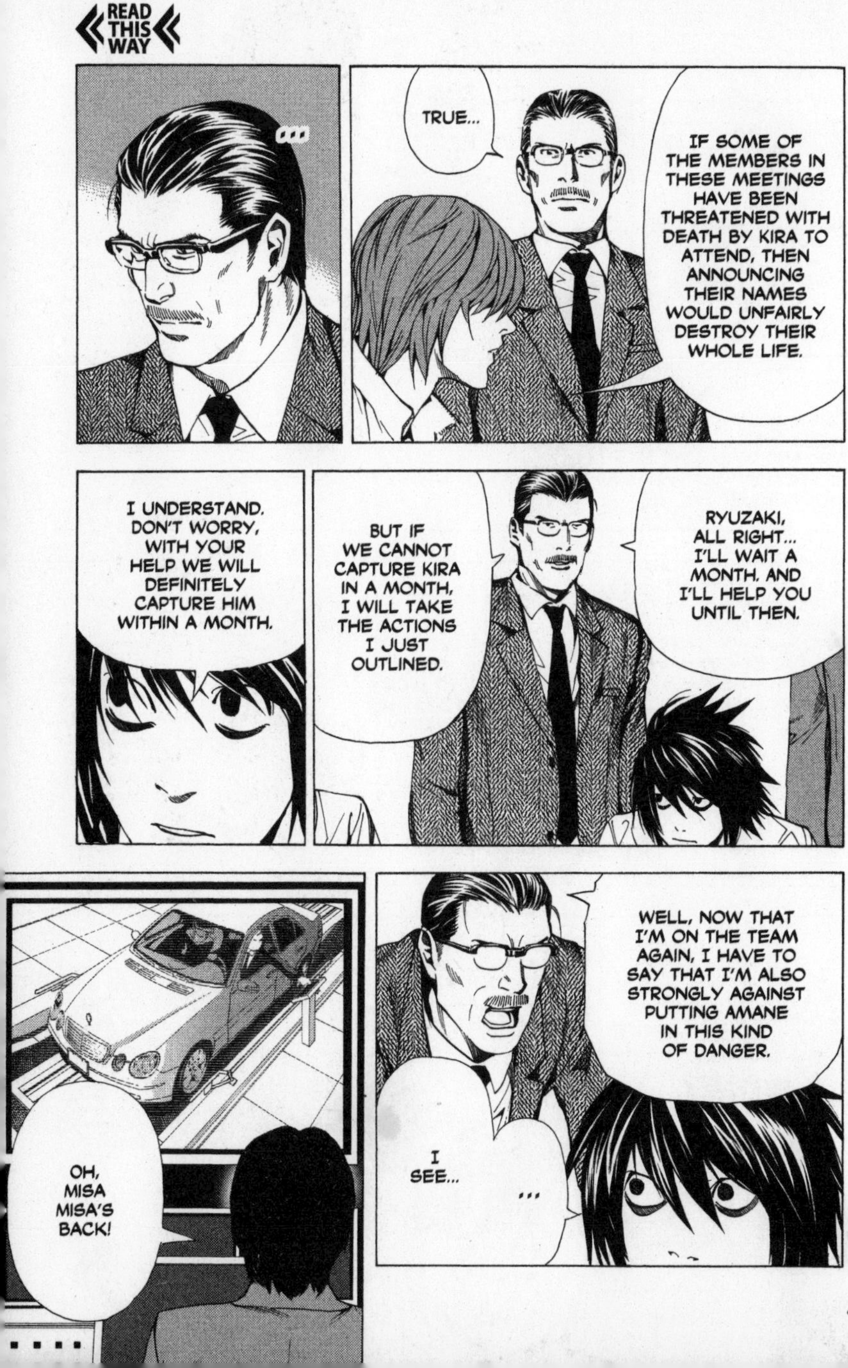
READ THIS WAY
IF SOME OF THE MEMBERS IN THESE MEETINGS HAVE BEEN THREATENED WITH DEATH BY KIRA TO ATTEND, THEN ANNOUNCING THEIR NAMES WOULD UNFAIRLY DESTROY THEIR WHOLE LIFE.
TRUE...
...
RYUZAKI, ALL RIGHT... I'LL WAIT A MONTH. AND I'LL HELP YOU UNTIL THEN.
BUT IF WE CANNOT CAPTURE KIRA IN A MONTH, I WILL TAKE THE ACTIONS I JUST OUTLINED.
I UNDERSTAND. DON'T WORRY, WITH YOUR HELP WE WILL DEFINITELY CAPTURE HIM WITHIN A MONTH.
WELL, NOW THAT I'M ON THE TEAM AGAIN, I HAVE TO SAY THAT I'M ALSO STRONGLY AGAINST PUTTING AMANE IN THIS KIND OF DANGER.
...
I SEE...
OH, MISA MISA'S BACK!

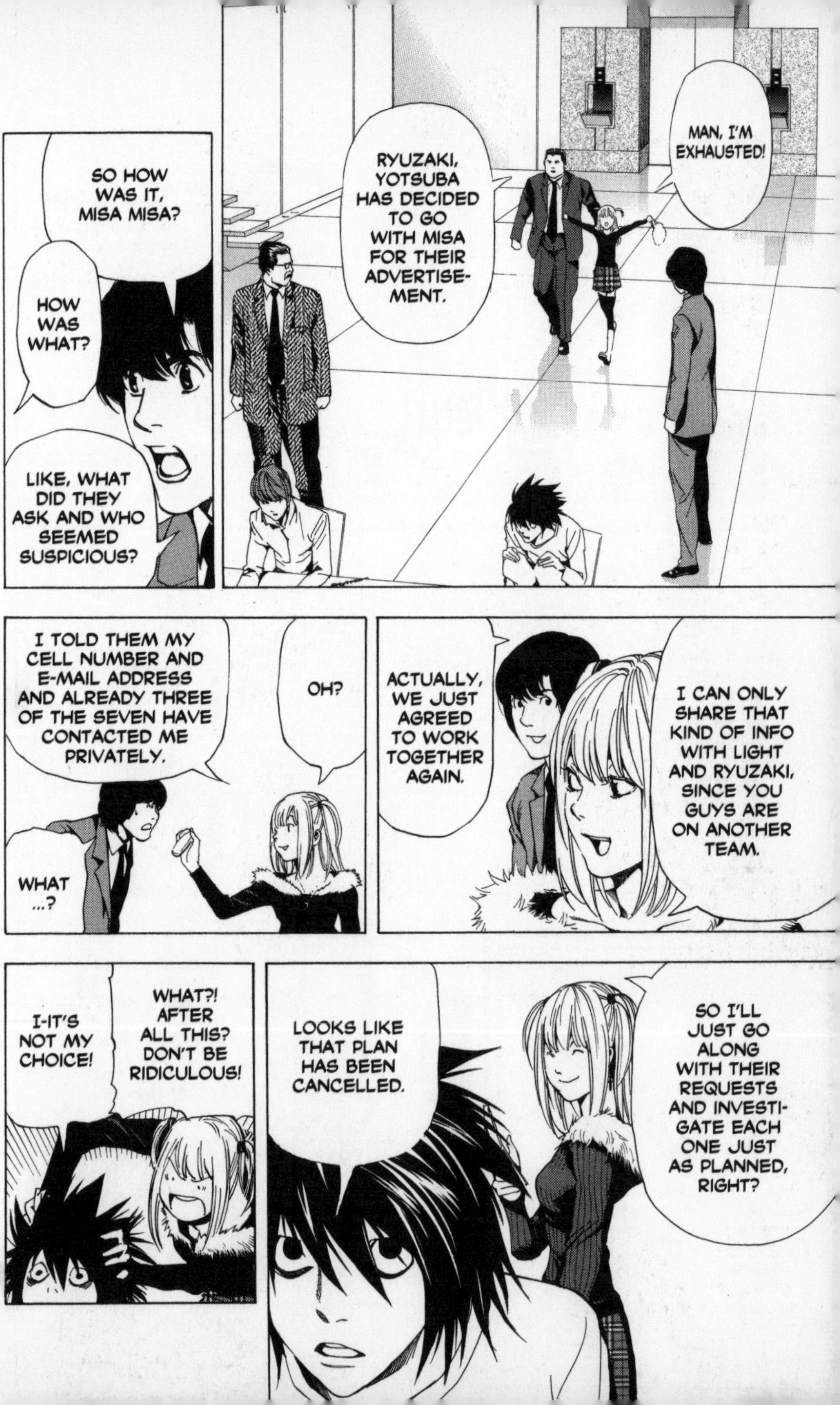
MAN, I'M EXHAUSTED!
RYUZAKI, YOTSUBA HAS DECIDED TO GO WITH MISA FOR THEIR ADVERTISE-MENT.
SO HOW WAS IT, MISA MISA?
HOW WAS WHAT?
LIKE, WHAT DID THEY ASK AND WHO SEEMED SUSPICIOUS?
I CAN ONLY SHARE THAT KIND OF INFO WITH LIGHT AND RYUZAKI, SINCE YOU GUYS ARE ON ANOTHER TEAM.
ACTUALLY, WE JUST AGREED TO WORK TOGETHER AGAIN.
OH?
I TOLD THEM MY CELL NUMBER AND E-MAIL ADDRESS AND ALREADY THREE OF THE SEVEN HAVE CONTACTED ME PRIVATELY.
WHAT ...?
SO I'LL JUST GO ALONG WITH THEIR REQUESTS AND INVESTI-GATE EACH ONE JUST AS PLANNED, RIGHT?
LOOKS LIKE THAT PLAN HAS BEEN CANCELLED.
WHAT?! AFTER ALL THIS? DON'T BE RIDICULOUS!
I-IT'S NOT MY CHOICE!

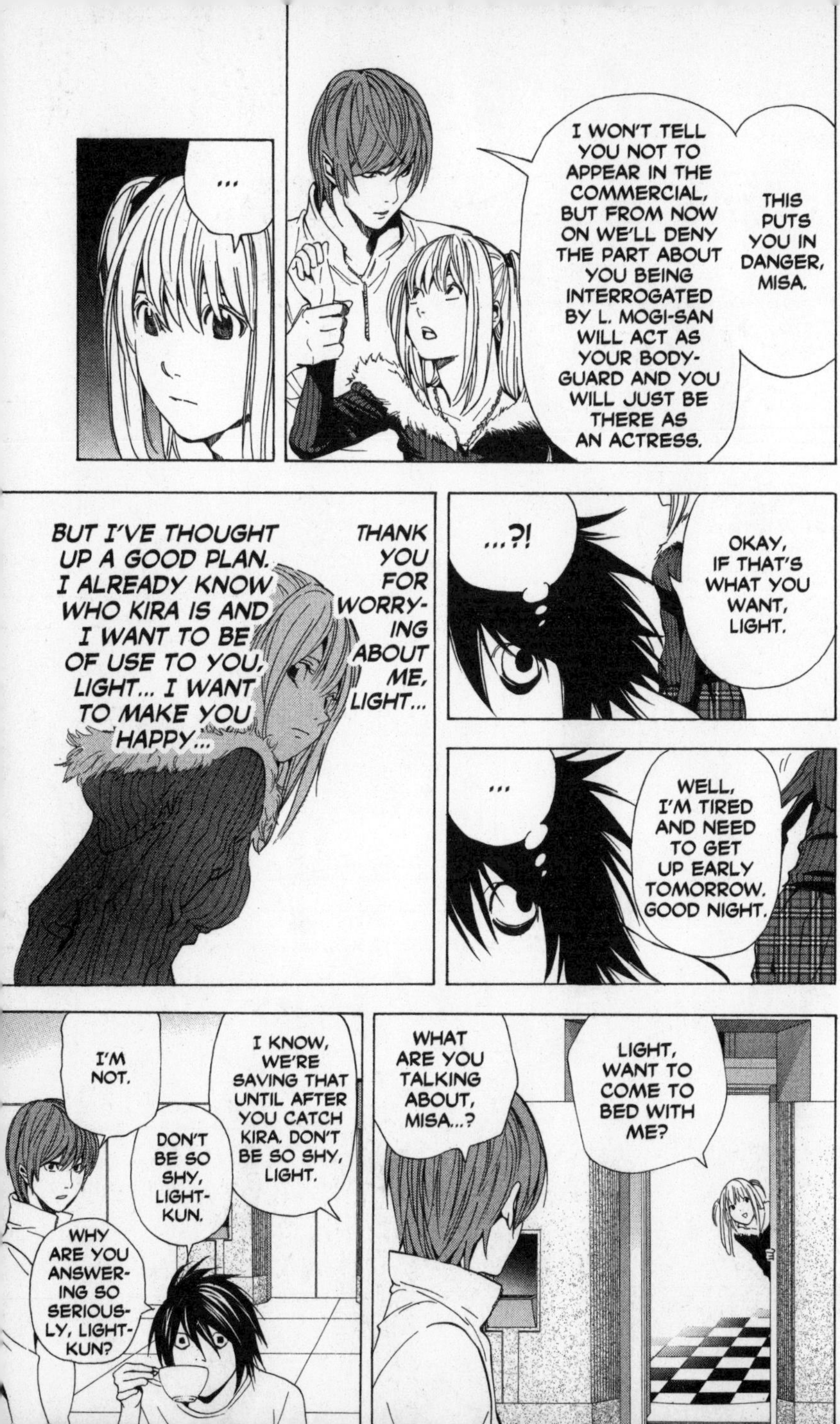
THIS PUTS YOU IN DANGER, MISA.
I WON'T TELL YOU NOT TO APPEAR IN THE COMMERCIAL, BUT FROM NOW ON WE'LL DENY THE PART ABOUT YOU BEING INTERROGATED BY L. MOGI-SAN WILL ACT AS YOUR BODY-GUARD AND YOU WILL JUST BE THERE AS AN ACTRESS.
...
OKAY, IF THAT'S WHAT YOU WANT, LIGHT.
...?!
WELL, I'M TIRED AND NEED TO GET UP EARLY TOMORROW. GOOD NIGHT.
...
THANK YOU FOR WORRY-ING ABOUT ME, LIGHT...
BUT I'VE THOUGHT UP A GOOD PLAN. I ALREADY KNOW WHO KIRA IS AND I WANT TO BE OF USE TO YOU, LIGHT... I WANT TO MAKE YOU HAPPY...
LIGHT, WANT TO COME TO BED WITH ME?
WHAT ARE YOU TALKING ABOUT, MISA...?
I KNOW, WE'RE SAVING THAT UNTIL AFTER YOU CATCH KIRA. DON'T BE SO SHY, LIGHT.
I'M NOT.
DON'T BE SO SHY, LIGHT-KUN.
WHY ARE YOU ANSWER-ING SO SERIOUS-LY, LIGHT-KUN?

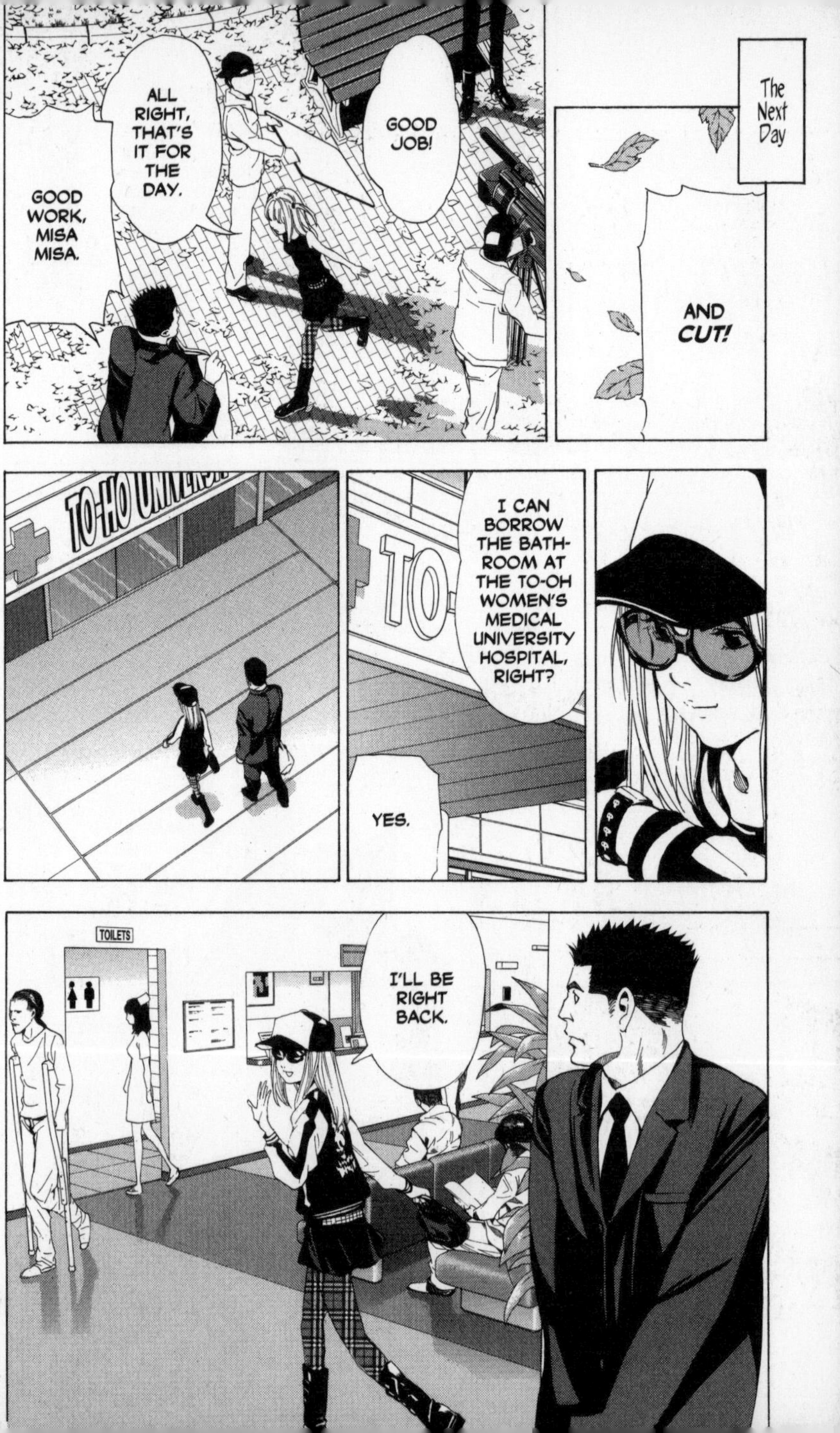
The Next Day
AND CUT!
GOOD JOB!
ALL RIGHT, THAT'S IT FOR THE DAY.
GOOD WORK, MISA MISA.
I CAN BORROW THE BATH-ROOM AT THE TO-OH WOMEN'S MEDICAL UNIVERSITY HOSPITAL, RIGHT?
YES.
I'LL BE RIGHT BACK.
TOILETS

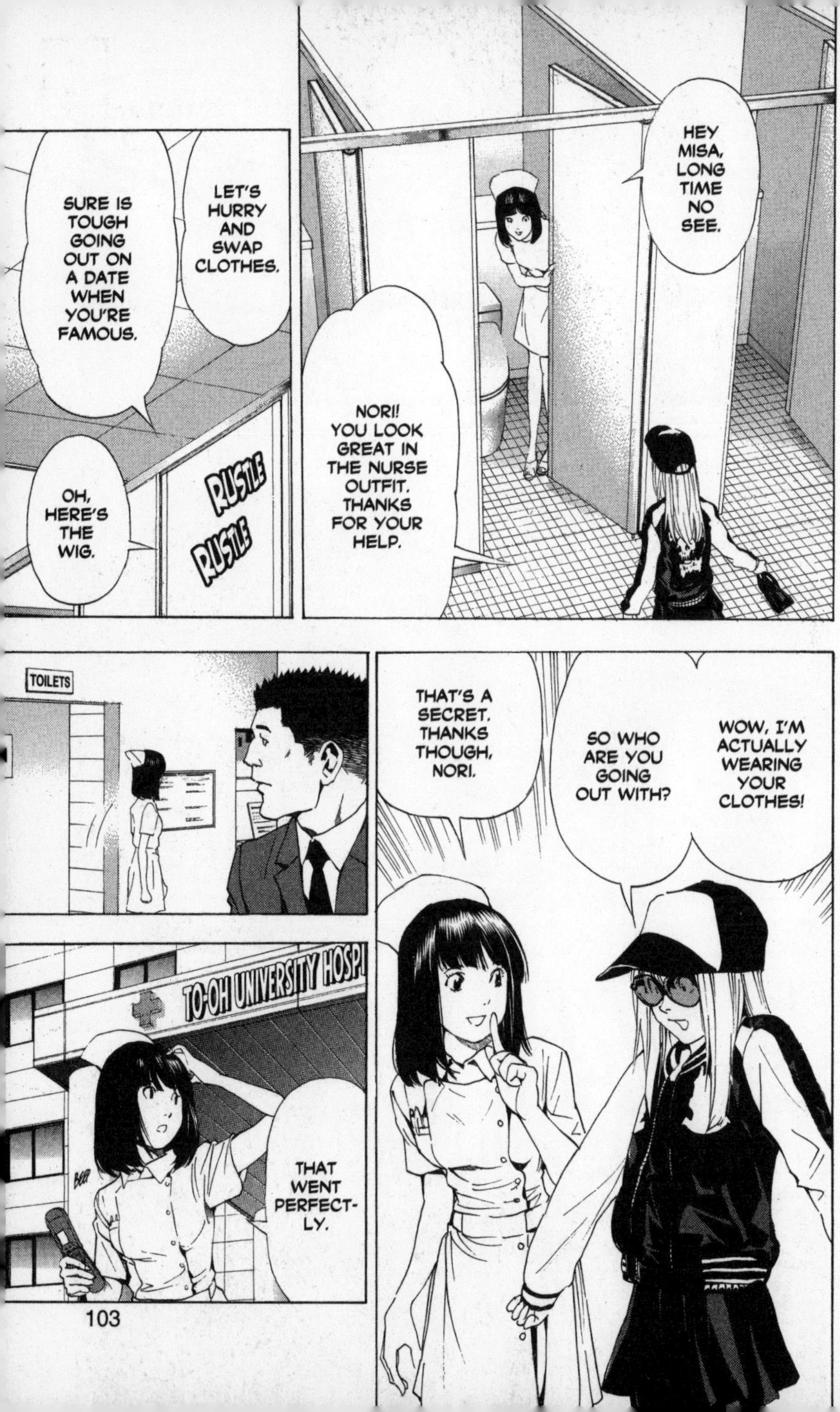
HEY MISA, LONG TIME NO SEE.
NORI! YOU LOOK GREAT IN THE NURSE OUTFIT. THANKS FOR YOUR HELP.
LET'S HURRY AND SWAP CLOTHES.
SURE IS TOUGH GOING OUT ON A DATE WHEN YOU'RE FAMOUS.
RUSTLE
RUSTLE
OH, HERE'S THE WIG.
WOW, I'M ACTUALLY WEARING YOUR CLOTHES!
SO WHO ARE YOU GOING OUT WITH?
THAT'S A SECRET. THANKS THOUGH, NORI.
TOILETS
TO-OH UNIVERSITY HOSP
BEEP
THAT WENT PERFECT-LY.

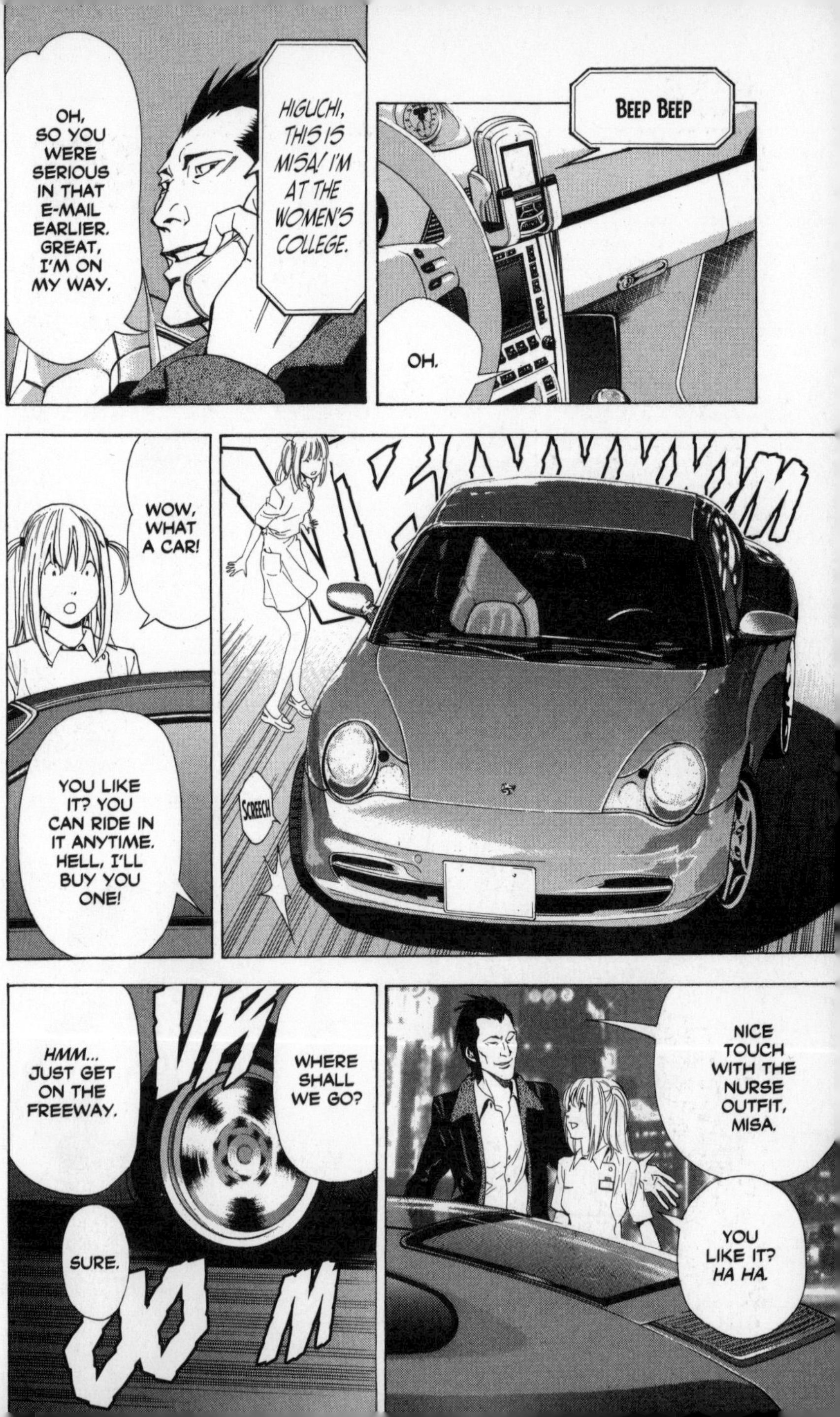

BEEP BEEP
OH.
HIGUCHI, THIS IS MISA! I'M AT THE WOMEN'S COLLEGE.
OH, SO YOU WERE SERIOUS IN THAT E-MAIL EARLIER. GREAT, I'M ON MY WAY.
SCREECH
WOW, WHAT A CAR!
YOU LIKE IT? YOU CAN RIDE IN IT ANYTIME. HELL, I'LL BUY YOU ONE!
NICE TOUCH WITH THE NURSE OUTFIT, MISA.
YOU LIKE IT? HA HA.
WHERE SHALL WE GO?
HMM... JUST GET ON THE FREEWAY.
SURE.

READ THIS WAY

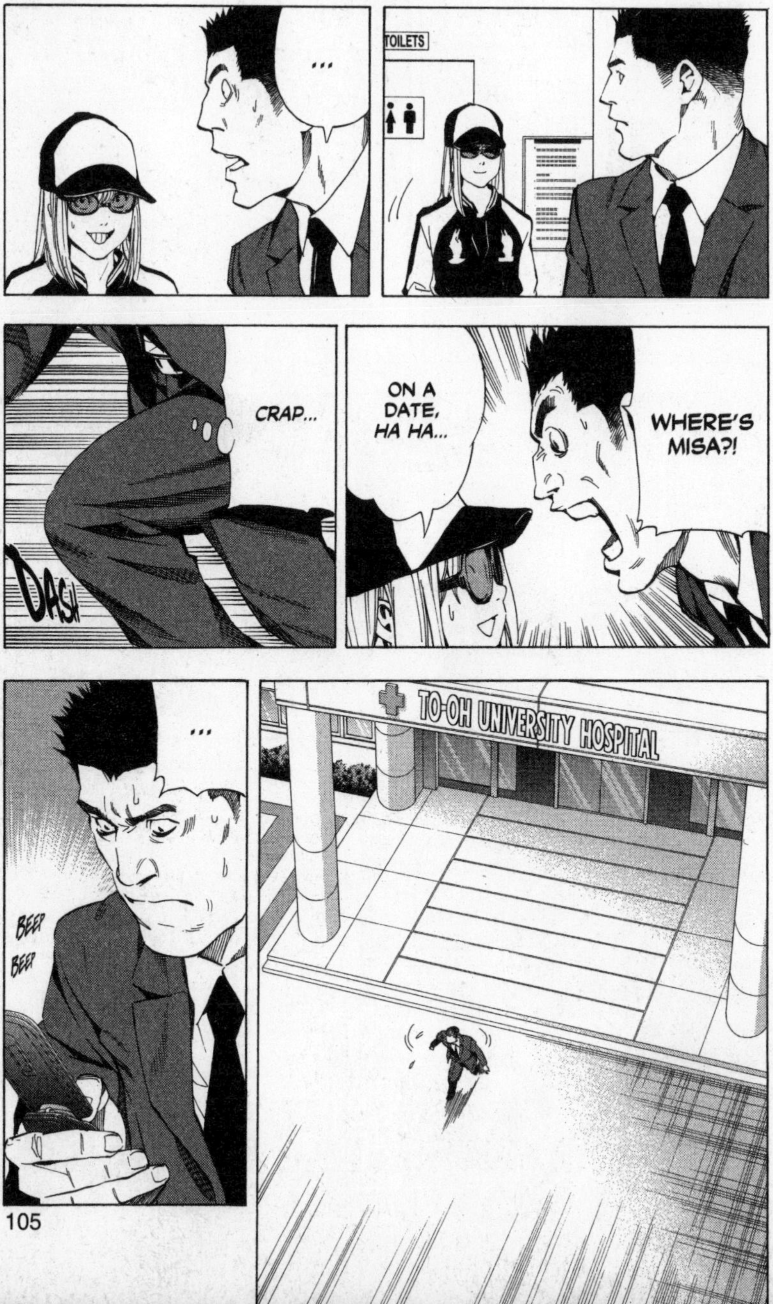

TOILETS
...
WHERE'S MISA?!
ON A DATE, HA HA...
CRAP...
DASH
TO-OH UNIVERSITY HOSPITAL
...
BEEP
BEEP

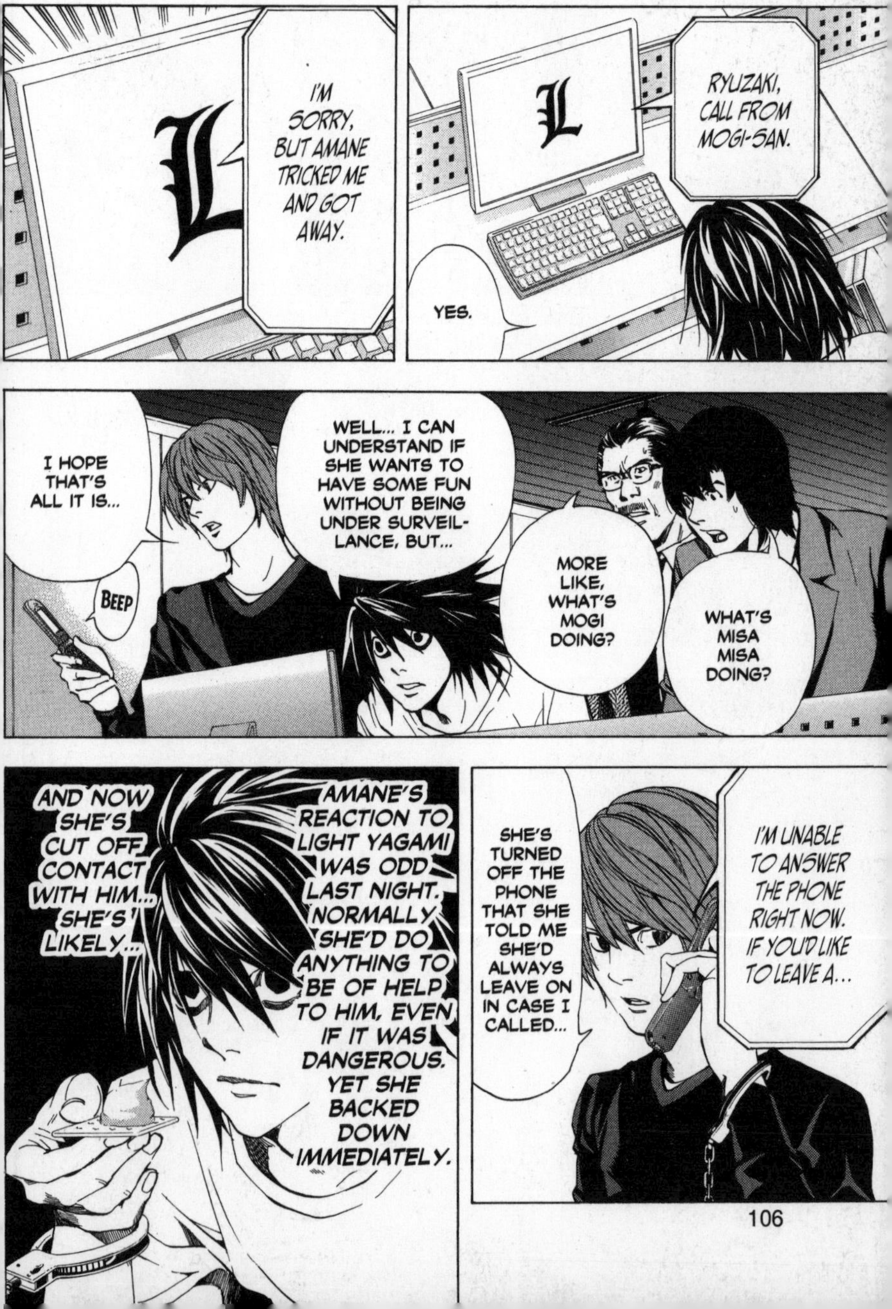
RYUZAKI, CALL FROM MOGI-SAN.
YES.
I'M SORRY, BUT AMANE TRICKED ME AND GOT AWAY.
WHAT'S MISA MISA DOING?
MORE LIKE, WHAT'S MOGI DOING?
WELL... I CAN UNDERSTAND IF SHE WANTS TO HAVE SOME FUN WITHOUT BEING UNDER SURVEIL-LANCE, BUT...
I HOPE THAT'S ALL IT IS...
BEEP
I'M UNABLE TO ANSWER THE PHONE RIGHT NOW. IF YOU'D LIKE TO LEAVE A...
SHE'S TURNED OFF THE PHONE THAT SHE TOLD ME SHE'D ALWAYS LEAVE ON IN CASE I CALLED...
AMANE'S REACTION TO LIGHT YAGAMI WAS ODD LAST NIGHT. NORMALLY SHE'D DO ANYTHING TO BE OF HELP TO HIM, EVEN IF IT WAS DANGEROUS. YET SHE BACKED DOWN IMMEDIATELY.
AND NOW SHE'S CUT OFF CONTACT WITH HIM... SHE'S LIKELY...

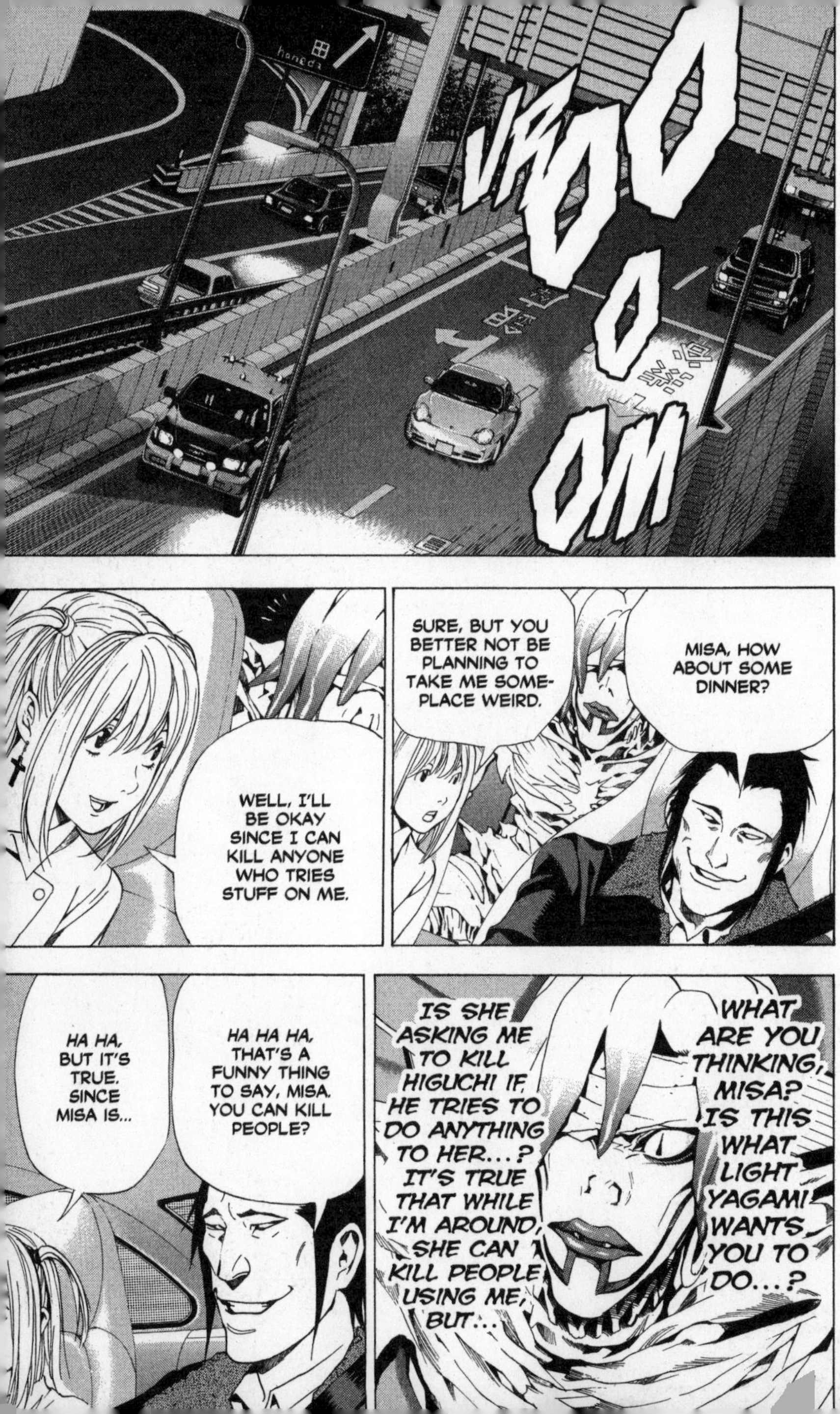
haneda
VROOOOM
MISA, HOW ABOUT SOME DINNER?
SURE, BUT YOU BETTER NOT BE PLANNING TO TAKE ME SOME-PLACE WEIRD.
WELL, I'LL BE OKAY SINCE I CAN KILL ANYONE WHO TRIES STUFF ON ME.
WHAT ARE YOU THINKING, MISA? IS THIS WHAT LIGHT YAGAMI WANTS YOU TO DO...?
IS SHE ASKING ME TO KILL HIGUCHI IF HE TRIES TO DO ANYTHING TO HER...? IT'S TRUE THAT WHILE I'M AROUND, SHE CAN KILL PEOPLE USING ME, BUT...
HA HA HA, THAT'S A FUNNY THING TO SAY, MISA. YOU CAN KILL PEOPLE?
HA HA, BUT IT'S TRUE. SINCE MISA IS...

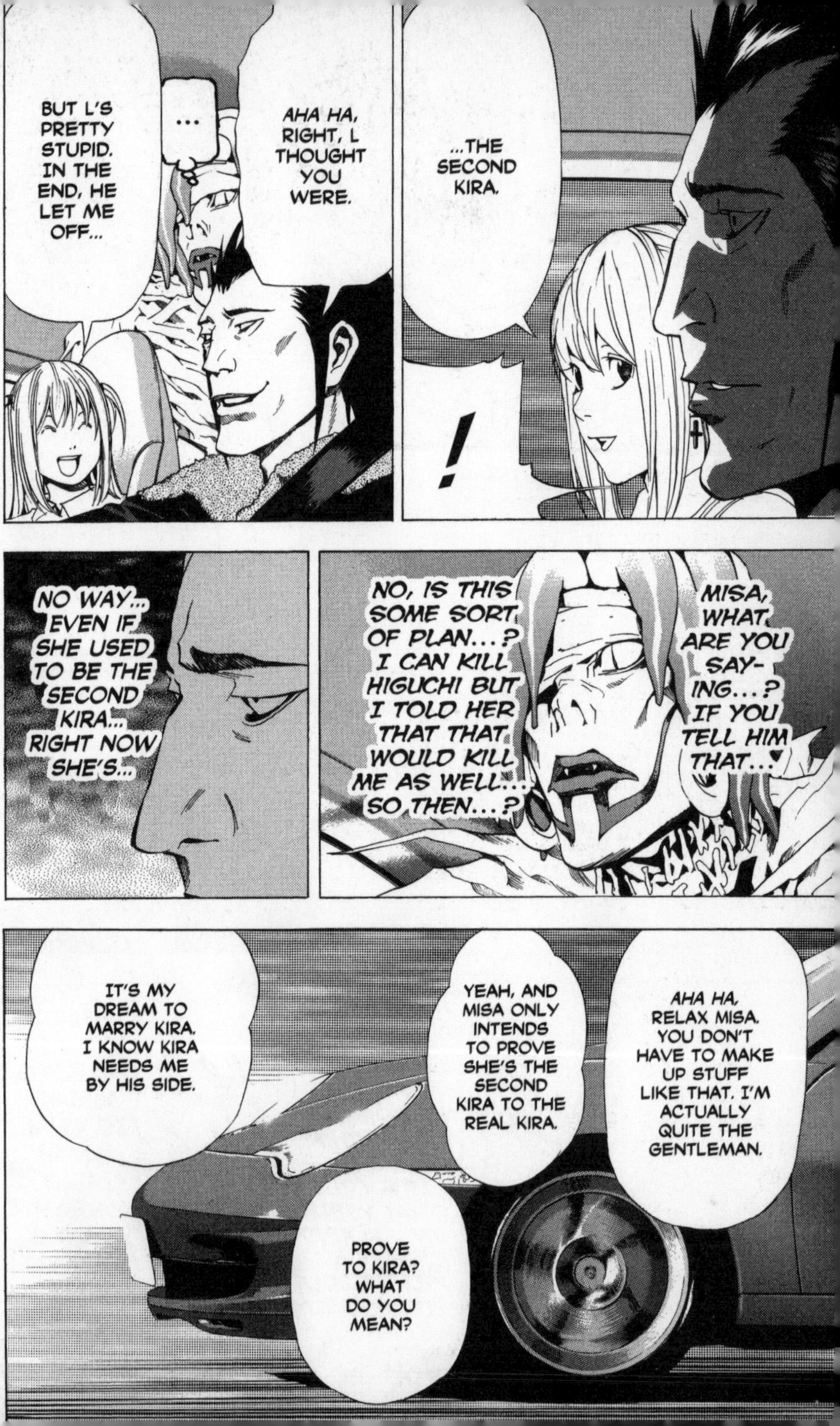
...THE SECOND KIRA.
!
AHA HA, RIGHT, L THOUGHT YOU WERE.
...
BUT L'S PRETTY STUPID. IN THE END, HE LET ME OFF...
MISA, WHAT ARE YOU SAYING...? IF YOU TELL HIM THAT...
NO, IS THIS SOME SORT OF PLAN...? I CAN KILL HIGUCHI BUT I TOLD HER THAT THAT WOULD KILL ME AS WELL... SO THEN...?
NO WAY... EVEN IF SHE USED TO BE THE SECOND KIRA... RIGHT NOW SHE'S...
AHA HA, RELAX MISA. YOU DON'T HAVE TO MAKE UP STUFF LIKE THAT. I'M ACTUALLY QUITE THE GENTLEMAN.
YEAH, AND MISA ONLY INTENDS TO PROVE SHE'S THE SECOND KIRA TO THE REAL KIRA.
IT'S MY DREAM TO MARRY KIRA. I KNOW KIRA NEEDS ME BY HIS SIDE.
PROVE TO KIRA? WHAT DO YOU MEAN?

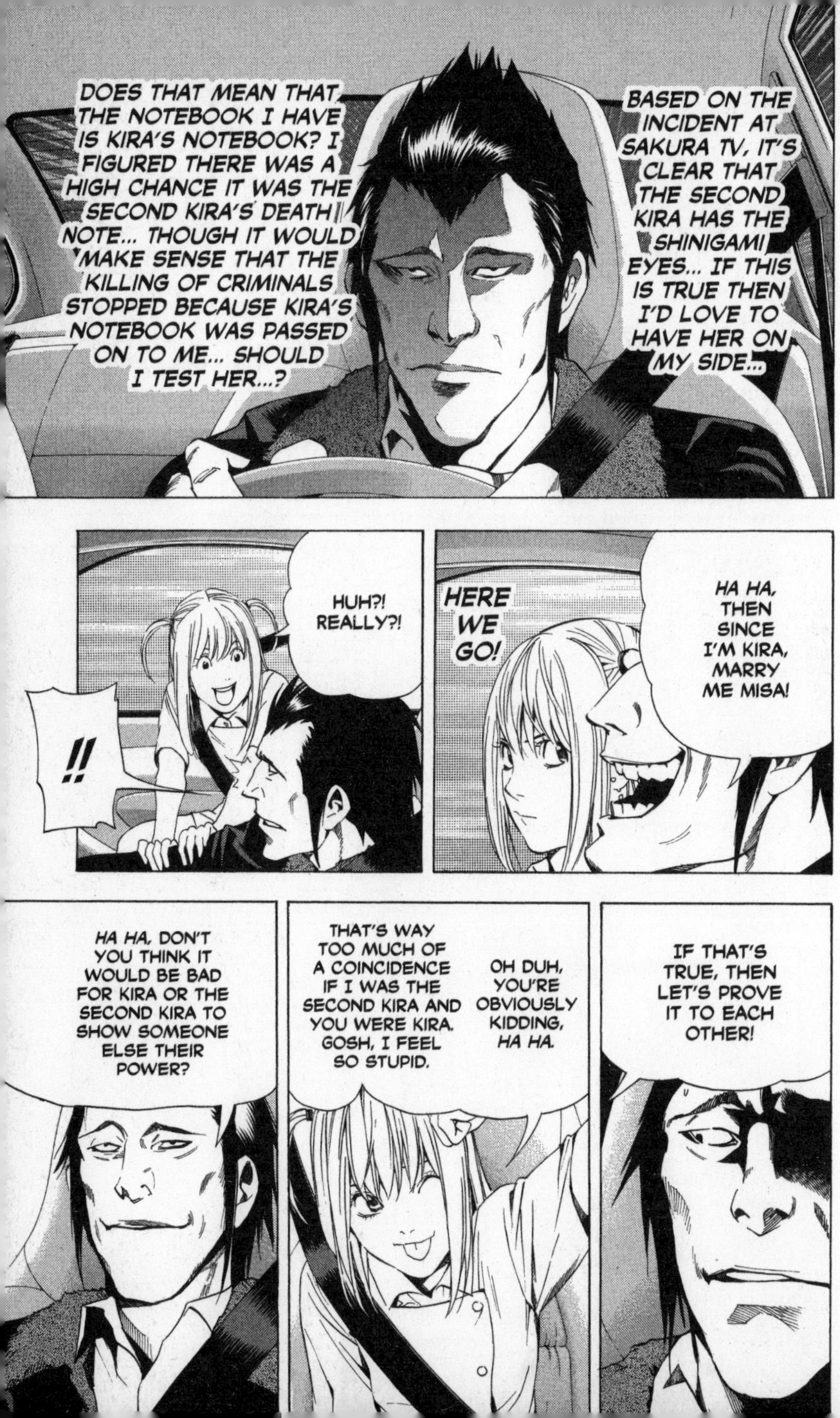
BASED ON THE INCIDENT AT SAKURA TV, IT'S CLEAR THAT THE SECOND KIRA HAS THE SHINIGAMI EYES... IF THIS IS TRUE THEN I'D LOVE TO HAVE HER ON MY SIDE...
DOES THAT MEAN THAT THE NOTEBOOK I HAVE IS KIRA'S NOTEBOOK? I FIGURED THERE WAS A HIGH CHANCE IT WAS THE SECOND KIRA'S DEATH NOTE... THOUGH IT WOULD MAKE SENSE THAT THE KILLING OF CRIMINALS STOPPED BECAUSE KIRA'S NOTEBOOK WAS PASSED ON TO ME... SHOULD I TEST HER...?
HA HA, THEN SINCE I'M KIRA, MARRY ME MISA!
HERE WE GO!
HUH?! REALLY?!
!!
IF THAT'S TRUE, THEN LET'S PROVE IT TO EACH OTHER!
OH DUH, YOU'RE OBVIOUSLY KIDDING, HA HA.
THAT'S WAY TOO MUCH OF A COINCIDENCE IF I WAS THE SECOND KIRA AND YOU WERE KIRA. GOSH, I FEEL SO STUPID.
HA HA, DON'T YOU THINK IT WOULD BE BAD FOR KIRA OR THE SECOND KIRA TO SHOW SOMEONE ELSE THEIR POWER?

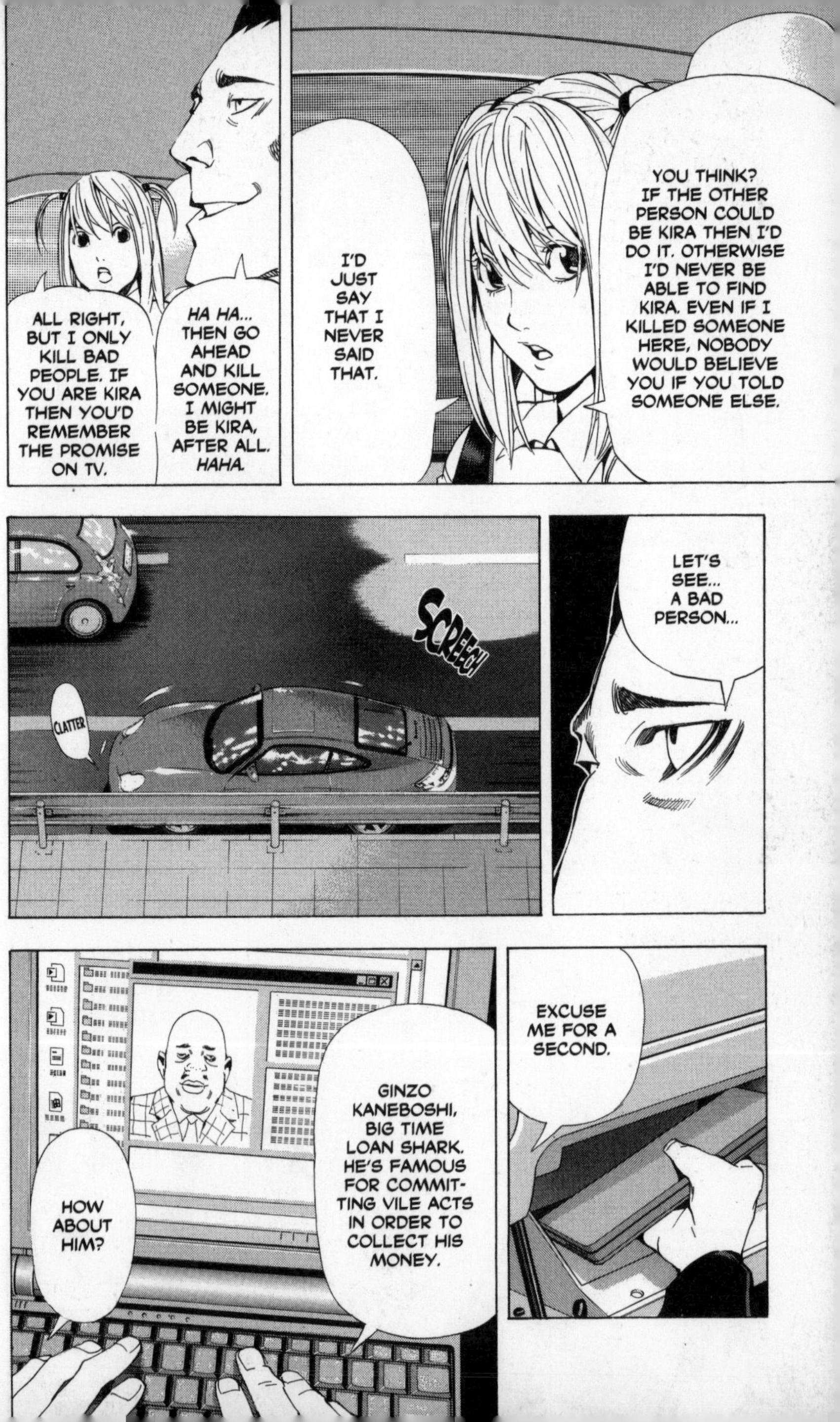
YOU THINK? IF THE OTHER PERSON COULD BE KIRA THEN I'D DO IT. OTHERWISE I'D NEVER BE ABLE TO FIND KIRA. EVEN IF I KILLED SOMEONE HERE, NOBODY WOULD BELIEVE YOU IF YOU TOLD SOMEONE ELSE.
I'D JUST SAY THAT I NEVER SAID THAT.
HA HA... THEN GO AHEAD AND KILL SOMEONE. I MIGHT BE KIRA, AFTER ALL. *HAHA.*
ALL RIGHT, BUT I ONLY KILL BAD PEOPLE. IF YOU ARE KIRA THEN YOU'D REMEMBER THE PROMISE ON TV.
LET'S SEE... A BAD PERSON...
SCREECH
CLATTER
EXCUSE ME FOR A SECOND.
GINZO KANEBOSHI, BIG TIME LOAN SHARK. HE'S FAMOUS FOR COMMIT-TING VILE ACTS IN ORDER TO COLLECT HIS MONEY.
HOW ABOUT HIM?

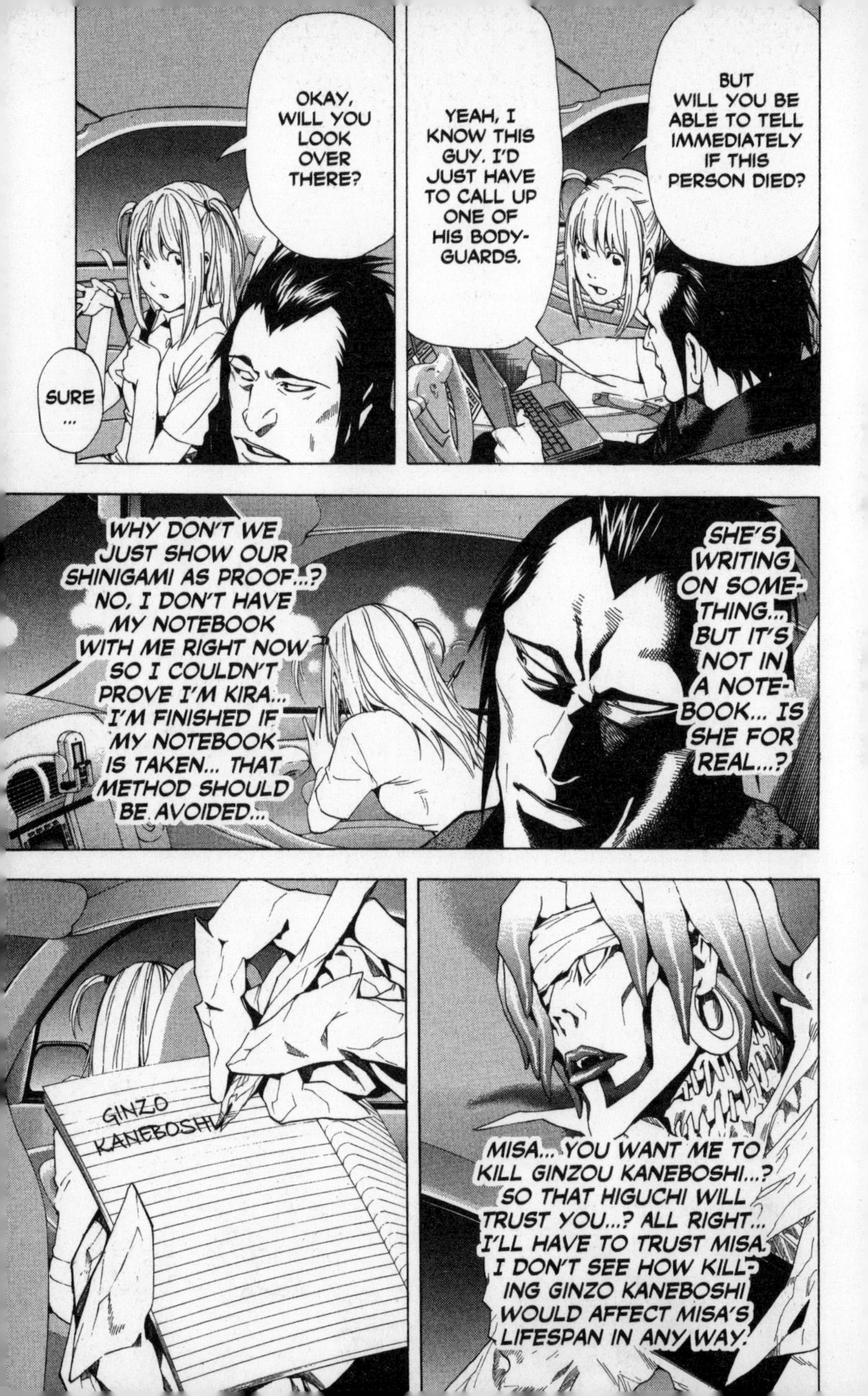
BUT WILL YOU BE ABLE TO TELL IMMEDIATELY IF THIS PERSON DIED?
YEAH, I KNOW THIS GUY. I'D JUST HAVE TO CALL UP ONE OF HIS BODY-GUARDS.
OKAY, WILL YOU LOOK OVER THERE?
SURE ...
SHE'S WRITING ON SOME-THING... BUT IT'S NOT IN A NOTE-BOOK... IS SHE FOR REAL...?
WHY DON'T WE JUST SHOW OUR SHINIGAMI AS PROOF...? NO, I DON'T HAVE MY NOTEBOOK WITH ME RIGHT NOW SO I COULDN'T PROVE I'M KIRA... I'M FINISHED IF MY NOTEBOOK IS TAKEN... THAT METHOD SHOULD BE AVOIDED...
MISA... YOU WANT ME TO KILL GINZOU KANEBOSHI...? SO THAT HIGUCHI WILL TRUST YOU...? ALL RIGHT... I'LL HAVE TO TRUST MISA. I DON'T SEE HOW KILL-ING GINZO KANEBOSHI WOULD AFFECT MISA'S LIFESPAN IN ANY WAY.
GINZO KANEBOSHI

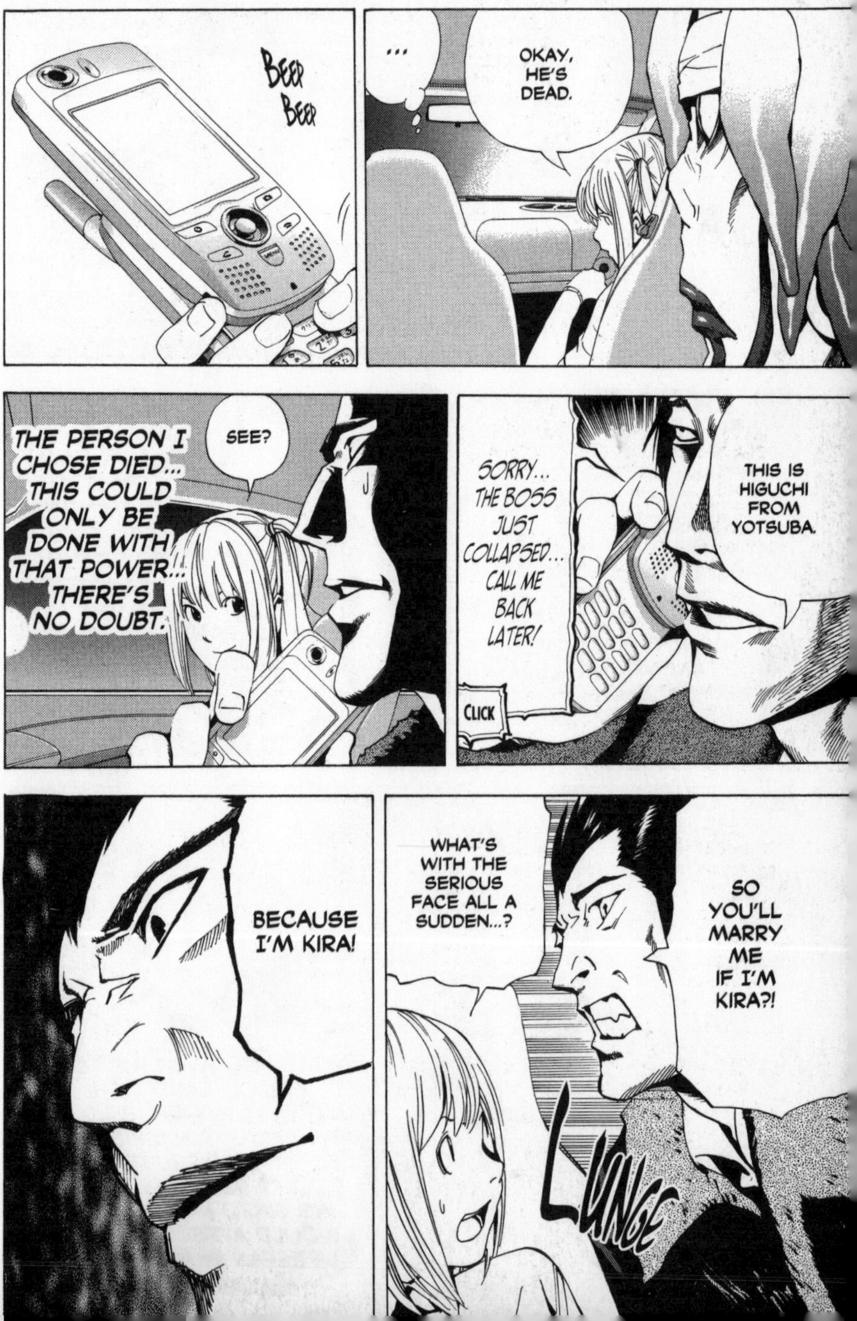
...
OKAY, HE'S DEAD.
BEEP BEEP
THIS IS HIGUCHI FROM YOTSUBA.
SORRY... THE BOSS JUST COLLAPSED... CALL ME BACK LATER!
CLICK
SEE?
THE PERSON I CHOSE DIED... THIS COULD ONLY BE DONE WITH THAT POWER... THERE'S NO DOUBT.
SO YOU'LL MARRY ME IF I'M KIRA?!
WHAT'S WITH THE SERIOUS FACE ALL A SUDDEN...?
LUNGE
BECAUSE I'M KIRA!

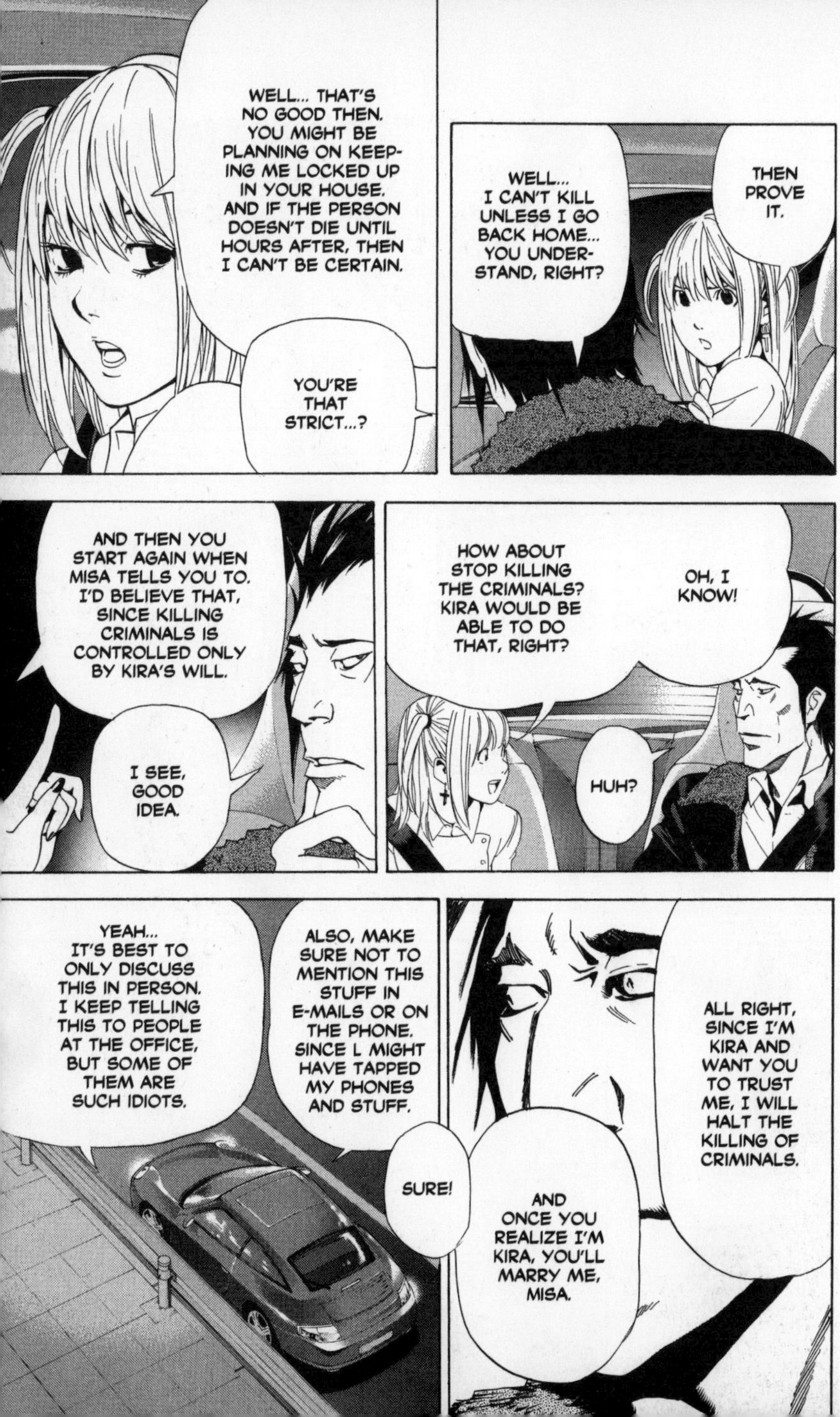
THEN PROVE IT.
WELL... I CAN'T KILL UNLESS I GO BACK HOME... YOU UNDERSTAND, RIGHT?
WELL... THAT'S NO GOOD THEN. YOU MIGHT BE PLANNING ON KEEPING ME LOCKED UP IN YOUR HOUSE. AND IF THE PERSON DOESN'T DIE UNTIL HOURS AFTER, THEN I CAN'T BE CERTAIN.
YOU'RE THAT STRICT...?
OH, I KNOW!
HOW ABOUT STOP KILLING THE CRIMINALS? KIRA WOULD BE ABLE TO DO THAT, RIGHT?
HUH?
AND THEN YOU START AGAIN WHEN MISA TELLS YOU TO. I'D BELIEVE THAT, SINCE KILLING CRIMINALS IS CONTROLLED ONLY BY KIRA'S WILL.
I SEE, GOOD IDEA.
ALL RIGHT, SINCE I'M KIRA AND WANT YOU TO TRUST ME, I WILL HALT THE KILLING OF CRIMINALS.
AND ONCE YOU REALIZE I'M KIRA, YOU'LL MARRY ME, MISA.
ALSO, MAKE SURE NOT TO MENTION THIS STUFF IN E-MAILS OR ON THE PHONE. SINCE L MIGHT HAVE TAPPED MY PHONES AND STUFF.
SURE!
YEAH... IT'S BEST TO ONLY DISCUSS THIS IN PERSON. I KEEP TELLING THIS TO PEOPLE AT THE OFFICE, BUT SOME OF THEM ARE SUCH IDIOTS.

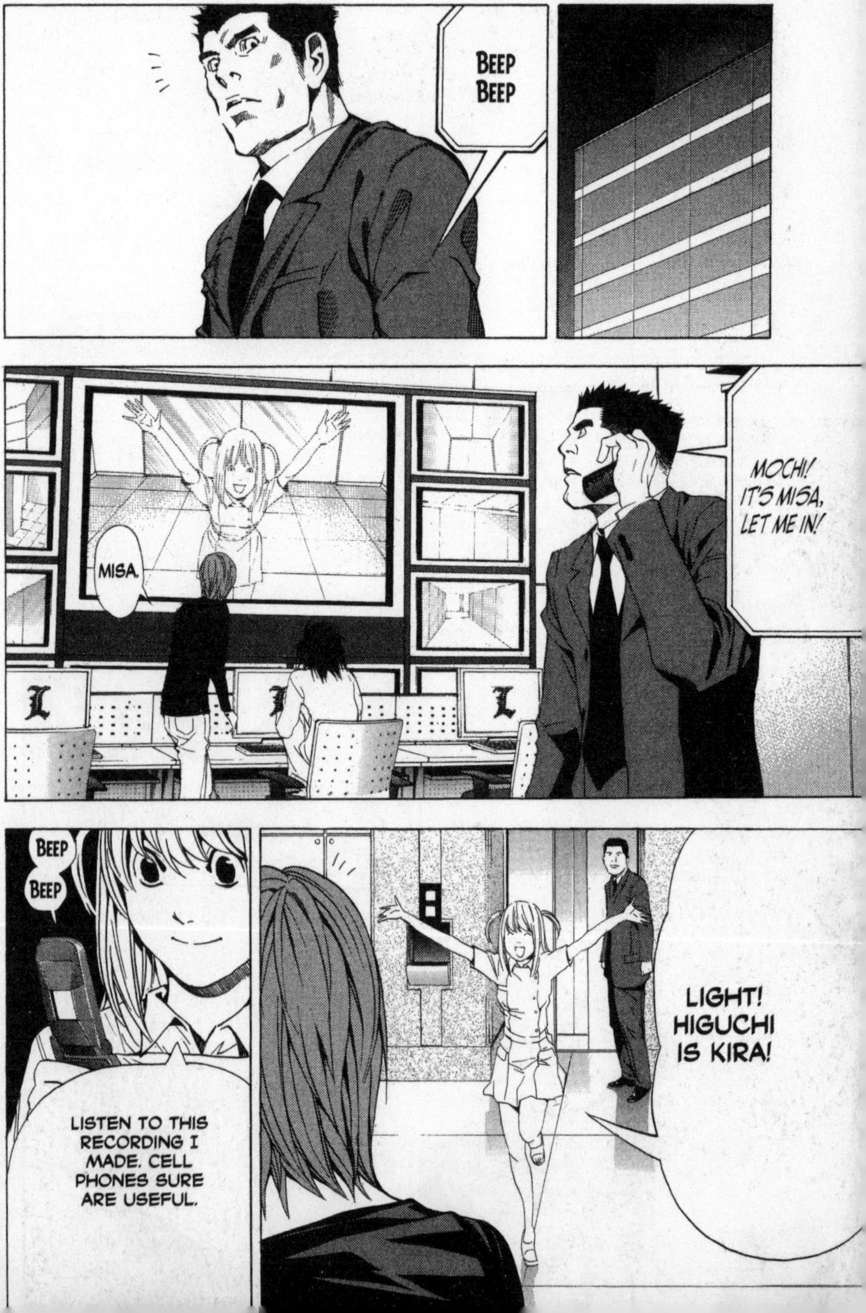
BEEP BEEP
MOCHI! IT'S MISA, LET ME IN!
MISA.
LIGHT! HIGUCHI IS KIRA!
BEEP BEEP
LISTEN TO THIS RECORDING I MADE. CELL PHONES SURE ARE USEFUL.

DEATH NOTE
How to Use It
XXXIV

- The owner of the DEATH NOTE cannot be killed by a god of death who is living in the world of the gods of death.

  デスノートを持った人間を死神界にいる死神が殺す事はできない。

- Also, a god of death who comes to the human world, in the objective to kill the owner of the DEATH NOTE, will not be able to do so.

  デスノートを持った人間を殺す目的で、死神が人間界に下り、その人間を殺す事もできない。

- Only a god of death that has passed on their DEATH NOTE to a human is able to kill the owner of the DEATH NOTE.

  デスノートを持った人間を殺せるのは人間界にデスノートを譲渡している死神だけである。

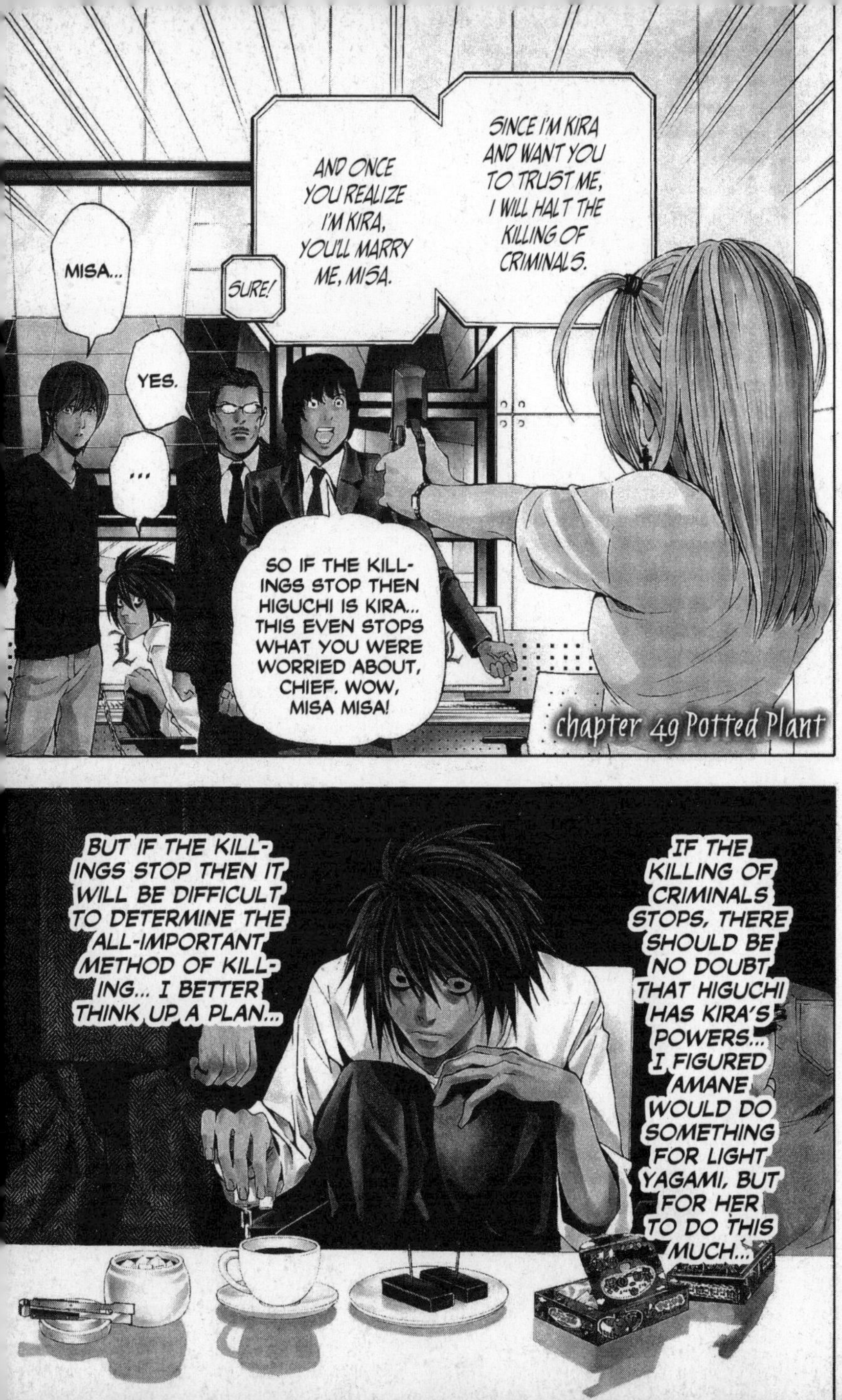
SINCE I'M KIRA AND WANT YOU TO TRUST ME, I WILL HALT THE KILLING OF CRIMINALS.
AND ONCE YOU REALIZE I'M KIRA, YOU'LL MARRY ME, MISA.
SURE!
MISA...
YES.
...
SO IF THE KILL-INGS STOP THEN HIGUCHI IS KIRA... THIS EVEN STOPS WHAT YOU WERE WORRIED ABOUT, CHIEF. WOW, MISA MISA!
chapter 49 Potted Plant
IF THE KILLING OF CRIMINALS STOPS, THERE SHOULD BE NO DOUBT THAT HIGUCHI HAS KIRA'S POWERS... I FIGURED AMANE WOULD DO SOMETHING FOR LIGHT YAGAMI, BUT FOR HER TO DO THIS MUCH...
BUT IF THE KILL-INGS STOP THEN IT WILL BE DIFFICULT TO DETERMINE THE ALL-IMPORTANT METHOD OF KILL-ING... I BETTER THINK UP A PLAN...

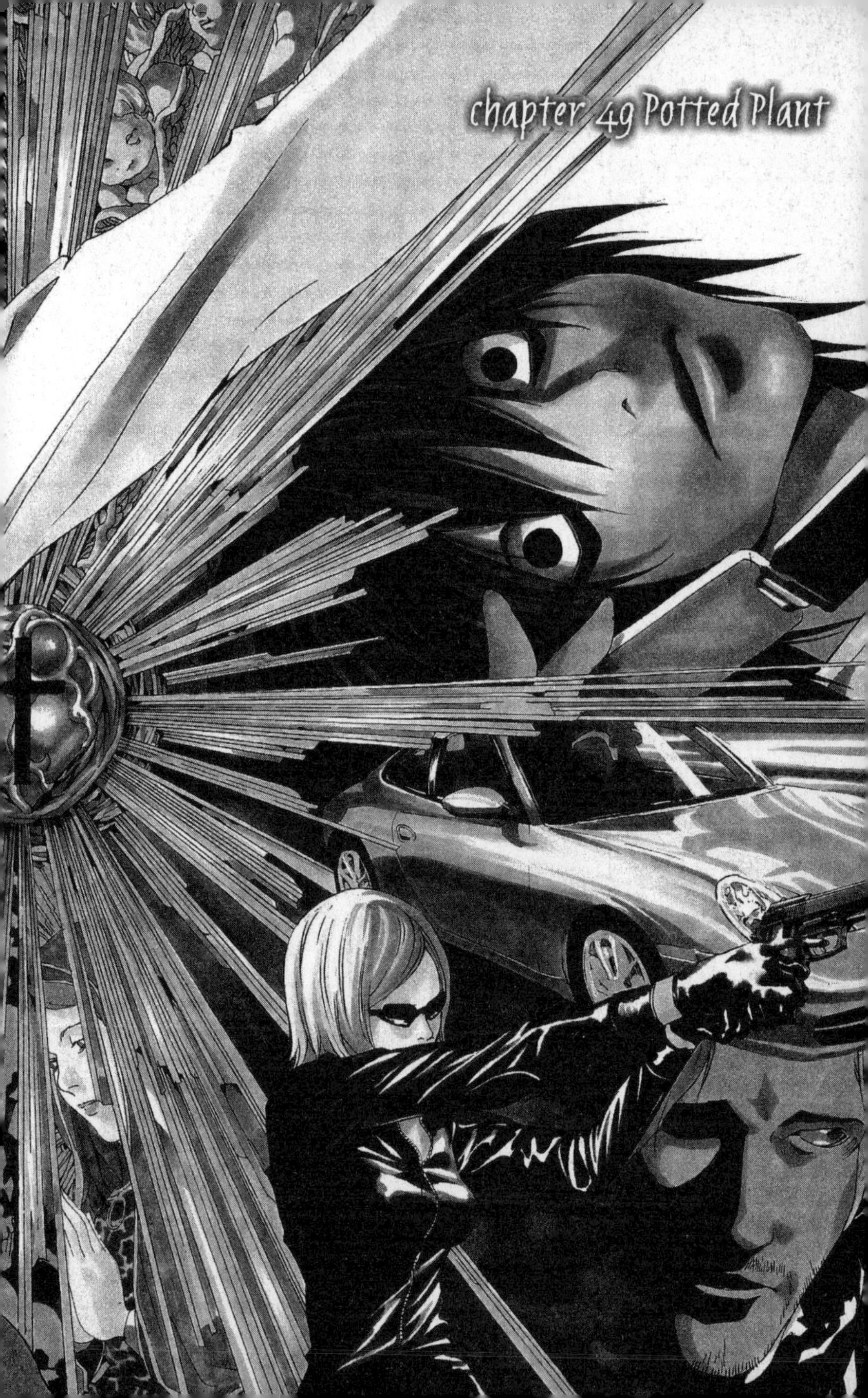
chapter 49 Potted Plant

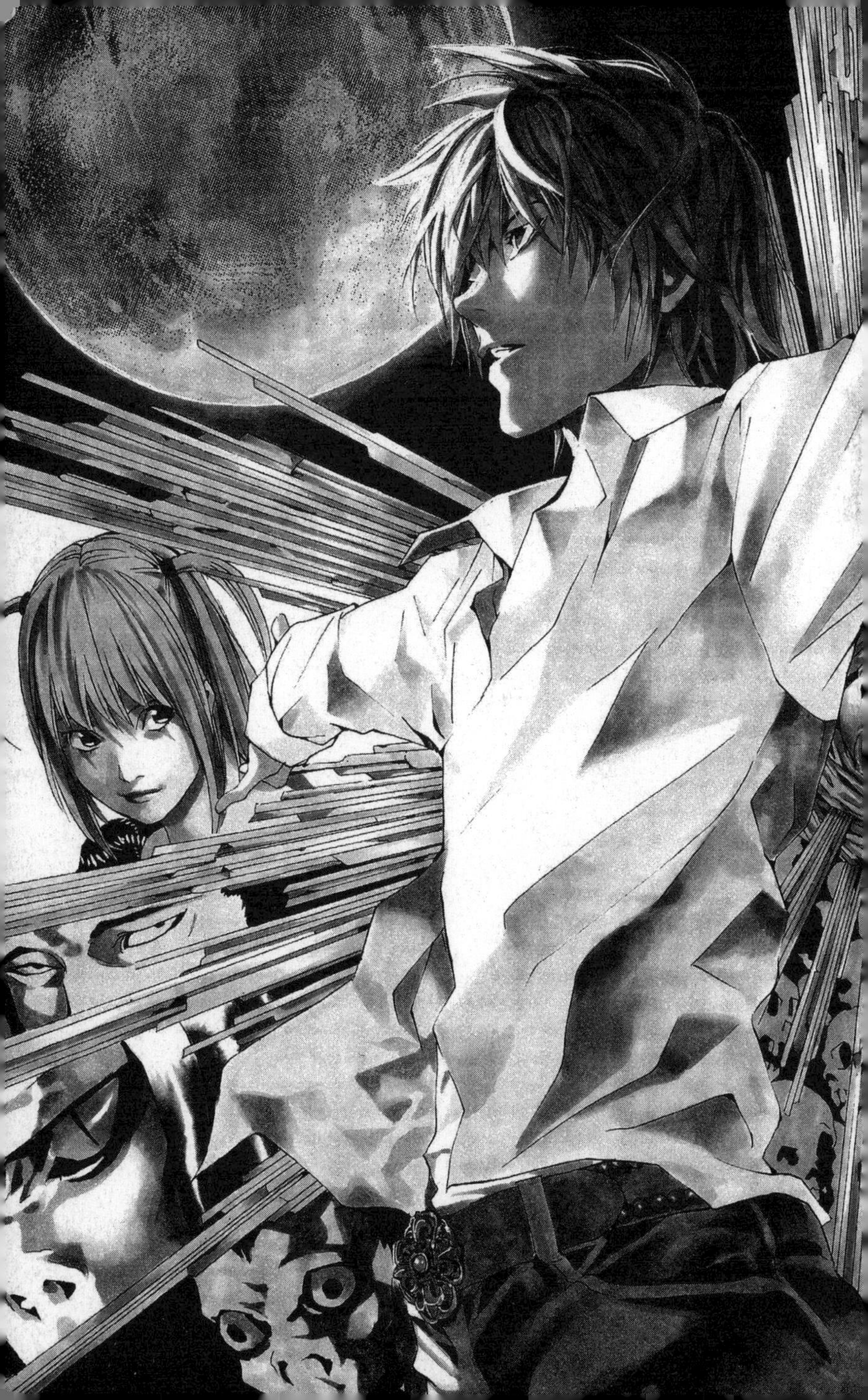

READ THIS WAY

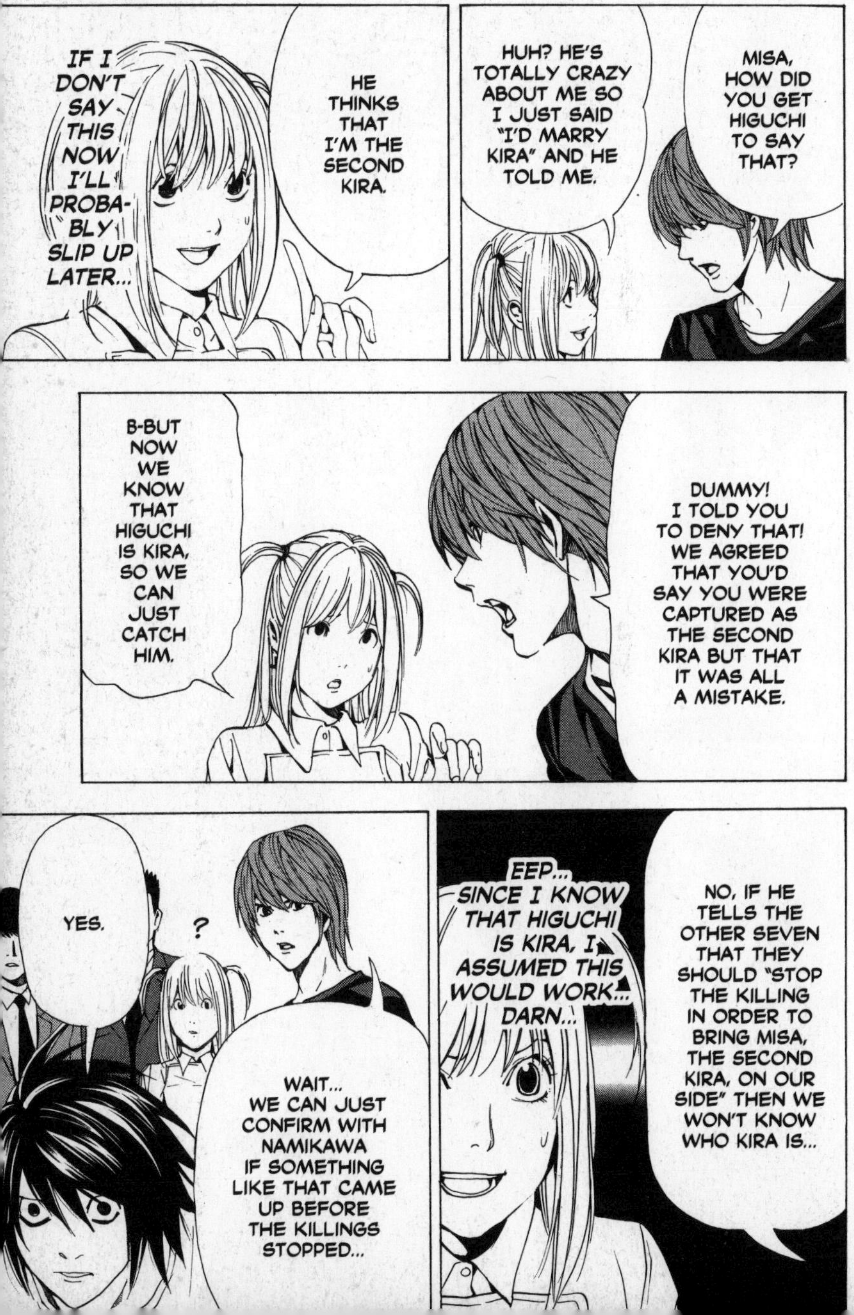
MISA, HOW DID YOU GET HIGUCHI TO SAY THAT?
HUH? HE'S TOTALLY CRAZY ABOUT ME SO I JUST SAID "I'D MARRY KIRA" AND HE TOLD ME.
HE THINKS THAT I'M THE SECOND KIRA.
IF I DON'T SAY THIS NOW I'LL PROBABLY SLIP UP LATER...
DUMMY! I TOLD YOU TO DENY THAT! WE AGREED THAT YOU'D SAY YOU WERE CAPTURED AS THE SECOND KIRA BUT THAT IT WAS ALL A MISTAKE.
B-BUT NOW WE KNOW THAT HIGUCHI IS KIRA, SO WE CAN JUST CATCH HIM.
NO, IF HE TELLS THE OTHER SEVEN THAT THEY SHOULD "STOP THE KILLING IN ORDER TO BRING MISA, THE SECOND KIRA, ON OUR SIDE" THEN WE WON'T KNOW WHO KIRA IS...
EEP... SINCE I KNOW THAT HIGUCHI IS KIRA, I ASSUMED THIS WOULD WORK... DARN...
?
WAIT... WE CAN JUST CONFIRM WITH NAMIKAWA IF SOMETHING LIKE THAT CAME UP BEFORE THE KILLINGS STOPPED...
YES.

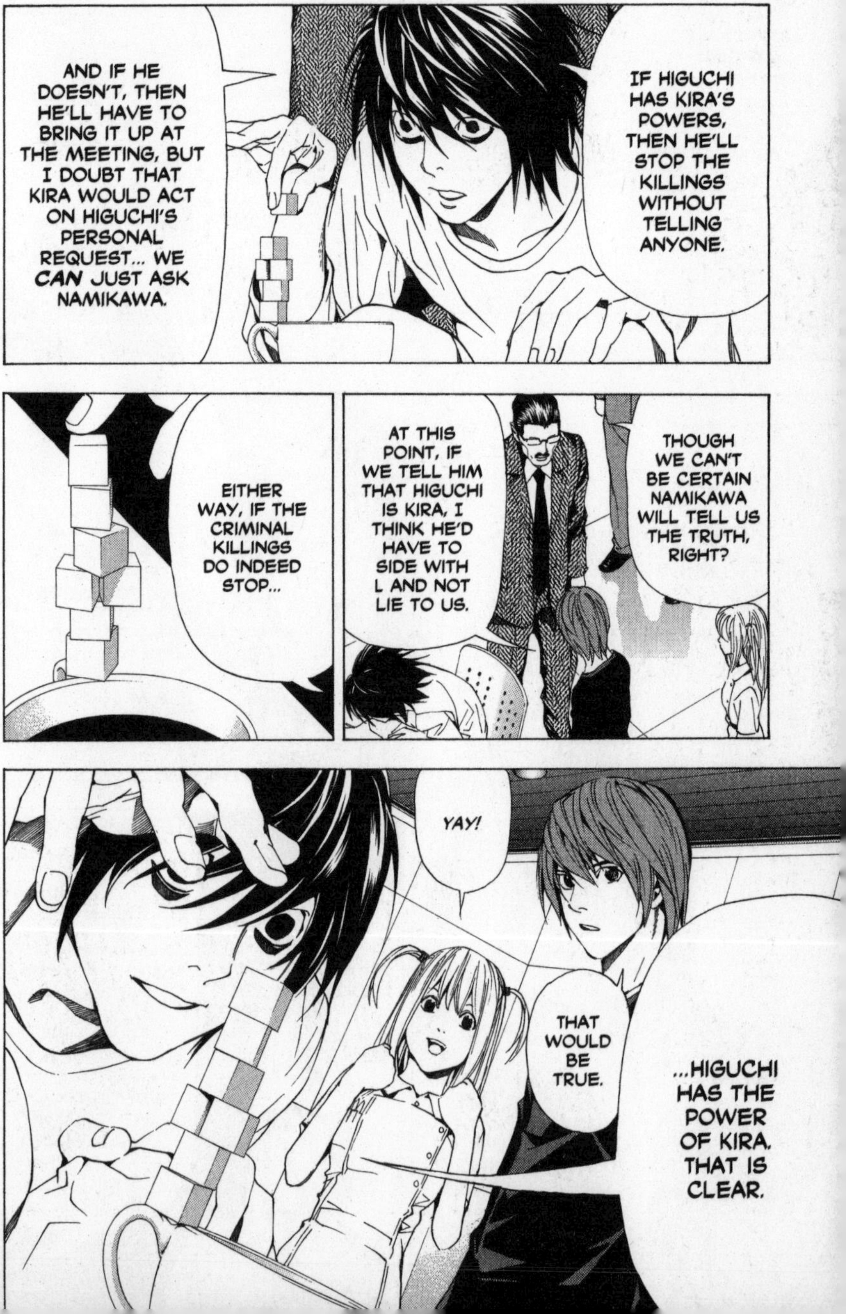

IF HIGUCHI HAS KIRA'S POWERS, THEN HE'LL STOP THE KILLINGS WITHOUT TELLING ANYONE.
AND IF HE DOESN'T, THEN HE'LL HAVE TO BRING IT UP AT THE MEETING, BUT I DOUBT THAT KIRA WOULD ACT ON HIGUCHI'S PERSONAL REQUEST... WE *CAN* JUST ASK NAMIKAWA.
THOUGH WE CAN'T BE CERTAIN NAMIKAWA WILL TELL US THE TRUTH, RIGHT?
AT THIS POINT, IF WE TELL HIM THAT HIGUCHI IS KIRA, I THINK HE'D HAVE TO SIDE WITH L AND NOT LIE TO US.
EITHER WAY, IF THE CRIMINAL KILLINGS DO INDEED STOP...
...HIGUCHI HAS THE POWER OF KIRA. THAT IS CLEAR.
THAT WOULD BE TRUE.
YAY!

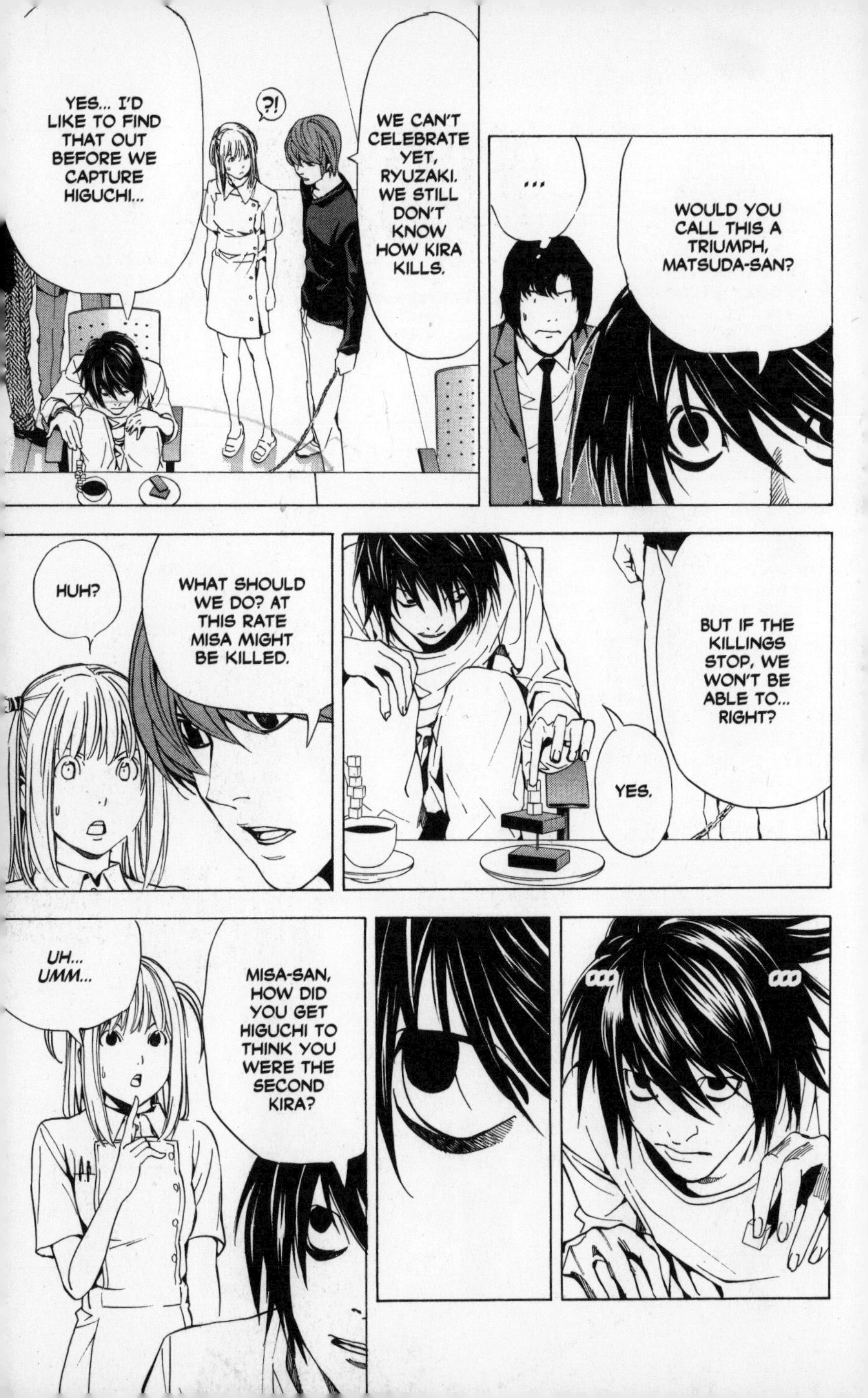
WOULD YOU CALL THIS A TRIUMPH, MATSUDA-SAN?
...
WE CAN'T CELEBRATE YET, RYUZAKI. WE STILL DON'T KNOW HOW KIRA KILLS.
?!
YES... I'D LIKE TO FIND THAT OUT BEFORE WE CAPTURE HIGUCHI...
BUT IF THE KILLINGS STOP, WE WON'T BE ABLE TO... RIGHT?
YES.
WHAT SHOULD WE DO? AT THIS RATE MISA MIGHT BE KILLED.
HUH?
MISA-SAN, HOW DID YOU GET HIGUCHI TO THINK YOU WERE THE SECOND KIRA?
UH... UMM...

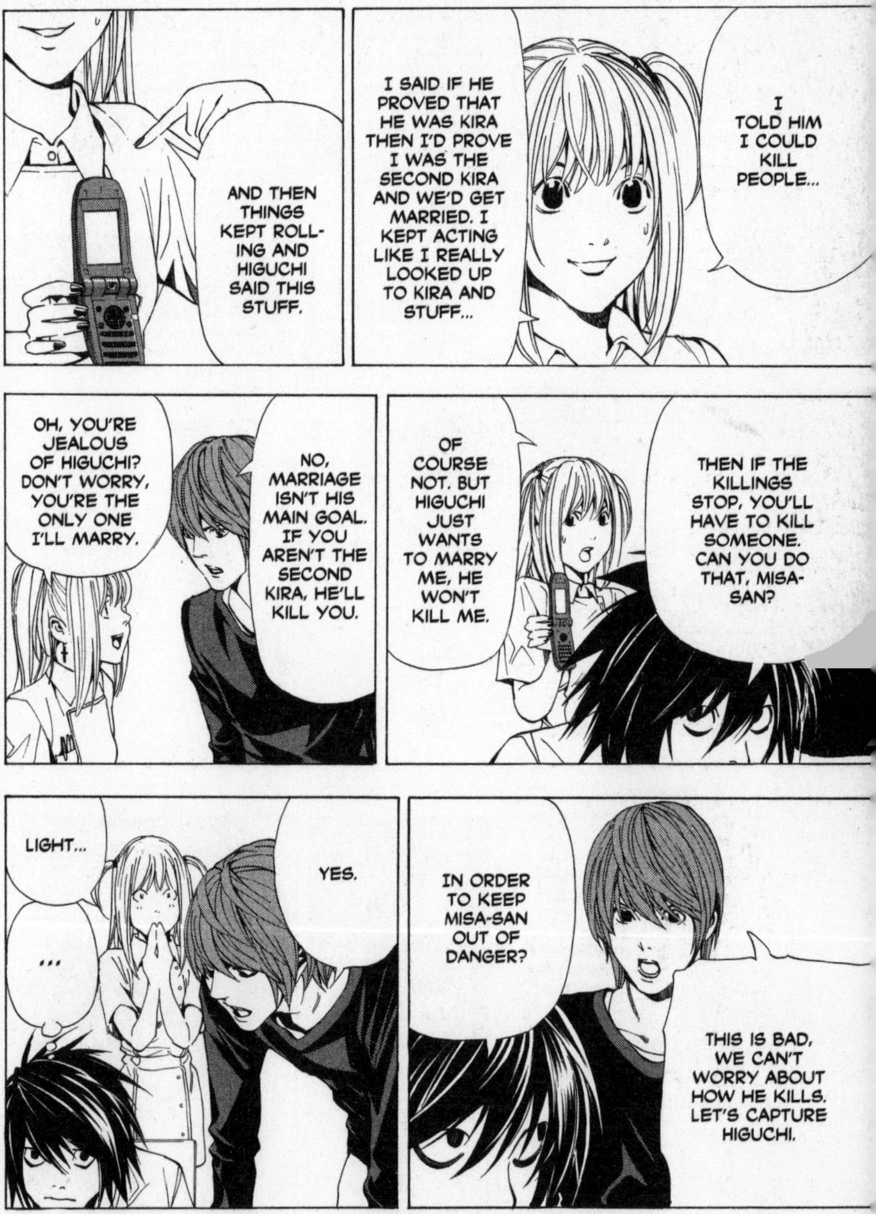
I TOLD HIM I COULD KILL PEOPLE...
I SAID IF HE PROVED THAT HE WAS KIRA THEN I'D PROVE I WAS THE SECOND KIRA AND WE'D GET MARRIED. I KEPT ACTING LIKE I REALLY LOOKED UP TO KIRA AND STUFF...
AND THEN THINGS KEPT ROLL-ING AND HIGUCHI SAID THIS STUFF.
THEN IF THE KILLINGS STOP, YOU'LL HAVE TO KILL SOMEONE. CAN YOU DO THAT, MISA-SAN?
OF COURSE NOT. BUT HIGUCHI JUST WANTS TO MARRY ME, HE WON'T KILL ME.
NO, MARRIAGE ISN'T HIS MAIN GOAL. IF YOU AREN'T THE SECOND KIRA, HE'LL KILL YOU.
OH, YOU'RE JEALOUS OF HIGUCHI? DON'T WORRY, YOU'RE THE ONLY ONE I'LL MARRY.
THIS IS BAD, WE CAN'T WORRY ABOUT HOW HE KILLS. LET'S CAPTURE HIGUCHI.
IN ORDER TO KEEP MISA-SAN OUT OF DANGER?
YES.
LIGHT...
...

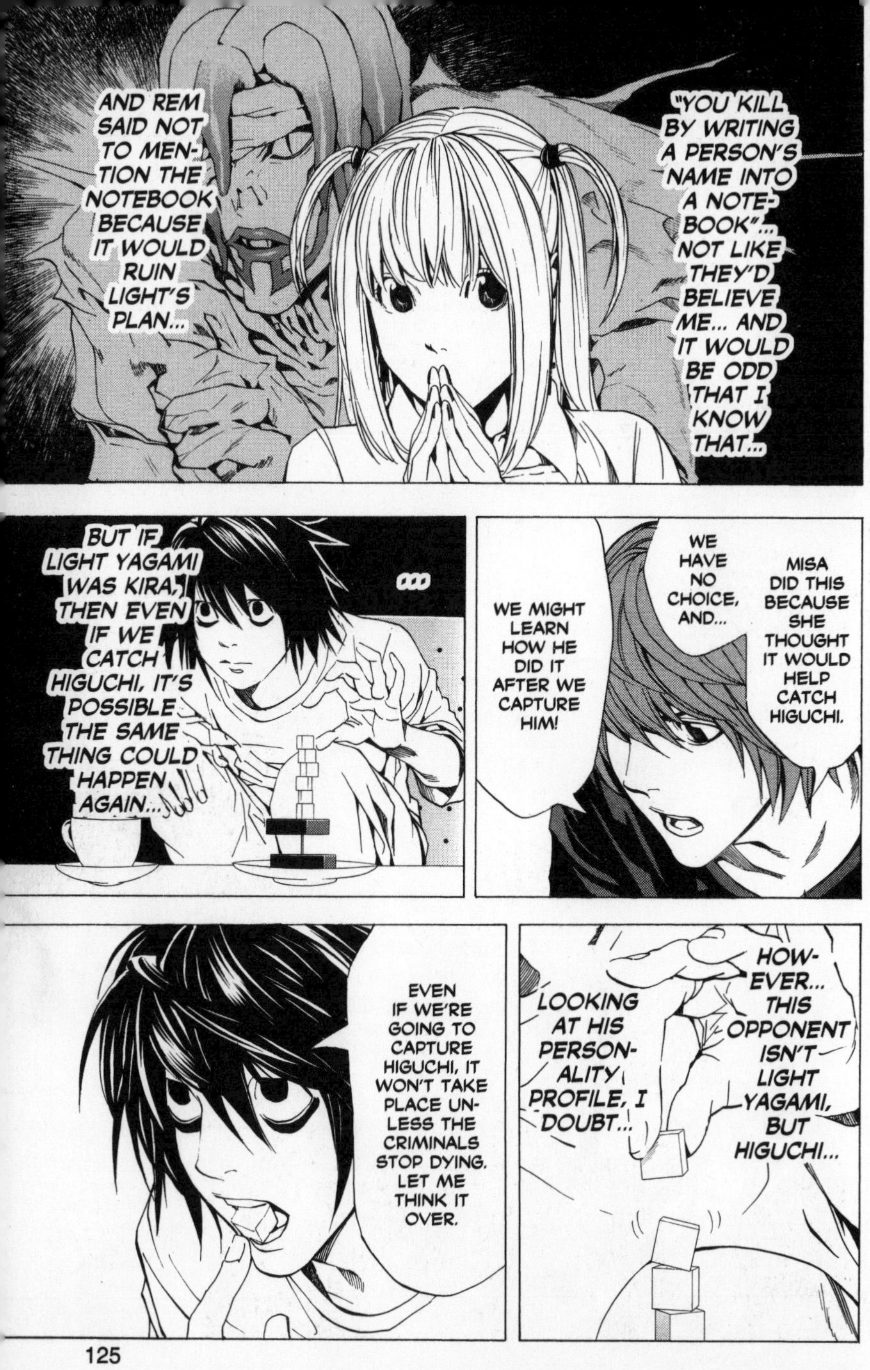
"YOU KILL BY WRITING A PERSON'S NAME INTO A NOTEBOOK"... NOT LIKE THEY'D BELIEVE ME... AND IT WOULD BE ODD THAT I KNOW THAT...
AND REM SAID NOT TO MENTION THE NOTEBOOK BECAUSE IT WOULD RUIN LIGHT'S PLAN...
MISA DID THIS BECAUSE SHE THOUGHT IT WOULD HELP CATCH HIGUCHI.
WE HAVE NO CHOICE, AND...
WE MIGHT LEARN HOW HE DID IT AFTER WE CAPTURE HIM!
...
BUT IF LIGHT YAGAMI WAS KIRA, THEN EVEN IF WE CATCH HIGUCHI, IT'S POSSIBLE THE SAME THING COULD HAPPEN AGAIN...
HOWEVER... THIS OPPONENT ISN'T LIGHT YAGAMI, BUT HIGUCHI...
LOOKING AT HIS PERSONALITY PROFILE, I DOUBT...
EVEN IF WE'RE GOING TO CAPTURE HIGUCHI, IT WON'T TAKE PLACE UNLESS THE CRIMINALS STOP DYING. LET ME THINK IT OVER.

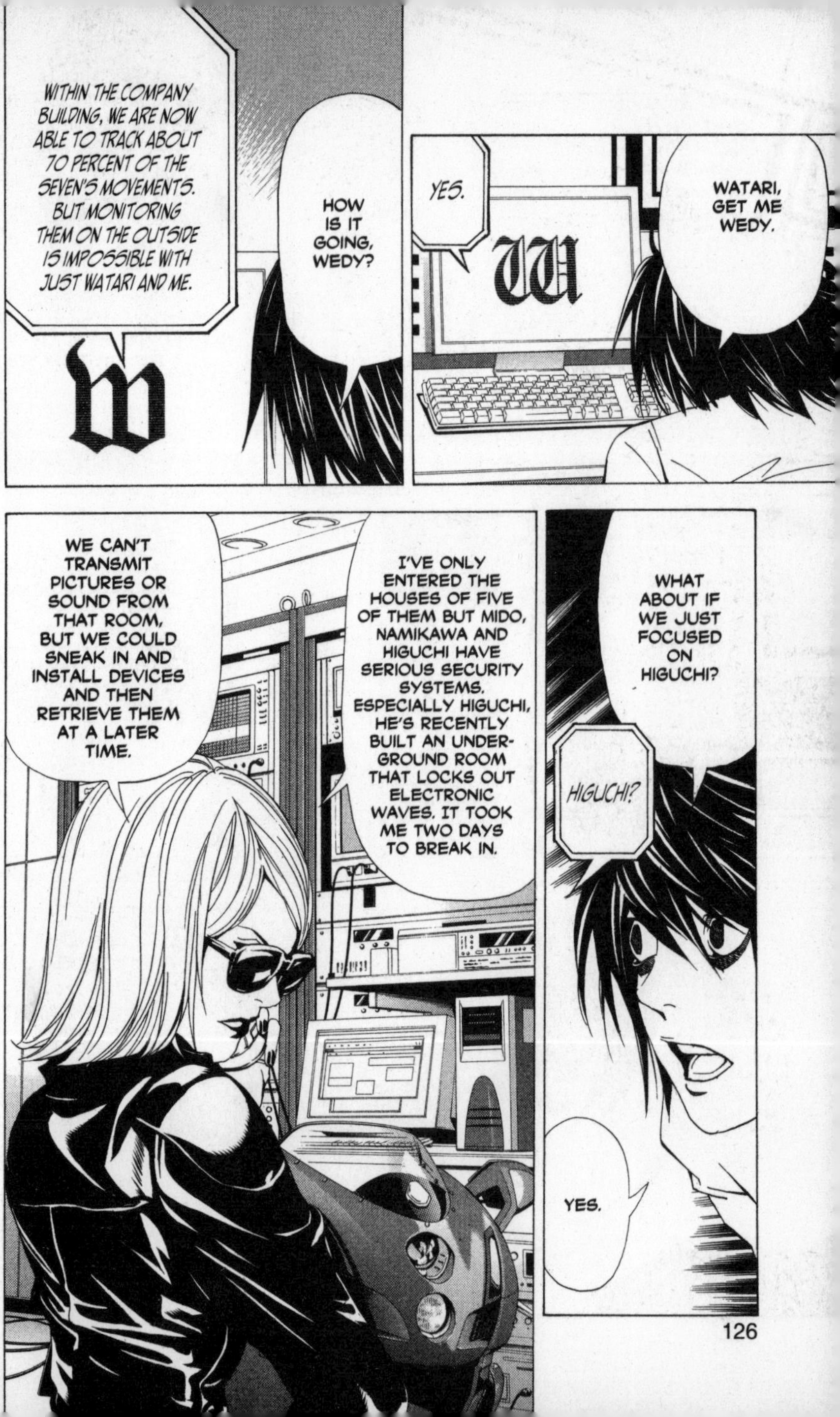
WATARI, GET ME WEDY.
YES.
HOW IS IT GOING, WEDY?
WITHIN THE COMPANY BUILDING, WE ARE NOW ABLE TO TRACK ABOUT 70 PERCENT OF THE SEVEN'S MOVEMENTS. BUT MONITORING THEM ON THE OUTSIDE IS IMPOSSIBLE WITH JUST WATARI AND ME.
I'VE ONLY ENTERED THE HOUSES OF FIVE OF THEM BUT MIDO, NAMIKAWA AND HIGUCHI HAVE SERIOUS SECURITY SYSTEMS. ESPECIALLY HIGUCHI, HE'S RECENTLY BUILT AN UNDER-GROUND ROOM THAT LOCKS OUT ELECTRONIC WAVES. IT TOOK ME TWO DAYS TO BREAK IN.
WE CAN'T TRANSMIT PICTURES OR SOUND FROM THAT ROOM, BUT WE COULD SNEAK IN AND INSTALL DEVICES AND THEN RETRIEVE THEM AT A LATER TIME.
WHAT ABOUT IF WE JUST FOCUSED ON HIGUCHI?
HIGUCHI?
YES.

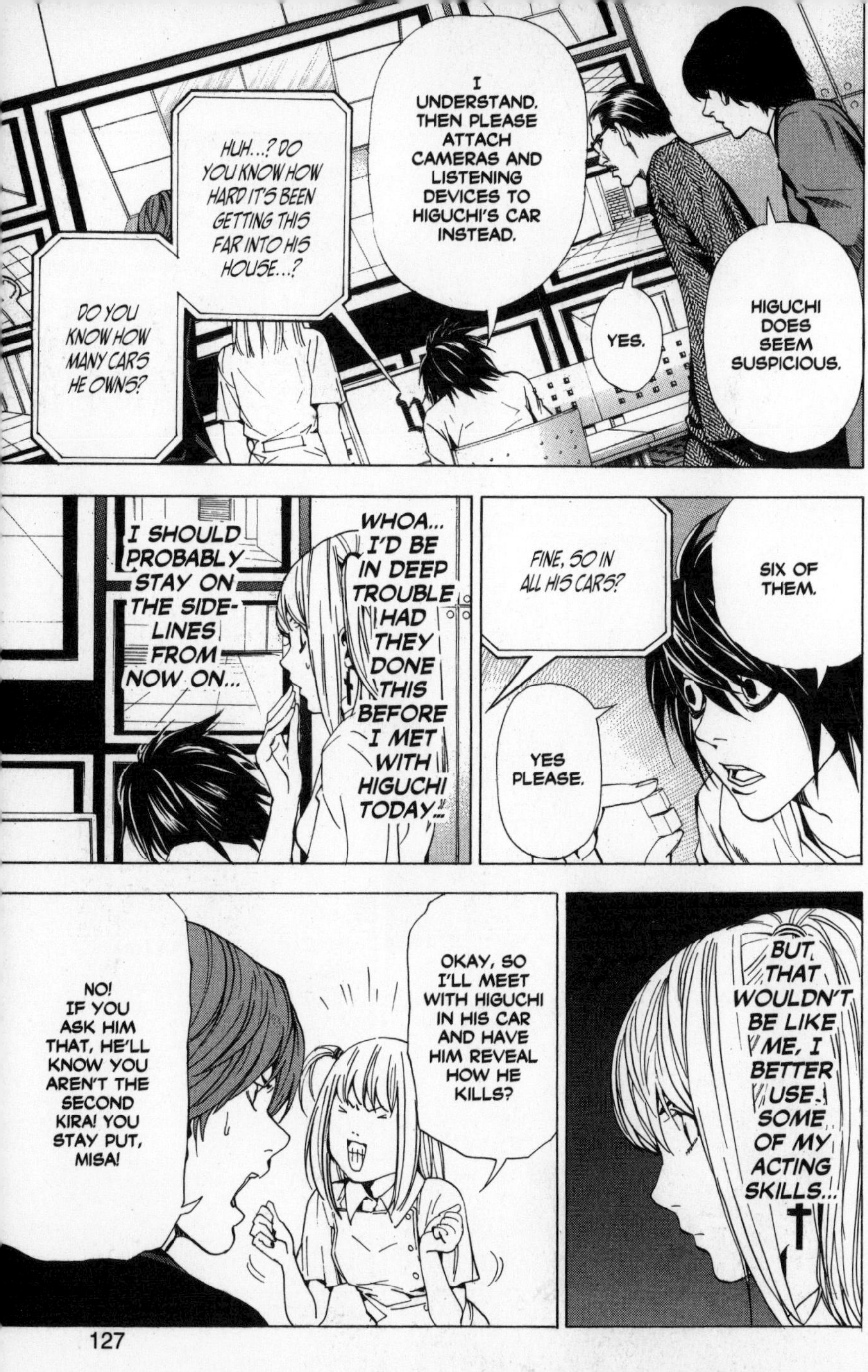
HIGUCHI DOES SEEM SUSPICIOUS.
YES.
I UNDERSTAND. THEN PLEASE ATTACH CAMERAS AND LISTENING DEVICES TO HIGUCHI'S CAR INSTEAD.
HUH...? DO YOU KNOW HOW HARD IT'S BEEN GETTING THIS FAR INTO HIS HOUSE...?
DO YOU KNOW HOW MANY CARS HE OWNS?
SIX OF THEM.
FINE, SO IN ALL HIS CARS?
YES PLEASE.
WHOA... I'D BE IN DEEP TROUBLE HAD THEY DONE THIS BEFORE I MET WITH HIGUCHI TODAY...
I SHOULD PROBABLY STAY ON THE SIDE-LINES FROM NOW ON...
BUT, THAT WOULDN'T BE LIKE ME, I BETTER USE SOME OF MY ACTING SKILLS...
OKAY, SO I'LL MEET WITH HIGUCHI IN HIS CAR AND HAVE HIM REVEAL HOW HE KILLS?
NO! IF YOU ASK HIM THAT, HE'LL KNOW YOU AREN'T THE SECOND KIRA! YOU STAY PUT, MISA!

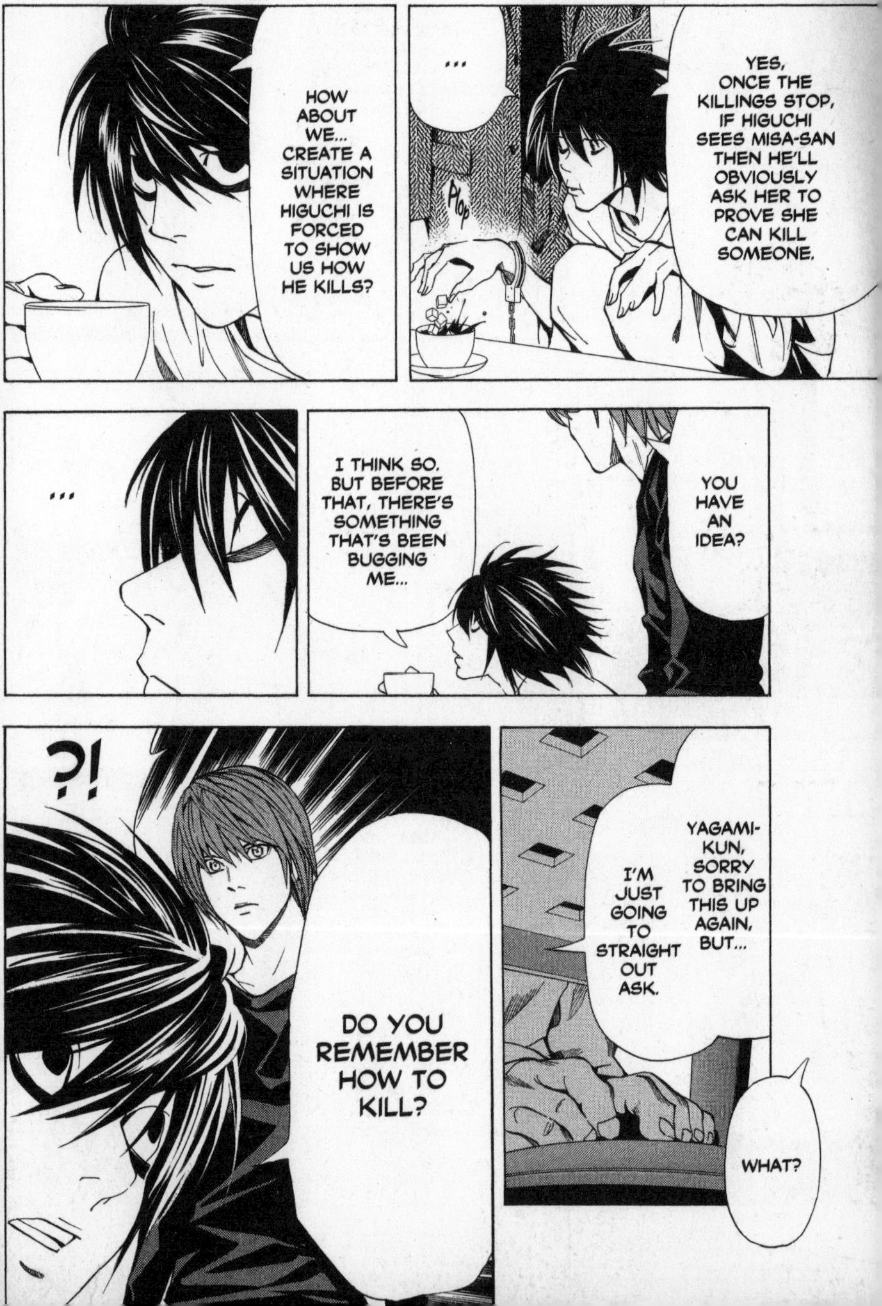
YES, ONCE THE KILLINGS STOP, IF HIGUCHI SEES MISA-SAN THEN HE'LL OBVIOUSLY ASK HER TO PROVE SHE CAN KILL SOMEONE.
...
Plop
HOW ABOUT WE... CREATE A SITUATION WHERE HIGUCHI IS FORCED TO SHOW US HOW HE KILLS?
YOU HAVE AN IDEA?
I THINK SO. BUT BEFORE THAT, THERE'S SOMETHING THAT'S BEEN BUGGING ME...
...
YAGAMI-KUN, SORRY TO BRING THIS UP AGAIN, BUT...
I'M JUST GOING TO STRAIGHT OUT ASK.
WHAT?
?!
DO YOU REMEMBER HOW TO KILL?

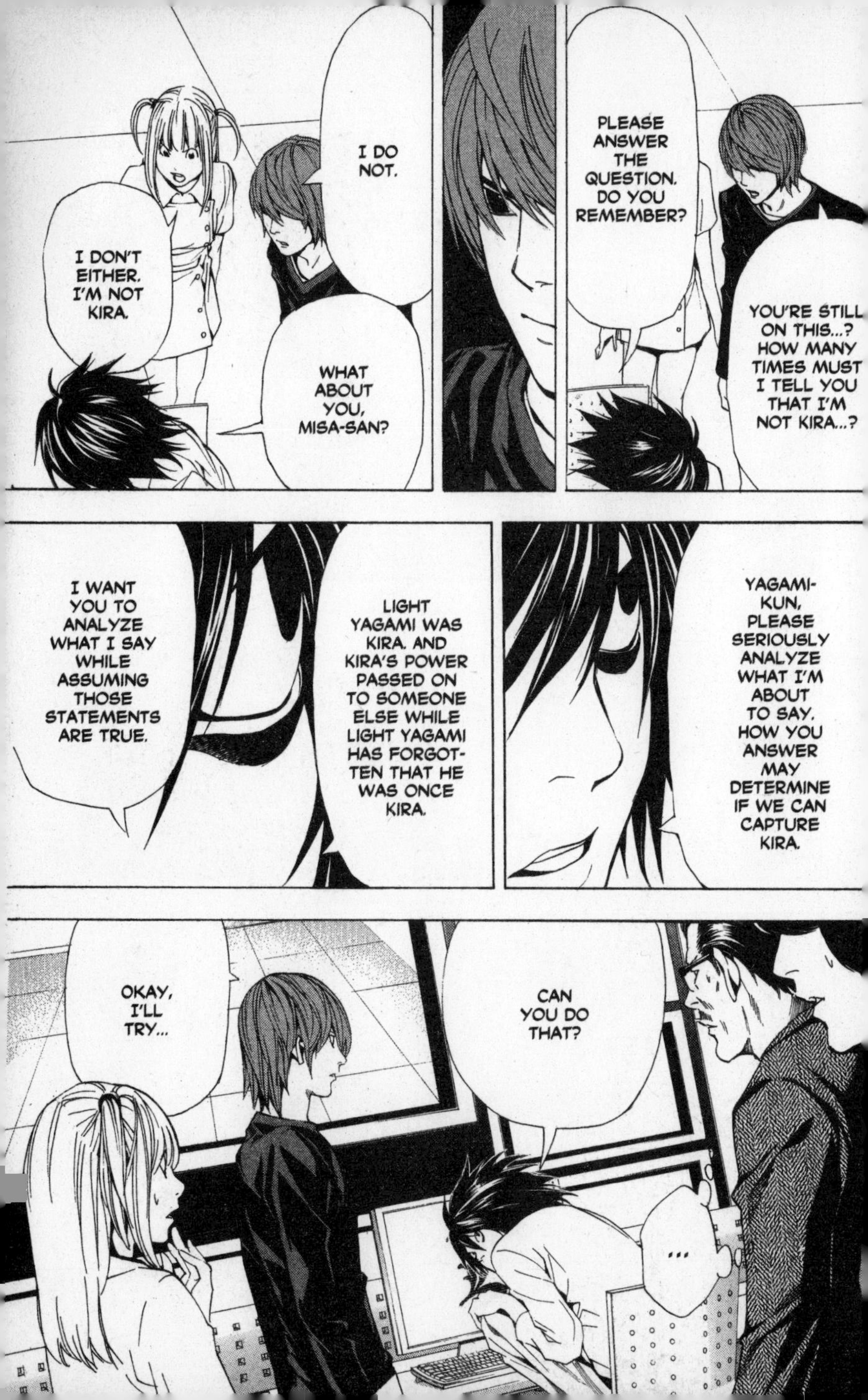
YOU'RE STILL ON THIS...? HOW MANY TIMES MUST I TELL YOU THAT I'M NOT KIRA...?
PLEASE ANSWER THE QUESTION. DO YOU REMEMBER?
I DO NOT.
WHAT ABOUT YOU, MISA-SAN?
I DON'T EITHER. I'M NOT KIRA.
YAGAMI-KUN, PLEASE SERIOUSLY ANALYZE WHAT I'M ABOUT TO SAY. HOW YOU ANSWER MAY DETERMINE IF WE CAN CAPTURE KIRA.
LIGHT YAGAMI WAS KIRA. AND KIRA'S POWER PASSED ON TO SOMEONE ELSE WHILE LIGHT YAGAMI HAS FORGOTTEN THAT HE WAS ONCE KIRA.
I WANT YOU TO ANALYZE WHAT I SAY WHILE ASSUMING THOSE STATEMENTS ARE TRUE.
CAN YOU DO THAT?
...
OKAY, I'LL TRY...

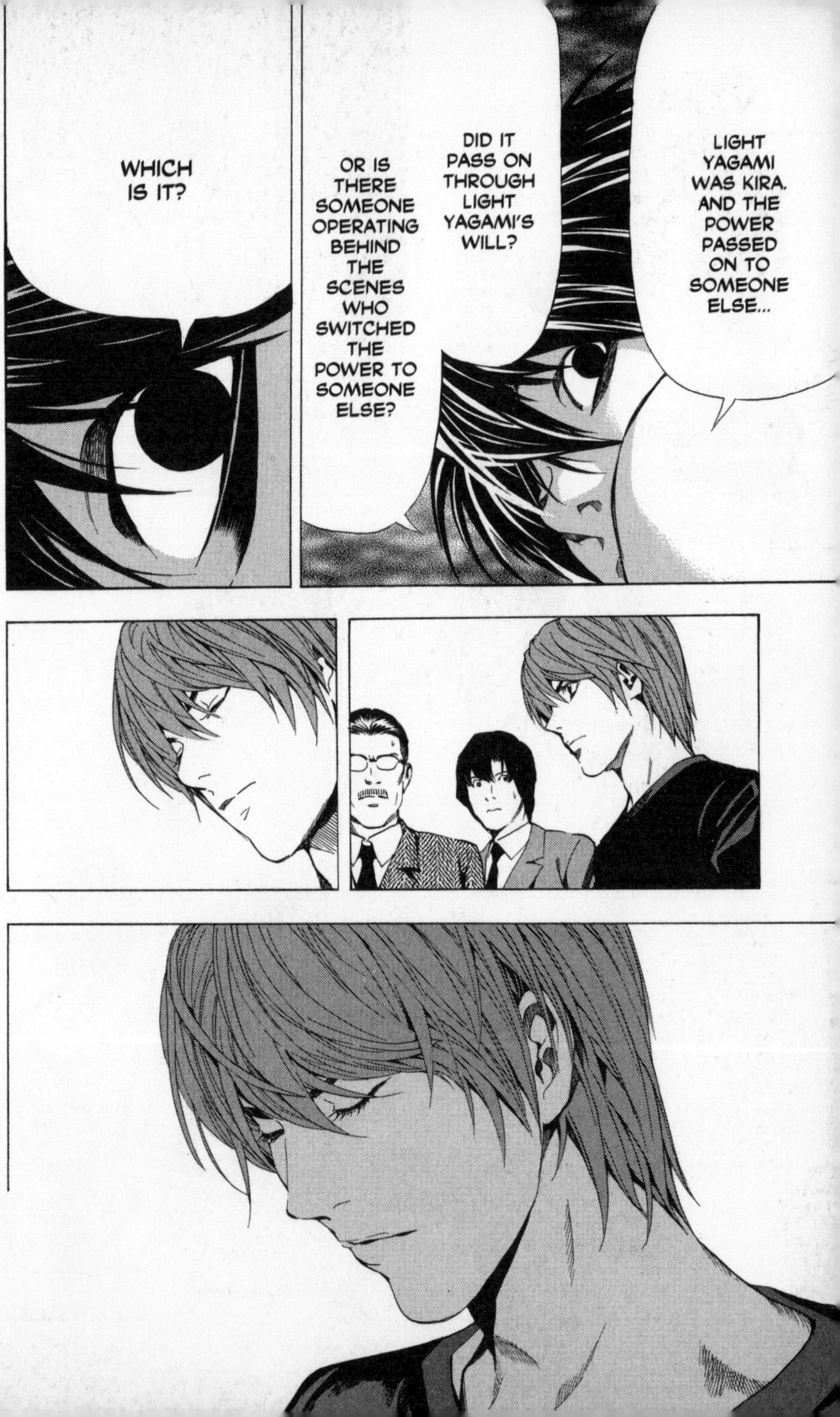
LIGHT YAGAMI WAS KIRA. AND THE POWER PASSED ON TO SOMEONE ELSE...
DID IT PASS ON THROUGH LIGHT YAGAMI'S WILL?
OR IS THERE SOMEONE OPERATING BEHIND THE SCENES WHO SWITCHED THE POWER TO SOMEONE ELSE?
WHICH IS IT?

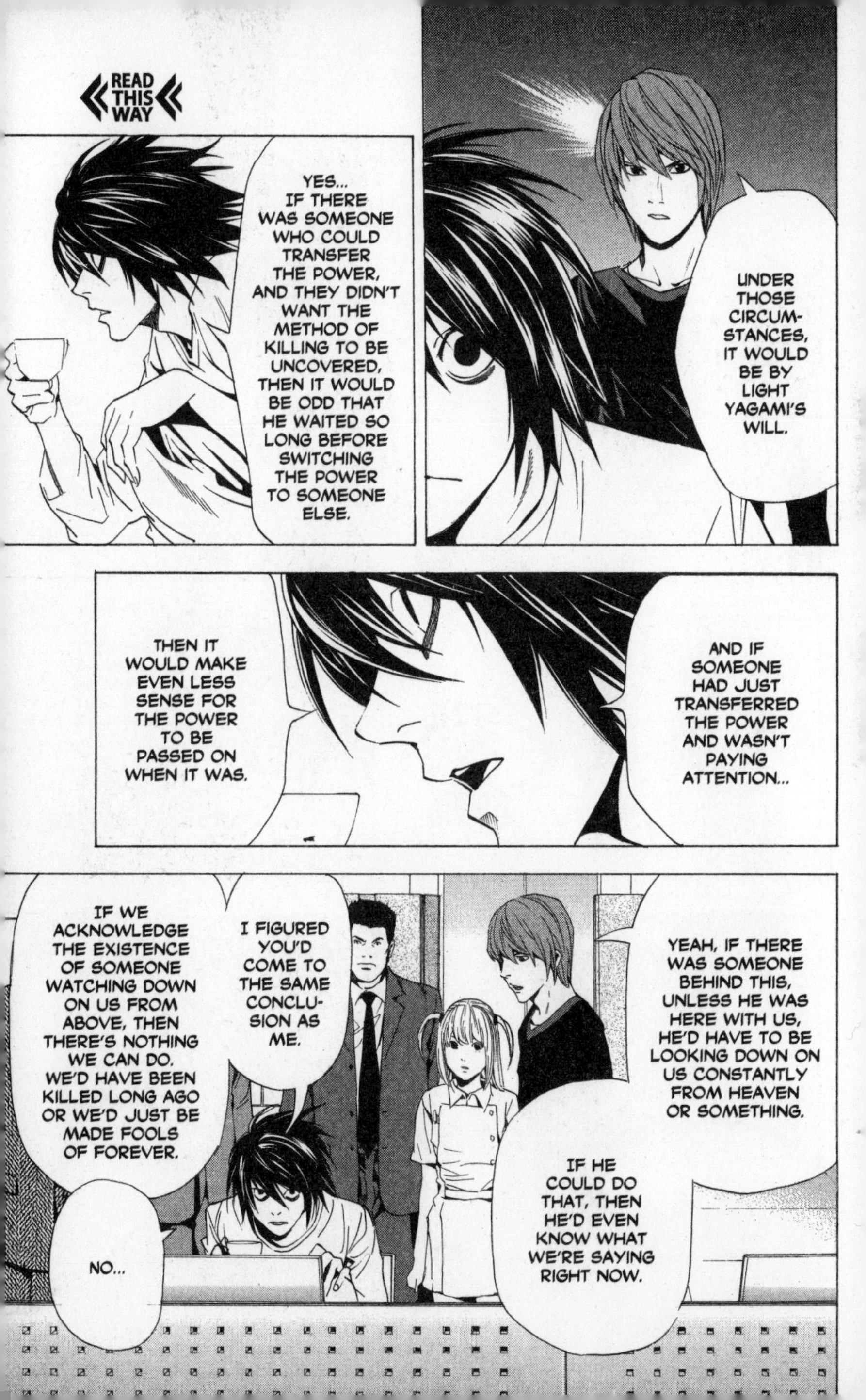
READ THIS WAY
UNDER THOSE CIRCUMSTANCES, IT WOULD BE BY LIGHT YAGAMI'S WILL.
YES... IF THERE WAS SOMEONE WHO COULD TRANSFER THE POWER, AND THEY DIDN'T WANT THE METHOD OF KILLING TO BE UNCOVERED, THEN IT WOULD BE ODD THAT HE WAITED SO LONG BEFORE SWITCHING THE POWER TO SOMEONE ELSE.
AND IF SOMEONE HAD JUST TRANSFERRED THE POWER AND WASN'T PAYING ATTENTION...
THEN IT WOULD MAKE EVEN LESS SENSE FOR THE POWER TO BE PASSED ON WHEN IT WAS.
YEAH, IF THERE WAS SOMEONE BEHIND THIS, UNLESS HE WAS HERE WITH US, HE'D HAVE TO BE LOOKING DOWN ON US CONSTANTLY FROM HEAVEN OR SOMETHING.
IF HE COULD DO THAT, THEN HE'D EVEN KNOW WHAT WE'RE SAYING RIGHT NOW.
NO...
IF WE ACKNOWLEDGE THE EXISTENCE OF SOMEONE WATCHING DOWN ON US FROM ABOVE, THEN THERE'S NOTHING WE CAN DO. WE'D HAVE BEEN KILLED LONG AGO OR WE'D JUST BE MADE FOOLS OF FOREVER.
I FIGURED YOU'D COME TO THE SAME CONCLUSION AS ME.

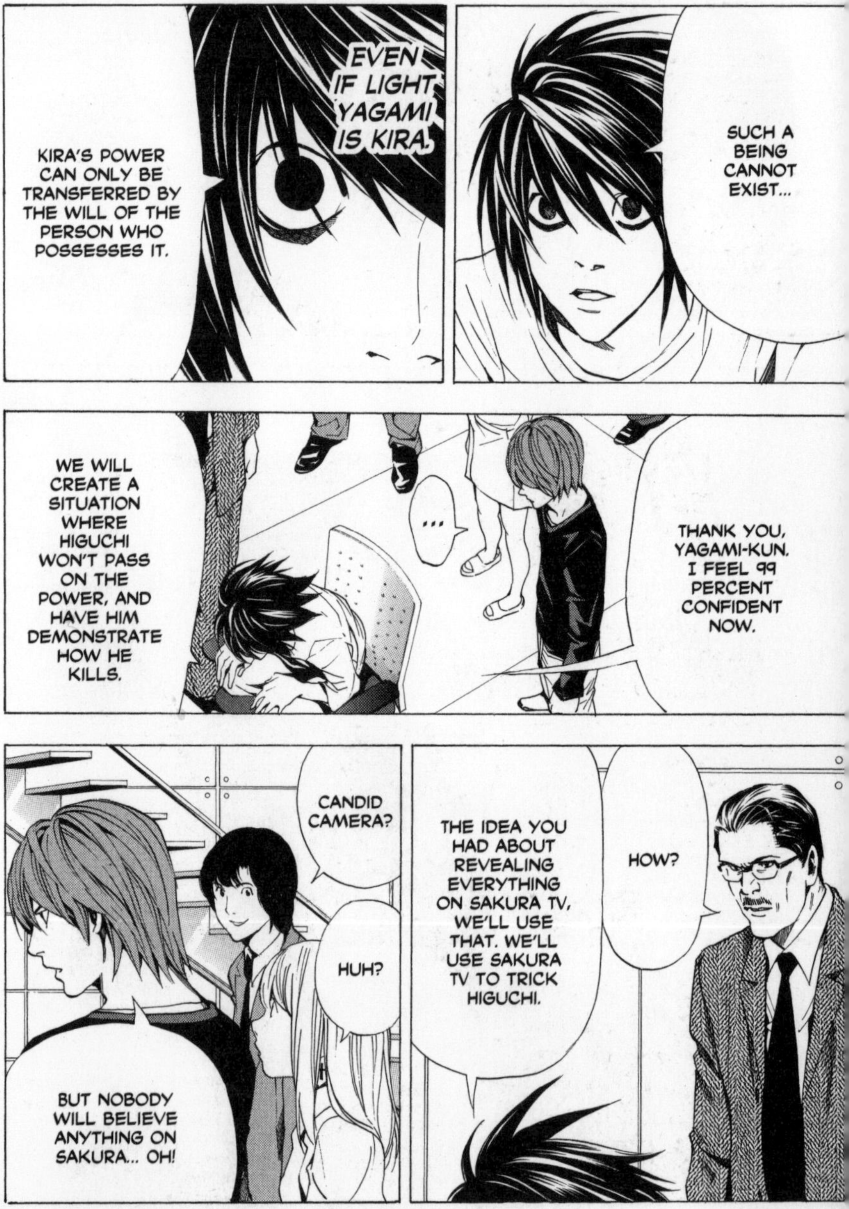
SUCH A BEING CANNOT EXIST...
EVEN IF LIGHT YAGAMI IS KIRA.
KIRA'S POWER CAN ONLY BE TRANSFERRED BY THE WILL OF THE PERSON WHO POSSESSES IT.
THANK YOU, YAGAMI-KUN. I FEEL 99 PERCENT CONFIDENT NOW.
...
WE WILL CREATE A SITUATION WHERE HIGUCHI WON'T PASS ON THE POWER, AND HAVE HIM DEMONSTRATE HOW HE KILLS.
HOW?
THE IDEA YOU HAD ABOUT REVEALING EVERYTHING ON SAKURA TV, WE'LL USE THAT. WE'LL USE SAKURA TV TO TRICK HIGUCHI.
CANDID CAMERA?
HUH?
BUT NOBODY WILL BELIEVE ANYTHING ON SAKURA... OH!

READ THIS WAY

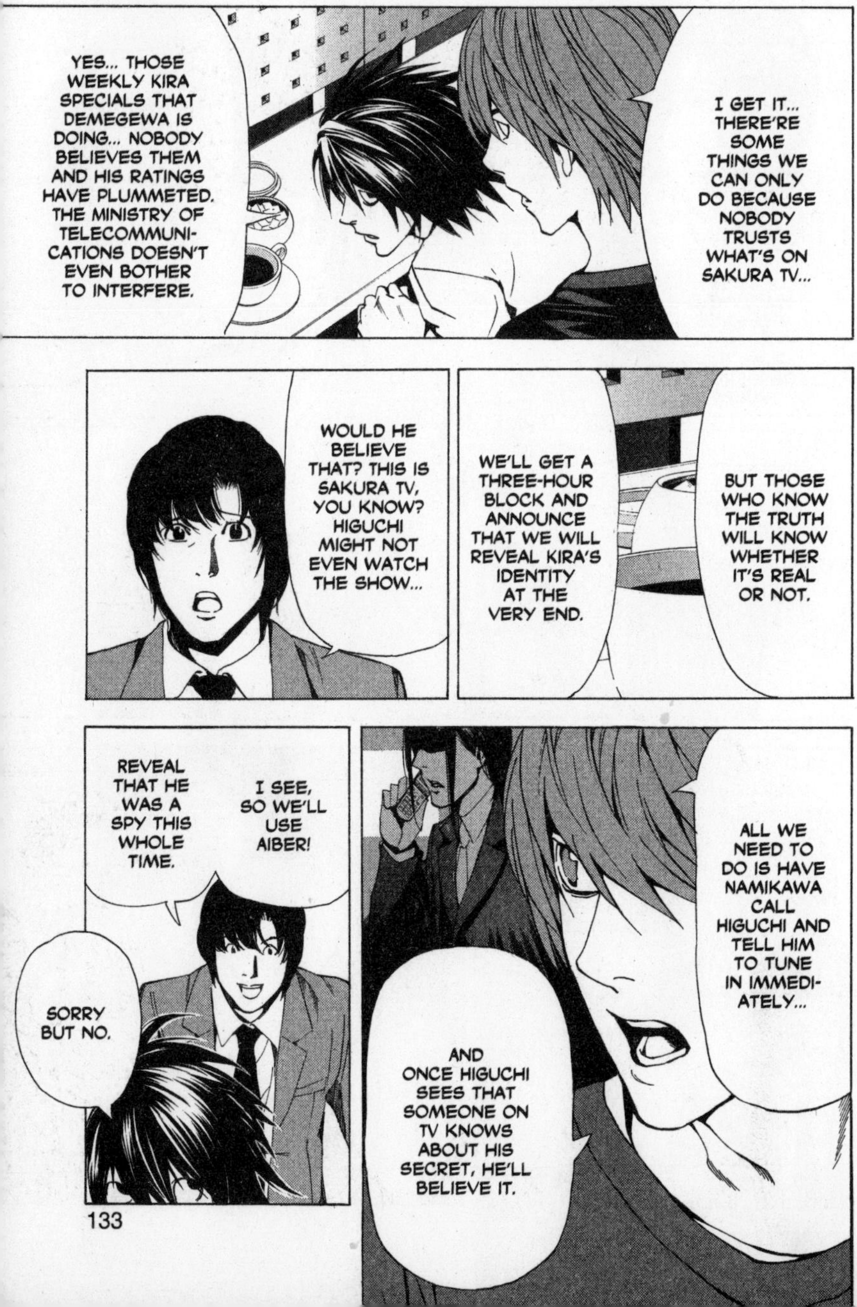
I GET IT... THERE'RE SOME THINGS WE CAN ONLY DO BECAUSE NOBODY TRUSTS WHAT'S ON SAKURA TV...
YES... THOSE WEEKLY KIRA SPECIALS THAT DEMEGEWA IS DOING... NOBODY BELIEVES THEM AND HIS RATINGS HAVE PLUMMETED. THE MINISTRY OF TELECOMMUNI-CATIONS DOESN'T EVEN BOTHER TO INTERFERE.
BUT THOSE WHO KNOW THE TRUTH WILL KNOW WHETHER IT'S REAL OR NOT.
WE'LL GET A THREE-HOUR BLOCK AND ANNOUNCE THAT WE WILL REVEAL KIRA'S IDENTITY AT THE VERY END.
WOULD HE BELIEVE THAT? THIS IS SAKURA TV, YOU KNOW? HIGUCHI MIGHT NOT EVEN WATCH THE SHOW...
ALL WE NEED TO DO IS HAVE NAMIKAWA CALL HIGUCHI AND TELL HIM TO TUNE IN IMMEDI-ATELY...
AND ONCE HIGUCHI SEES THAT SOMEONE ON TV KNOWS ABOUT HIS SECRET, HE'LL BELIEVE IT.
I SEE, SO WE'LL USE AIBER!
REVEAL THAT HE WAS A SPY THIS WHOLE TIME.
SORRY BUT NO.

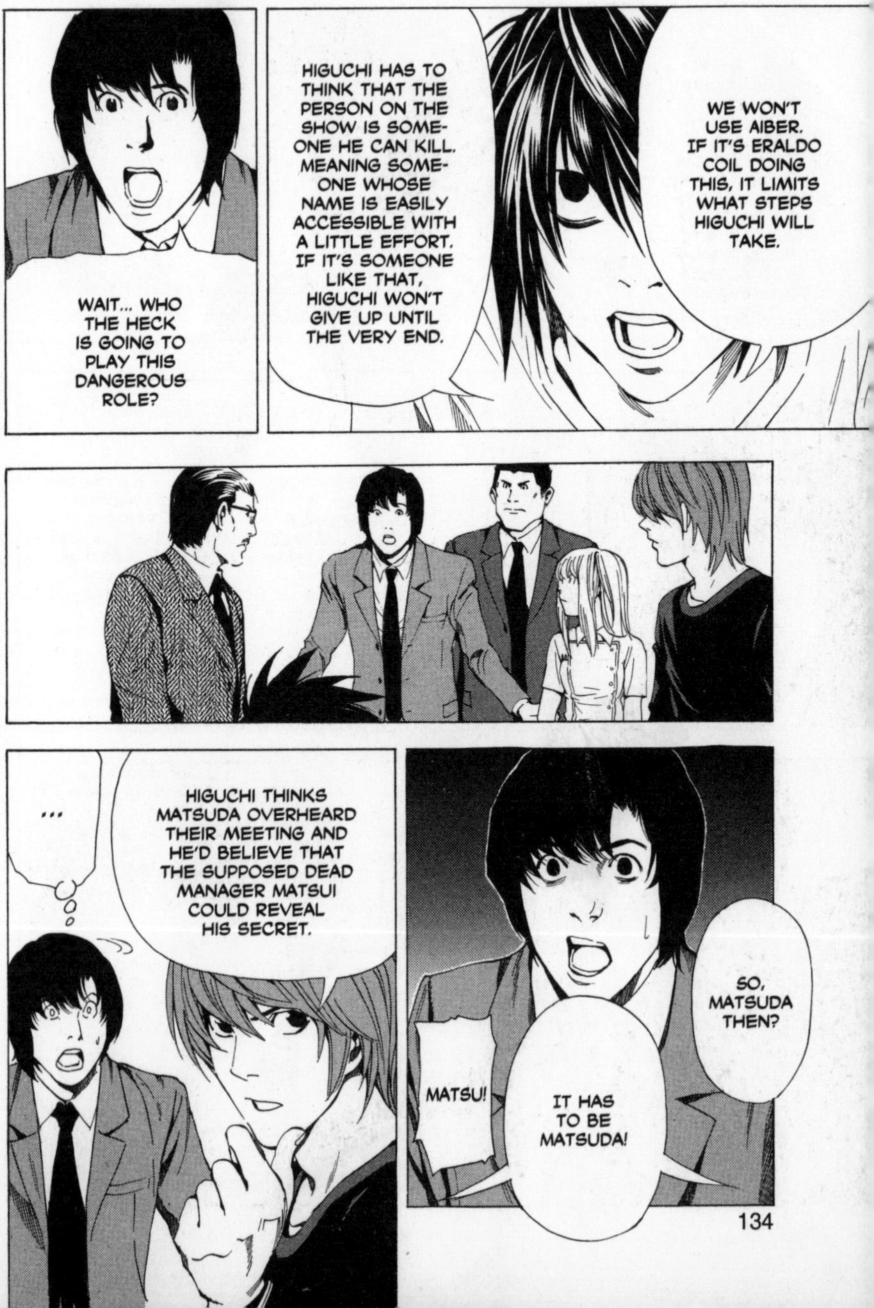
WE WON'T USE AIBER. IF IT'S ERALDO COIL DOING THIS, IT LIMITS WHAT STEPS HIGUCHI WILL TAKE.
HIGUCHI HAS TO THINK THAT THE PERSON ON THE SHOW IS SOME-ONE HE CAN KILL. MEANING SOME-ONE WHOSE NAME IS EASILY ACCESSIBLE WITH A LITTLE EFFORT. IF IT'S SOMEONE LIKE THAT, HIGUCHI WON'T GIVE UP UNTIL THE VERY END.
WAIT... WHO THE HECK IS GOING TO PLAY THIS DANGEROUS ROLE?
SO, MATSUDA THEN?
IT HAS TO BE MATSUDA!
MATSU!
HIGUCHI THINKS MATSUDA OVERHEARD THEIR MEETING AND HE'D BELIEVE THAT THE SUPPOSED DEAD MANAGER MATSUI COULD REVEAL HIS SECRET.
...

READ THIS WAY

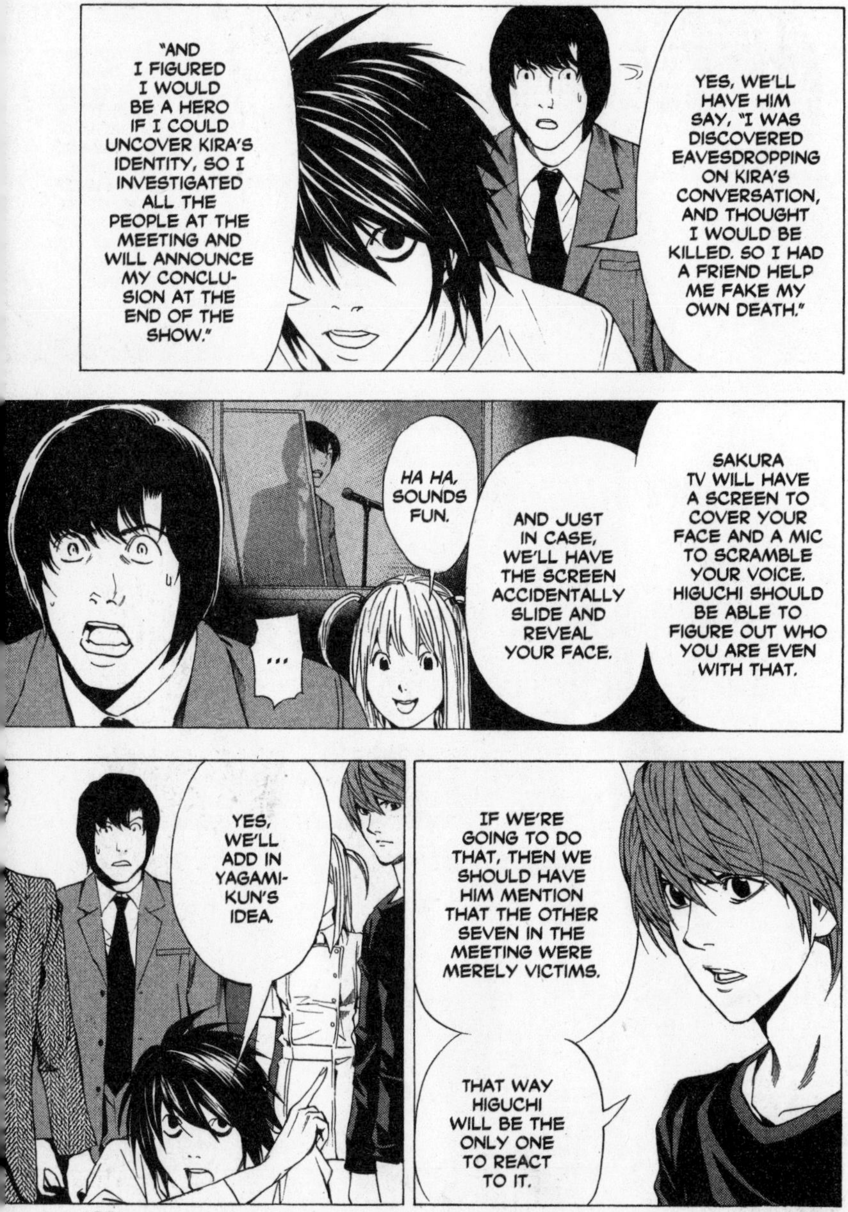
YES, WE'LL HAVE HIM SAY, "I WAS DISCOVERED EAVESDROPPING ON KIRA'S CONVERSATION, AND THOUGHT I WOULD BE KILLED. SO I HAD A FRIEND HELP ME FAKE MY OWN DEATH."
"AND I FIGURED I WOULD BE A HERO IF I COULD UNCOVER KIRA'S IDENTITY, SO I INVESTIGATED ALL THE PEOPLE AT THE MEETING AND WILL ANNOUNCE MY CONCLUSION AT THE END OF THE SHOW."
SAKURA TV WILL HAVE A SCREEN TO COVER YOUR FACE AND A MIC TO SCRAMBLE YOUR VOICE. HIGUCHI SHOULD BE ABLE TO FIGURE OUT WHO YOU ARE EVEN WITH THAT.
AND JUST IN CASE, WE'LL HAVE THE SCREEN ACCIDENTALLY SLIDE AND REVEAL YOUR FACE.
HA HA, SOUNDS FUN.
...
IF WE'RE GOING TO DO THAT, THEN WE SHOULD HAVE HIM MENTION THAT THE OTHER SEVEN IN THE MEETING WERE MERELY VICTIMS.
THAT WAY HIGUCHI WILL BE THE ONLY ONE TO REACT TO IT.
YES, WE'LL ADD IN YAGAMI-KUN'S IDEA.

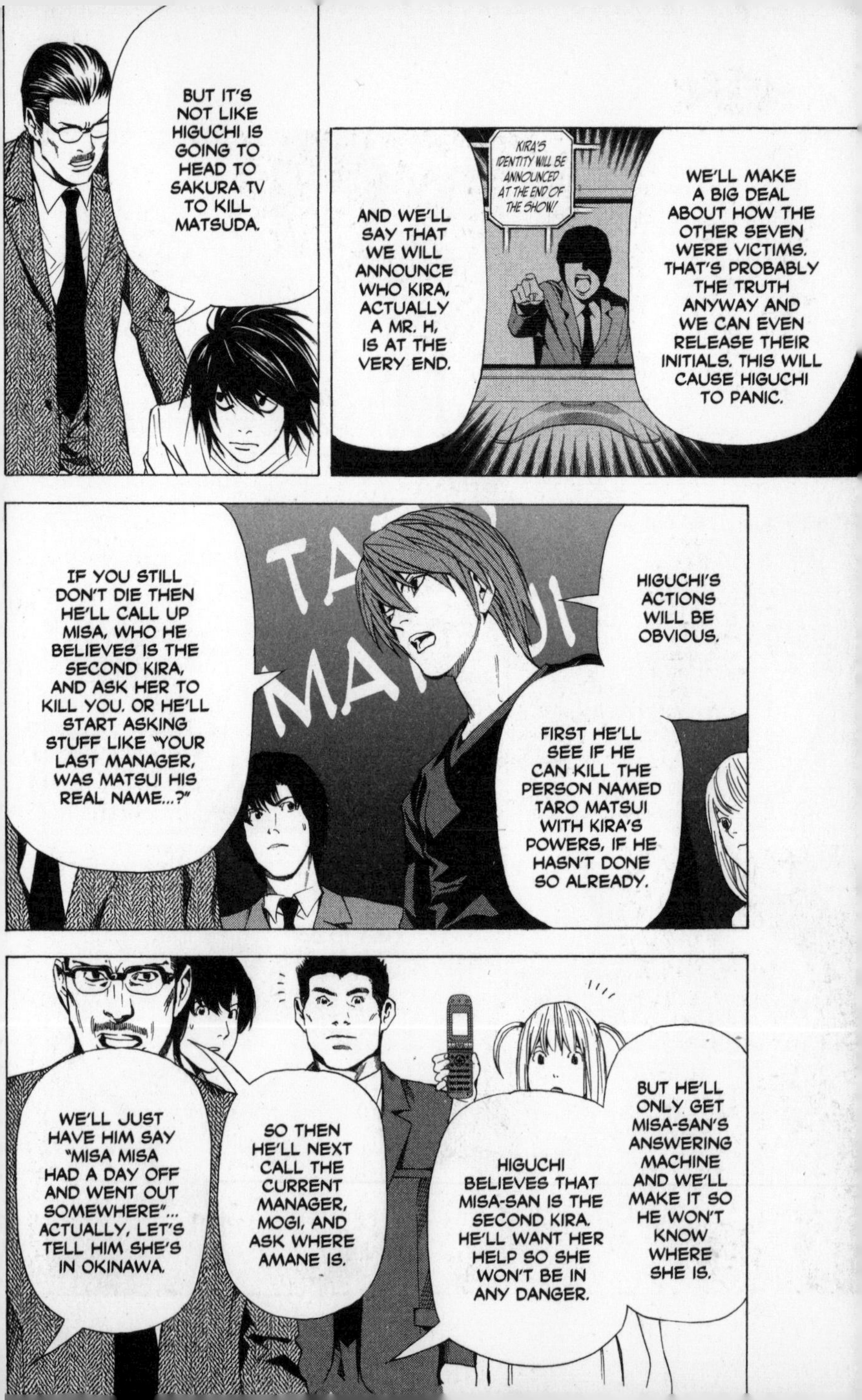
WE'LL MAKE A BIG DEAL ABOUT HOW THE OTHER SEVEN WERE VICTIMS. THAT'S PROBABLY THE TRUTH ANYWAY AND WE CAN EVEN RELEASE THEIR INITIALS. THIS WILL CAUSE HIGUCHI TO PANIC.
KIRA'S IDENTITY WILL BE ANNOUNCED AT THE END OF THE SHOW!
AND WE'LL SAY THAT WE WILL ANNOUNCE WHO KIRA, ACTUALLY A MR. H, IS AT THE VERY END.
BUT IT'S NOT LIKE HIGUCHI IS GOING TO HEAD TO SAKURA TV TO KILL MATSUDA.
HIGUCHI'S ACTIONS WILL BE OBVIOUS.
FIRST HE'LL SEE IF HE CAN KILL THE PERSON NAMED TARO MATSUI WITH KIRA'S POWERS, IF HE HASN'T DONE SO ALREADY.
IF YOU STILL DON'T DIE THEN HE'LL CALL UP MISA, WHO HE BELIEVES IS THE SECOND KIRA, AND ASK HER TO KILL YOU. OR HE'LL START ASKING STUFF LIKE "YOUR LAST MANAGER, WAS MATSUI HIS REAL NAME...?"
BUT HE'LL ONLY GET MISA-SAN'S ANSWERING MACHINE AND WE'LL MAKE IT SO HE WON'T KNOW WHERE SHE IS.
HIGUCHI BELIEVES THAT MISA-SAN IS THE SECOND KIRA. HE'LL WANT HER HELP SO SHE WON'T BE IN ANY DANGER.
SO THEN HE'LL NEXT CALL THE CURRENT MANAGER, MOGI, AND ASK WHERE AMANE IS.
WE'LL JUST HAVE HIM SAY "MISA MISA HAD A DAY OFF AND WENT OUT SOMEWHERE"... ACTUALLY, LET'S TELL HIM SHE'S IN OKINAWA.

READ THIS WAY

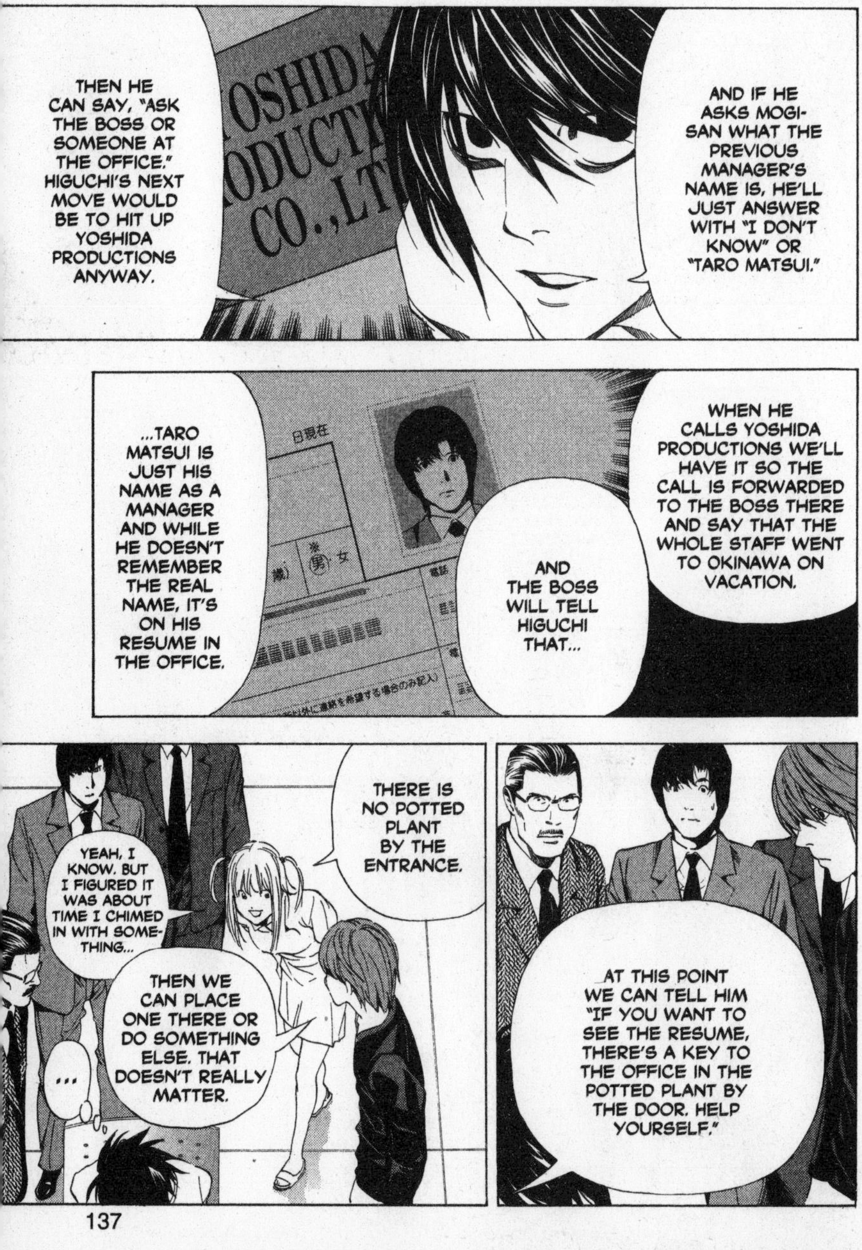

AND IF HE ASKS MOGI-SAN WHAT THE PREVIOUS MANAGER'S NAME IS, HE'LL JUST ANSWER WITH "I DON'T KNOW" OR "TARO MATSUI."
THEN HE CAN SAY, "ASK THE BOSS OR SOMEONE AT THE OFFICE." HIGUCHI'S NEXT MOVE WOULD BE TO HIT UP YOSHIDA PRODUCTIONS ANYWAY.
YOSHIDA PRODUCTI CO.,LT
WHEN HE CALLS YOSHIDA PRODUCTIONS WE'LL HAVE IT SO THE CALL IS FORWARDED TO THE BOSS THERE AND SAY THAT THE WHOLE STAFF WENT TO OKINAWA ON VACATION.
AND THE BOSS WILL TELL HIGUCHI THAT...
...TARO MATSUI IS JUST HIS NAME AS A MANAGER AND WHILE HE DOESN'T REMEMBER THE REAL NAME, IT'S ON HIS RESUME IN THE OFFICE.
...AT THIS POINT WE CAN TELL HIM "IF YOU WANT TO SEE THE RESUME, THERE'S A KEY TO THE OFFICE IN THE POTTED PLANT BY THE DOOR. HELP YOURSELF."
THERE IS NO POTTED PLANT BY THE ENTRANCE.
YEAH, I KNOW. BUT I FIGURED IT WAS ABOUT TIME I CHIMED IN WITH SOMETHING...
THEN WE CAN PLACE ONE THERE OR DO SOMETHING ELSE. THAT DOESN'T REALLY MATTER.
...

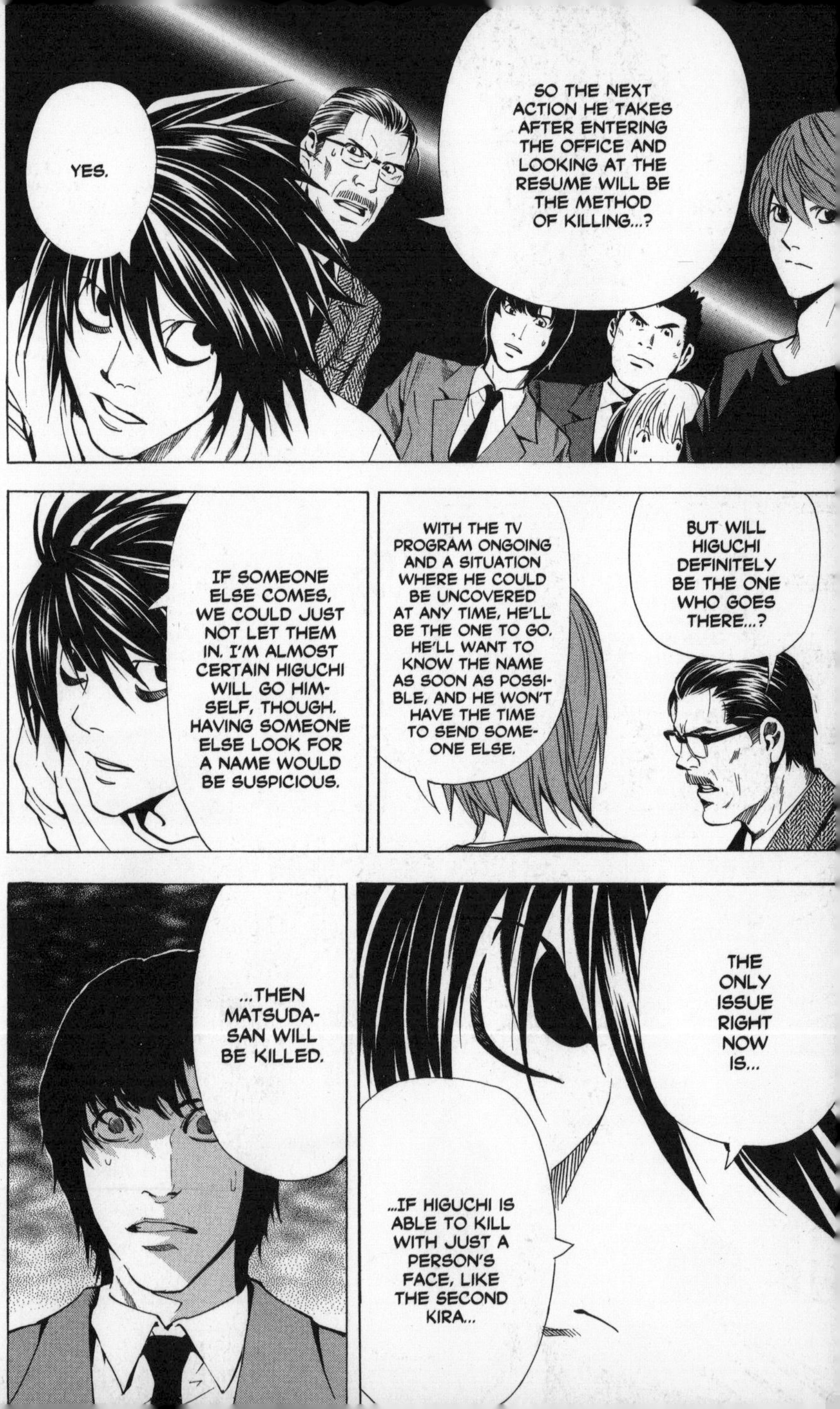
SO THE NEXT ACTION HE TAKES AFTER ENTERING THE OFFICE AND LOOKING AT THE RESUME WILL BE THE METHOD OF KILLING...?
YES.
BUT WILL HIGUCHI DEFINITELY BE THE ONE WHO GOES THERE...?
WITH THE TV PROGRAM ONGOING AND A SITUATION WHERE HE COULD BE UNCOVERED AT ANY TIME, HE'LL BE THE ONE TO GO. HE'LL WANT TO KNOW THE NAME AS SOON AS POSSIBLE, AND HE WON'T HAVE THE TIME TO SEND SOMEONE ELSE.
IF SOMEONE ELSE COMES, WE COULD JUST NOT LET THEM IN. I'M ALMOST CERTAIN HIGUCHI WILL GO HIMSELF, THOUGH. HAVING SOMEONE ELSE LOOK FOR A NAME WOULD BE SUSPICIOUS.
THE ONLY ISSUE RIGHT NOW IS...
...IF HIGUCHI IS ABLE TO KILL WITH JUST A PERSON'S FACE, LIKE THE SECOND KIRA...
...THEN MATSUDA-SAN WILL BE KILLED.

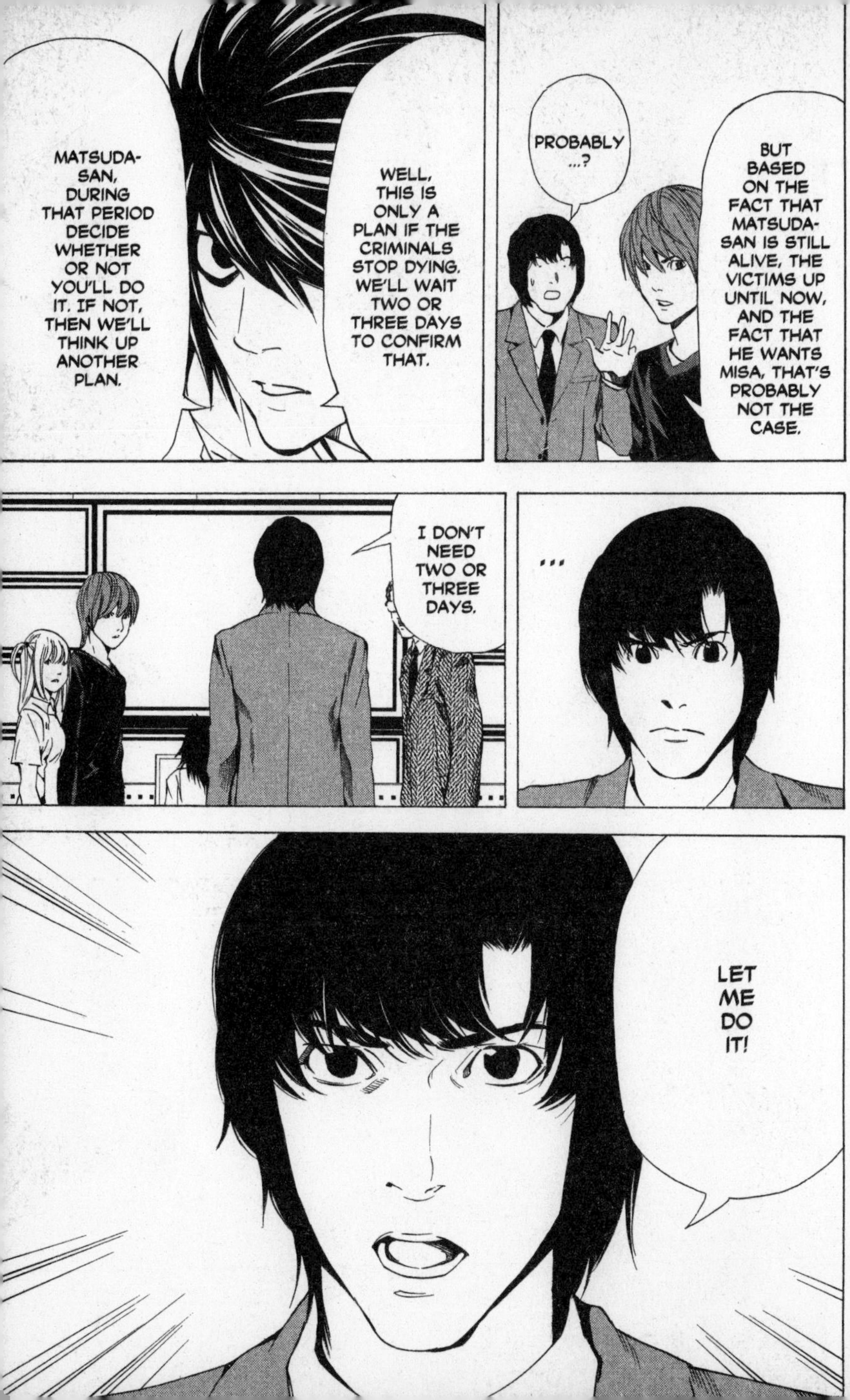
PROBABLY ...?
BUT BASED ON THE FACT THAT MATSUDA-SAN IS STILL ALIVE, THE VICTIMS UP UNTIL NOW, AND THE FACT THAT HE WANTS MISA, THAT'S PROBABLY NOT THE CASE.
WELL, THIS IS ONLY A PLAN IF THE CRIMINALS STOP DYING. WE'LL WAIT TWO OR THREE DAYS TO CONFIRM THAT.
MATSUDA-SAN, DURING THAT PERIOD DECIDE WHETHER OR NOT YOU'LL DO IT. IF NOT, THEN WE'LL THINK UP ANOTHER PLAN.
...
I DON'T NEED TWO OR THREE DAYS.
LET ME DO IT!

DEATH NOTE
How to use it
XXXV

- If a DEATH NOTE owner accidentally misspells a name four times, that person will be free from being killed by the DEATH NOTE. However, if they intentionally misspell the name four times, the DEATH NOTE owner will die.

デスノートに名前が書き込まれ死ぬ事を避ける為に
故意に4度名前を間違えて書くと、書き込んだ人間は死ぬ。

- The person whose name was misspelled four times on purpose will not be free of death by a DEATH NOTE.

故意に4度名前を間違えて書かれた人間は、
4度間違えて書かれた事になりデスノートに名前を書き込まれても
死ななくなる事にはならない。

chapter 50 Yotsuba

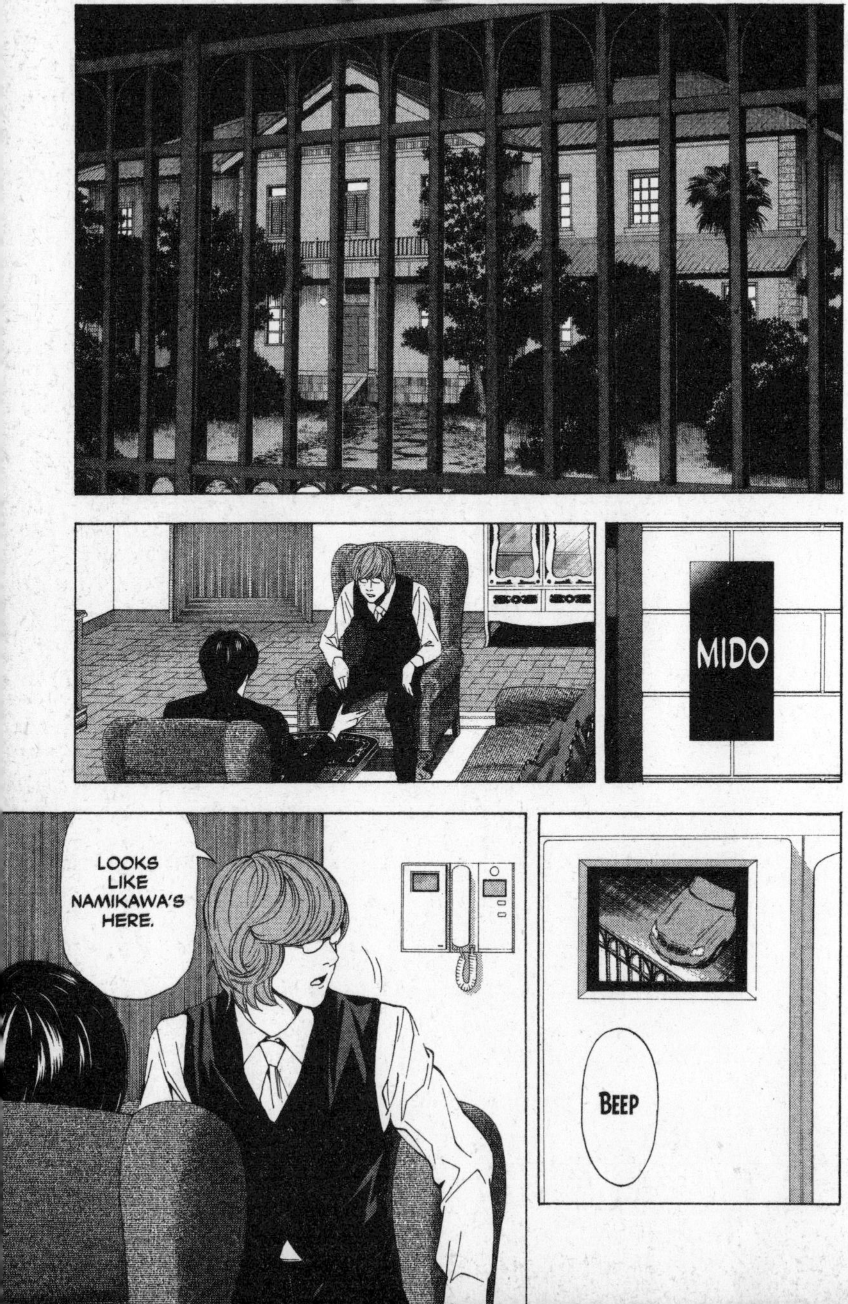
MIDO
BEEP
LOOKS LIKE NAMIKAWA'S HERE.

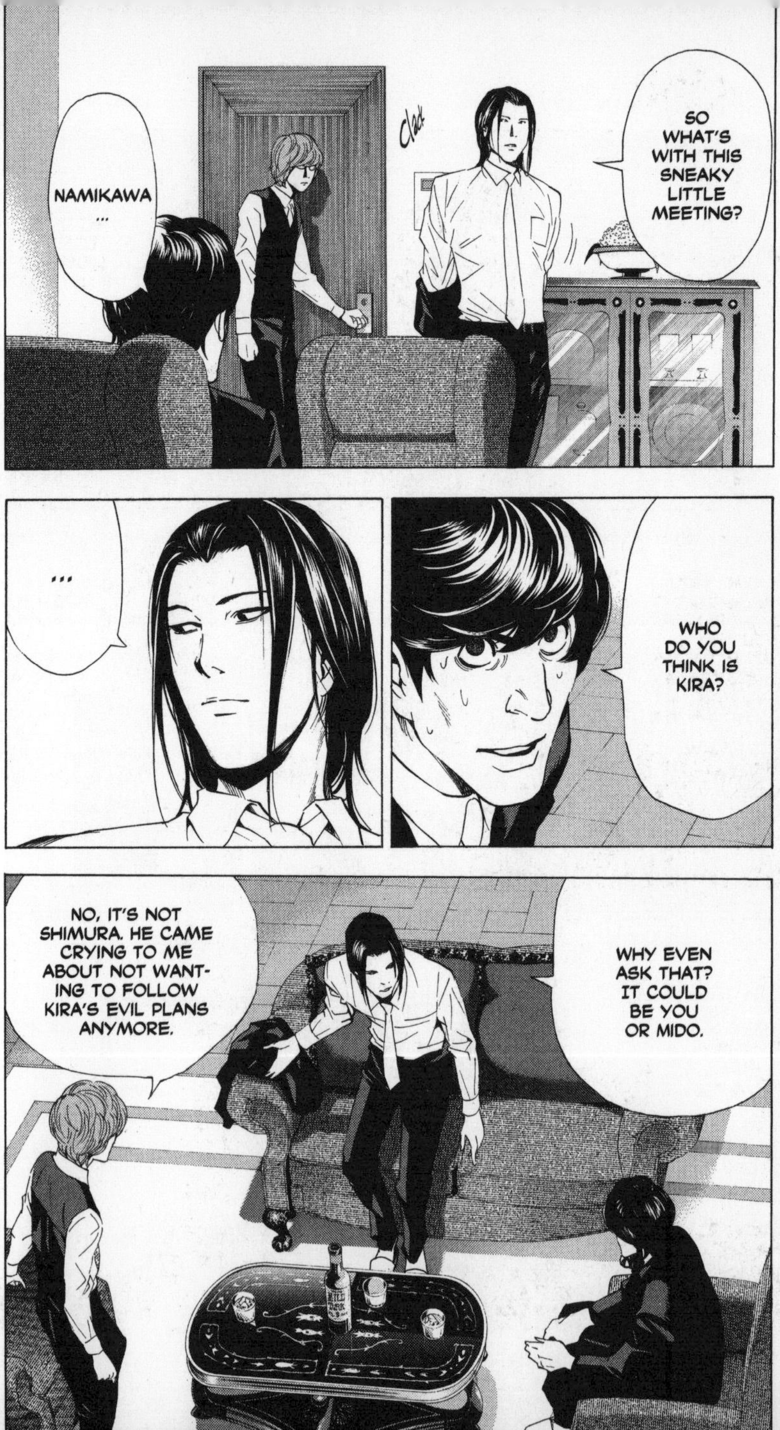
SO WHAT'S WITH THIS SNEAKY LITTLE MEETING?
Clack
NAMIKAWA ...
WHO DO YOU THINK IS KIRA?
...
WHY EVEN ASK THAT? IT COULD BE YOU OR MIDO.
NO, IT'S NOT SHIMURA. HE CAME CRYING TO ME ABOUT NOT WANTING TO FOLLOW KIRA'S EVIL PLANS ANYMORE.

READ THIS WAY

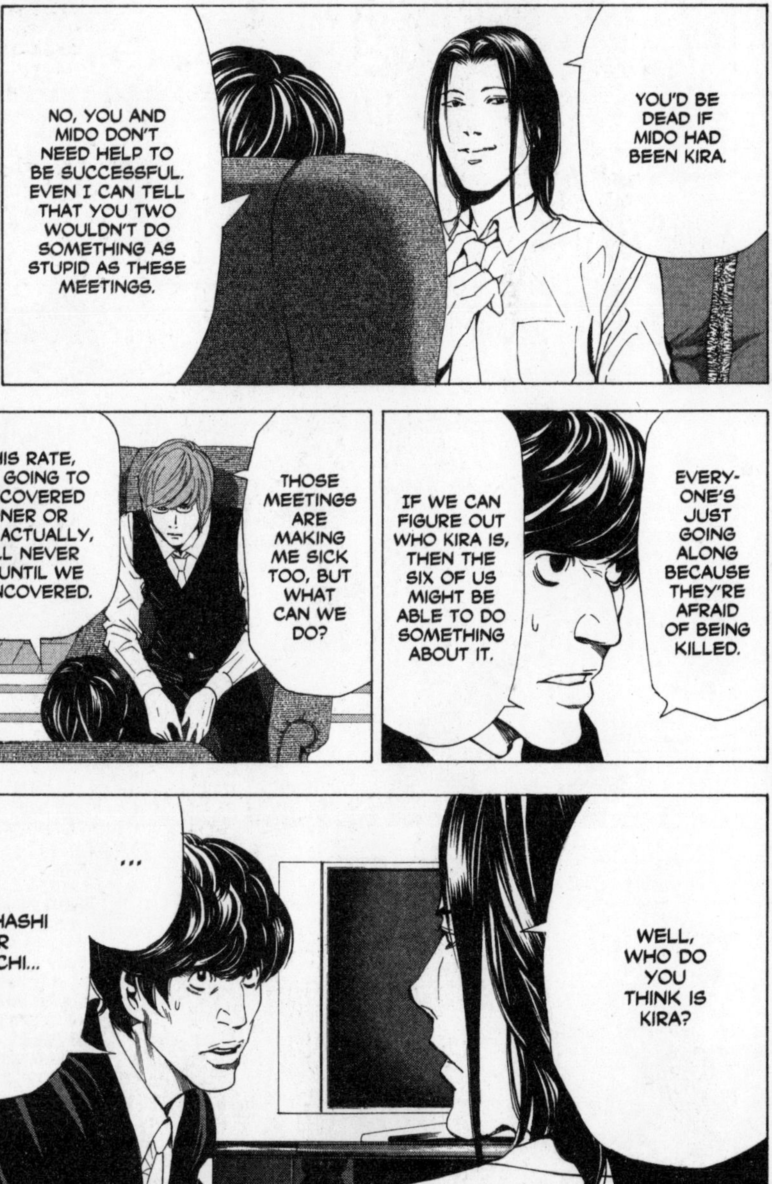

YOU'D BE DEAD IF MIDO HAD BEEN KIRA.
NO, YOU AND MIDO DON'T NEED HELP TO BE SUCCESSFUL. EVEN I CAN TELL THAT YOU TWO WOULDN'T DO SOMETHING AS STUPID AS THESE MEETINGS.
EVERY-ONE'S JUST GOING ALONG BECAUSE THEY'RE AFRAID OF BEING KILLED.
IF WE CAN FIGURE OUT WHO KIRA IS, THEN THE SIX OF US MIGHT BE ABLE TO DO SOMETHING ABOUT IT.
THOSE MEETINGS ARE MAKING ME SICK TOO, BUT WHAT CAN WE DO?
AT THIS RATE, WE'RE GOING TO BE UNCOVERED SOONER OR LATER. ACTUALLY, IT WILL NEVER STOP UNTIL WE ARE UNCOVERED.
WELL, WHO DO YOU THINK IS KIRA?
...
TAKAHASHI OR HIGUCHI...

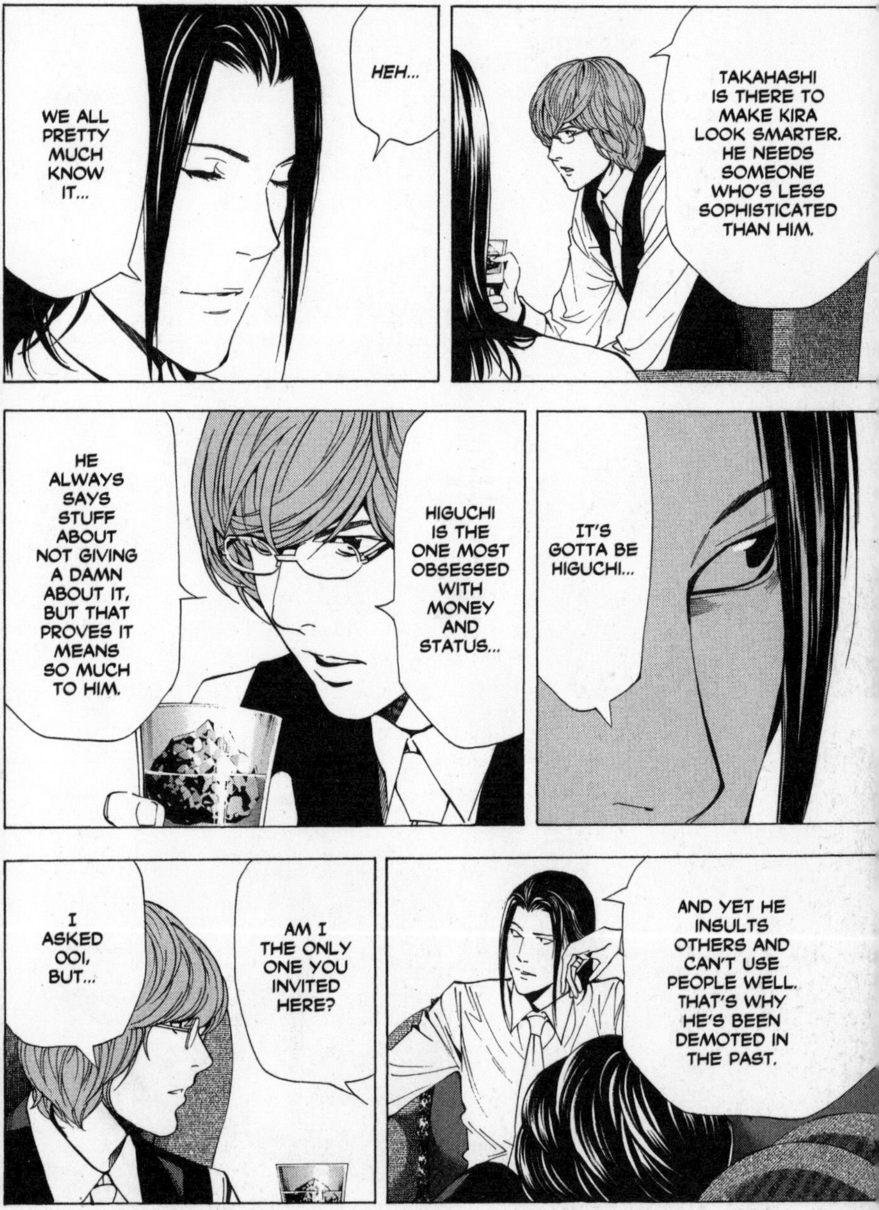
TAKAHASHI IS THERE TO MAKE KIRA LOOK SMARTER. HE NEEDS SOMEONE WHO'S LESS SOPHISTICATED THAN HIM.
HEH...
WE ALL PRETTY MUCH KNOW IT...
IT'S GOTTA BE HIGUCHI...
HIGUCHI IS THE ONE MOST OBSESSED WITH MONEY AND STATUS...
HE ALWAYS SAYS STUFF ABOUT NOT GIVING A DAMN ABOUT IT, BUT THAT PROVES IT MEANS SO MUCH TO HIM.
AND YET HE INSULTS OTHERS AND CAN'T USE PEOPLE WELL. THAT'S WHY HE'S BEEN DEMOTED IN THE PAST.
AM I THE ONLY ONE YOU INVITED HERE?
I ASKED OOI, BUT...

READ THIS WAY

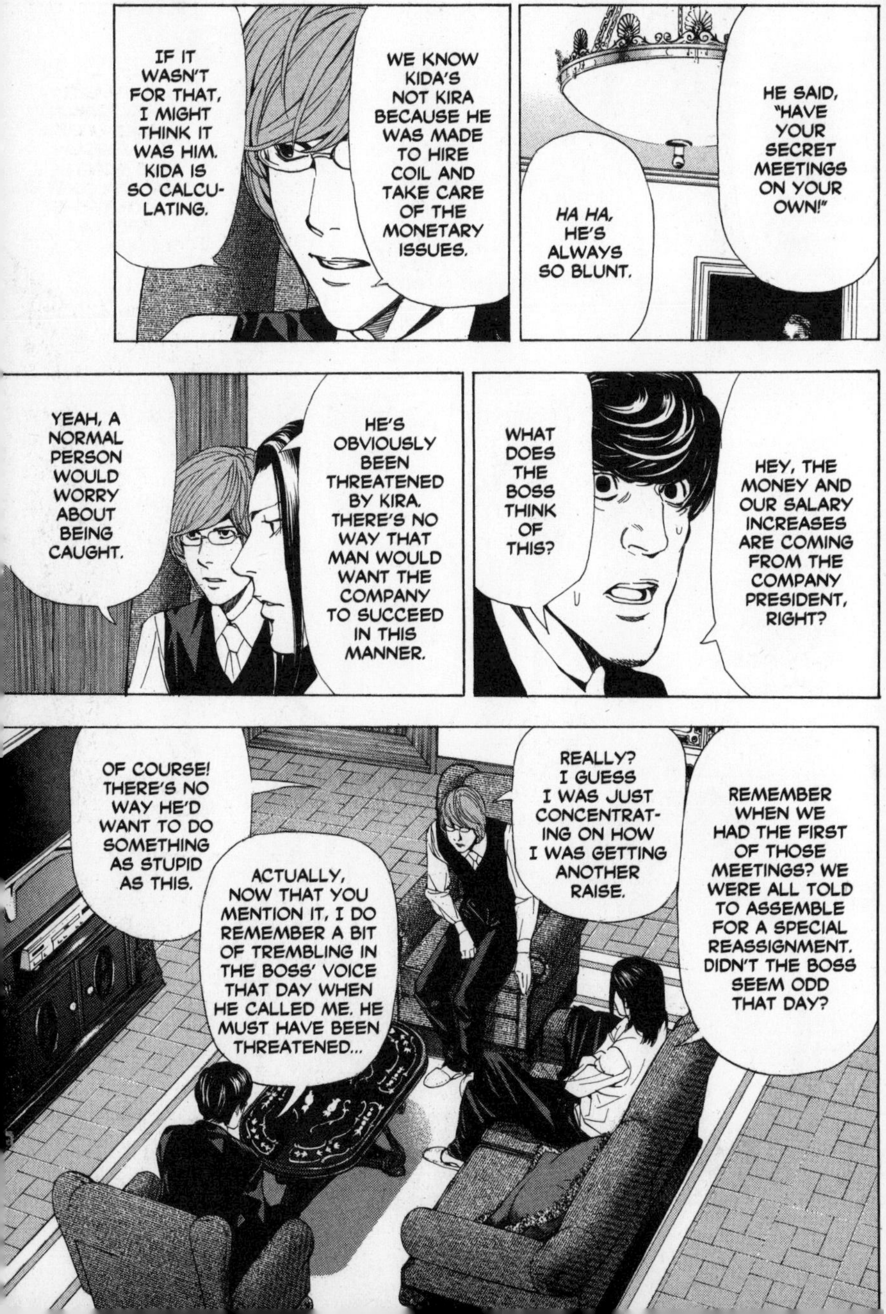
HE SAID, "HAVE YOUR SECRET MEETINGS ON YOUR OWN!"
HA HA, HE'S ALWAYS SO BLUNT.
WE KNOW KIDA'S NOT KIRA BECAUSE HE WAS MADE TO HIRE COIL AND TAKE CARE OF THE MONETARY ISSUES.
IF IT WASN'T FOR THAT, I MIGHT THINK IT WAS HIM. KIDA IS SO CALCU-LATING.
HEY, THE MONEY AND OUR SALARY INCREASES ARE COMING FROM THE COMPANY PRESIDENT, RIGHT?
WHAT DOES THE BOSS THINK OF THIS?
HE'S OBVIOUSLY BEEN THREATENED BY KIRA. THERE'S NO WAY THAT MAN WOULD WANT THE COMPANY TO SUCCEED IN THIS MANNER.
YEAH, A NORMAL PERSON WOULD WORRY ABOUT BEING CAUGHT.
REMEMBER WHEN WE HAD THE FIRST OF THOSE MEETINGS? WE WERE ALL TOLD TO ASSEMBLE FOR A SPECIAL REASSIGNMENT. DIDN'T THE BOSS SEEM ODD THAT DAY?
REALLY? I GUESS I WAS JUST CONCENTRAT-ING ON HOW I WAS GETTING ANOTHER RAISE.
ACTUALLY, NOW THAT YOU MENTION IT, I DO REMEMBER A BIT OF TREMBLING IN THE BOSS' VOICE THAT DAY WHEN HE CALLED ME. HE MUST HAVE BEEN THREATENED...
OF COURSE! THERE'S NO WAY HE'D WANT TO DO SOMETHING AS STUPID AS THIS.

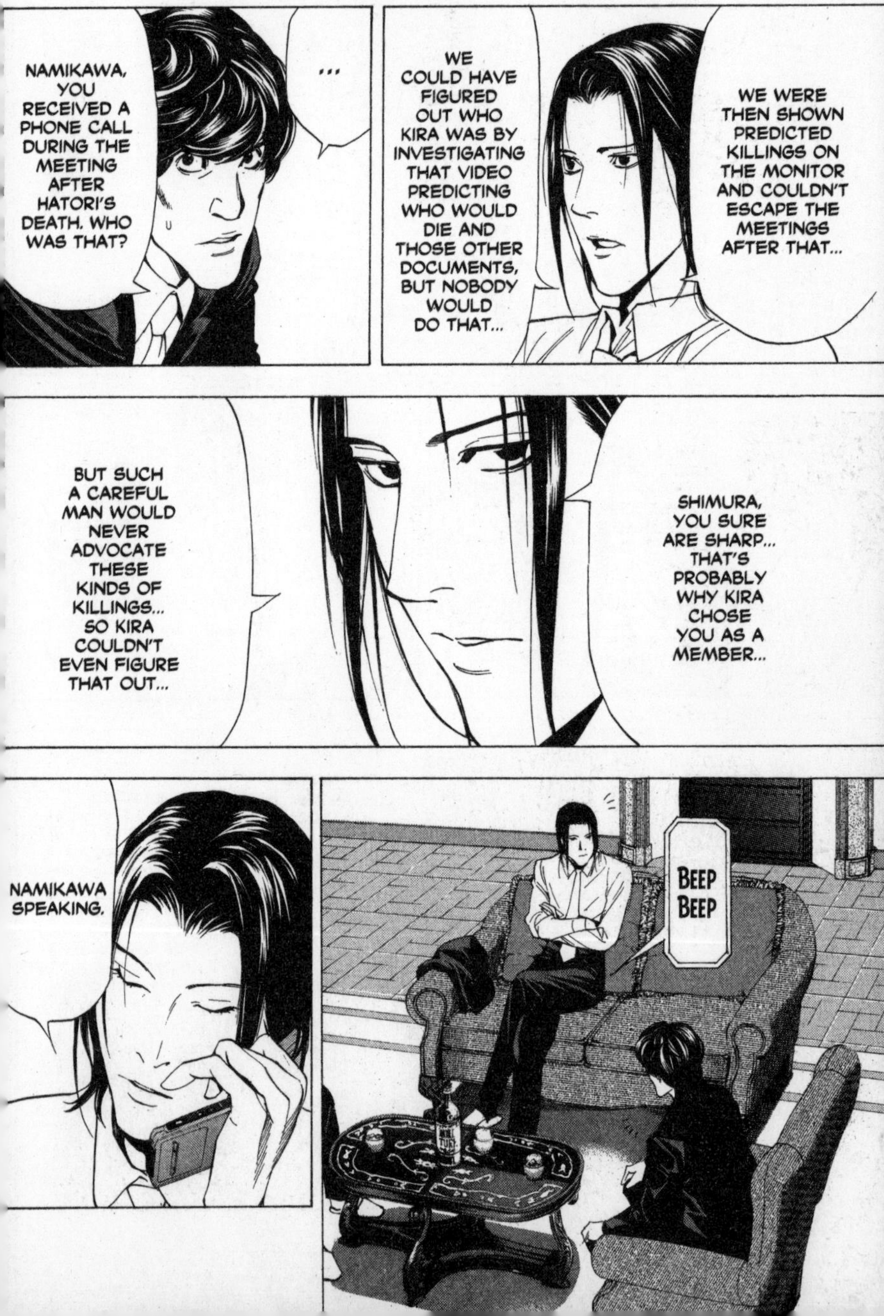
WE WERE THEN SHOWN PREDICTED KILLINGS ON THE MONITOR AND COULDN'T ESCAPE THE MEETINGS AFTER THAT...
WE COULD HAVE FIGURED OUT WHO KIRA WAS BY INVESTIGATING THAT VIDEO PREDICTING WHO WOULD DIE AND THOSE OTHER DOCUMENTS, BUT NOBODY WOULD DO THAT...
...
NAMIKAWA, YOU RECEIVED A PHONE CALL DURING THE MEETING AFTER HATORI'S DEATH. WHO WAS THAT?
SHIMURA, YOU SURE ARE SHARP... THAT'S PROBABLY WHY KIRA CHOSE YOU AS A MEMBER...
BUT SUCH A CAREFUL MAN WOULD NEVER ADVOCATE THESE KINDS OF KILLINGS... SO KIRA COULDN'T EVEN FIGURE THAT OUT...
BEEP BEEP
NAMIKAWA SPEAKING.

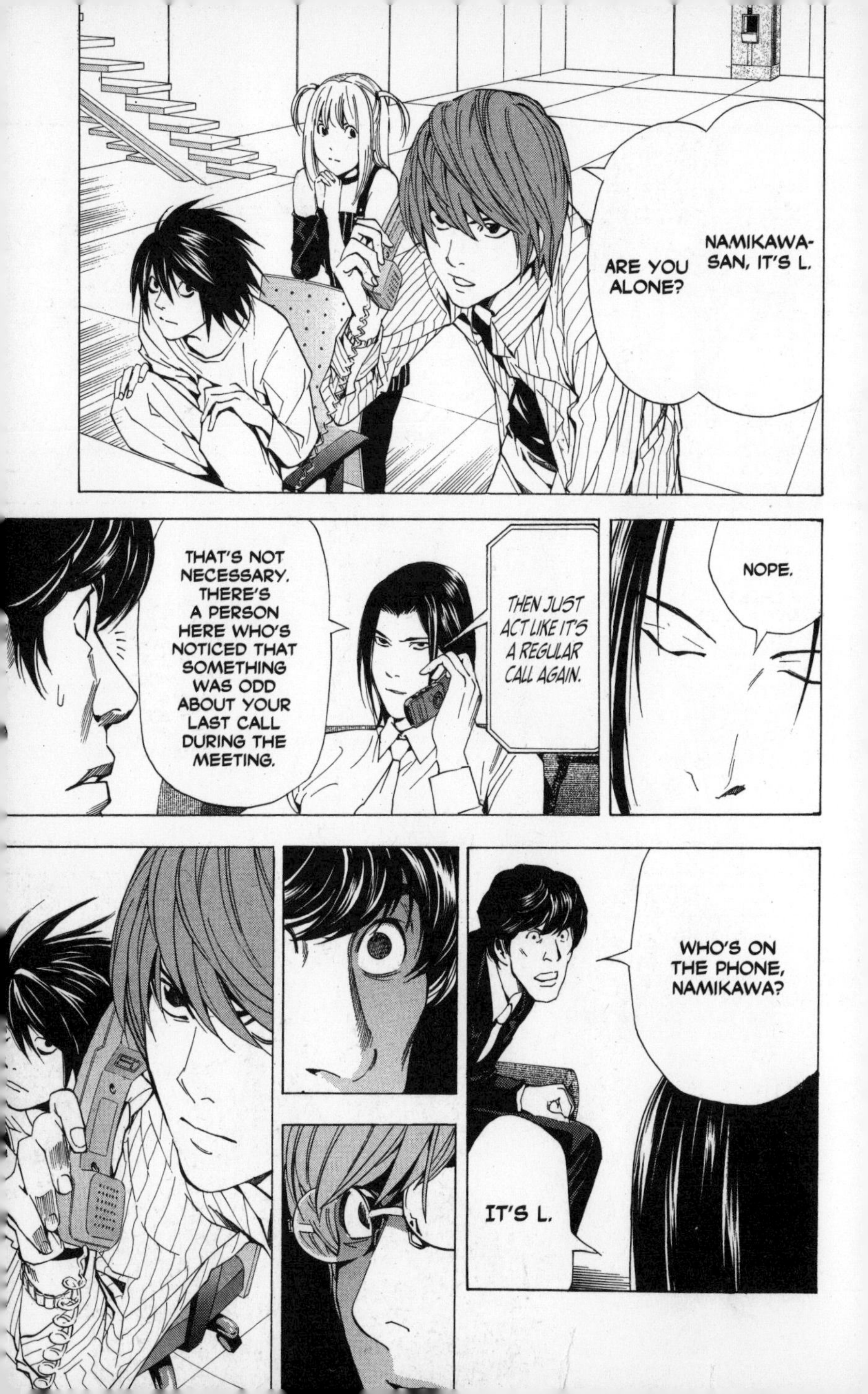
NAMIKAWA-SAN, IT'S L.
ARE YOU ALONE?
NOPE.
THEN JUST ACT LIKE IT'S A REGULAR CALL AGAIN.
THAT'S NOT NECESSARY. THERE'S A PERSON HERE WHO'S NOTICED THAT SOMETHING WAS ODD ABOUT YOUR LAST CALL DURING THE MEETING.
WHO'S ON THE PHONE, NAMIKAWA?
IT'S L.

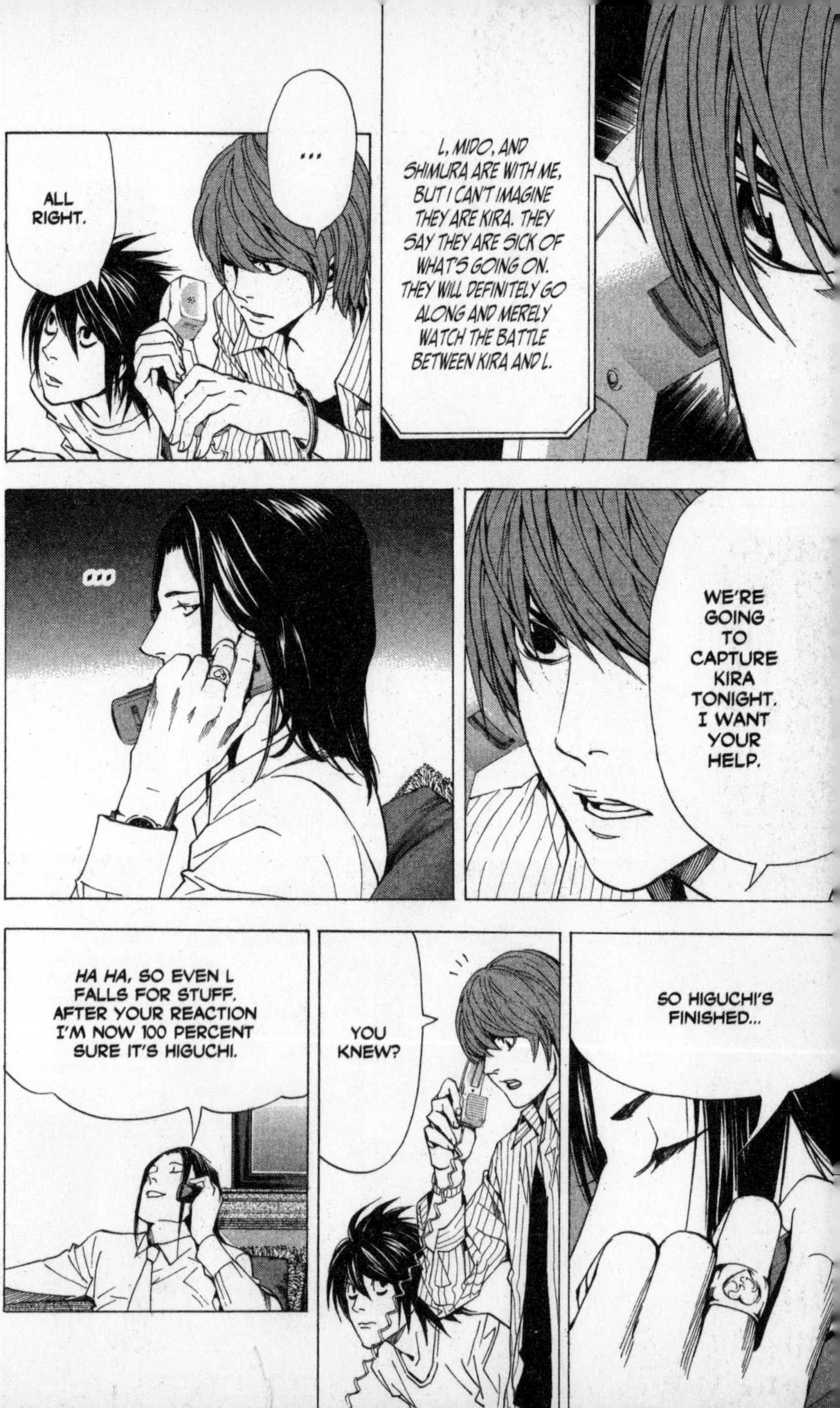
L, MIDO, AND SHIMURA ARE WITH ME, BUT I CAN'T IMAGINE THEY ARE KIRA. THEY SAY THEY ARE SICK OF WHAT'S GOING ON. THEY WILL DEFINITELY GO ALONG AND MERELY WATCH THE BATTLE BETWEEN KIRA AND L.
...
ALL RIGHT.
WE'RE GOING TO CAPTURE KIRA TONIGHT. I WANT YOUR HELP.
...
SO HIGUCHI'S FINISHED...
YOU KNEW?
HA HA, SO EVEN L FALLS FOR STUFF. AFTER YOUR REACTION I'M NOW 100 PERCENT SURE IT'S HIGUCHI.

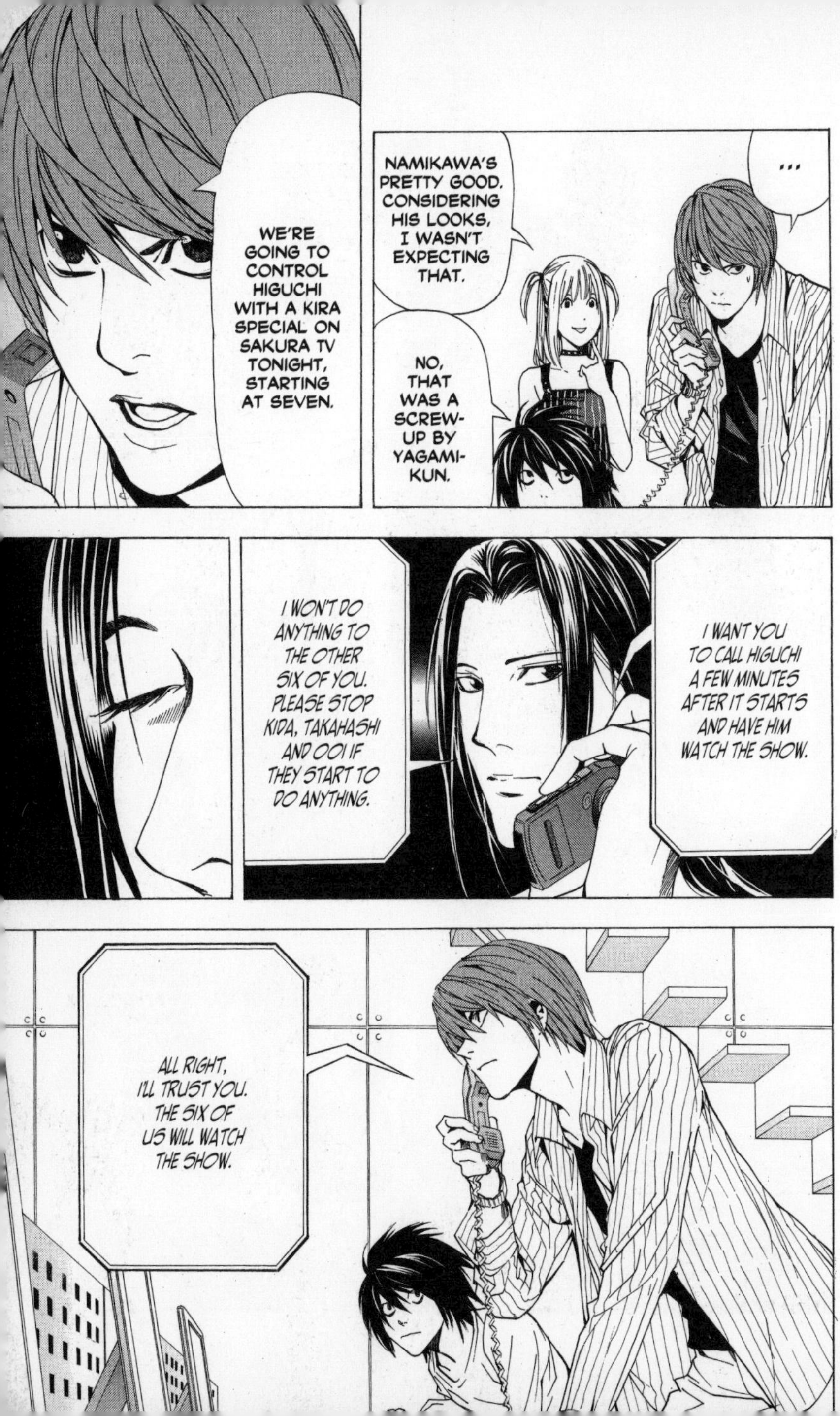
...
NAMIKAWA'S PRETTY GOOD. CONSIDERING HIS LOOKS, I WASN'T EXPECTING THAT.
NO, THAT WAS A SCREW-UP BY YAGAMI-KUN.
WE'RE GOING TO CONTROL HIGUCHI WITH A KIRA SPECIAL ON SAKURA TV TONIGHT, STARTING AT SEVEN.
I WANT YOU TO CALL HIGUCHI A FEW MINUTES AFTER IT STARTS AND HAVE HIM WATCH THE SHOW.
I WON'T DO ANYTHING TO THE OTHER SIX OF YOU. PLEASE STOP KIDA, TAKAHASHI AND OOI IF THEY START TO DO ANYTHING.
ALL RIGHT, I'LL TRUST YOU. THE SIX OF US WILL WATCH THE SHOW.

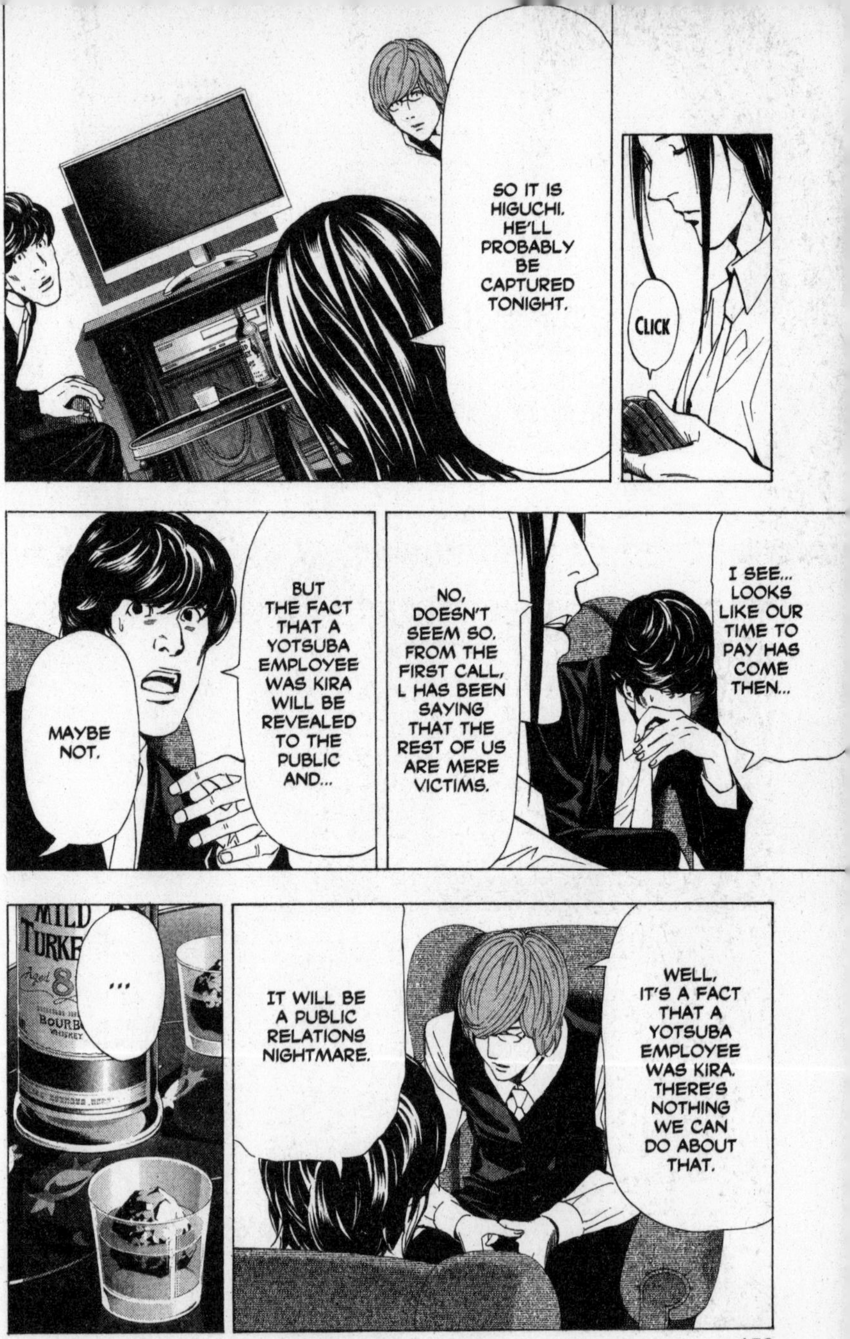
CLICK
SO IT IS HIGUCHI. HE'LL PROBABLY BE CAPTURED TONIGHT.
I SEE... LOOKS LIKE OUR TIME TO PAY HAS COME THEN...
NO, DOESN'T SEEM SO. FROM THE FIRST CALL, L HAS BEEN SAYING THAT THE REST OF US ARE MERE VICTIMS.
BUT THE FACT THAT A YOTSUBA EMPLOYEE WAS KIRA WILL BE REVEALED TO THE PUBLIC AND...
MAYBE NOT.
WELL, IT'S A FACT THAT A YOTSUBA EMPLOYEE WAS KIRA. THERE'S NOTHING WE CAN DO ABOUT THAT.
IT WILL BE A PUBLIC RELATIONS NIGHTMARE.
...

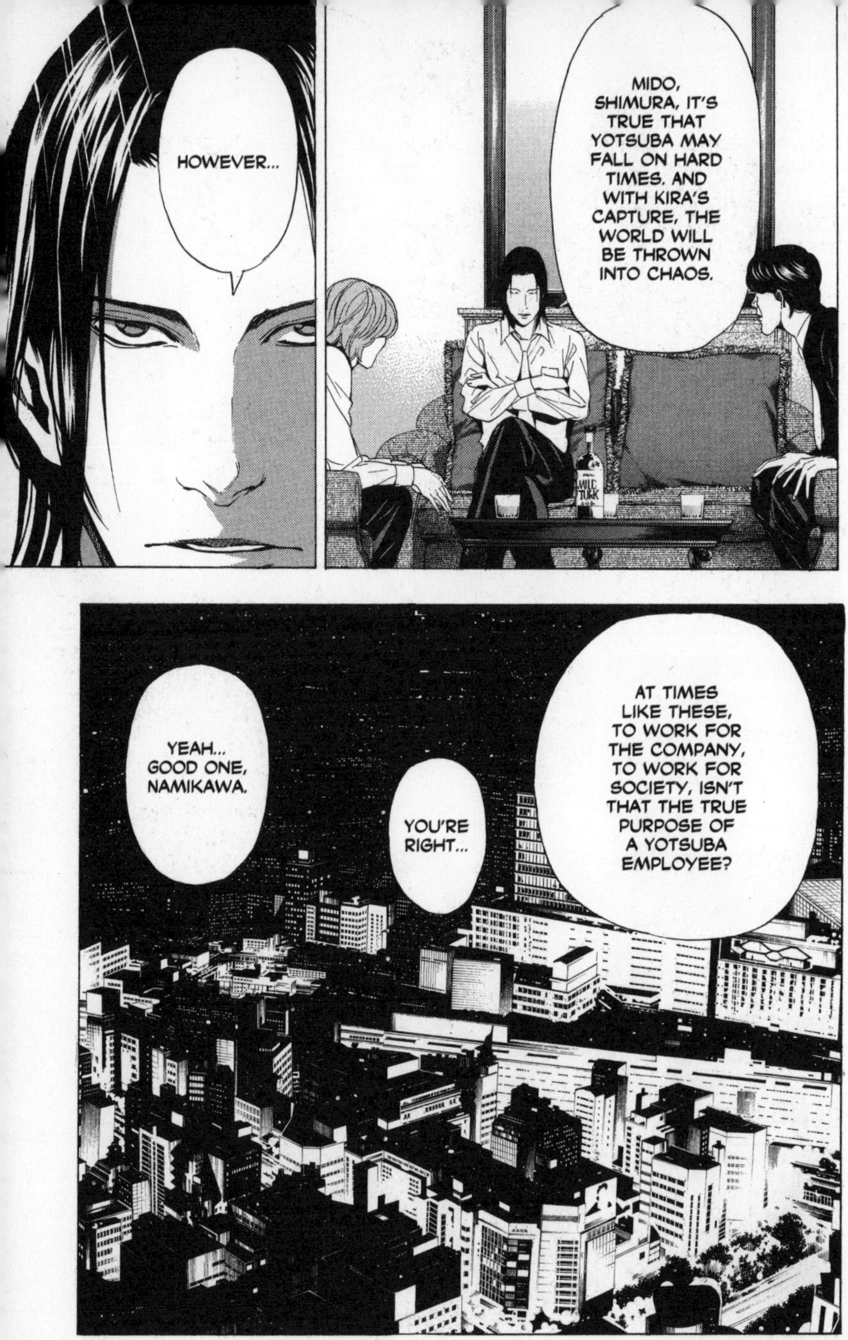
MIDO, SHIMURA, IT'S TRUE THAT YOTSUBA MAY FALL ON HARD TIMES. AND WITH KIRA'S CAPTURE, THE WORLD WILL BE THROWN INTO CHAOS.
WILD TURK
HOWEVER...
AT TIMES LIKE THESE, TO WORK FOR THE COMPANY, TO WORK FOR SOCIETY, ISN'T THAT THE TRUE PURPOSE OF A YOTSUBA EMPLOYEE?
YOU'RE RIGHT...
YEAH... GOOD ONE, NAMIKAWA.

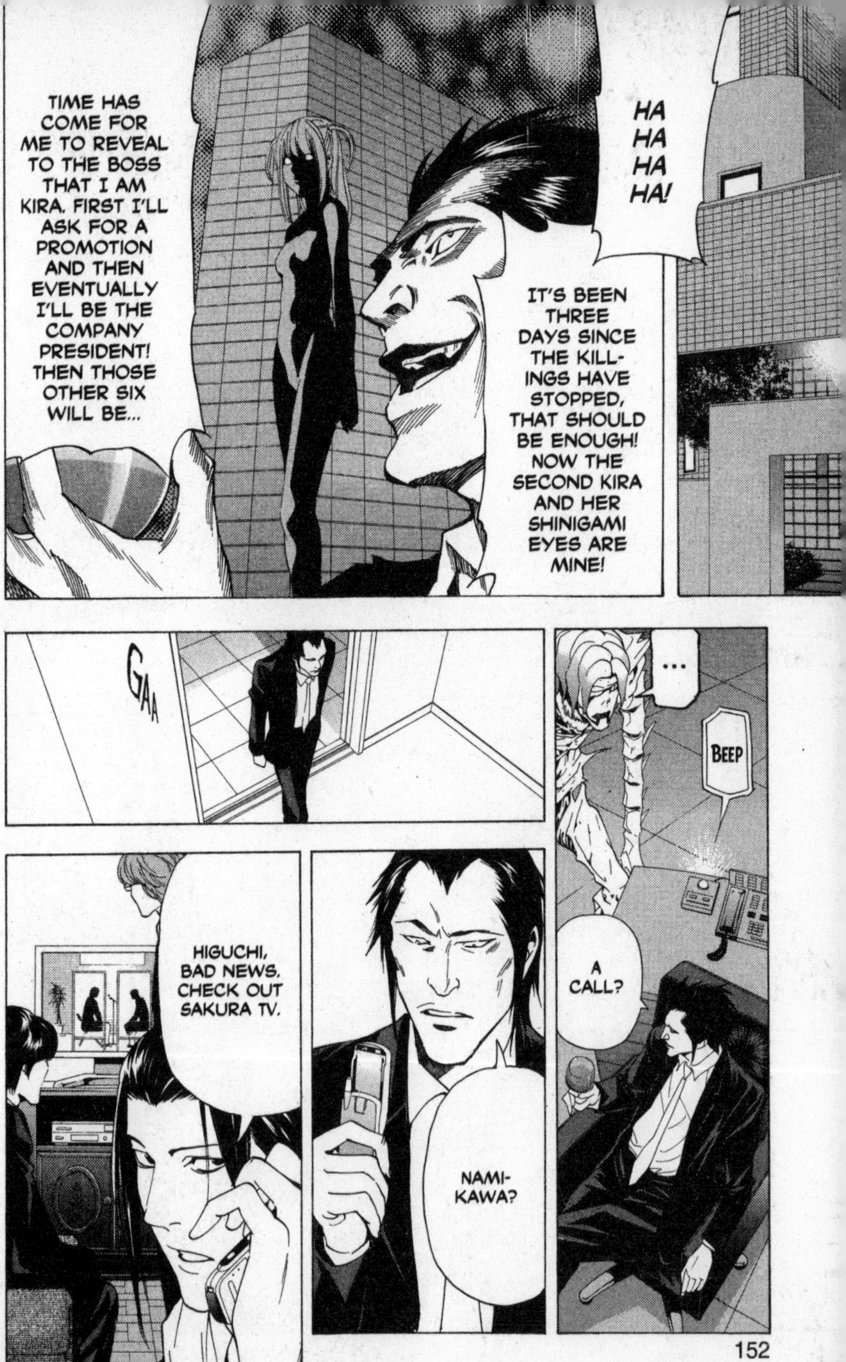
HA HA HA HA!
IT'S BEEN THREE DAYS SINCE THE KILL-INGS HAVE STOPPED, THAT SHOULD BE ENOUGH! NOW THE SECOND KIRA AND HER SHINIGAMI EYES ARE MINE!
TIME HAS COME FOR ME TO REVEAL TO THE BOSS THAT I AM KIRA. FIRST I'LL ASK FOR A PROMOTION AND THEN EVENTUALLY I'LL BE THE COMPANY PRESIDENT! THEN THOSE OTHER SIX WILL BE...
...
BEEP
A CALL?
GAA
NAMI-KAWA?
HIGUCHI, BAD NEWS. CHECK OUT SAKURA TV.

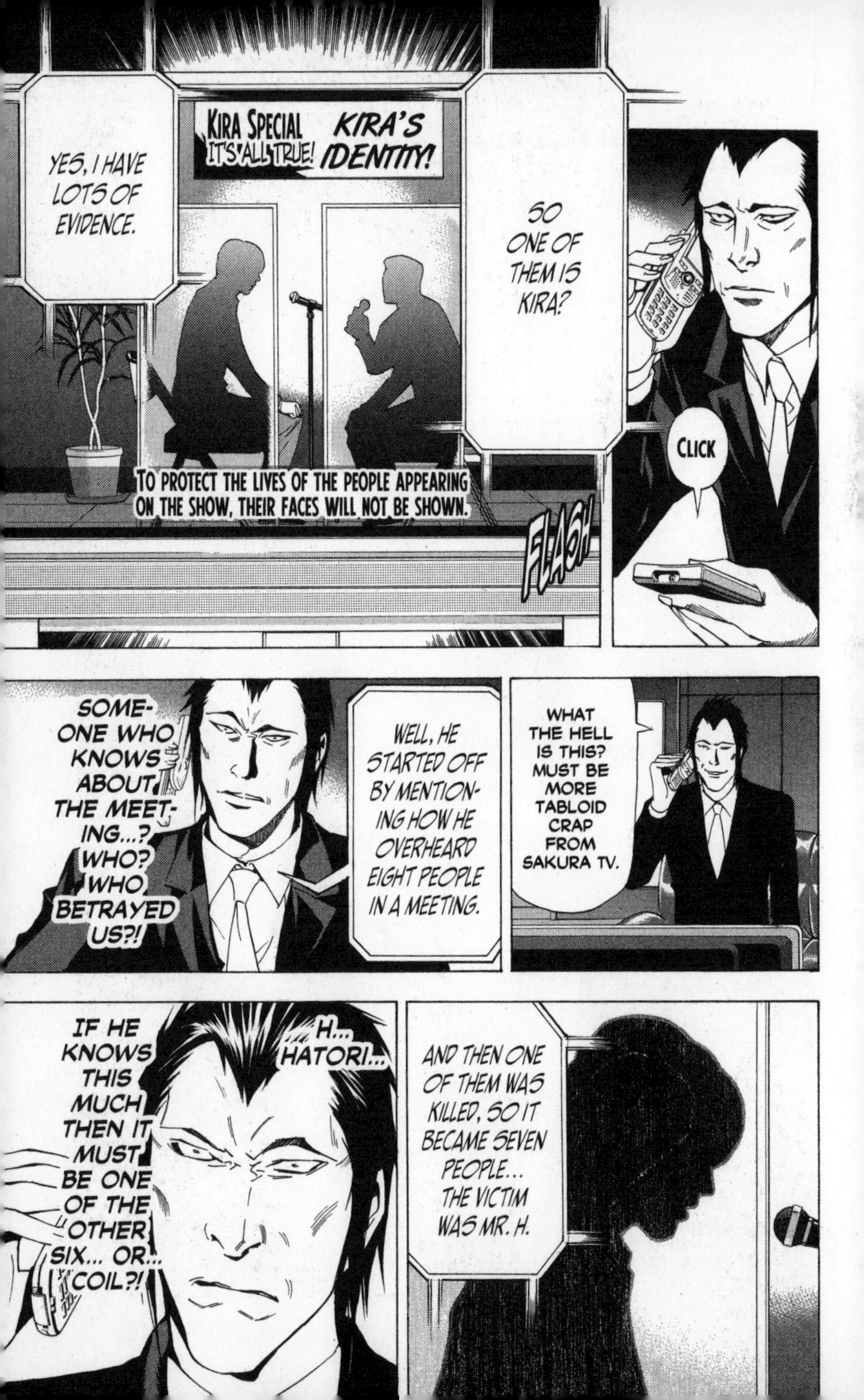
CLICK
SO ONE OF THEM IS KIRA?
KIRA SPECIAL IT'S ALL TRUE! KIRA'S IDENTITY!
YES, I HAVE LOTS OF EVIDENCE.
TO PROTECT THE LIVES OF THE PEOPLE APPEARING ON THE SHOW, THEIR FACES WILL NOT BE SHOWN.
FLASH
WHAT THE HELL IS THIS? MUST BE MORE TABLOID CRAP FROM SAKURA TV.
WELL, HE STARTED OFF BY MENTIONING HOW HE OVERHEARD EIGHT PEOPLE IN A MEETING.
SOMEONE WHO KNOWS ABOUT THE MEETING...? WHO? WHO BETRAYED US?!
AND THEN ONE OF THEM WAS KILLED, SO IT BECAME SEVEN PEOPLE... THE VICTIM WAS MR. H.
H... HATORI...
IF HE KNOWS THIS MUCH THEN IT MUST BE ONE OF THE OTHER SIX... OR... COIL?!

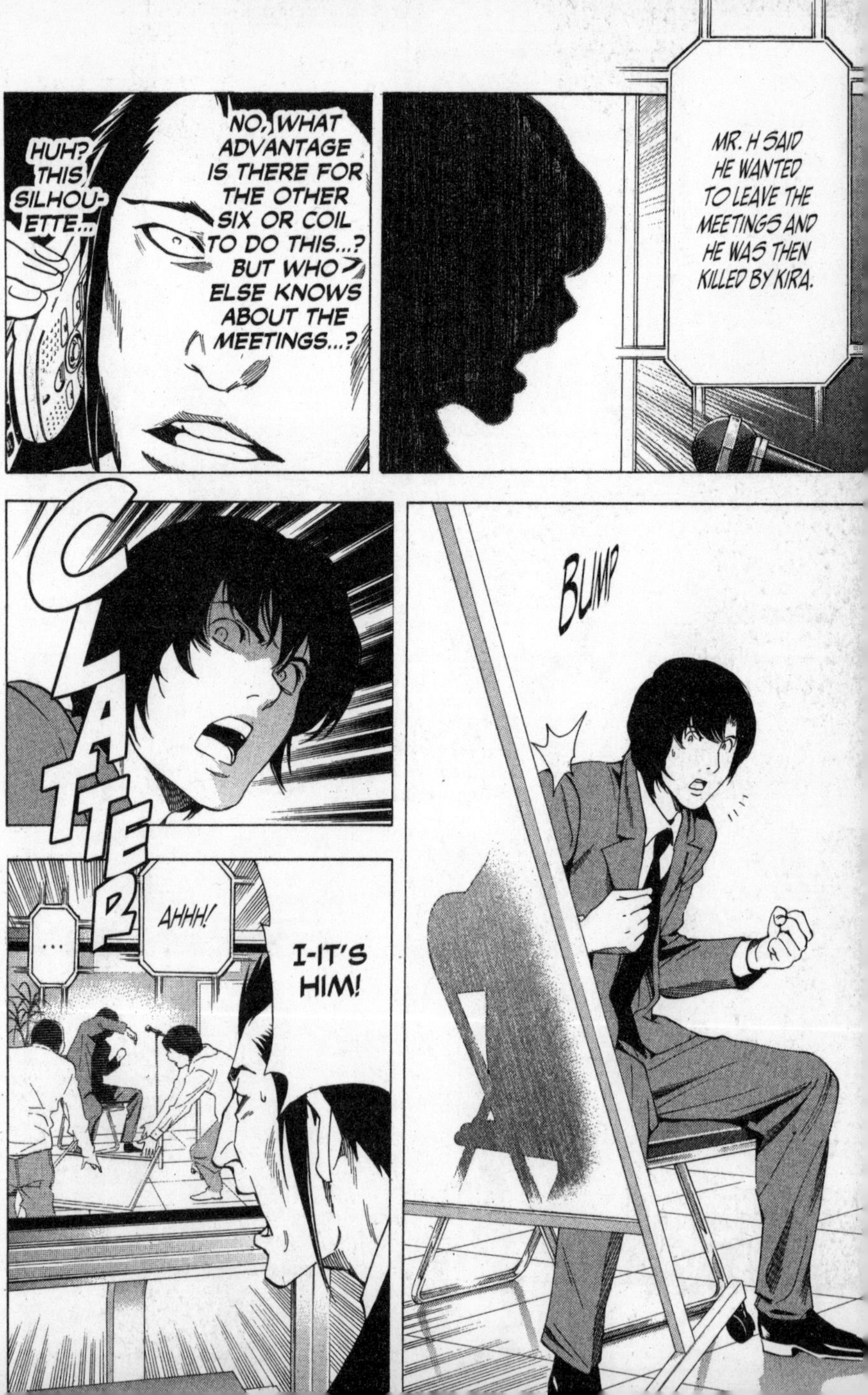
MR. H SAID HE WANTED TO LEAVE THE MEETINGS AND HE WAS THEN KILLED BY KIRA.
NO, WHAT ADVANTAGE IS THERE FOR THE OTHER SIX OR COIL TO DO THIS...? BUT WHO ELSE KNOWS ABOUT THE MEETINGS...?
HUH? THIS SILHOU-ETTE...
BUMP
CLATTER
I-IT'S HIM!
AHHH!
...

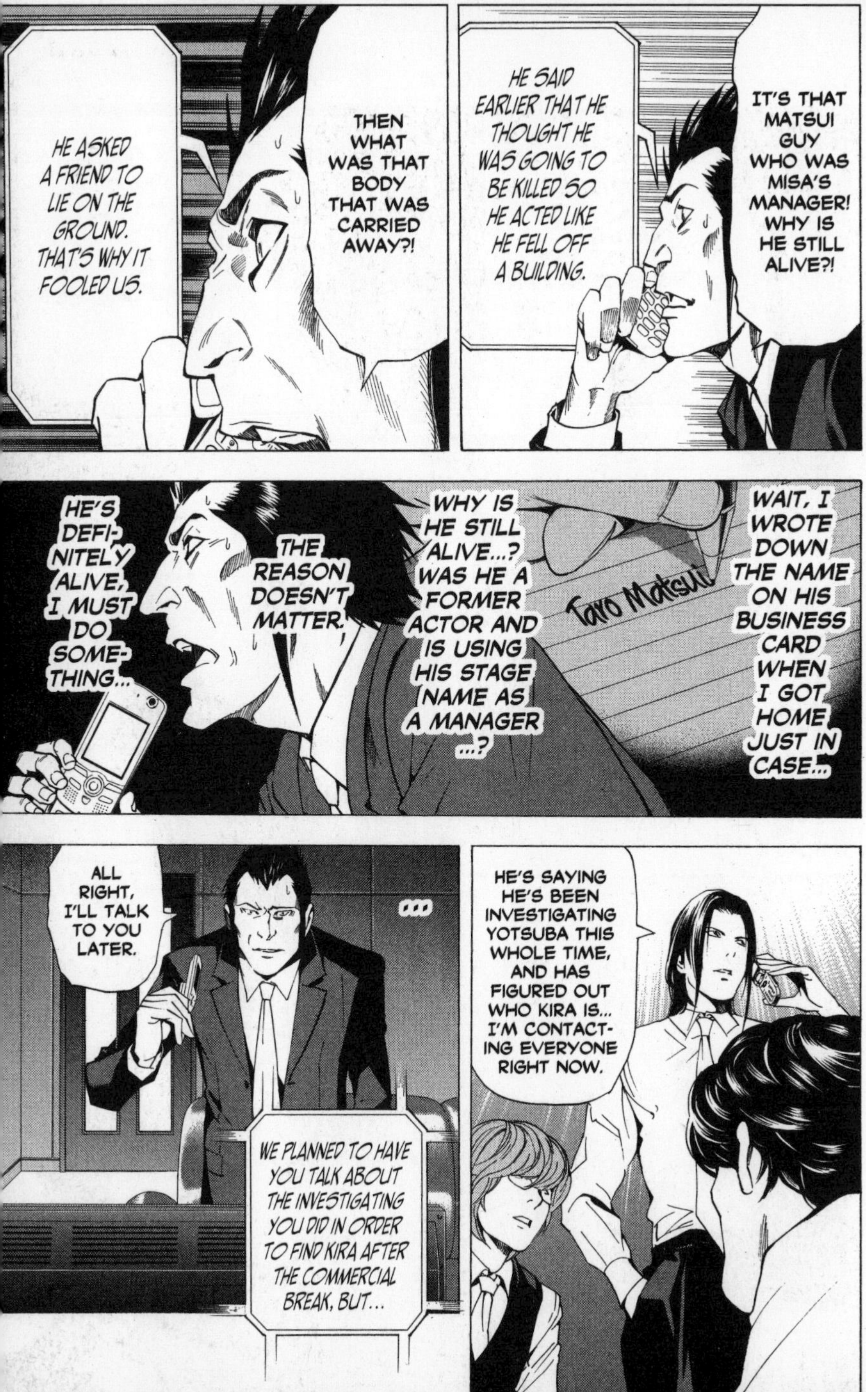
IT'S THAT MATSUI GUY WHO WAS MISA'S MANAGER! WHY IS HE STILL ALIVE?!
HE SAID EARLIER THAT HE THOUGHT HE WAS GOING TO BE KILLED SO HE ACTED LIKE HE FELL OFF A BUILDING.
THEN WHAT WAS THAT BODY THAT WAS CARRIED AWAY?!
HE ASKED A FRIEND TO LIE ON THE GROUND. THAT'S WHY IT FOOLED US.
WAIT, I WROTE DOWN THE NAME ON HIS BUSINESS CARD WHEN I GOT HOME JUST IN CASE...
Taro Matsui
WHY IS HE STILL ALIVE...? WAS HE A FORMER ACTOR AND IS USING HIS STAGE NAME AS A MANAGER ...?
THE REASON DOESN'T MATTER.
HE'S DEFINITELY ALIVE, I MUST DO SOMETHING...
HE'S SAYING HE'S BEEN INVESTIGATING YOTSUBA THIS WHOLE TIME, AND HAS FIGURED OUT WHO KIRA IS... I'M CONTACTING EVERYONE RIGHT NOW.
...
ALL RIGHT, I'LL TALK TO YOU LATER.
WE PLANNED TO HAVE YOU TALK ABOUT THE INVESTIGATING YOU DID IN ORDER TO FIND KIRA AFTER THE COMMERCIAL BREAK, BUT...

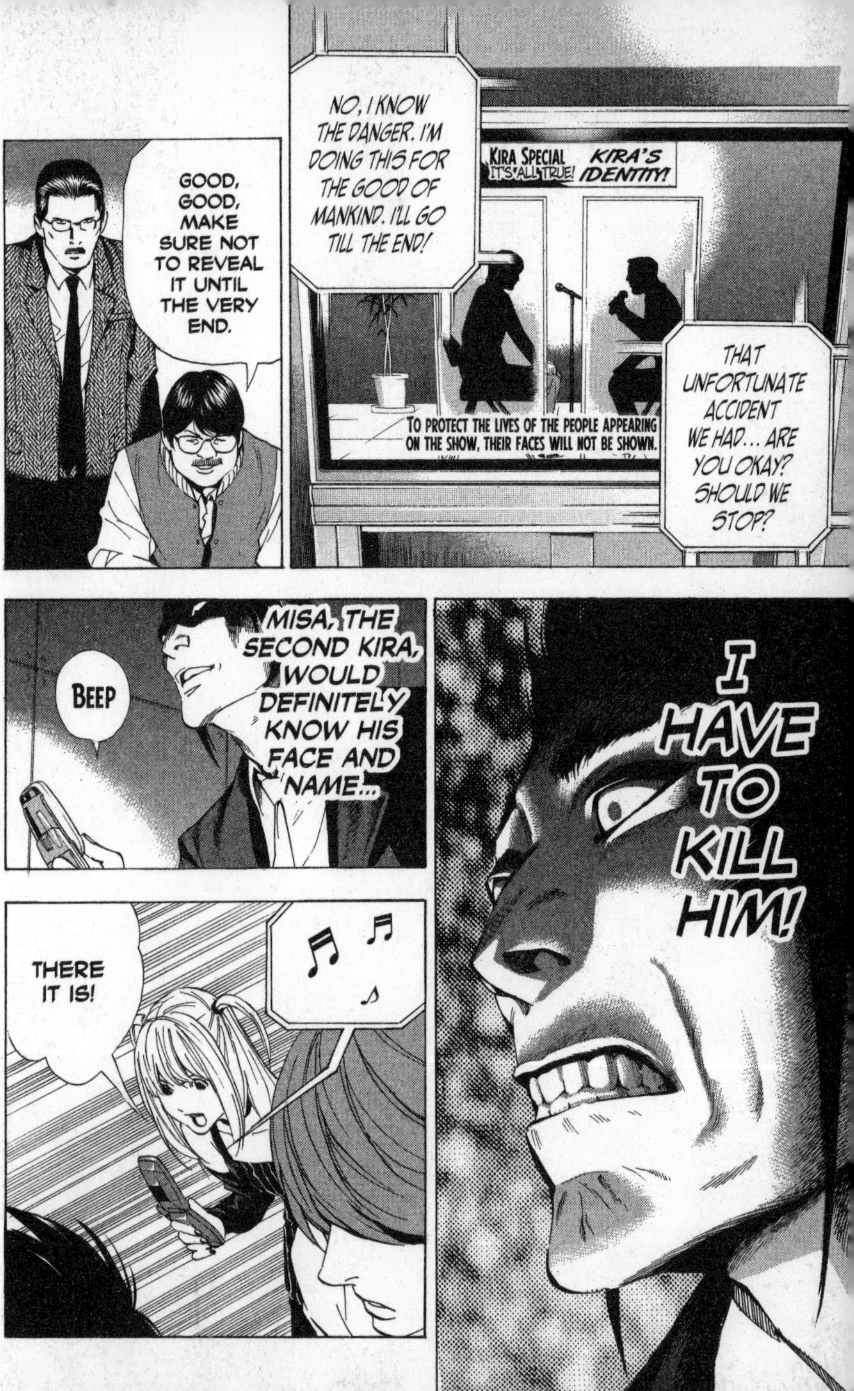
KIRA SPECIAL
IT'S ALL TRUE!
KIRA'S IDENTITY!
THAT UNFORTUNATE ACCIDENT WE HAD... ARE YOU OKAY? SHOULD WE STOP?
NO, I KNOW THE DANGER. I'M DOING THIS FOR THE GOOD OF MANKIND. I'LL GO TILL THE END!
TO PROTECT THE LIVES OF THE PEOPLE APPEARING ON THE SHOW, THEIR FACES WILL NOT BE SHOWN.
GOOD, GOOD, MAKE SURE NOT TO REVEAL IT UNTIL THE VERY END.
I HAVE TO KILL HIM!
MISA, THE SECOND KIRA, WOULD DEFINITELY KNOW HIS FACE AND NAME...
BEEP
♫ ♫ ♪
THERE IT IS!

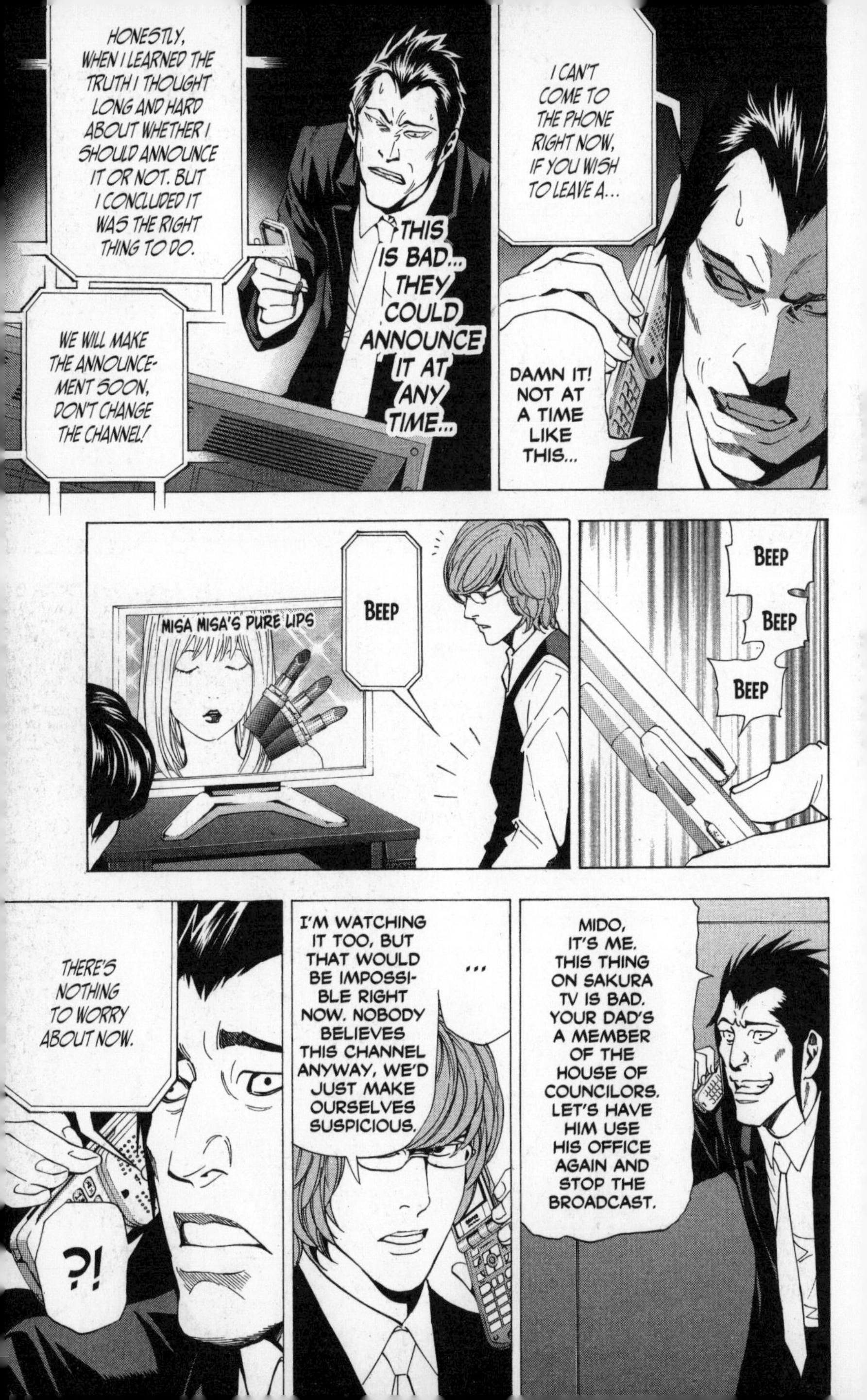
I CAN'T COME TO THE PHONE RIGHT NOW, IF YOU WISH TO LEAVE A...
DAMN IT! NOT AT A TIME LIKE THIS...
HONESTLY, WHEN I LEARNED THE TRUTH I THOUGHT LONG AND HARD ABOUT WHETHER I SHOULD ANNOUNCE IT OR NOT. BUT I CONCLUDED IT WAS THE RIGHT THING TO DO.
THIS IS BAD... THEY COULD ANNOUNCE IT AT ANY TIME...
WE WILL MAKE THE ANNOUNCE-MENT SOON, DON'T CHANGE THE CHANNEL!
BEEP
BEEP
BEEP
BEEP
MISA MISA'S PURE LIPS
MIDO, IT'S ME. THIS THING ON SAKURA TV IS BAD. YOUR DAD'S A MEMBER OF THE HOUSE OF COUNCILORS. LET'S HAVE HIM USE HIS OFFICE AGAIN AND STOP THE BROADCAST.
...
I'M WATCHING IT TOO, BUT THAT WOULD BE IMPOSSI-BLE RIGHT NOW. NOBODY BELIEVES THIS CHANNEL ANYWAY, WE'D JUST MAKE OURSELVES SUSPICIOUS.
THERE'S NOTHING TO WORRY ABOUT NOW.
?!

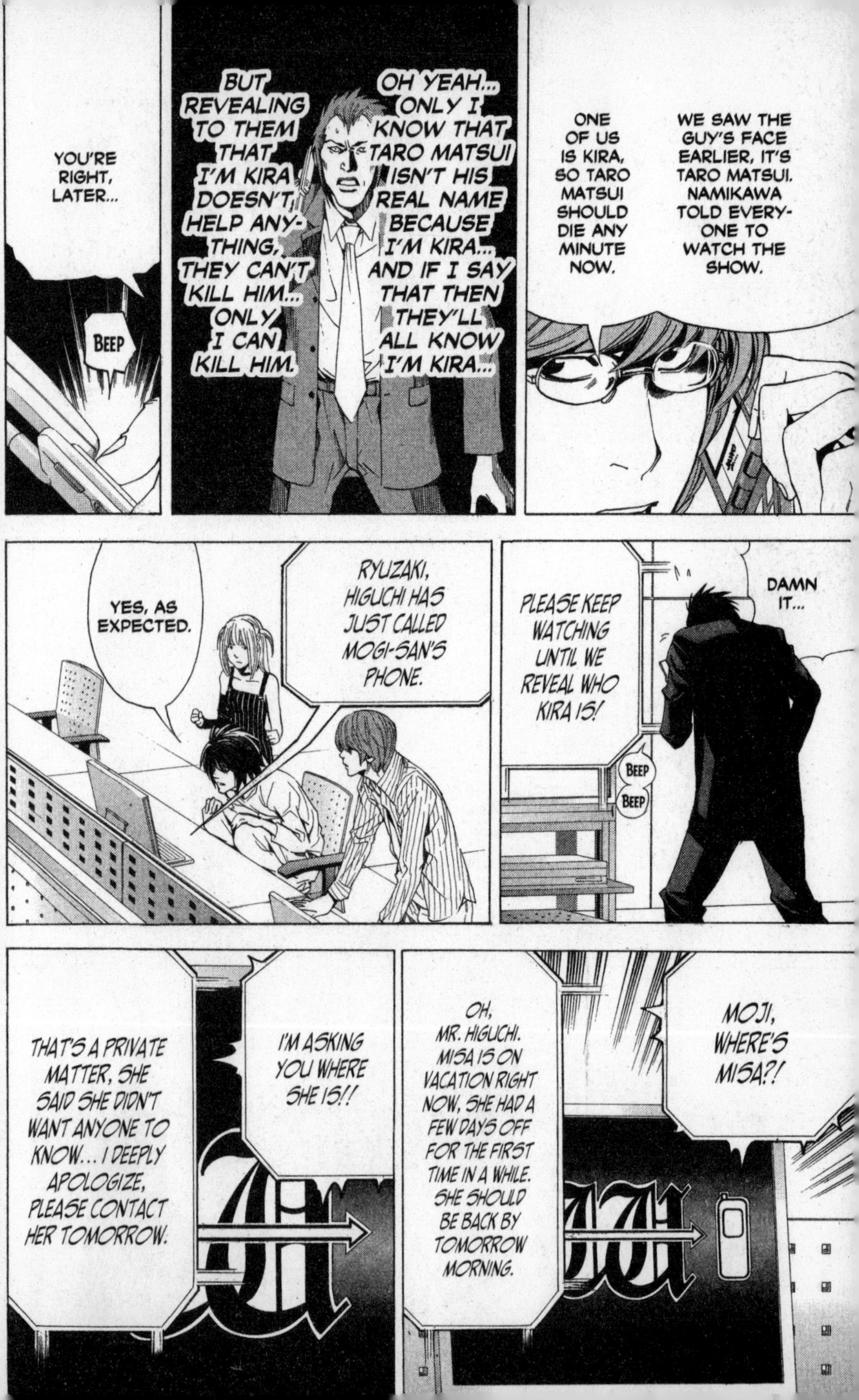
WE SAW THE GUY'S FACE EARLIER, IT'S TARO MATSUI. NAMIKAWA TOLD EVERYONE TO WATCH THE SHOW.
ONE OF US IS KIRA, SO TARO MATSUI SHOULD DIE ANY MINUTE NOW.
OH YEAH... ONLY I KNOW THAT TARO MATSUI ISN'T HIS REAL NAME BECAUSE I'M KIRA... AND IF I SAY THAT THEN THEY'LL ALL KNOW I'M KIRA...
BUT REVEALING TO THEM THAT I'M KIRA DOESN'T HELP ANYTHING, THEY CAN'T KILL HIM... ONLY I CAN KILL HIM.
YOU'RE RIGHT, LATER...
BEEP
DAMN IT...
PLEASE KEEP WATCHING UNTIL WE REVEAL WHO KIRA IS!
BEEP
BEEP
RYUZAKI, HIGUCHI HAS JUST CALLED MOGI-SAN'S PHONE.
YES, AS EXPECTED.
MOJI, WHERE'S MISA?!
OH, MR. HIGUCHI. MISA IS ON VACATION RIGHT NOW, SHE HAD A FEW DAYS OFF FOR THE FIRST TIME IN A WHILE. SHE SHOULD BE BACK BY TOMORROW MORNING.
I'M ASKING YOU WHERE SHE IS!!
THAT'S A PRIVATE MATTER, SHE SAID SHE DIDN'T WANT ANYONE TO KNOW... I DEEPLY APOLOGIZE, PLEASE CONTACT HER TOMORROW.

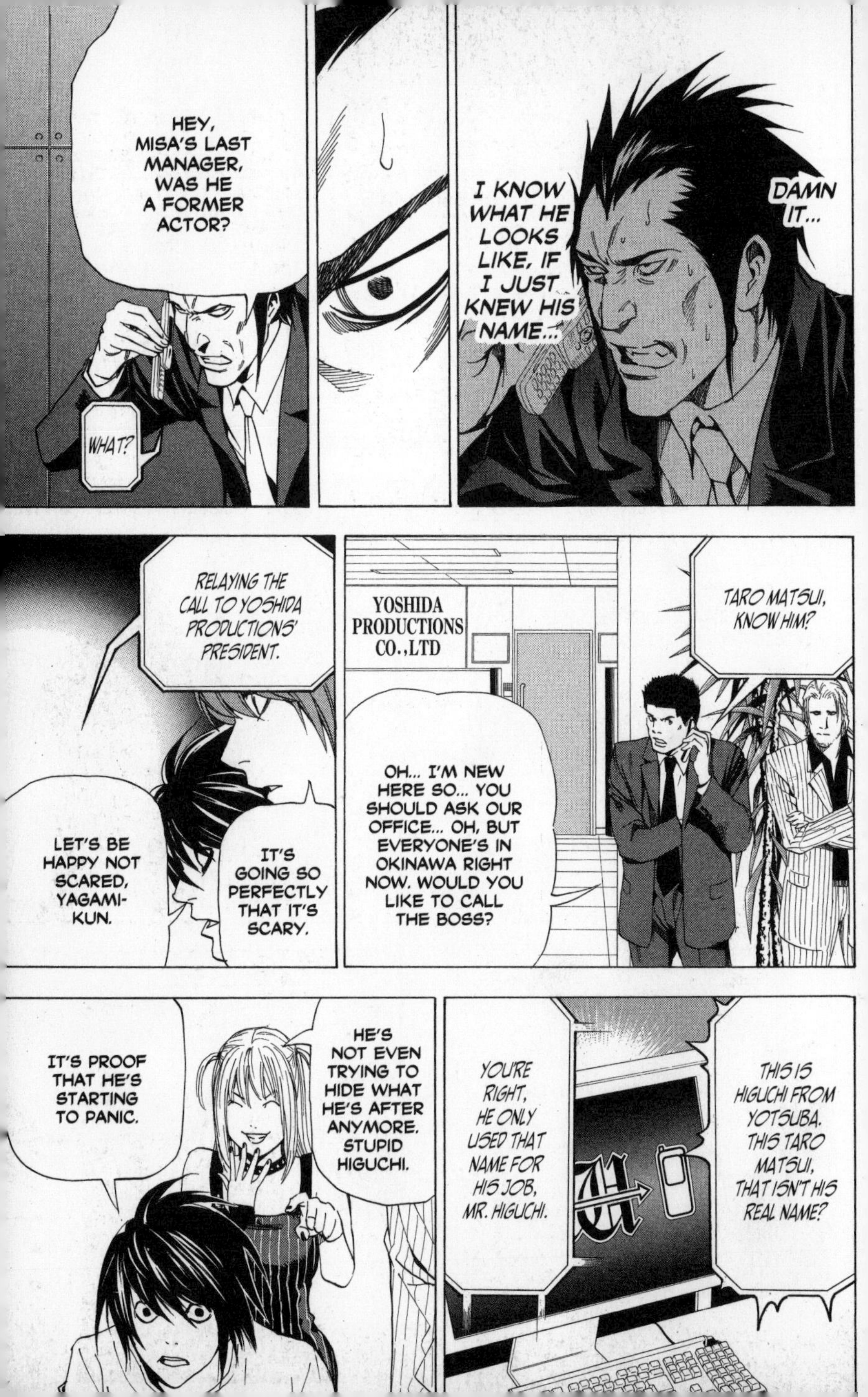
DAMN IT...
I KNOW WHAT HE LOOKS LIKE, IF I JUST KNEW HIS NAME...
HEY, MISA'S LAST MANAGER, WAS HE A FORMER ACTOR?
WHAT?
TARO MATSUI, KNOW HIM?
YOSHIDA PRODUCTIONS CO.,LTD
OH... I'M NEW HERE SO... YOU SHOULD ASK OUR OFFICE... OH, BUT EVERYONE'S IN OKINAWA RIGHT NOW. WOULD YOU LIKE TO CALL THE BOSS?
RELAYING THE CALL TO YOSHIDA PRODUCTIONS' PRESIDENT.
IT'S GOING SO PERFECTLY THAT IT'S SCARY.
LET'S BE HAPPY NOT SCARED, YAGAMI-KUN.
THIS IS HIGUCHI FROM YOTSUBA. THIS TARO MATSUI, THAT ISN'T HIS REAL NAME?
YOU'RE RIGHT, HE ONLY USED THAT NAME FOR HIS JOB, MR. HIGUCHI.
HE'S NOT EVEN TRYING TO HIDE WHAT HE'S AFTER ANYMORE. STUPID HIGUCHI.
IT'S PROOF THAT HE'S STARTING TO PANIC.

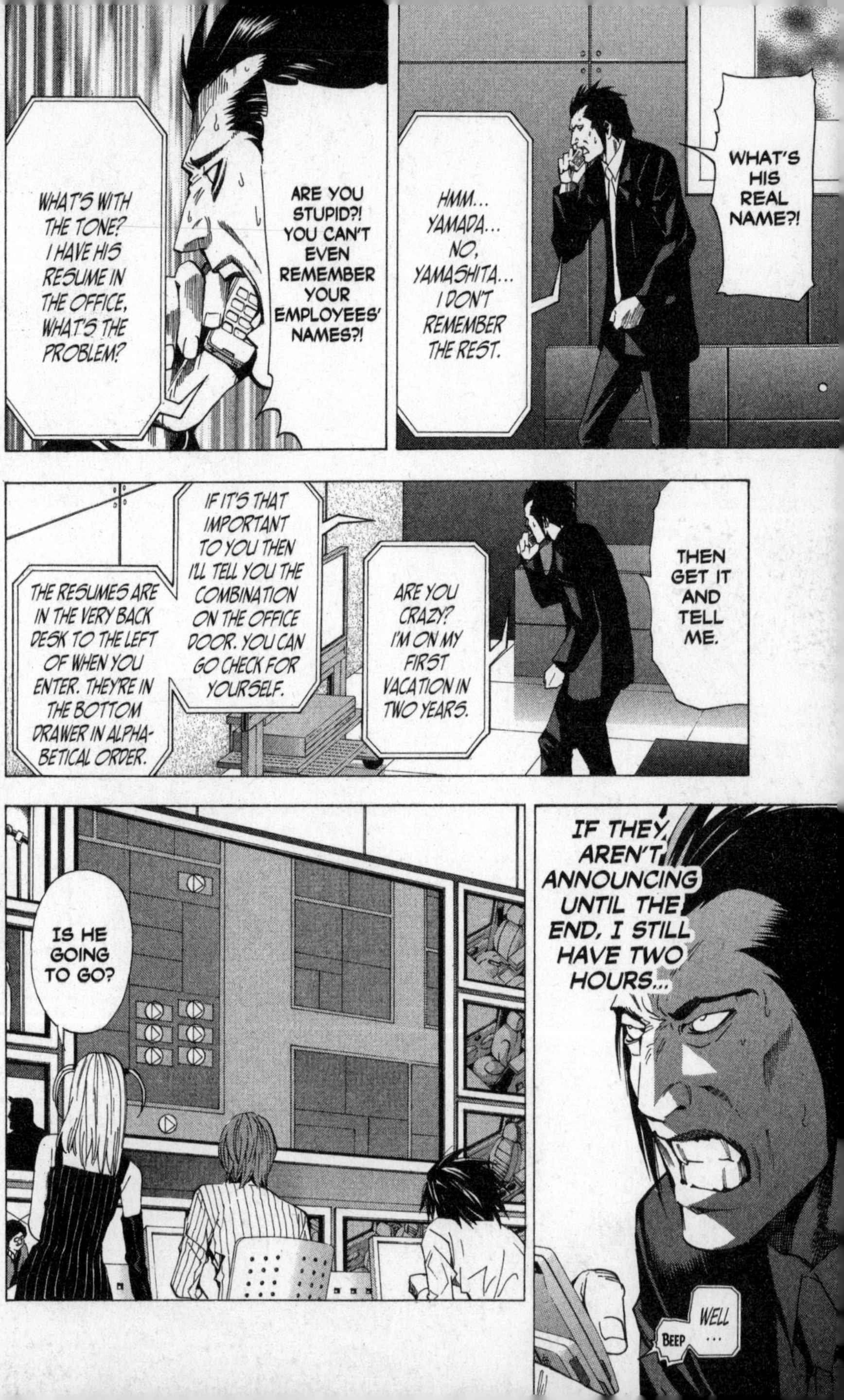
WHAT'S HIS REAL NAME?!
HMM... YAMADA... NO, YAMASHITA... I DON'T REMEMBER THE REST.
ARE YOU STUPID?! YOU CAN'T EVEN REMEMBER YOUR EMPLOYEES' NAMES?!
WHAT'S WITH THE TONE? I HAVE HIS RESUME IN THE OFFICE, WHAT'S THE PROBLEM?
THEN GET IT AND TELL ME.
ARE YOU CRAZY? I'M ON MY FIRST VACATION IN TWO YEARS.
IF IT'S THAT IMPORTANT TO YOU THEN I'LL TELL YOU THE COMBINATION ON THE OFFICE DOOR. YOU CAN GO CHECK FOR YOURSELF.
THE RESUMES ARE IN THE VERY BACK DESK TO THE LEFT OF WHEN YOU ENTER. THEY'RE IN THE BOTTOM DRAWER IN ALPHA-BETICAL ORDER.
IF THEY AREN'T ANNOUNCING UNTIL THE END, I STILL HAVE TWO HOURS...
WELL ...
BEEP
IS HE GOING TO GO?

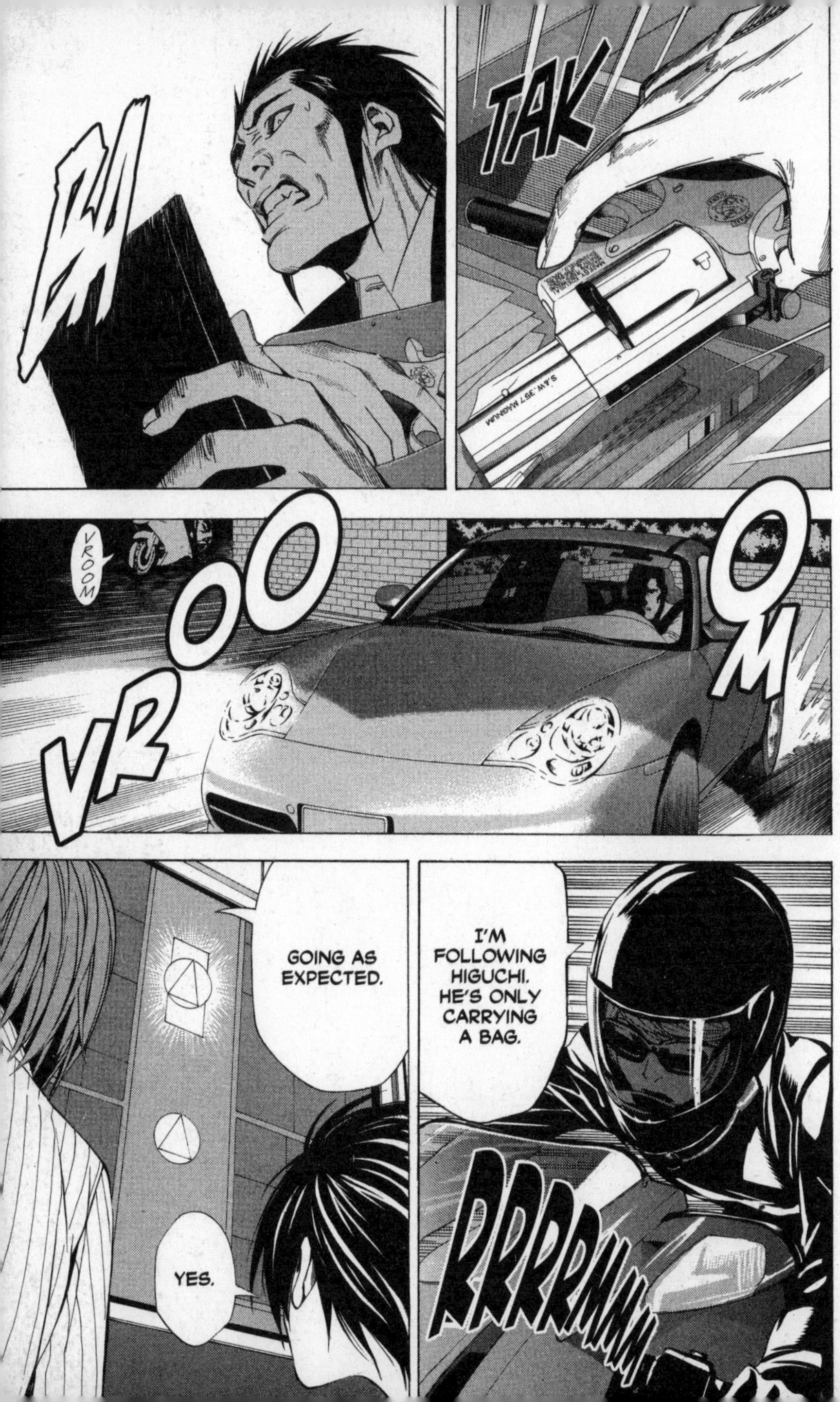
TAK
S.&W. .357 MAGNUM
BA
VROOM
VROOOOM
I'M FOLLOWING HIGUCHI. HE'S ONLY CARRYING A BAG.
RRRRMMMM
GOING AS EXPECTED.
YES.

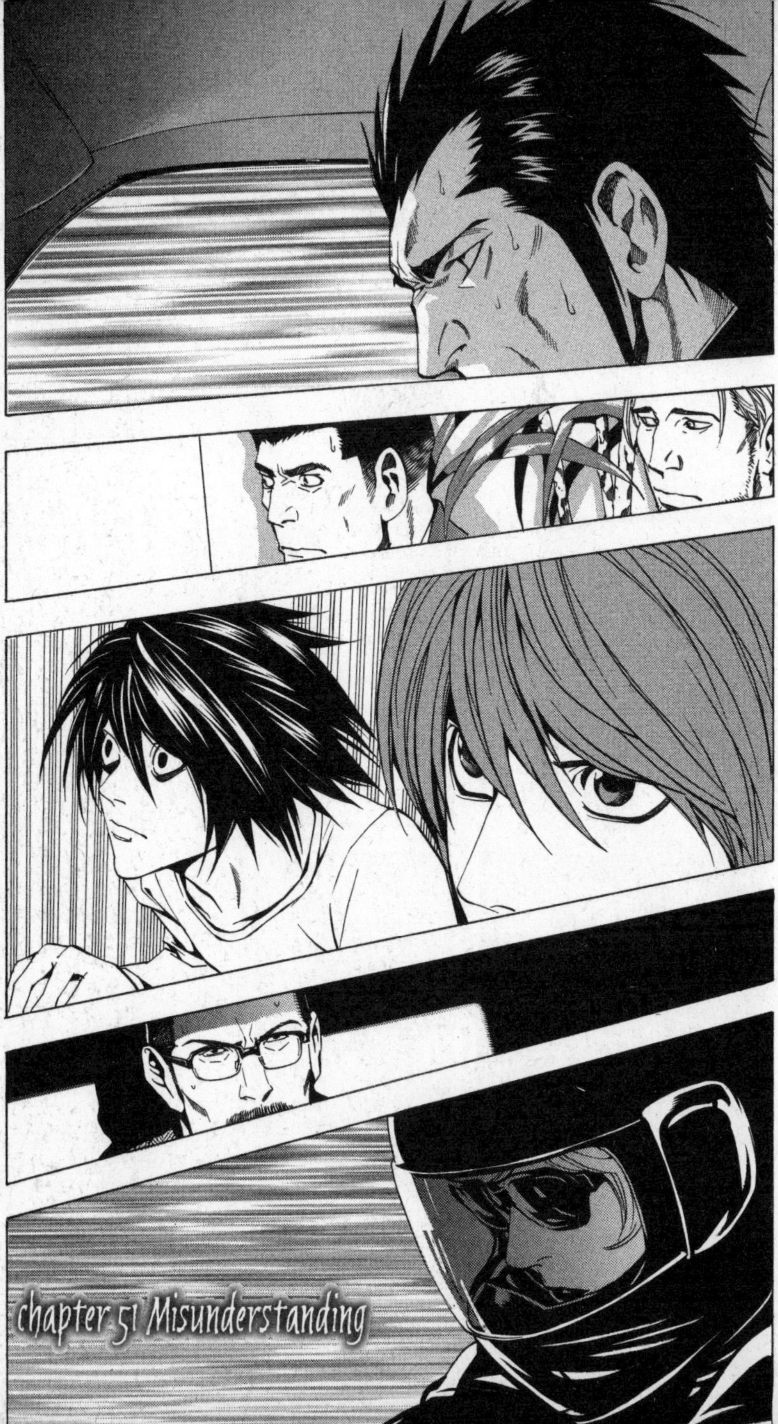
chapter 51 Misunderstanding

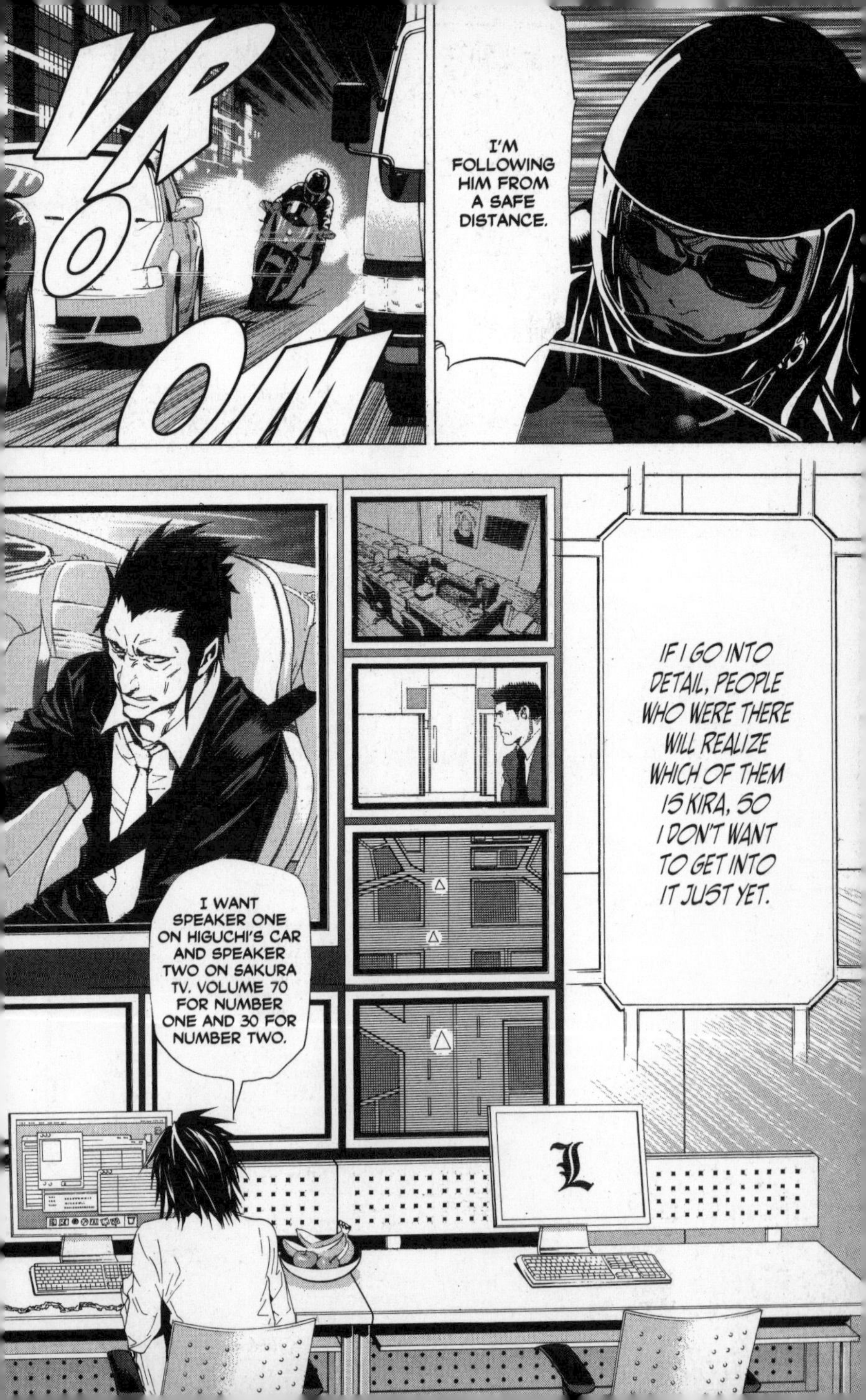
I'M FOLLOWING HIM FROM A SAFE DISTANCE.
VROOM
IF I GO INTO DETAIL, PEOPLE WHO WERE THERE WILL REALIZE WHICH OF THEM IS KIRA, SO I DON'T WANT TO GET INTO IT JUST YET.
I WANT SPEAKER ONE ON HIGUCHI'S CAR AND SPEAKER TWO ON SAKURA TV. VOLUME 70 FOR NUMBER ONE AND 30 FOR NUMBER TWO.
L

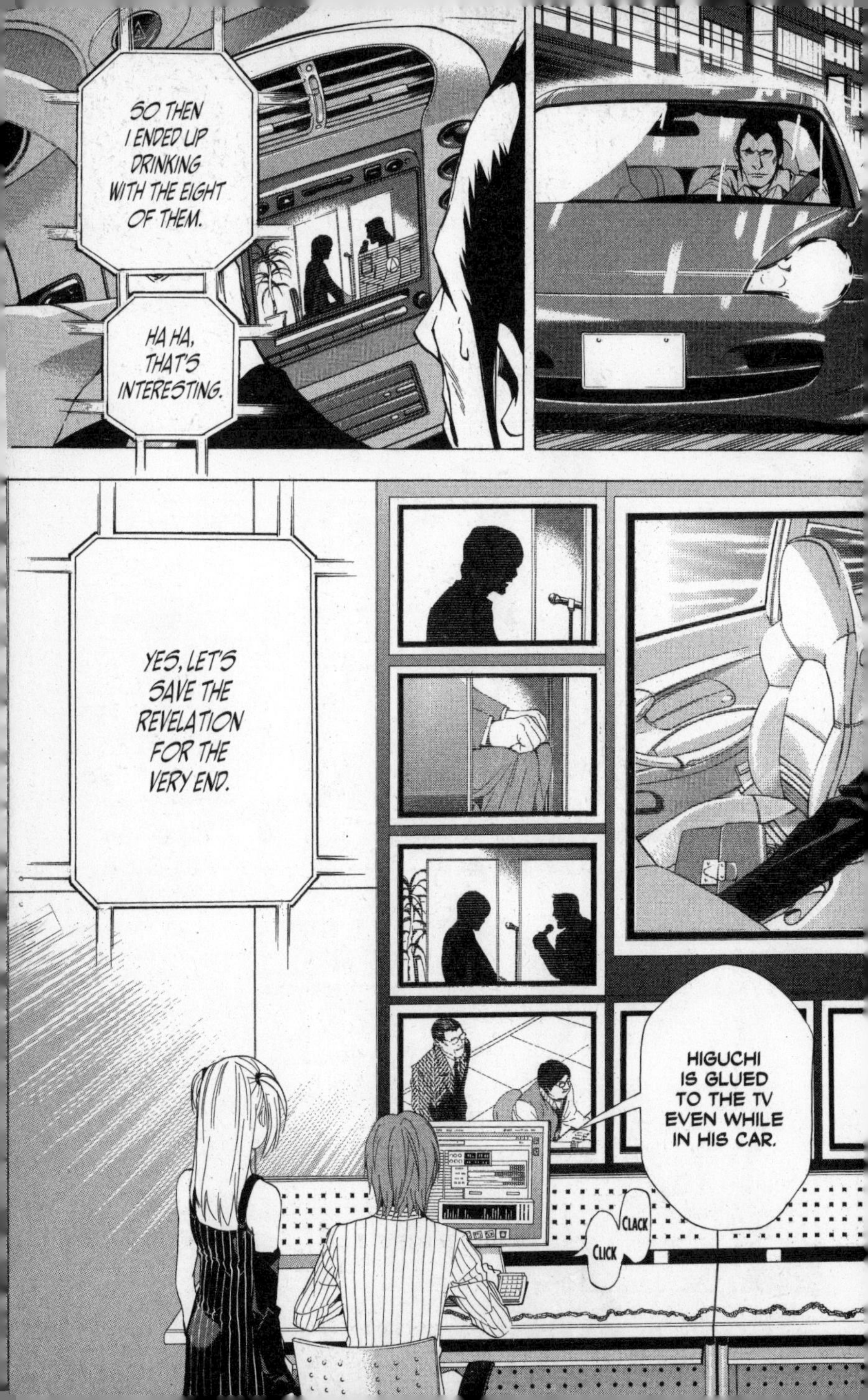
SO THEN I ENDED UP DRINKING WITH THE EIGHT OF THEM.
HA HA, THAT'S INTERESTING.
HIGUCHI IS GLUED TO THE TV EVEN WHILE IN HIS CAR.
CLACK
CLICK
YES, LET'S SAVE THE REVELATION FOR THE VERY END.

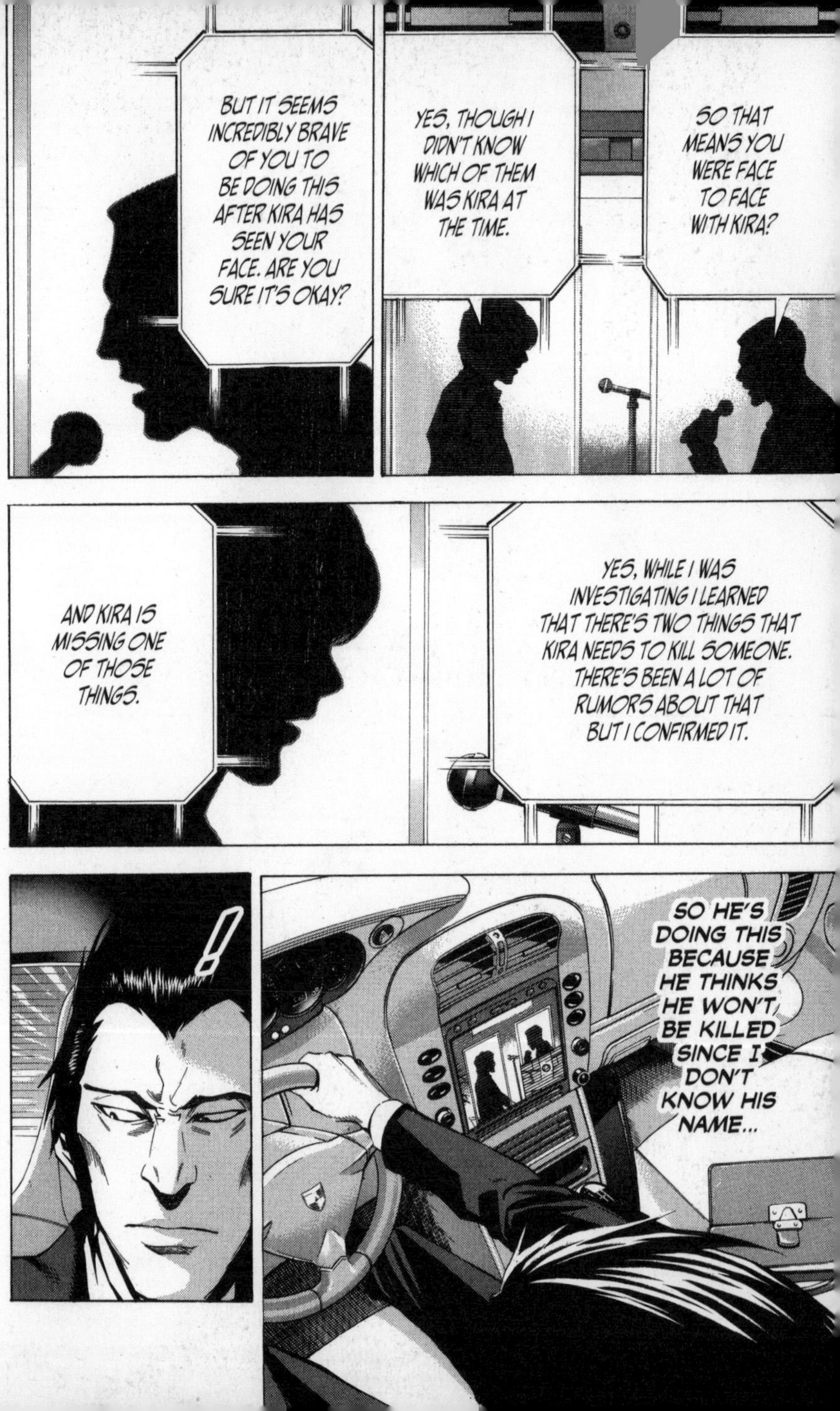
SO THAT MEANS YOU WERE FACE TO FACE WITH KIRA?
YES, THOUGH I DIDN'T KNOW WHICH OF THEM WAS KIRA AT THE TIME.
BUT IT SEEMS INCREDIBLY BRAVE OF YOU TO BE DOING THIS AFTER KIRA HAS SEEN YOUR FACE. ARE YOU SURE IT'S OKAY?
YES, WHILE I WAS INVESTIGATING I LEARNED THAT THERE'S TWO THINGS THAT KIRA NEEDS TO KILL SOMEONE. THERE'S BEEN A LOT OF RUMORS ABOUT THAT BUT I CONFIRMED IT.
AND KIRA IS MISSING ONE OF THOSE THINGS.
SO HE'S DOING THIS BECAUSE HE THINKS HE WON'T BE KILLED SINCE I DON'T KNOW HIS NAME...
!

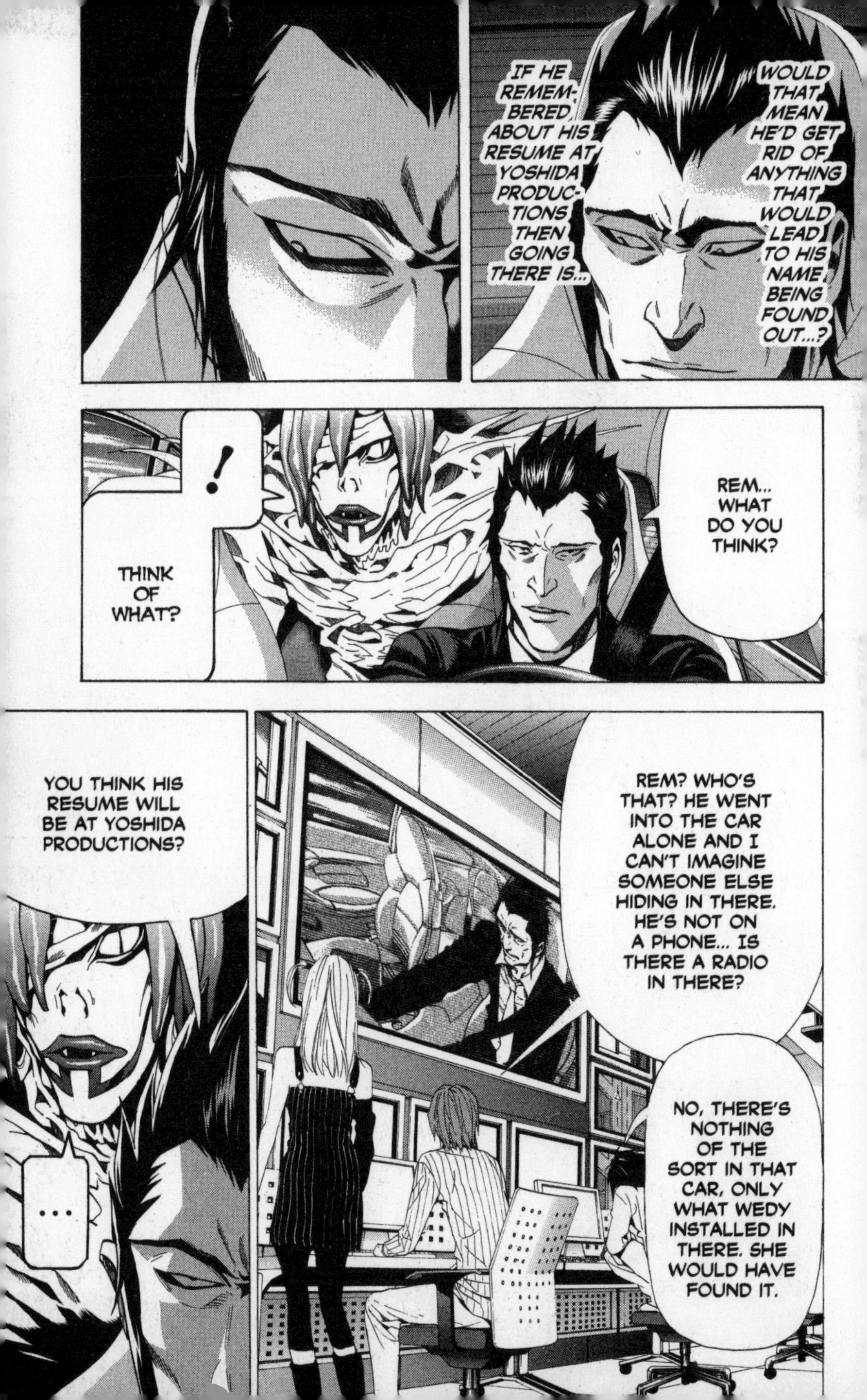
WOULD THAT MEAN HE'D GET RID OF ANYTHING THAT WOULD LEAD TO HIS NAME BEING FOUND OUT...?
IF HE REMEMBERED ABOUT HIS RESUME AT YOSHIDA PRODUCTIONS THEN GOING THERE IS...
REM... WHAT DO YOU THINK?
!
THINK OF WHAT?
REM? WHO'S THAT? HE WENT INTO THE CAR ALONE AND I CAN'T IMAGINE SOMEONE ELSE HIDING IN THERE. HE'S NOT ON A PHONE... IS THERE A RADIO IN THERE?
NO, THERE'S NOTHING OF THE SORT IN THAT CAR, ONLY WHAT WEDY INSTALLED IN THERE. SHE WOULD HAVE FOUND IT.
YOU THINK HIS RESUME WILL BE AT YOSHIDA PRODUCTIONS?
...

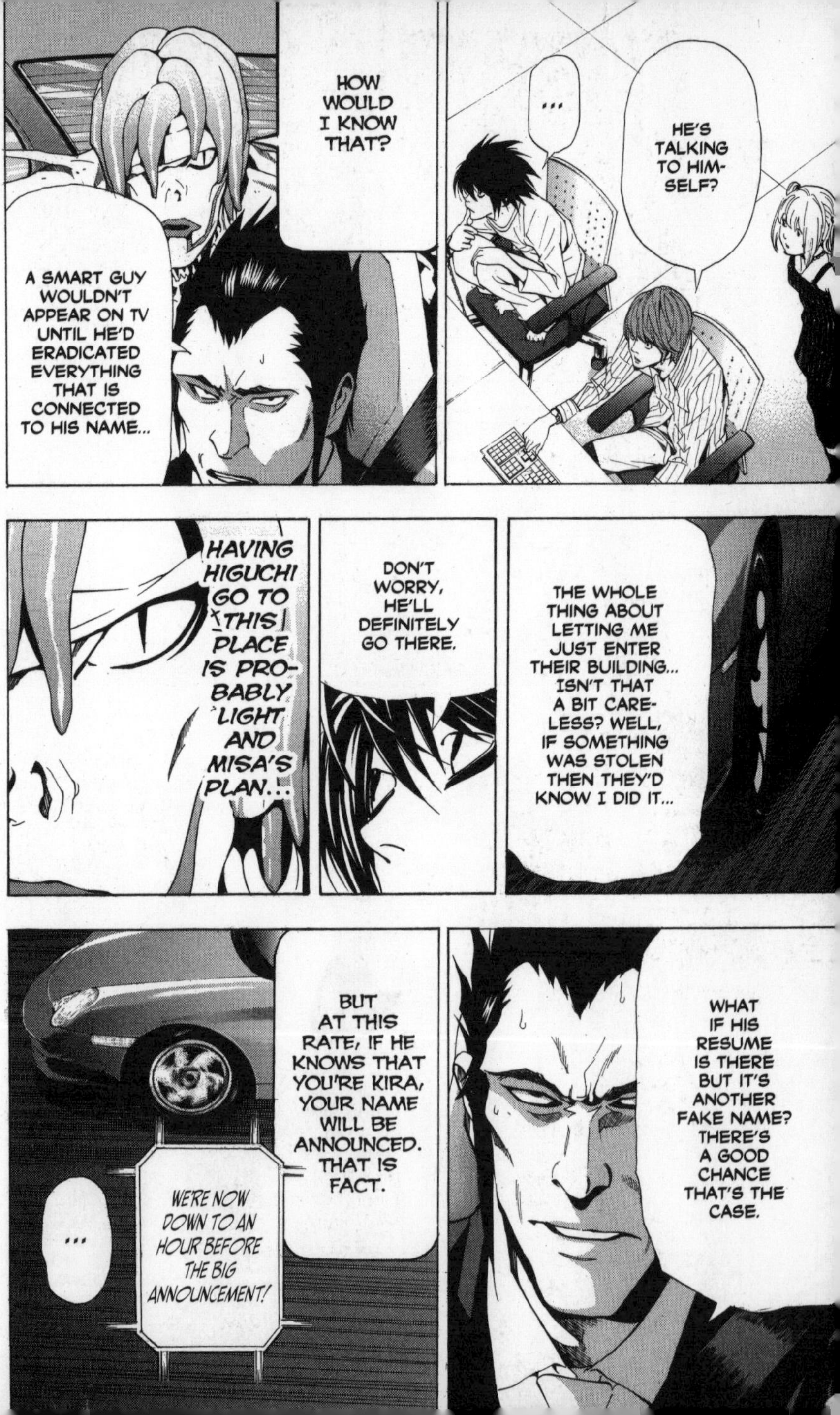
HE'S TALKING TO HIMSELF?
...
HOW WOULD I KNOW THAT?
A SMART GUY WOULDN'T APPEAR ON TV UNTIL HE'D ERADICATED EVERYTHING THAT IS CONNECTED TO HIS NAME...
THE WHOLE THING ABOUT LETTING ME JUST ENTER THEIR BUILDING... ISN'T THAT A BIT CARELESS? WELL, IF SOMETHING WAS STOLEN THEN THEY'D KNOW I DID IT...
DON'T WORRY, HE'LL DEFINITELY GO THERE.
HAVING HIGUCHI GO TO THIS PLACE IS PROBABLY LIGHT AND MISA'S PLAN...
WHAT IF HIS RESUME IS THERE BUT IT'S ANOTHER FAKE NAME? THERE'S A GOOD CHANCE THAT'S THE CASE.
BUT AT THIS RATE, IF HE KNOWS THAT YOU'RE KIRA, YOUR NAME WILL BE ANNOUNCED. THAT IS FACT.
WE'RE NOW DOWN TO AN HOUR BEFORE THE BIG ANNOUNCEMENT!
...

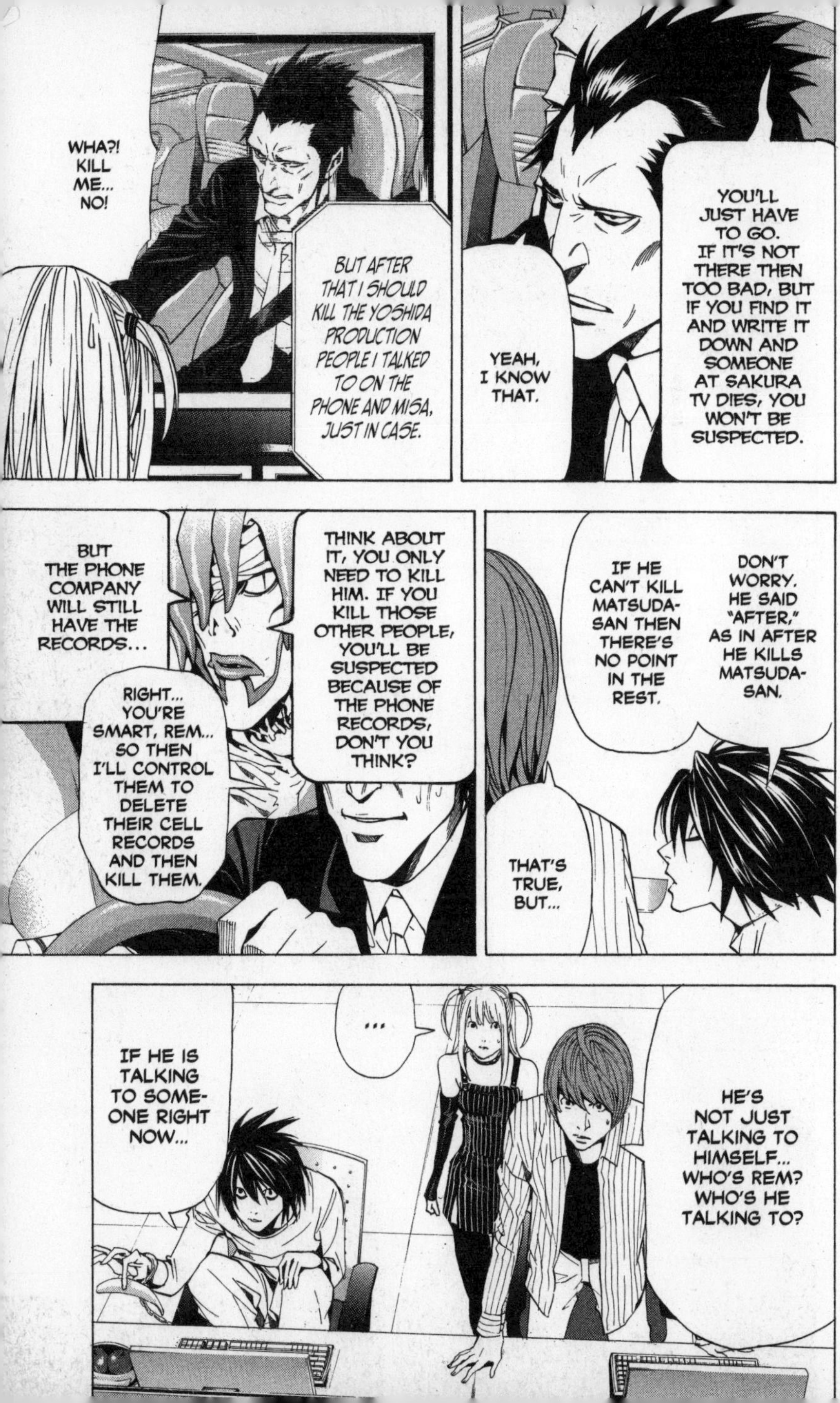
YOU'LL JUST HAVE TO GO. IF IT'S NOT THERE THEN TOO BAD, BUT IF YOU FIND IT AND WRITE IT DOWN AND SOMEONE AT SAKURA TV DIES, YOU WON'T BE SUSPECTED.
YEAH, I KNOW THAT.
BUT AFTER THAT I SHOULD KILL THE YOSHIDA PRODUCTION PEOPLE I TALKED TO ON THE PHONE AND MISA, JUST IN CASE.
WHA?! KILL ME... NO!
DON'T WORRY. HE SAID "AFTER," AS IN AFTER HE KILLS MATSUDA-SAN.
IF HE CAN'T KILL MATSUDA-SAN THEN THERE'S NO POINT IN THE REST.
THAT'S TRUE, BUT...
THINK ABOUT IT, YOU ONLY NEED TO KILL HIM. IF YOU KILL THOSE OTHER PEOPLE, YOU'LL BE SUSPECTED BECAUSE OF THE PHONE RECORDS, DON'T YOU THINK?
BUT THE PHONE COMPANY WILL STILL HAVE THE RECORDS...
RIGHT... YOU'RE SMART, REM... SO THEN I'LL CONTROL THEM TO DELETE THEIR CELL RECORDS AND THEN KILL THEM.
HE'S NOT JUST TALKING TO HIMSELF... WHO'S REM? WHO'S HE TALKING TO?
...
IF HE IS TALKING TO SOMEONE RIGHT NOW...

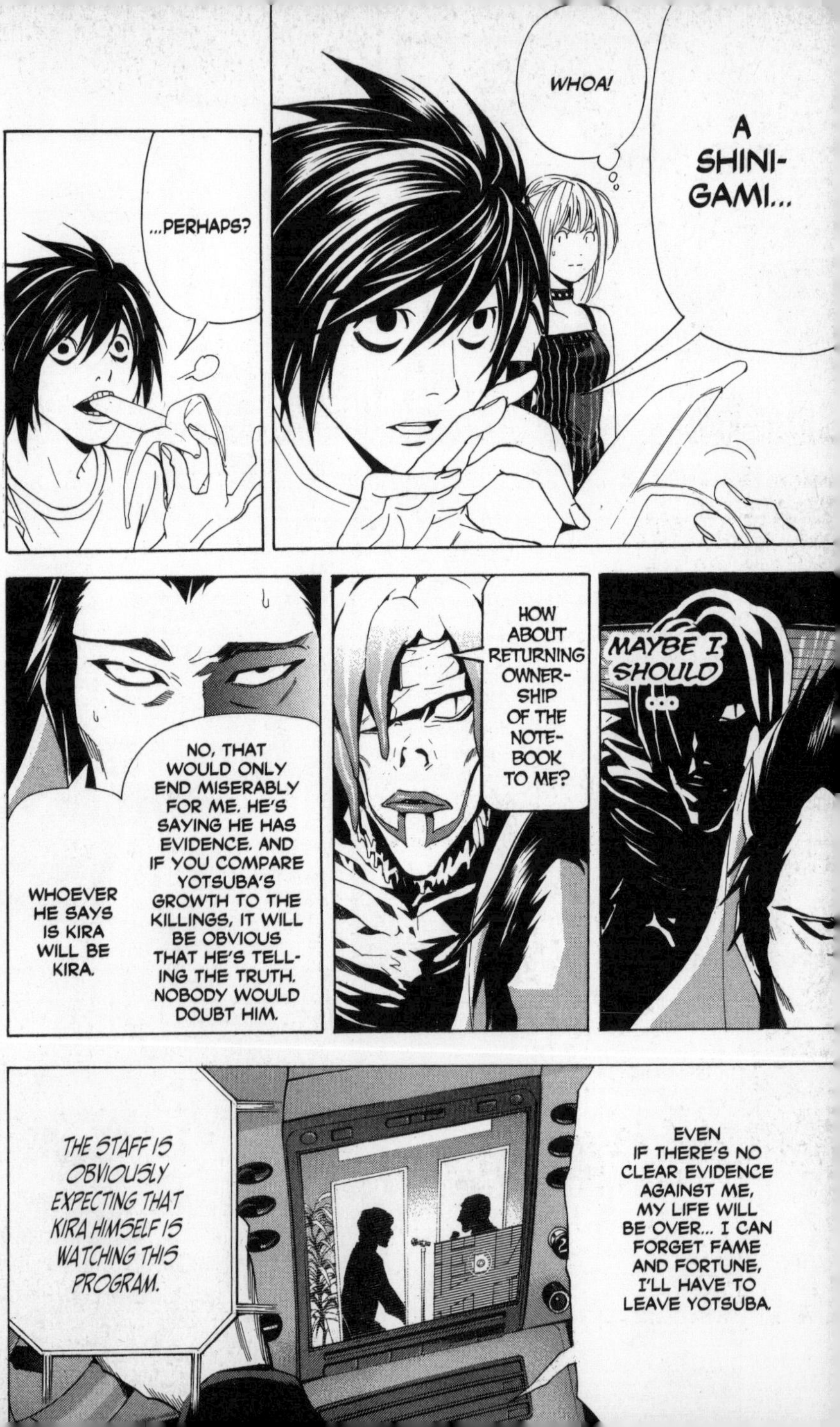
A SHINI-GAMI...
WHOA!
...PERHAPS?
MAYBE I SHOULD ...
HOW ABOUT RETURNING OWNERSHIP OF THE NOTEBOOK TO ME?
NO, THAT WOULD ONLY END MISERABLY FOR ME. HE'S SAYING HE HAS EVIDENCE. AND IF YOU COMPARE YOTSUBA'S GROWTH TO THE KILLINGS, IT WILL BE OBVIOUS THAT HE'S TELLING THE TRUTH. NOBODY WOULD DOUBT HIM.
WHOEVER HE SAYS IS KIRA WILL BE KIRA.
EVEN IF THERE'S NO CLEAR EVIDENCE AGAINST ME, MY LIFE WILL BE OVER... I CAN FORGET FAME AND FORTUNE, I'LL HAVE TO LEAVE YOTSUBA.
THE STAFF IS OBVIOUSLY EXPECTING THAT KIRA HIMSELF IS WATCHING THIS PROGRAM.

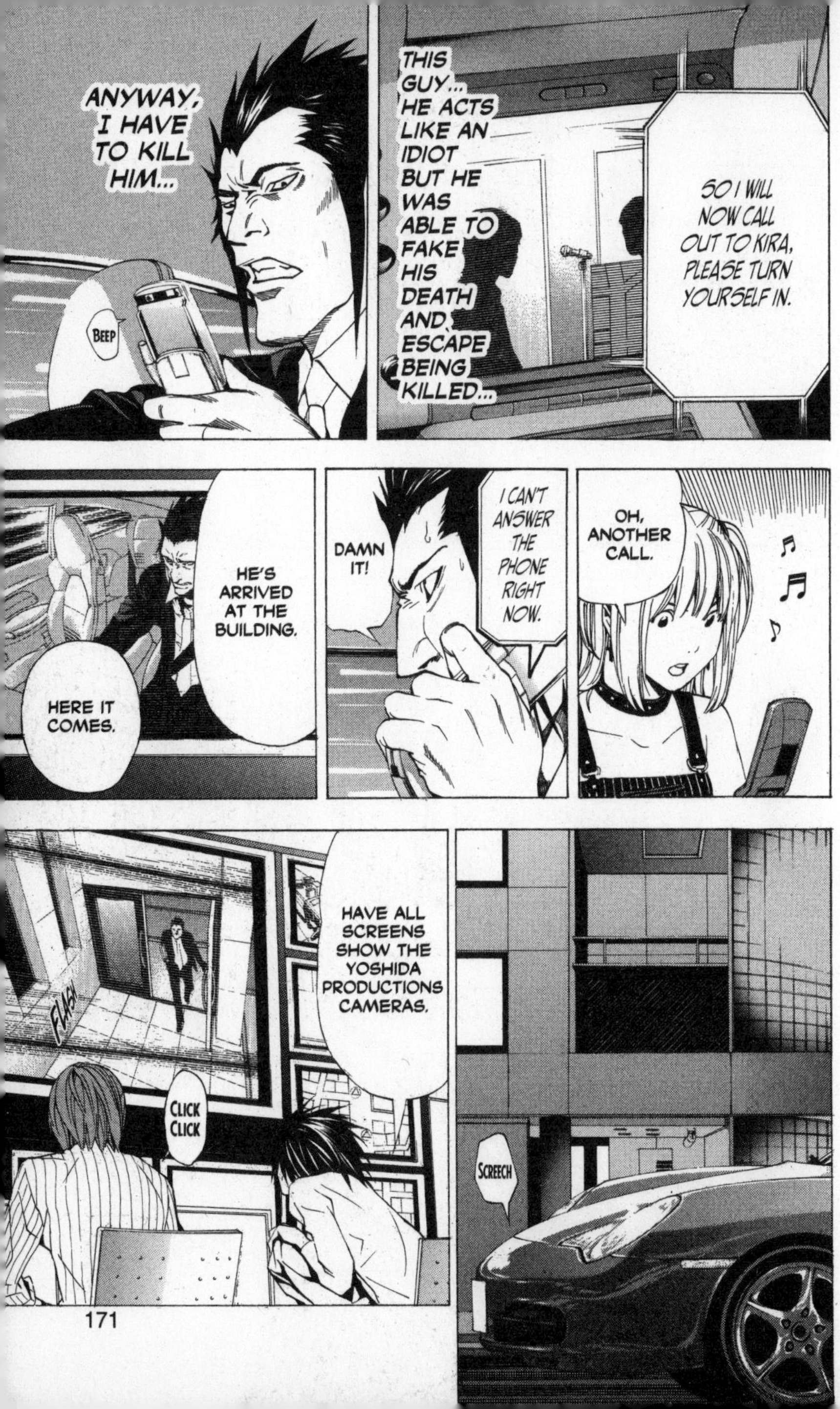
SO I WILL NOW CALL OUT TO KIRA, PLEASE TURN YOURSELF IN.
THIS GUY... HE ACTS LIKE AN IDIOT BUT HE WAS ABLE TO FAKE HIS DEATH AND ESCAPE BEING KILLED...
ANYWAY, I HAVE TO KILL HIM...
BEEP
OH, ANOTHER CALL.
I CAN'T ANSWER THE PHONE RIGHT NOW.
DAMN IT!
HE'S ARRIVED AT THE BUILDING.
HERE IT COMES.
SCREECH
HAVE ALL SCREENS SHOW THE YOSHIDA PRODUCTIONS CAMERAS.
FLASH
CLICK CLICK

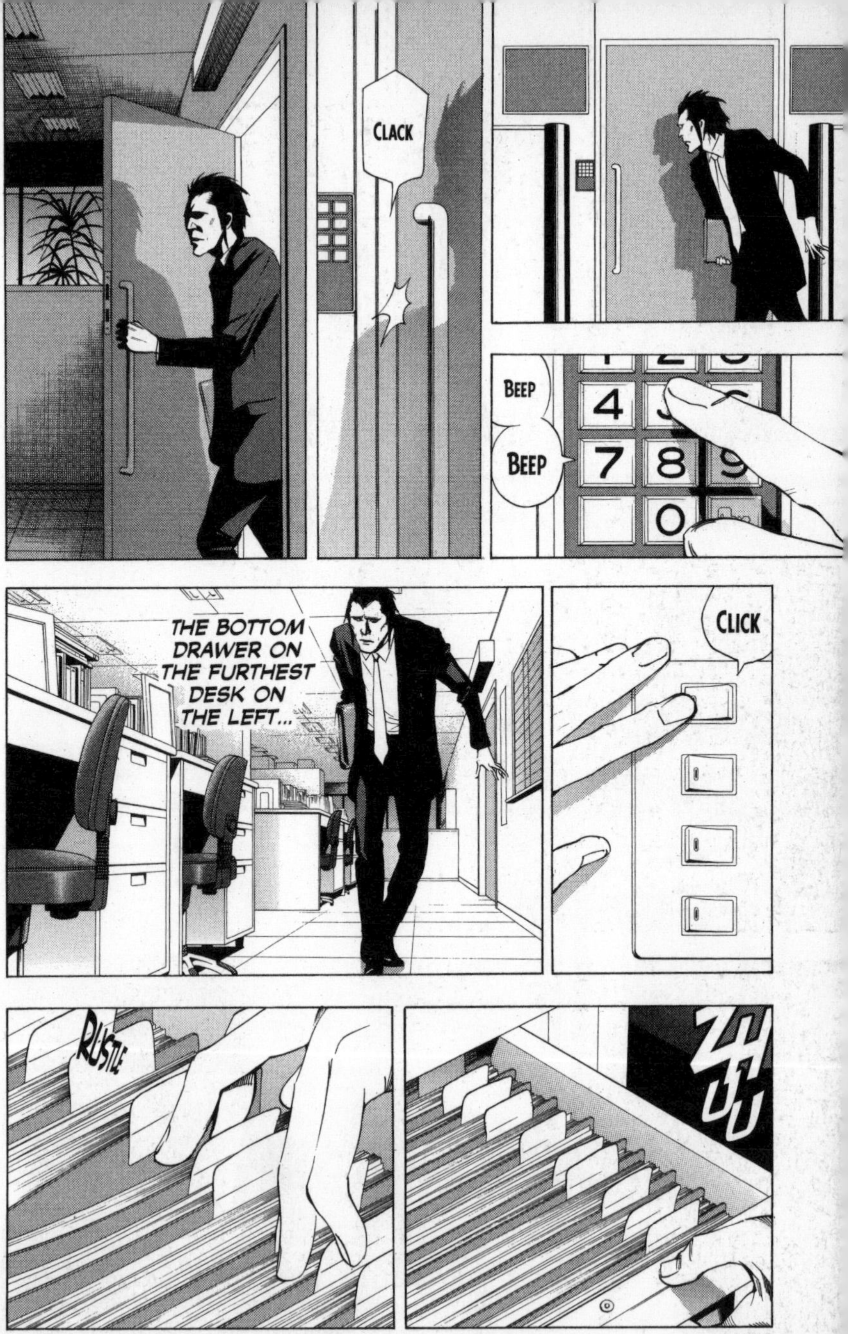
Beep
Beep
Clack
Click
The bottom drawer on the furthest desk on the left...
Rustle

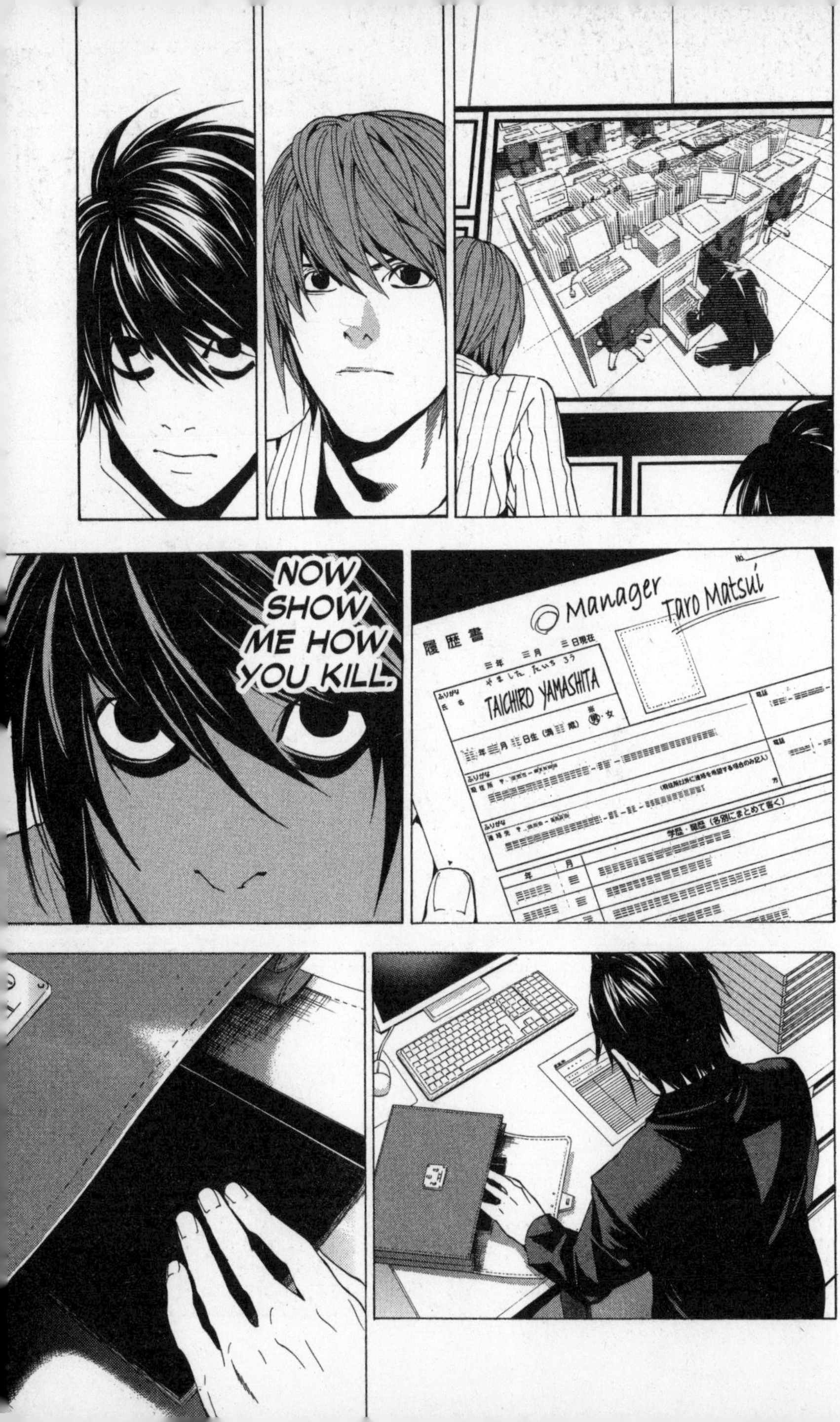
Manager
Taro Matsui
履歴書
日現在
TAICHIRO YAMASHITA
NOW SHOW ME HOW YOU KILL.

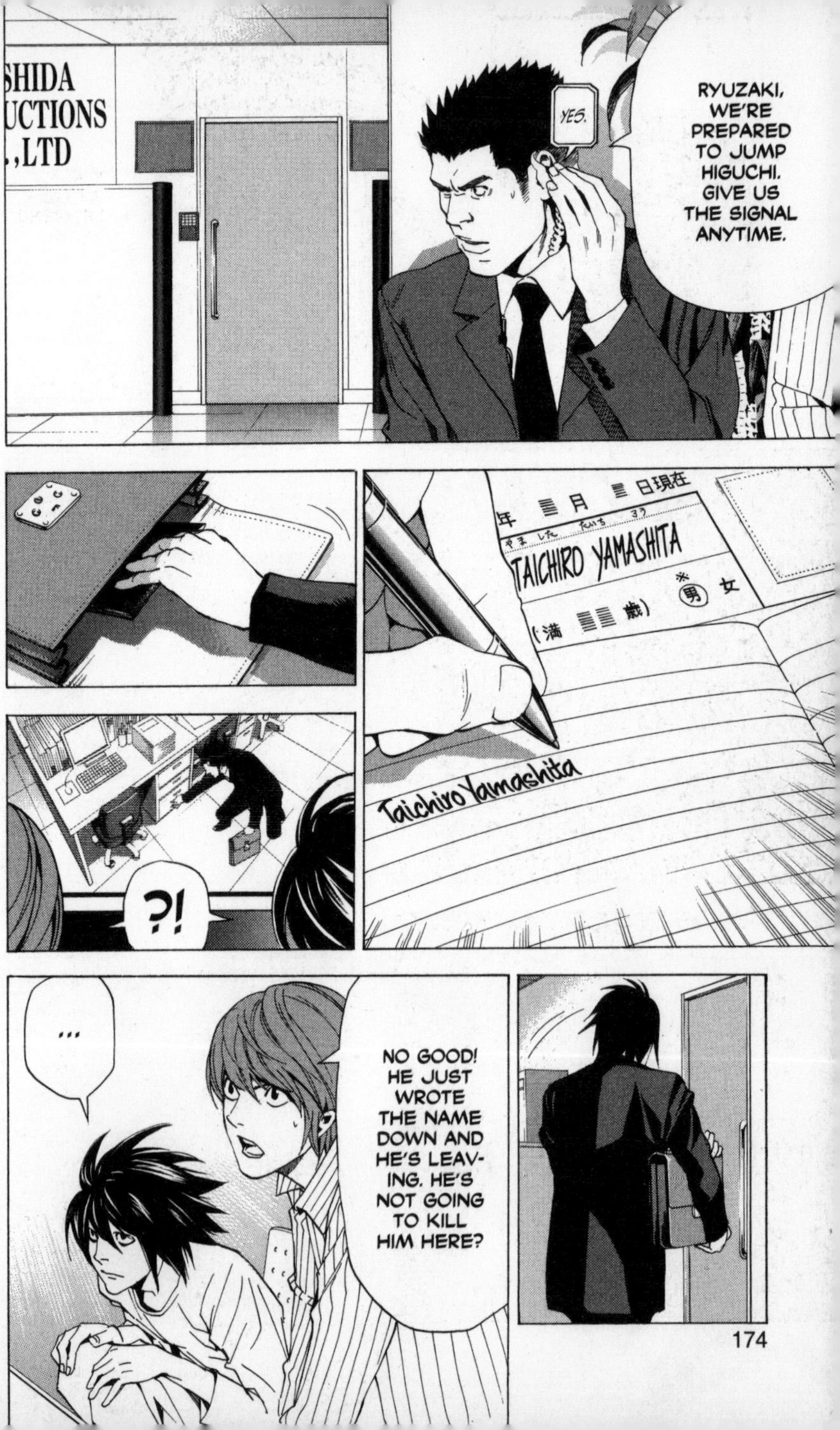
SHIDA
UCTIONS
.,LTD
RYUZAKI, WE'RE PREPARED TO JUMP HIGUCHI. GIVE US THE SIGNAL ANYTIME.
YES.
年 月 日現在
やました たいち ろう
TAICHIRO YAMASHITA
※ 男 女
(満 歳)
Taichiro Yamashita
?!
NO GOOD! HE JUST WROTE THE NAME DOWN AND HE'S LEAVING. HE'S NOT GOING TO KILL HIM HERE?
...

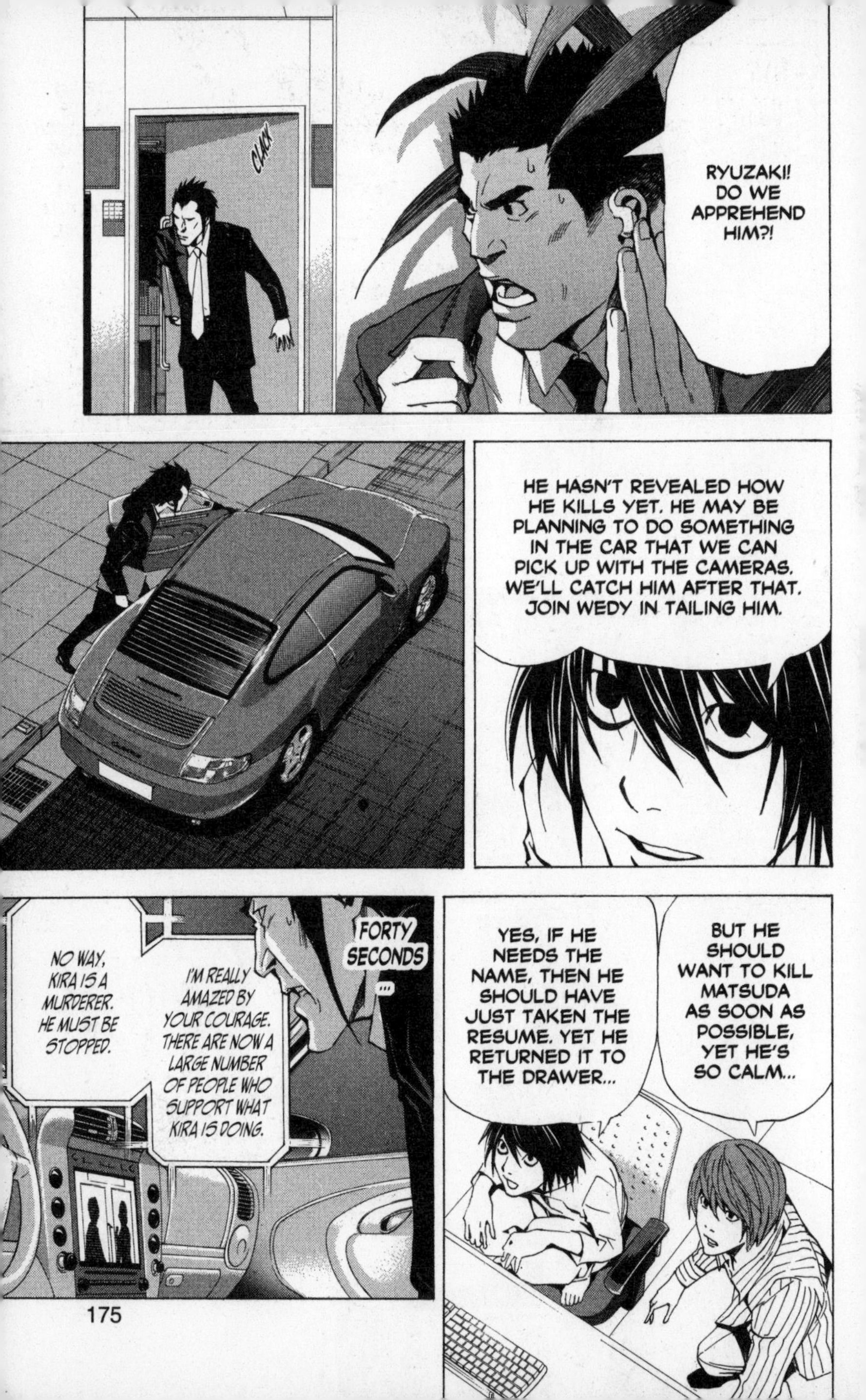
RYUZAKI! DO WE APPREHEND HIM?!
CLACK
HE HASN'T REVEALED HOW HE KILLS YET. HE MAY BE PLANNING TO DO SOMETHING IN THE CAR THAT WE CAN PICK UP WITH THE CAMERAS. WE'LL CATCH HIM AFTER THAT. JOIN WEDY IN TAILING HIM.
BUT HE SHOULD WANT TO KILL MATSUDA AS SOON AS POSSIBLE, YET HE'S SO CALM...
YES, IF HE NEEDS THE NAME, THEN HE SHOULD HAVE JUST TAKEN THE RESUME. YET HE RETURNED IT TO THE DRAWER...
FORTY SECONDS ...
I'M REALLY AMAZED BY YOUR COURAGE. THERE ARE NOW A LARGE NUMBER OF PEOPLE WHO SUPPORT WHAT KIRA IS DOING.
NO WAY, KIRA IS A MURDERER. HE MUST BE STOPPED.

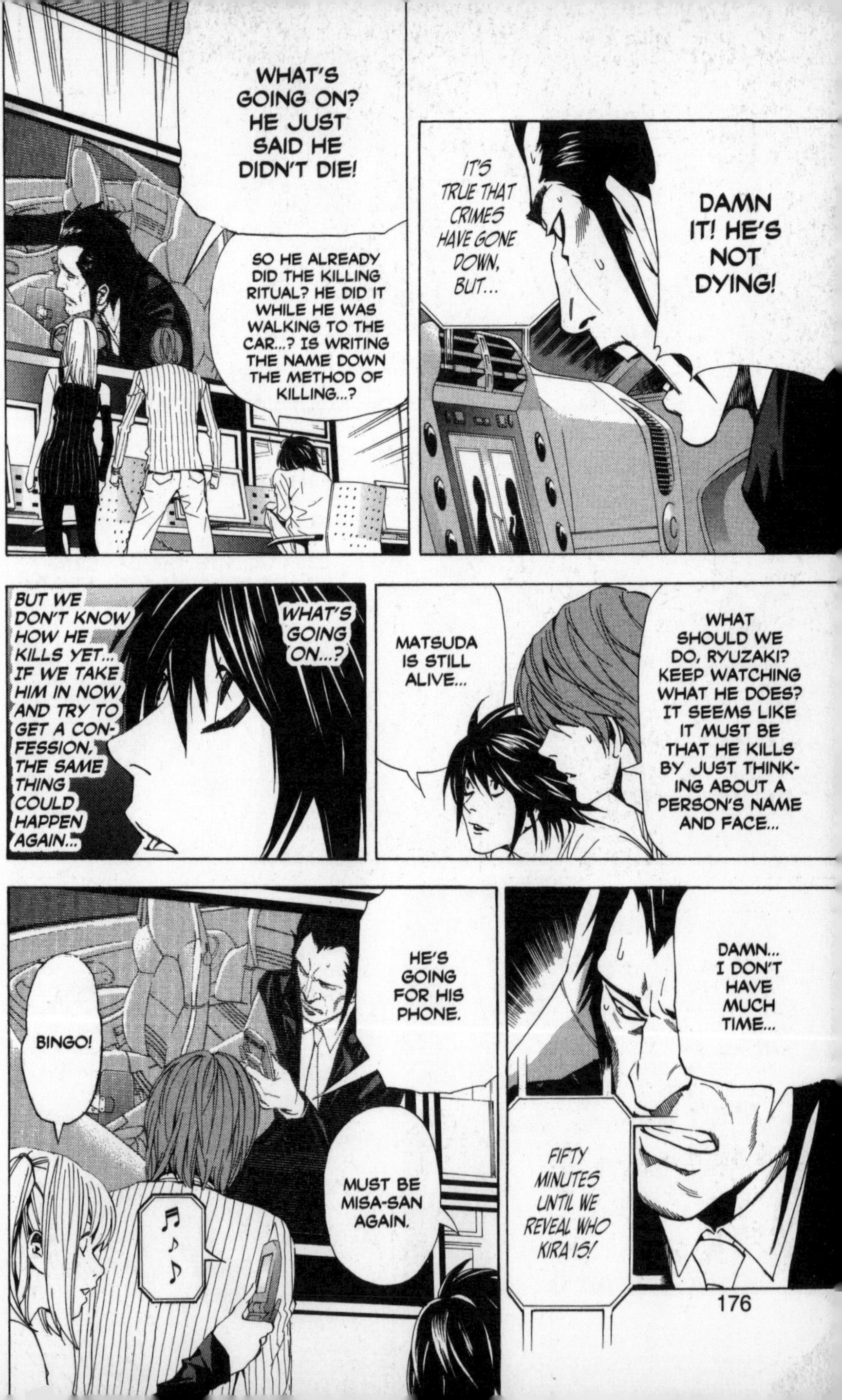
DAMN IT! HE'S NOT DYING!
IT'S TRUE THAT CRIMES HAVE GONE DOWN, BUT...
WHAT'S GOING ON? HE JUST SAID HE DIDN'T DIE!
SO HE ALREADY DID THE KILLING RITUAL? HE DID IT WHILE HE WAS WALKING TO THE CAR...? IS WRITING THE NAME DOWN THE METHOD OF KILLING...?
WHAT SHOULD WE DO, RYUZAKI? KEEP WATCHING WHAT HE DOES? IT SEEMS LIKE IT MUST BE THAT HE KILLS BY JUST THINKING ABOUT A PERSON'S NAME AND FACE...
MATSUDA IS STILL ALIVE...
WHAT'S GOING ON...?
BUT WE DON'T KNOW HOW HE KILLS YET... IF WE TAKE HIM IN NOW AND TRY TO GET A CONFESSION, THE SAME THING COULD HAPPEN AGAIN...
DAMN... I DON'T HAVE MUCH TIME...
FIFTY MINUTES UNTIL WE REVEAL WHO KIRA IS!
HE'S GOING FOR HIS PHONE.
BINGO!
MUST BE MISA-SAN AGAIN.
♪♪♪

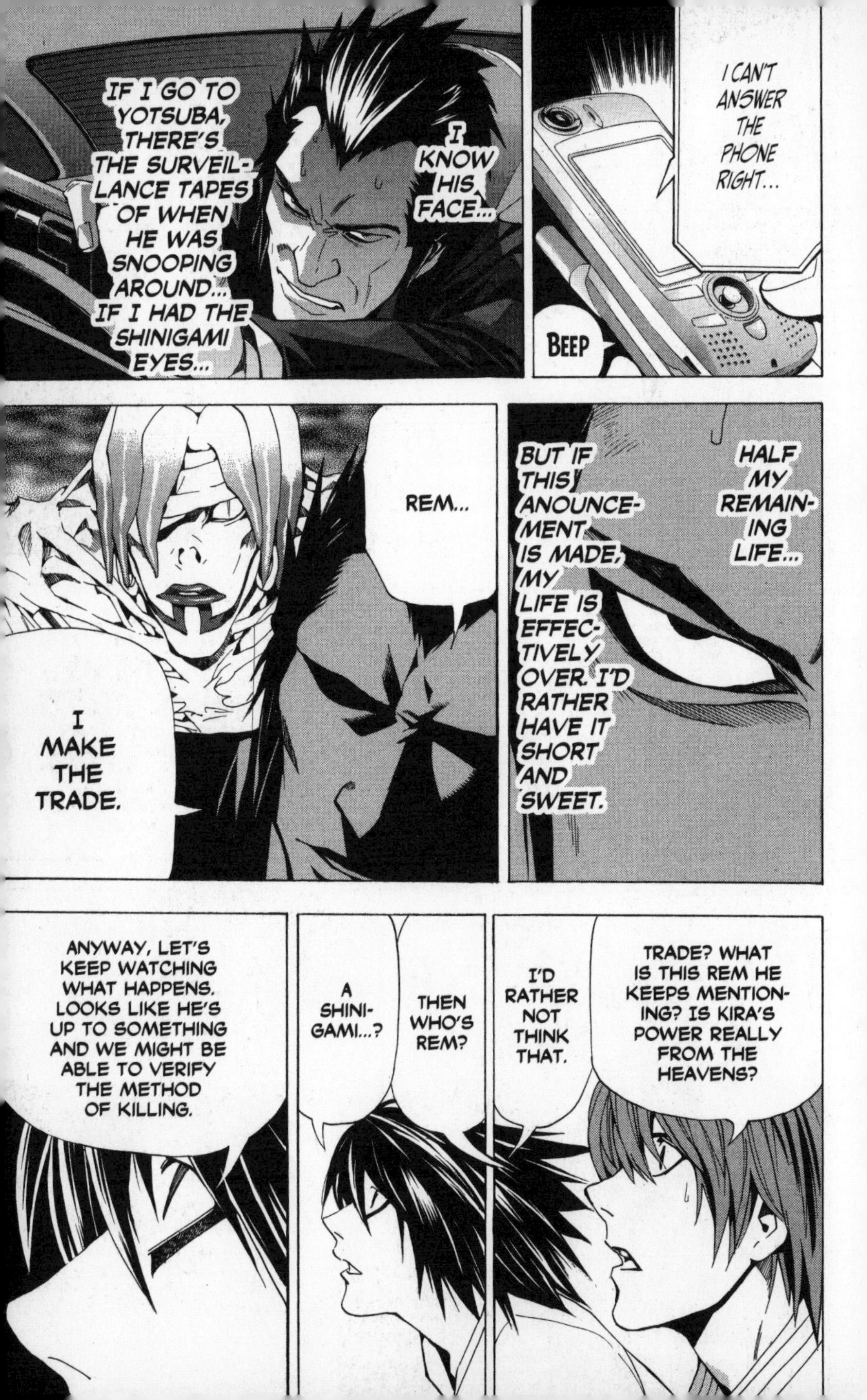
I CAN'T ANSWER THE PHONE RIGHT...
BEEP
I KNOW HIS FACE...
IF I GO TO YOTSUBA, THERE'S THE SURVEIL-LANCE TAPES OF WHEN HE WAS SNOOPING AROUND... IF I HAD THE SHINIGAMI EYES...
HALF MY REMAIN-ING LIFE...
BUT IF THIS ANOUNCE-MENT IS MADE, MY LIFE IS EFFEC-TIVELY OVER. I'D RATHER HAVE IT SHORT AND SWEET.
REM...
I MAKE THE TRADE.
TRADE? WHAT IS THIS REM HE KEEPS MENTION-ING? IS KIRA'S POWER REALLY FROM THE HEAVENS?
I'D RATHER NOT THINK THAT.
THEN WHO'S REM?
A SHINI-GAMI...?
ANYWAY, LET'S KEEP WATCHING WHAT HAPPENS. LOOKS LIKE HE'S UP TO SOMETHING AND WE MIGHT BE ABLE TO VERIFY THE METHOD OF KILLING.

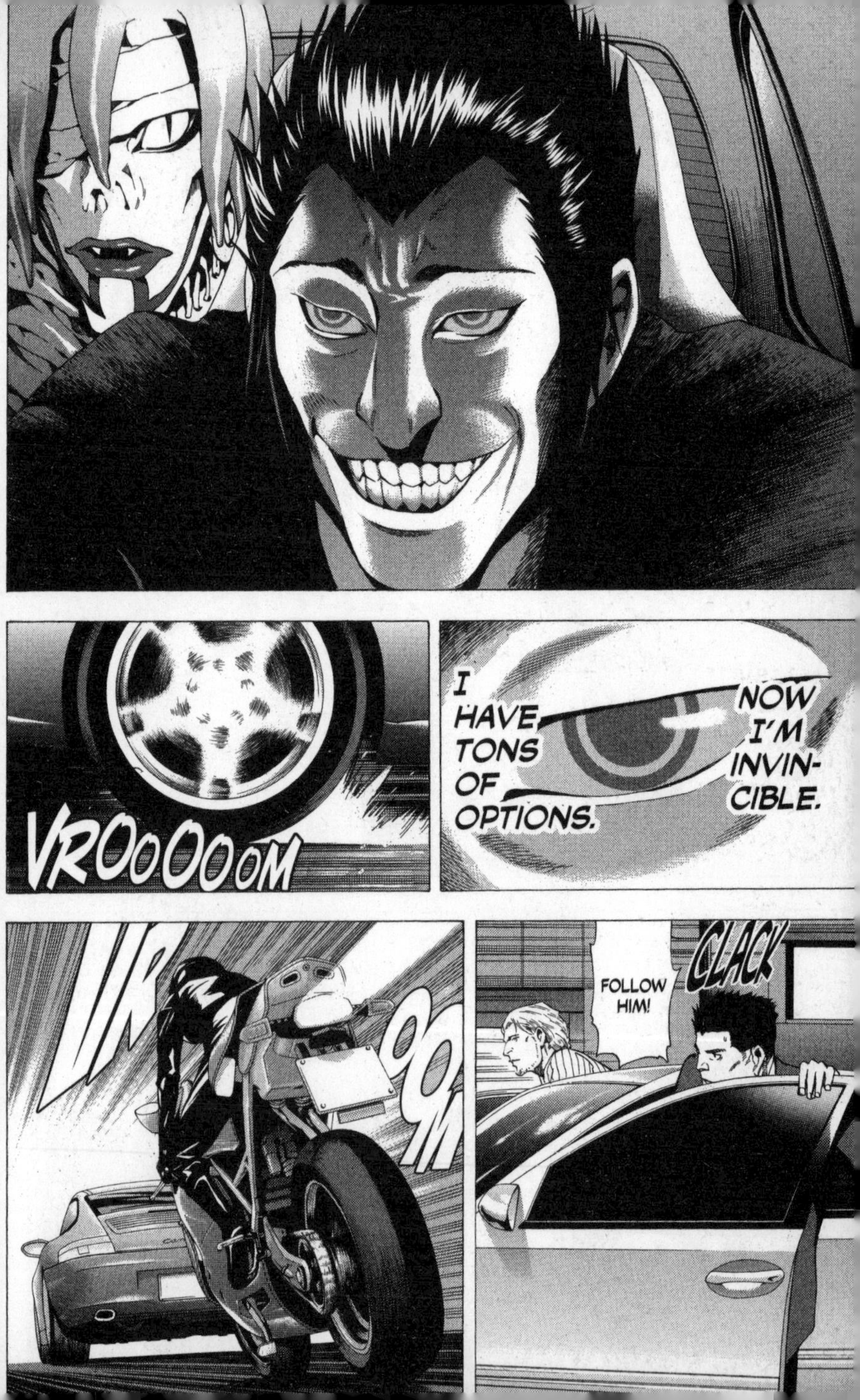
NOW I'M INVINCIBLE.
I HAVE TONS OF OPTIONS.
VROOOOOOM
CLACK
FOLLOW HIM!

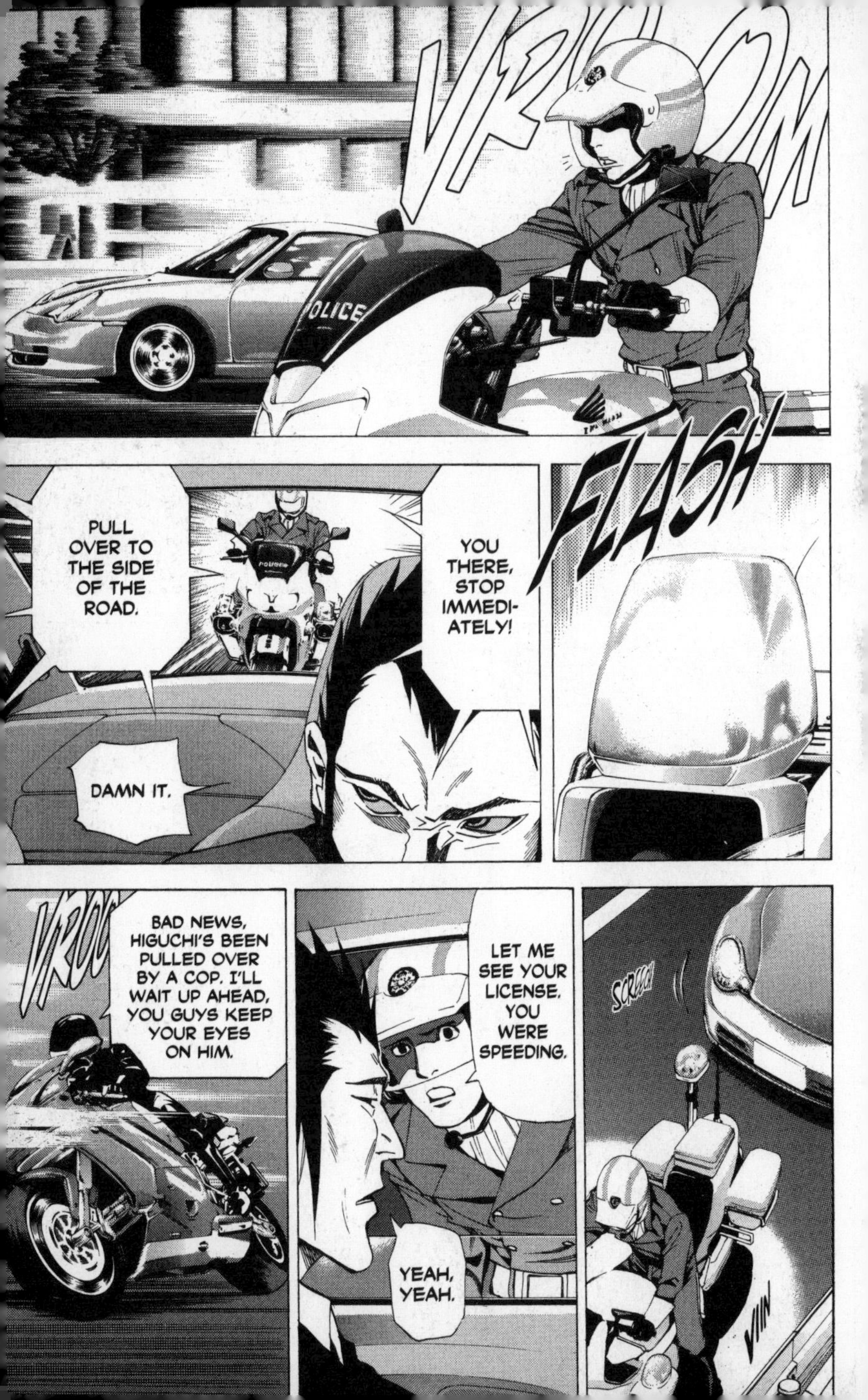
VROOOM
FLASH
YOU THERE, STOP IMMEDIATELY!
PULL OVER TO THE SIDE OF THE ROAD.
DAMN IT.
SCREECH
VIIN
LET ME SEE YOUR LICENSE. YOU WERE SPEEDING.
YEAH, YEAH.
BAD NEWS, HIGUCHI'S BEEN PULLED OVER BY A COP. I'LL WAIT UP AHEAD, YOU GUYS KEEP YOUR EYES ON HIM.

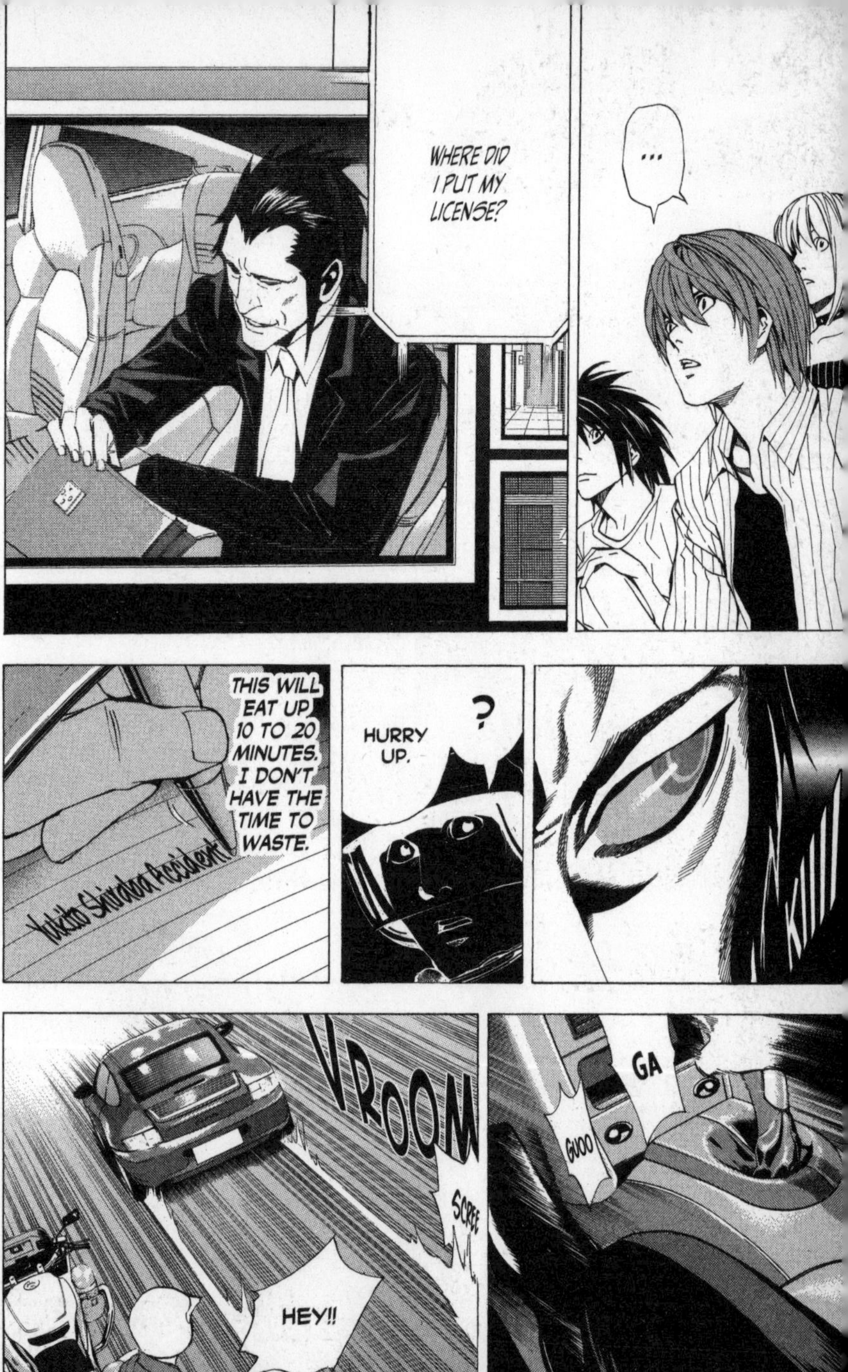
...
WHERE DID I PUT MY LICENSE?
?
HURRY UP.
THIS WILL EAT UP 10 TO 20 MINUTES. I DON'T HAVE THE TIME TO WASTE.
GA
GUOO
VROOM
SCREE
HEY!!

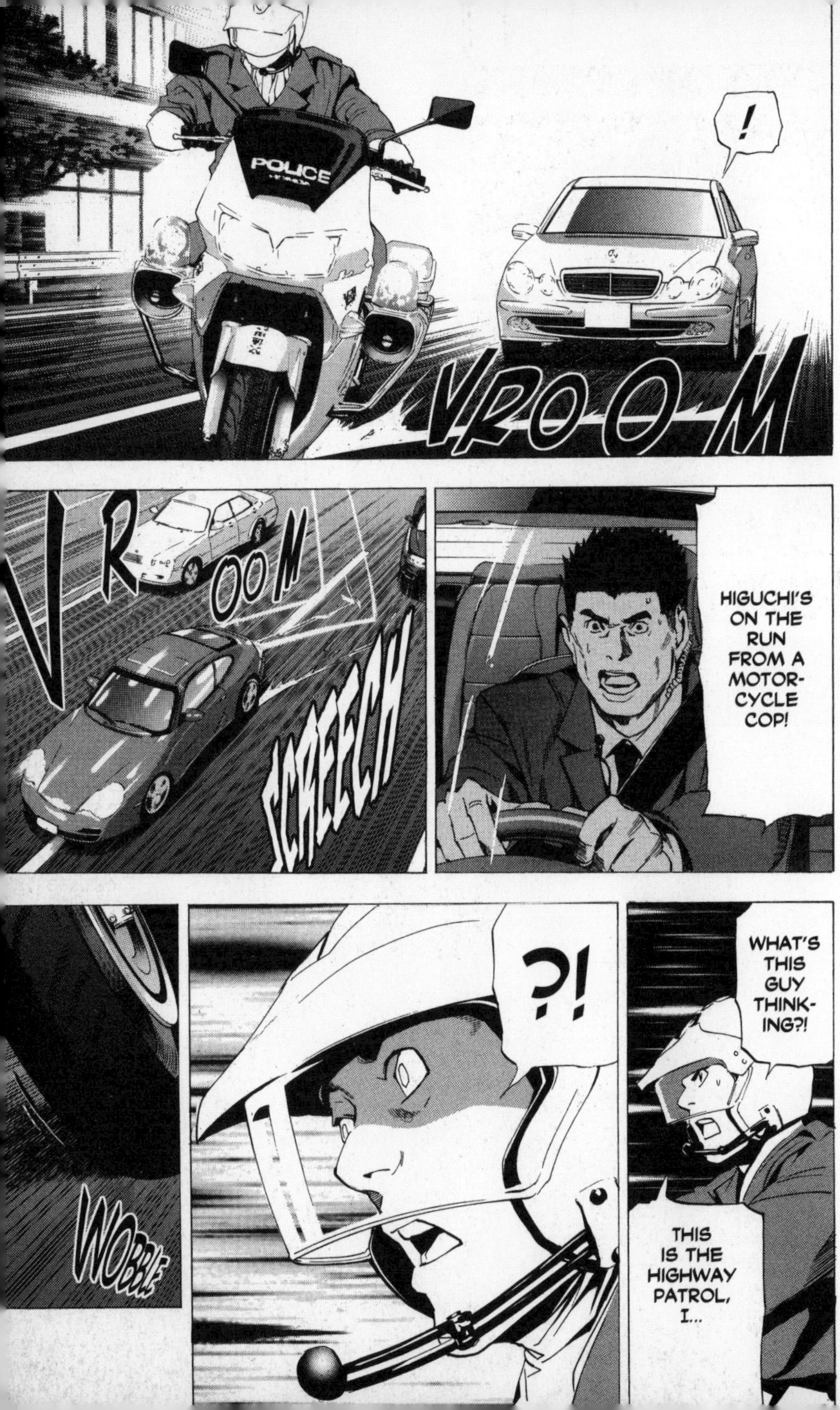
!
VROOM
HIGUCHI'S ON THE RUN FROM A MOTOR-CYCLE COP!
VROOM
SCREECH
WHAT'S THIS GUY THINKING?!
THIS IS THE HIGHWAY PATROL, I...
?!
WOBBLE

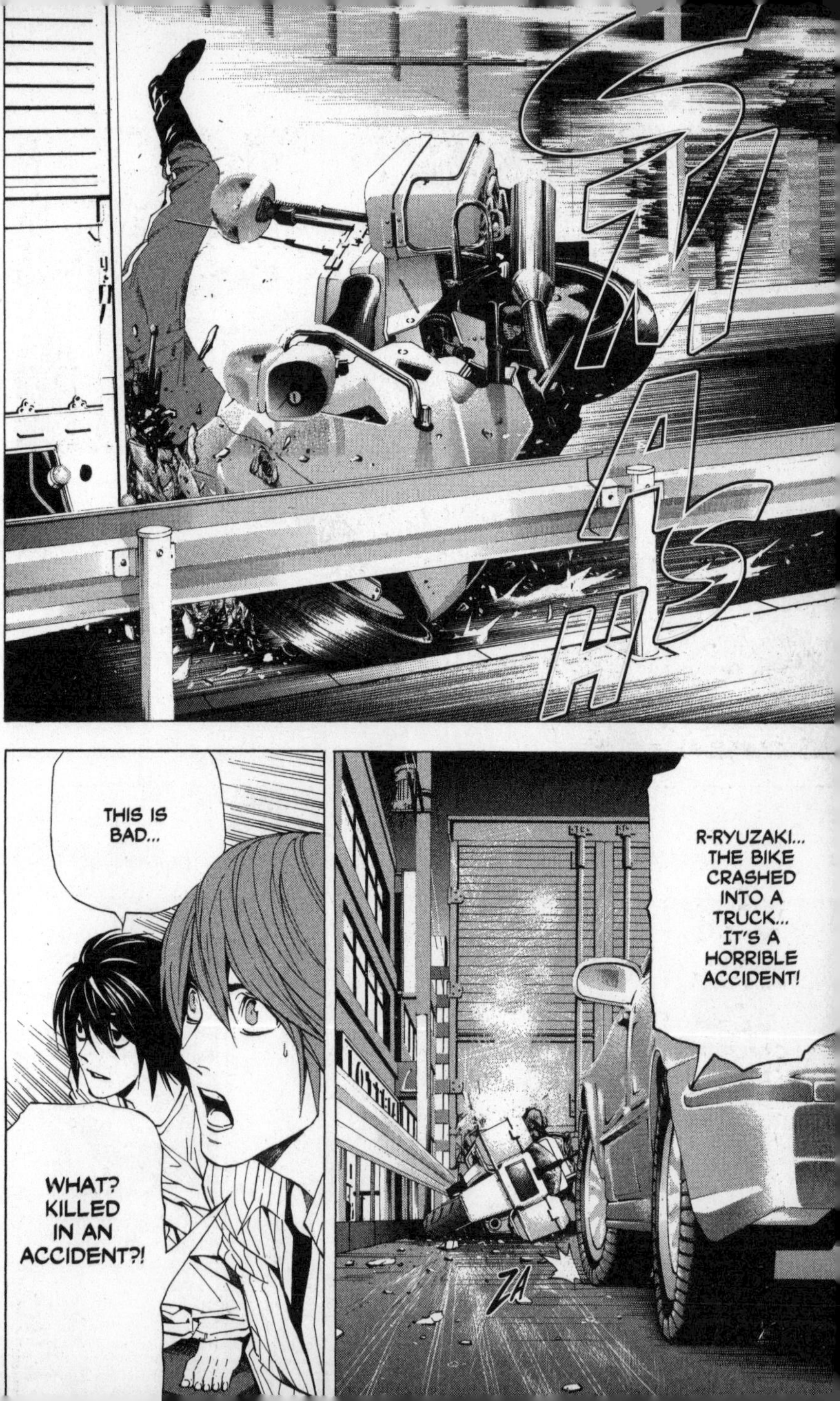
R-RYUZAKI... THE BIKE CRASHED INTO A TRUCK... IT'S A HORRIBLE ACCIDENT!
ZA
THIS IS BAD...
WHAT? KILLED IN AN ACCIDENT?!

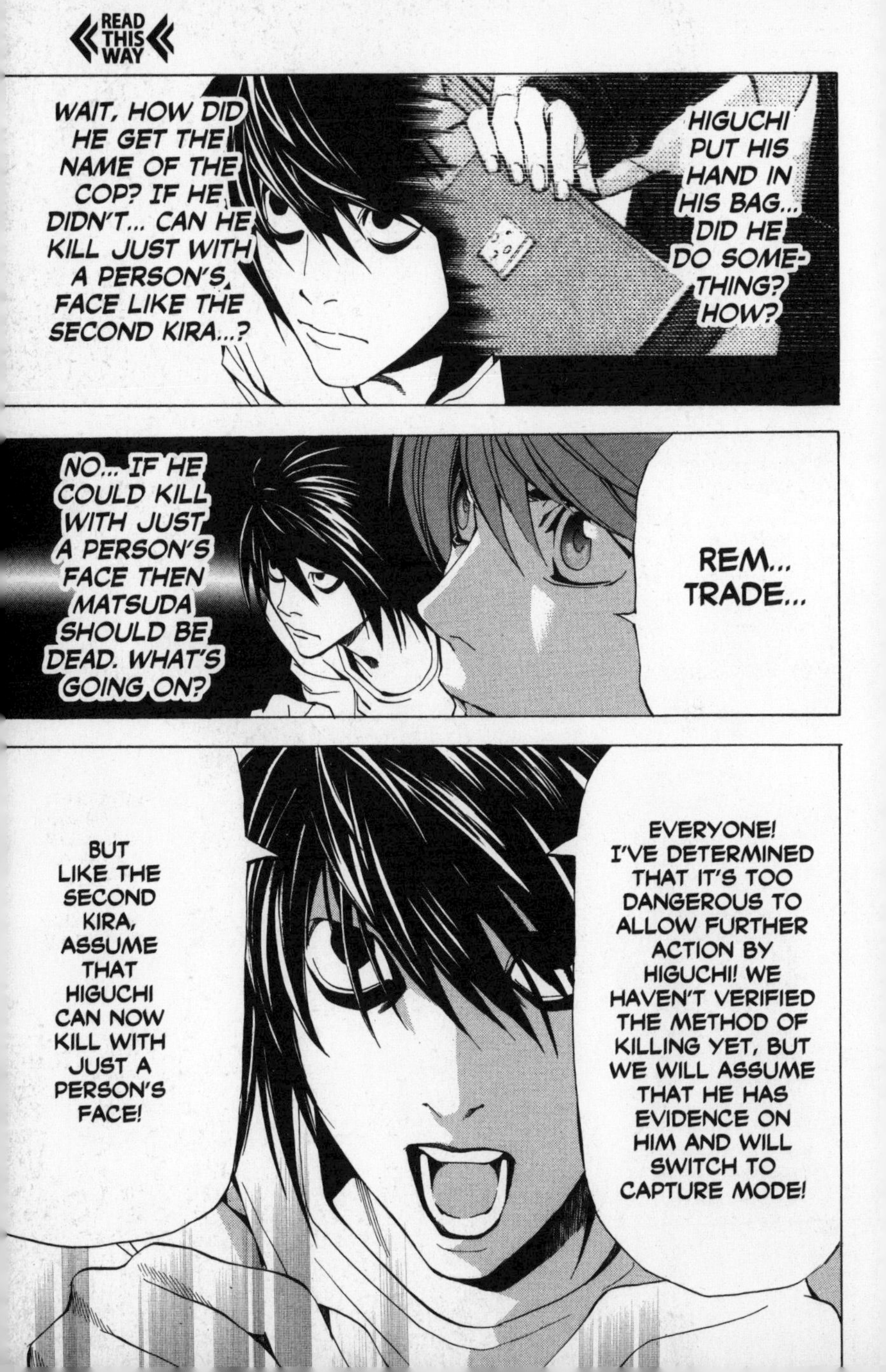
READ THIS WAY
HIGUCHI PUT HIS HAND IN HIS BAG... DID HE DO SOMETHING? HOW?
WAIT, HOW DID HE GET THE NAME OF THE COP? IF HE DIDN'T... CAN HE KILL JUST WITH A PERSON'S FACE LIKE THE SECOND KIRA...?
REM... TRADE...
NO... IF HE COULD KILL WITH JUST A PERSON'S FACE THEN MATSUDA SHOULD BE DEAD. WHAT'S GOING ON?
EVERYONE! I'VE DETERMINED THAT IT'S TOO DANGEROUS TO ALLOW FURTHER ACTION BY HIGUCHI! WE HAVEN'T VERIFIED THE METHOD OF KILLING YET, BUT WE WILL ASSUME THAT HE HAS EVIDENCE ON HIM AND WILL SWITCH TO CAPTURE MODE!
BUT LIKE THE SECOND KIRA, ASSUME THAT HIGUCHI CAN NOW KILL WITH JUST A PERSON'S FACE!

chapter 52 Split-Second

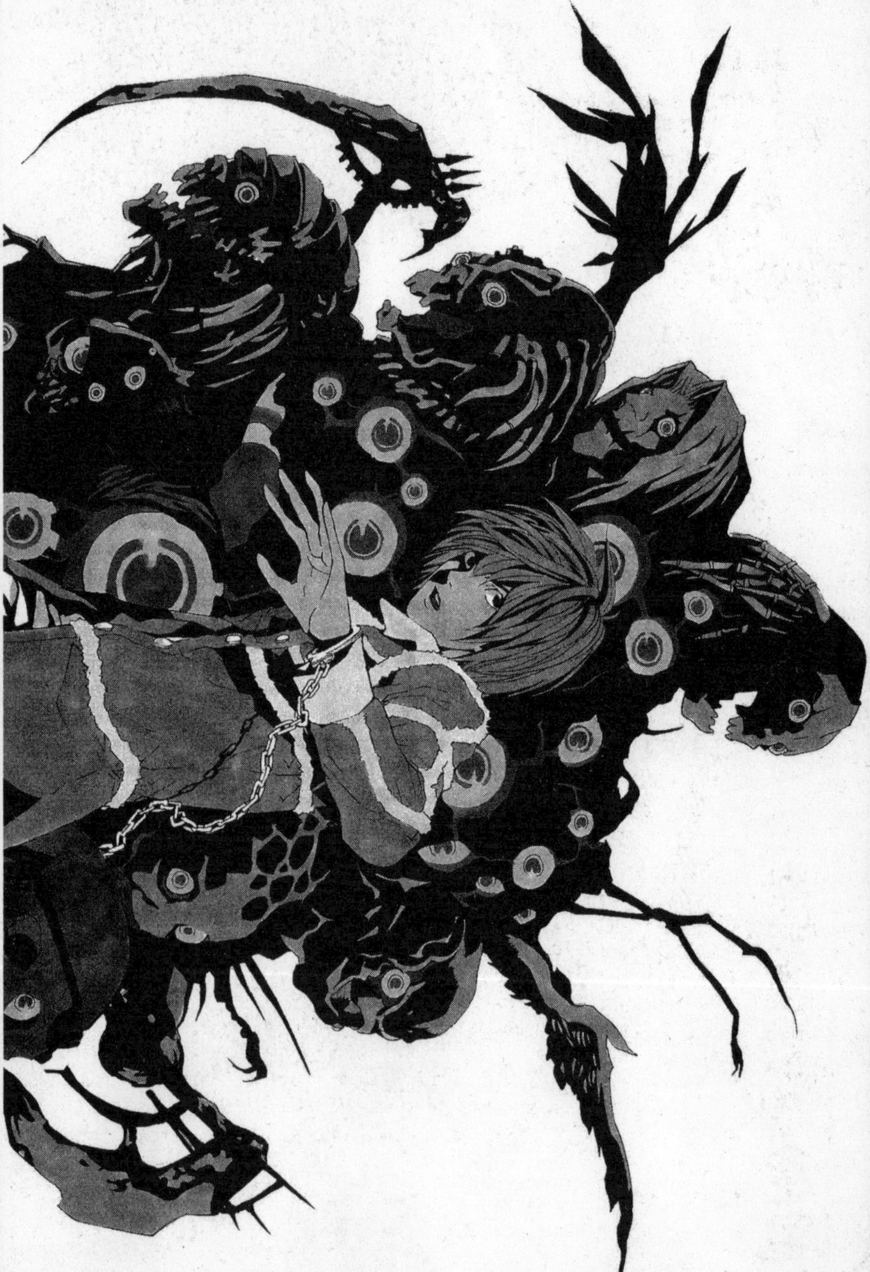

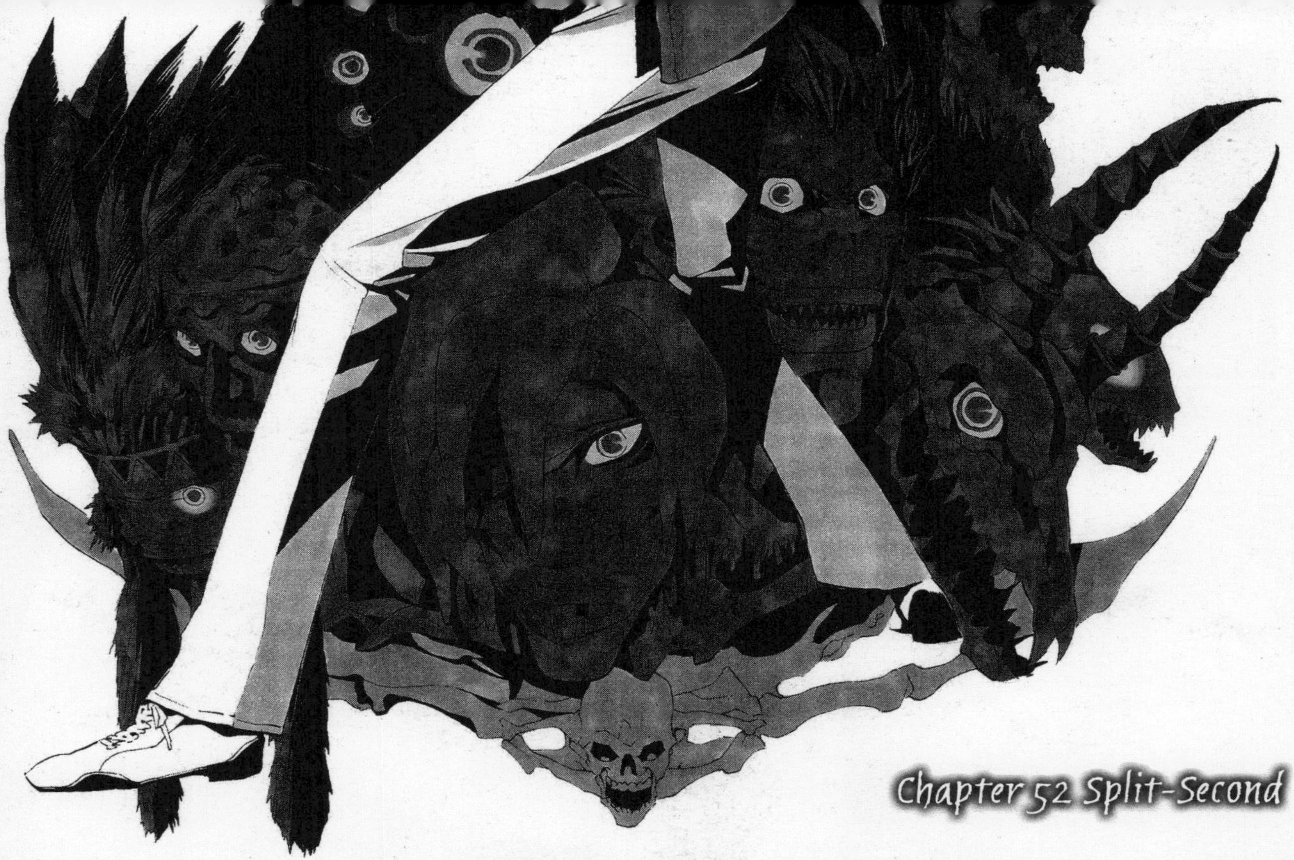

Chapter 52 Split-Second

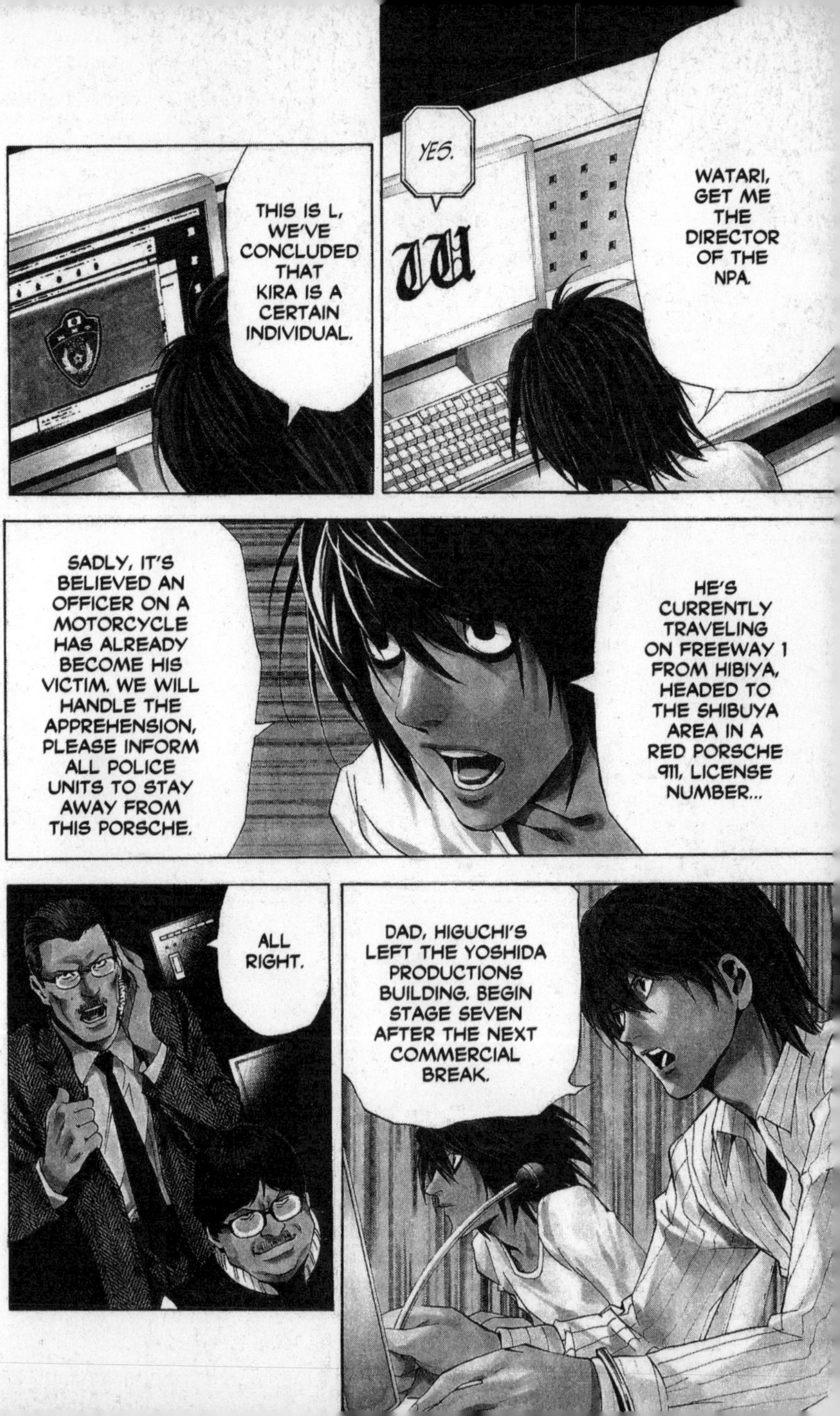
WATARI, GET ME THE DIRECTOR OF THE NPA.
YES.
THIS IS L, WE'VE CONCLUDED THAT KIRA IS A CERTAIN INDIVIDUAL.
HE'S CURRENTLY TRAVELING ON FREEWAY 1 FROM HIBIYA, HEADED TO THE SHIBUYA AREA IN A RED PORSCHE 911, LICENSE NUMBER...
SADLY, IT'S BELIEVED AN OFFICER ON A MOTORCYCLE HAS ALREADY BECOME HIS VICTIM. WE WILL HANDLE THE APPREHENSION, PLEASE INFORM ALL POLICE UNITS TO STAY AWAY FROM THIS PORSCHE.
DAD, HIGUCHI'S LEFT THE YOSHIDA PRODUCTIONS BUILDING. BEGIN STAGE SEVEN AFTER THE NEXT COMMERCIAL BREAK.
ALL RIGHT.

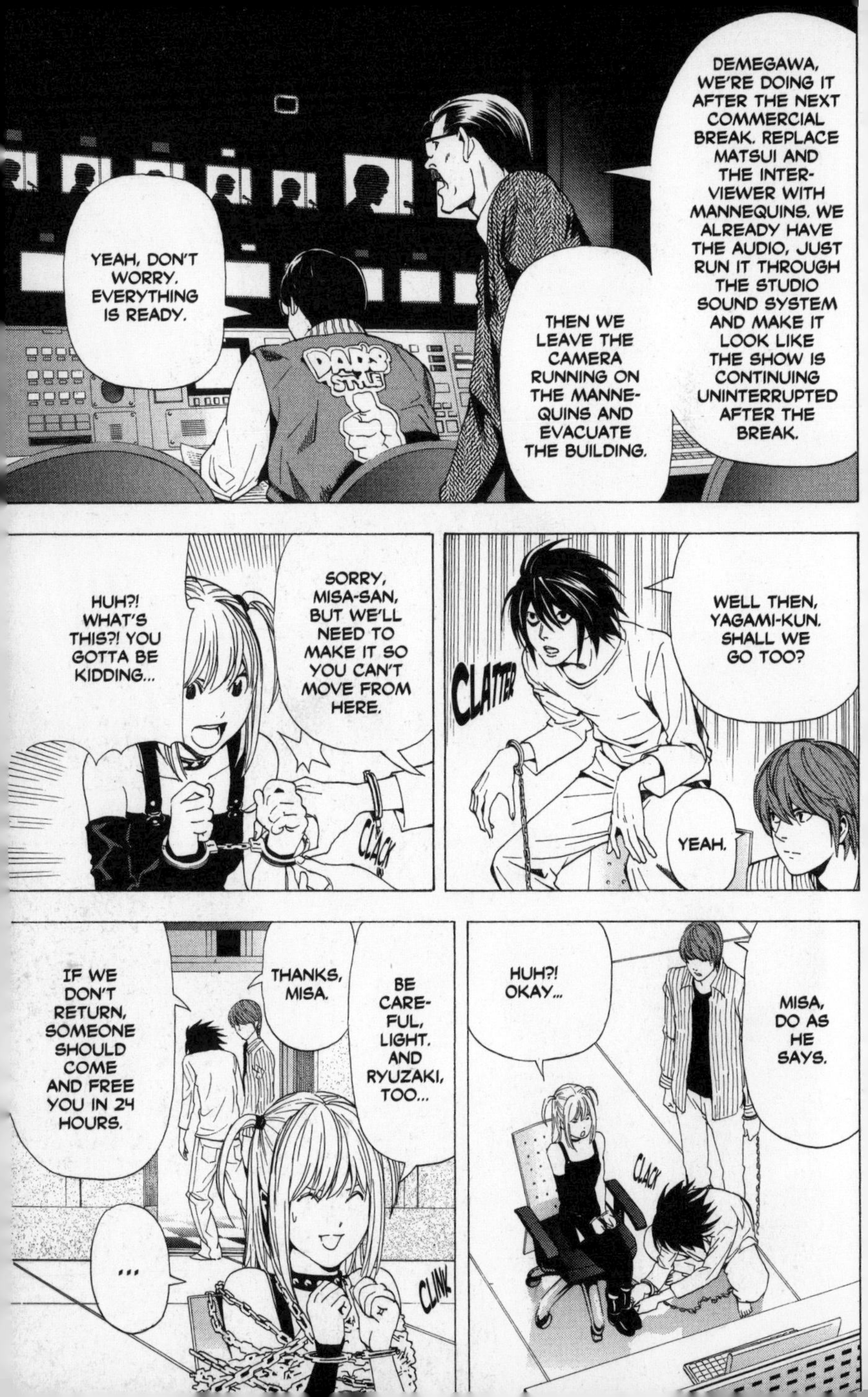
DEMEGAWA, WE'RE DOING IT AFTER THE NEXT COMMERCIAL BREAK. REPLACE MATSUI AND THE INTERVIEWER WITH MANNEQUINS. WE ALREADY HAVE THE AUDIO, JUST RUN IT THROUGH THE STUDIO SOUND SYSTEM AND MAKE IT LOOK LIKE THE SHOW IS CONTINUING UNINTERRUPTED AFTER THE BREAK.
THEN WE LEAVE THE CAMERA RUNNING ON THE MANNEQUINS AND EVACUATE THE BUILDING.
YEAH, DON'T WORRY. EVERYTHING IS READY.
DADS STYLE
WELL THEN, YAGAMI-KUN. SHALL WE GO TOO?
CLATTER
YEAH.
SORRY, MISA-SAN, BUT WE'LL NEED TO MAKE IT SO YOU CAN'T MOVE FROM HERE.
HUH?! WHAT'S THIS?! YOU GOTTA BE KIDDING...
CLACK
MISA, DO AS HE SAYS.
HUH?! OKAY...
CLACK
BE CAREFUL, LIGHT. AND RYUZAKI, TOO...
THANKS, MISA.
IF WE DON'T RETURN, SOMEONE SHOULD COME AND FREE YOU IN 24 HOURS.
...
CLINK

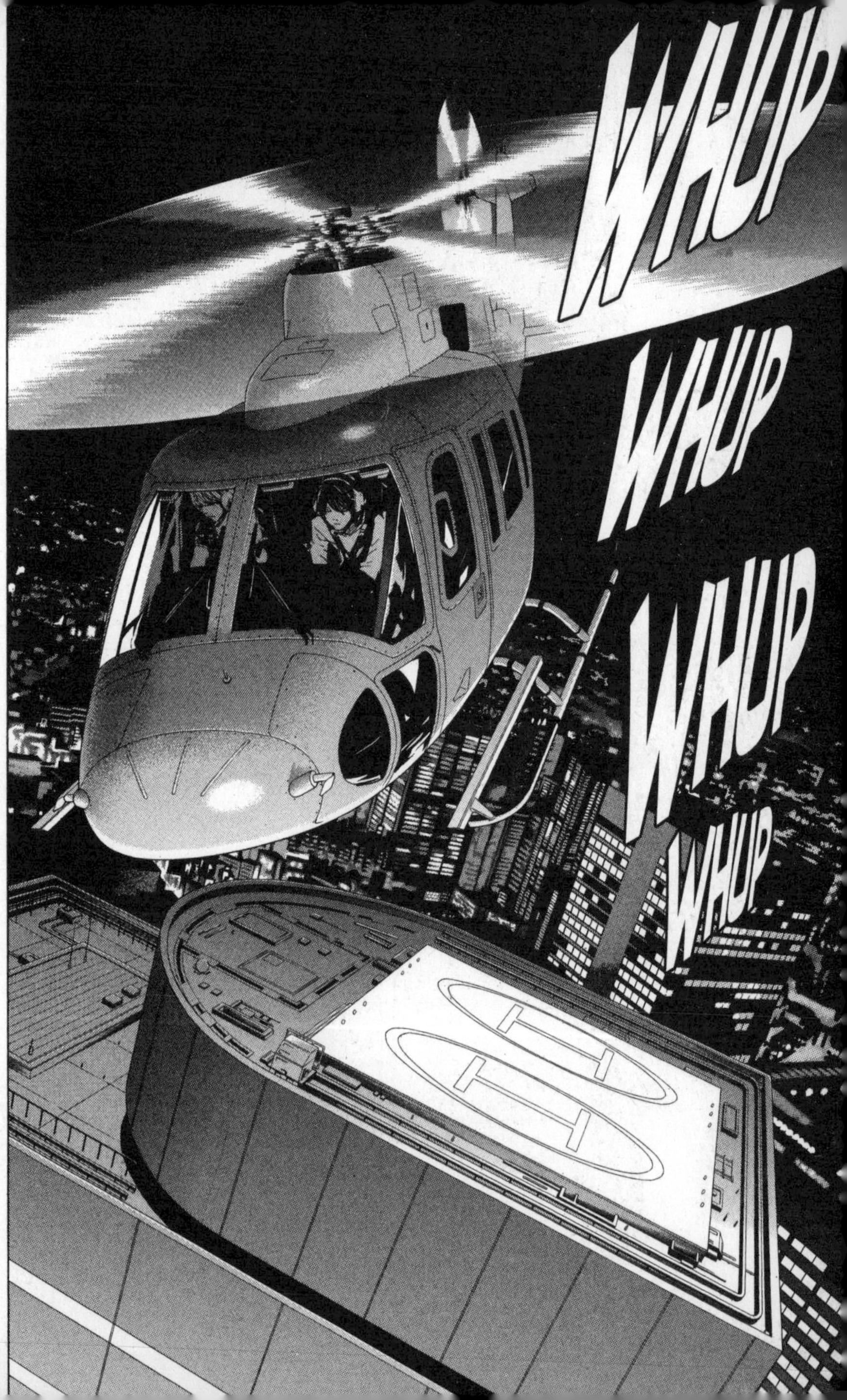
WHUP
WHUP
WHUP
WHUP

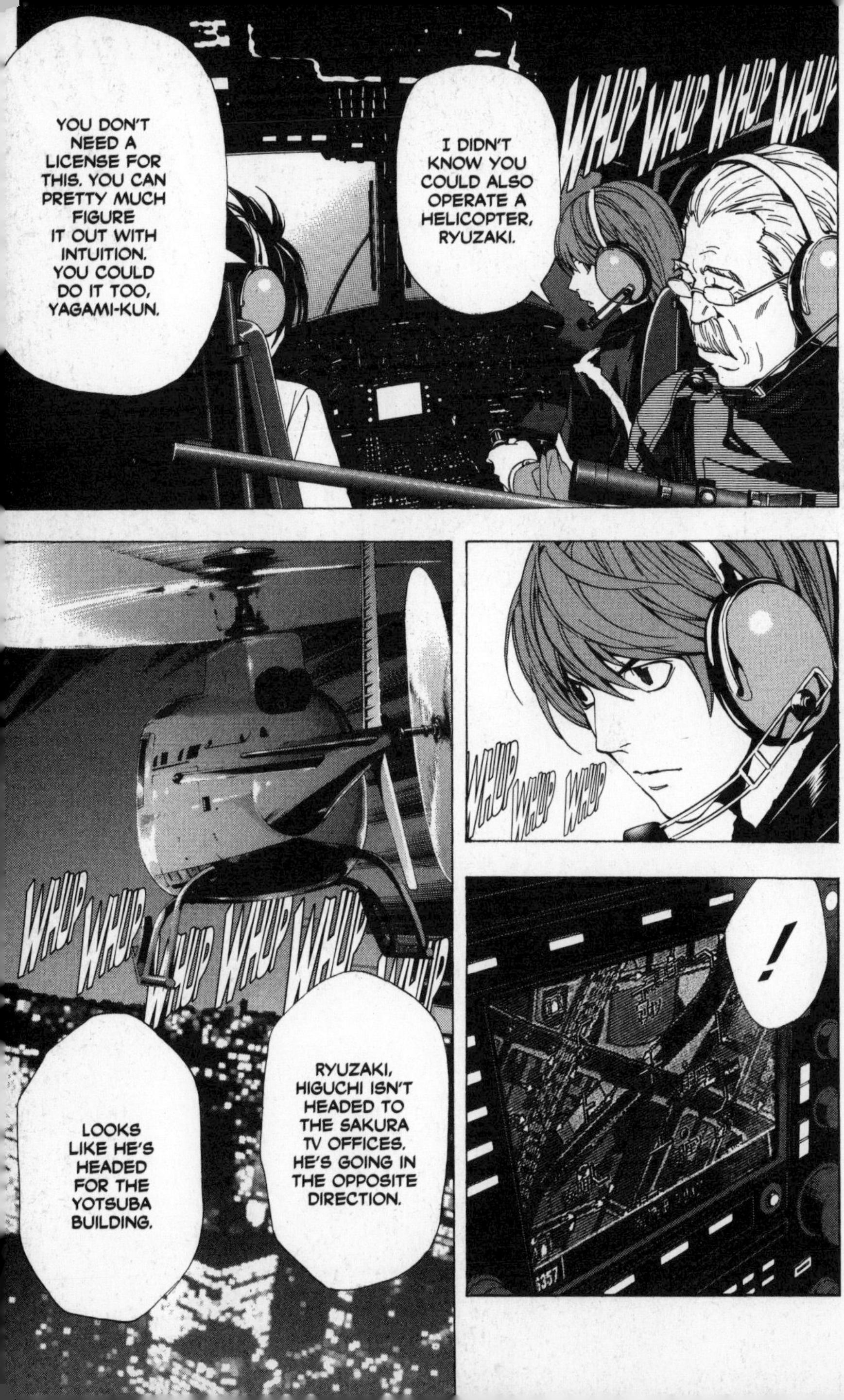
WHUP WHUP WHUP WHUP
I DIDN'T KNOW YOU COULD ALSO OPERATE A HELICOPTER, RYUZAKI.
YOU DON'T NEED A LICENSE FOR THIS. YOU CAN PRETTY MUCH FIGURE IT OUT WITH INTUITION. YOU COULD DO IT TOO, YAGAMI-KUN.
WHUP WHUP WHUP
!
WHUP WHUP WHUP WHUP WHUP
RYUZAKI, HIGUCHI ISN'T HEADED TO THE SAKURA TV OFFICES. HE'S GOING IN THE OPPOSITE DIRECTION.
LOOKS LIKE HE'S HEADED FOR THE YOTSUBA BUILDING.

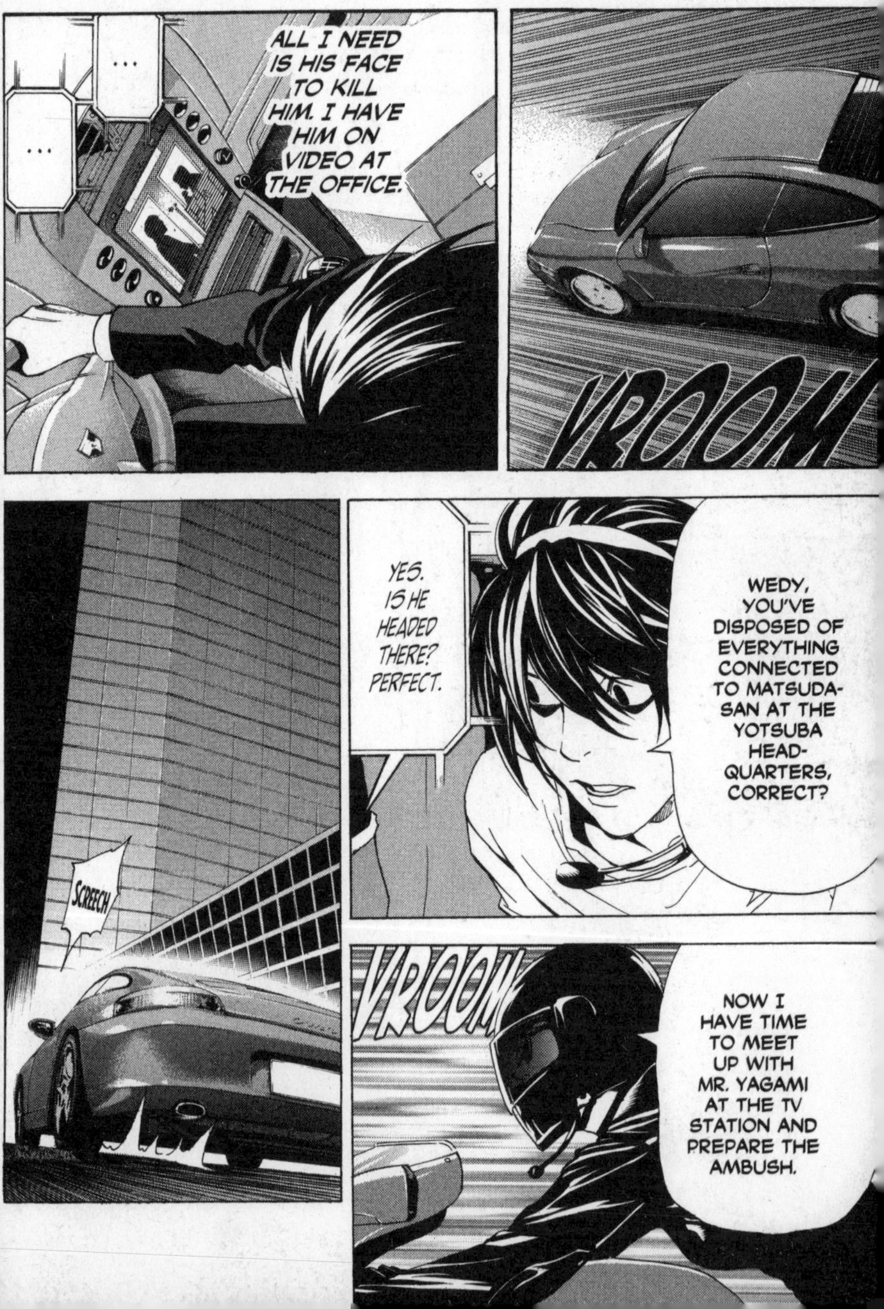
VROOM
...
...
ALL I NEED IS HIS FACE TO KILL HIM. I HAVE HIM ON VIDEO AT THE OFFICE.
WEDY, YOU'VE DISPOSED OF EVERYTHING CONNECTED TO MATSUDA-SAN AT THE YOTSUBA HEAD-QUARTERS, CORRECT?
YES. IS HE HEADED THERE? PERFECT.
VROOM
NOW I HAVE TIME TO MEET UP WITH MR. YAGAMI AT THE TV STATION AND PREPARE THE AMBUSH.
SCREECH

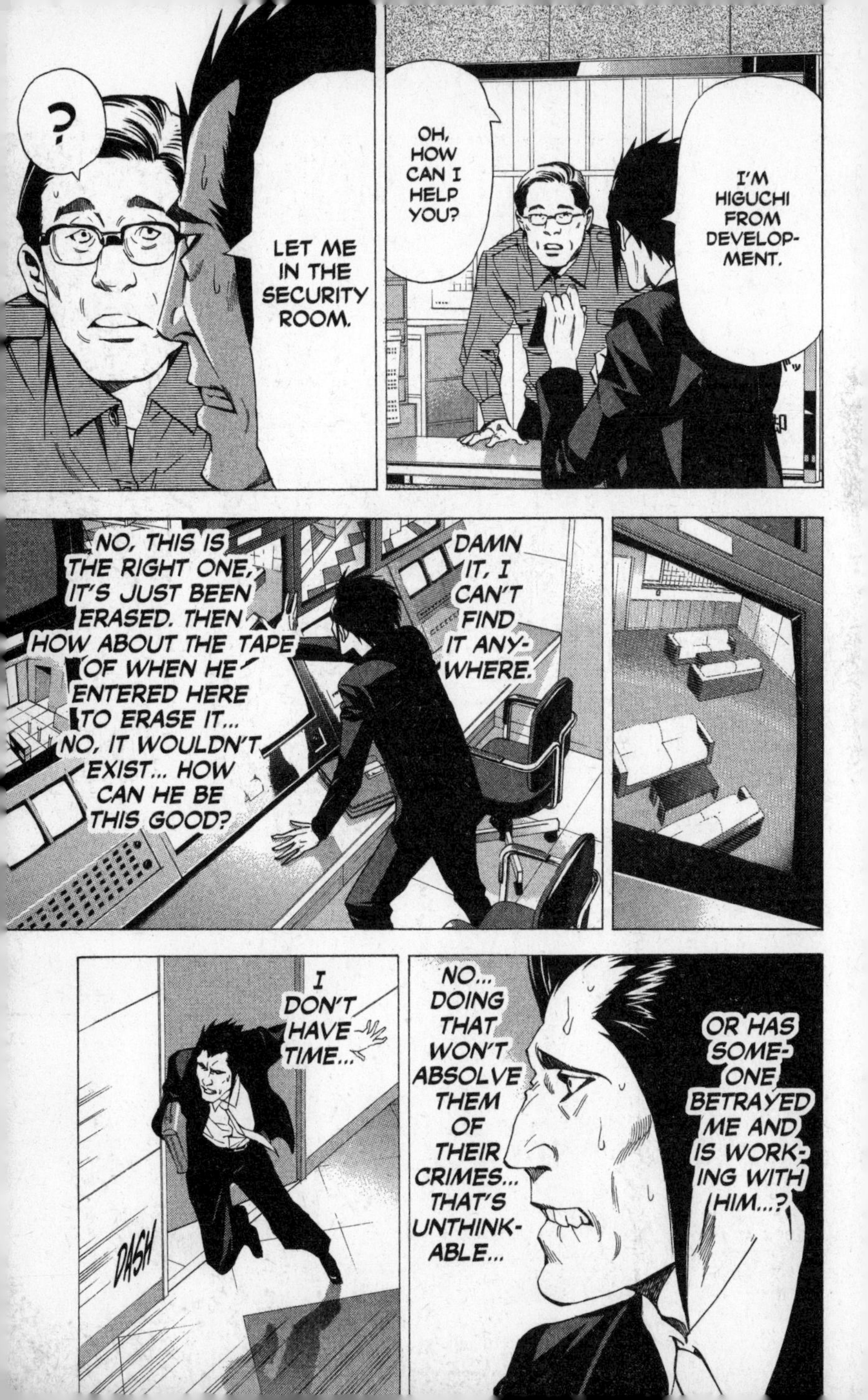
I'M HIGUCHI FROM DEVELOPMENT.
OH, HOW CAN I HELP YOU?
LET ME IN THE SECURITY ROOM.
?
DAMN IT, I CAN'T FIND IT ANYWHERE.
NO, THIS IS THE RIGHT ONE, IT'S JUST BEEN ERASED. THEN HOW ABOUT THE TAPE OF WHEN HE ENTERED HERE TO ERASE IT... NO, IT WOULDN'T EXIST... HOW CAN HE BE THIS GOOD?
OR HAS SOMEONE BETRAYED ME AND IS WORKING WITH HIM...?
NO... DOING THAT WON'T ABSOLVE THEM OF THEIR CRIMES... THAT'S UNTHINKABLE...
I DON'T HAVE TIME...
DASH

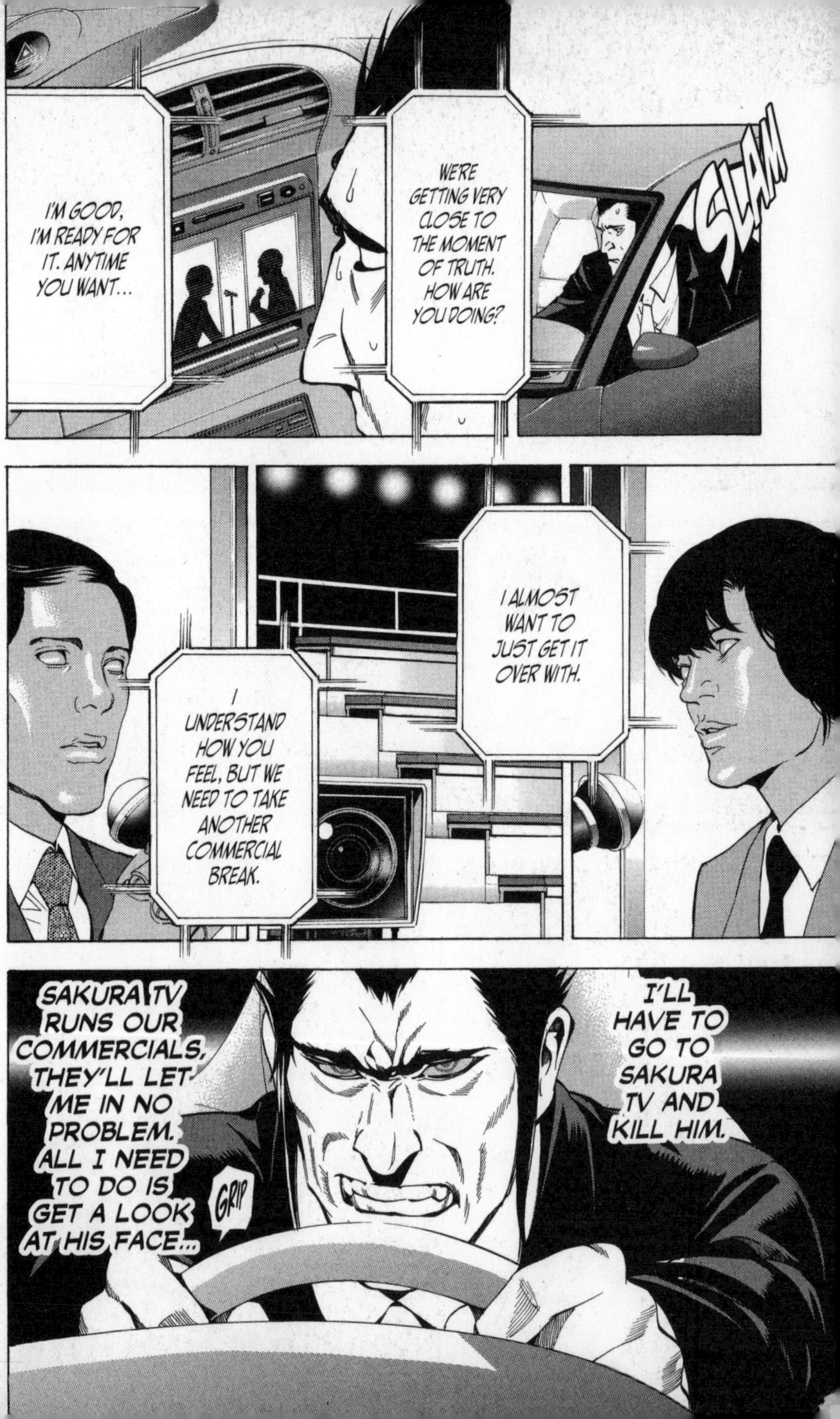
SLAM
WE'RE GETTING VERY CLOSE TO THE MOMENT OF TRUTH. HOW ARE YOU DOING?
I'M GOOD, I'M READY FOR IT. ANYTIME YOU WANT...
I ALMOST WANT TO JUST GET IT OVER WITH.
I UNDERSTAND HOW YOU FEEL, BUT WE NEED TO TAKE ANOTHER COMMERCIAL BREAK.
I'LL HAVE TO GO TO SAKURA TV AND KILL HIM.
SAKURA TV RUNS OUR COMMERCIALS, THEY'LL LET ME IN NO PROBLEM. ALL I NEED TO DO IS GET A LOOK AT HIS FACE...
GRIP

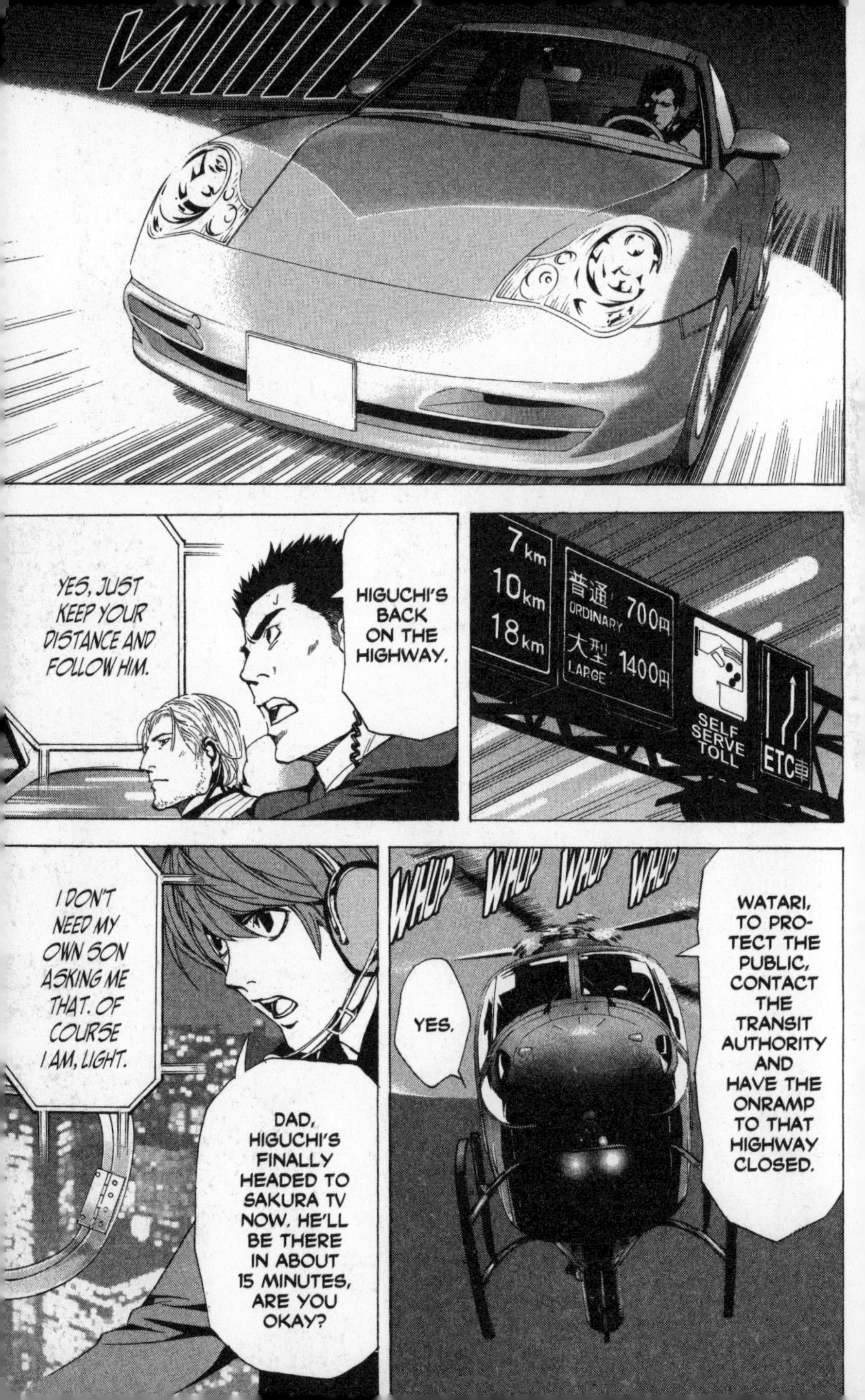
7km
10km
18km
普通 ORDINARY 700円
大型 LARGE 1400円
SELF SERVE TOLL
ETC車
HIGUCHI'S BACK ON THE HIGHWAY.
YES, JUST KEEP YOUR DISTANCE AND FOLLOW HIM.
WHUP WHUP WHUP WHUP
WATARI, TO PROTECT THE PUBLIC, CONTACT THE TRANSIT AUTHORITY AND HAVE THE ONRAMP TO THAT HIGHWAY CLOSED.
YES.
DAD, HIGUCHI'S FINALLY HEADED TO SAKURA TV NOW. HE'LL BE THERE IN ABOUT 15 MINUTES, ARE YOU OKAY?
I DON'T NEED MY OWN SON ASKING ME THAT. OF COURSE I AM, LIGHT.

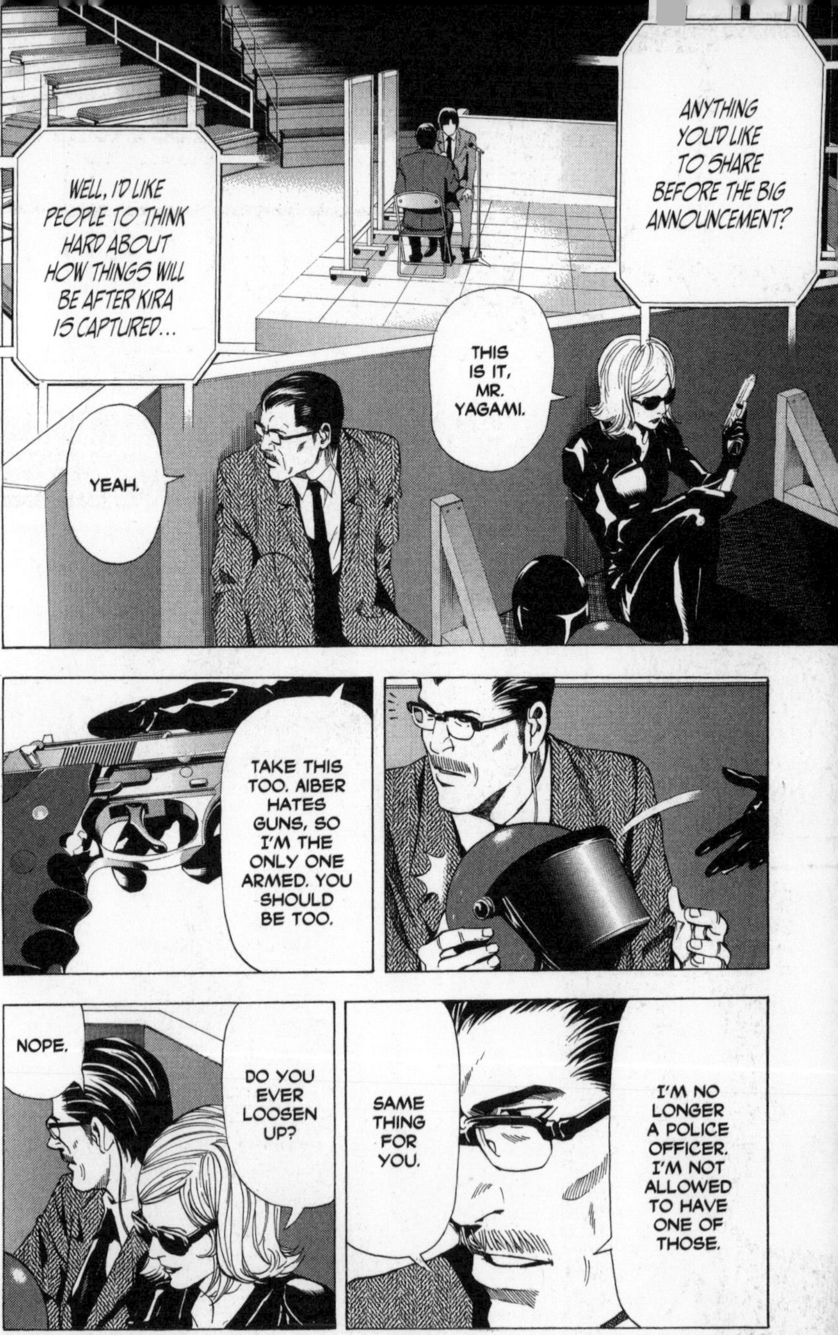
ANYTHING YOU'D LIKE TO SHARE BEFORE THE BIG ANNOUNCEMENT?
WELL, I'D LIKE PEOPLE TO THINK HARD ABOUT HOW THINGS WILL BE AFTER KIRA IS CAPTURED...
THIS IS IT, MR. YAGAMI.
YEAH.
TAKE THIS TOO. AIBER HATES GUNS, SO I'M THE ONLY ONE ARMED. YOU SHOULD BE TOO.
I'M NO LONGER A POLICE OFFICER. I'M NOT ALLOWED TO HAVE ONE OF THOSE.
SAME THING FOR YOU.
DO YOU EVER LOOSEN UP?
NOPE.

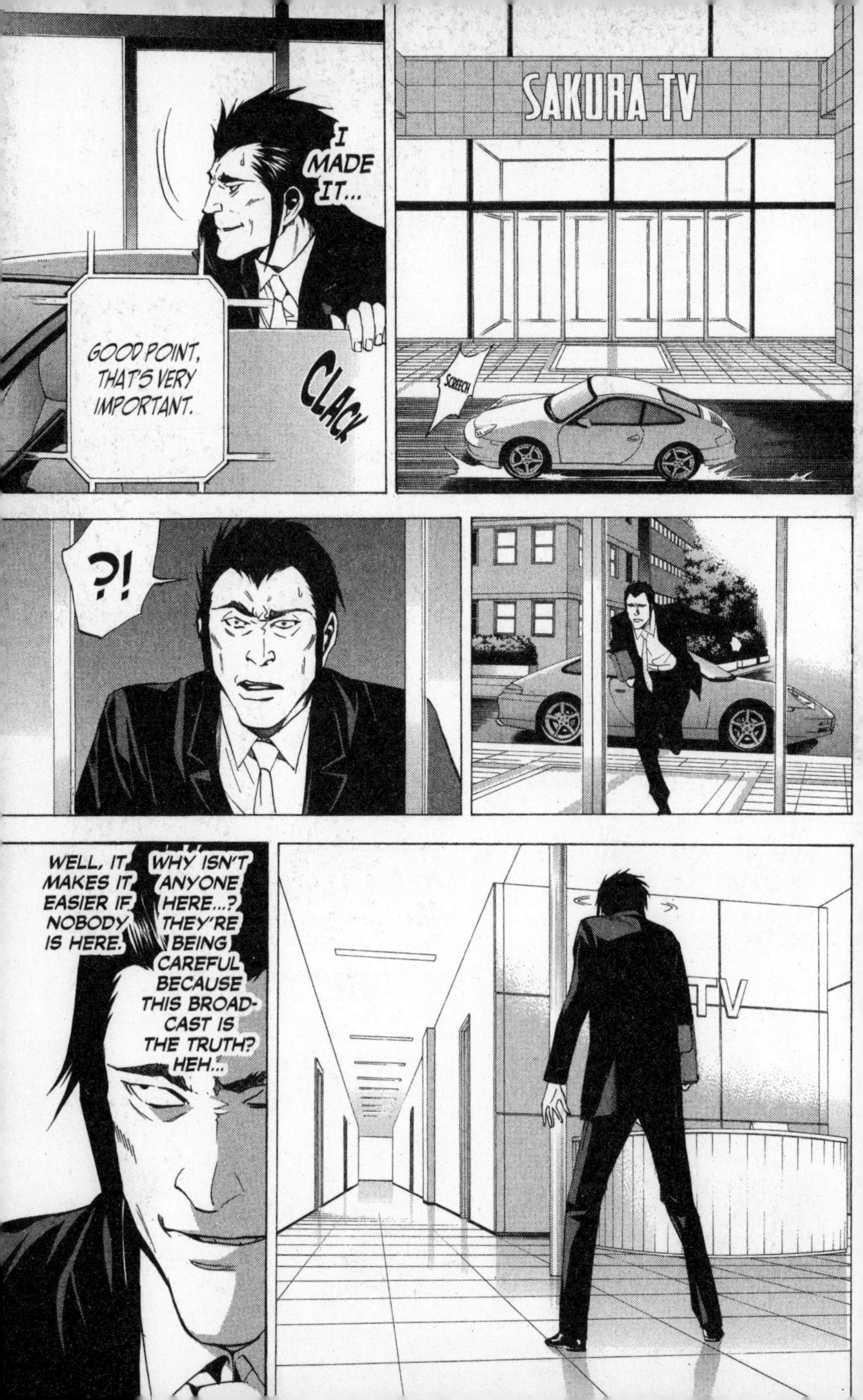
SAKURA TV
SCREECH
I MADE IT...
GOOD POINT, THAT'S VERY IMPORTANT.
CLACK
?!
TV
WHY ISN'T ANYONE HERE...? THEY'RE BEING CAREFUL BECAUSE THIS BROAD-CAST IS THE TRUTH? HEH...
WELL, IT MAKES IT EASIER IF NOBODY IS HERE.

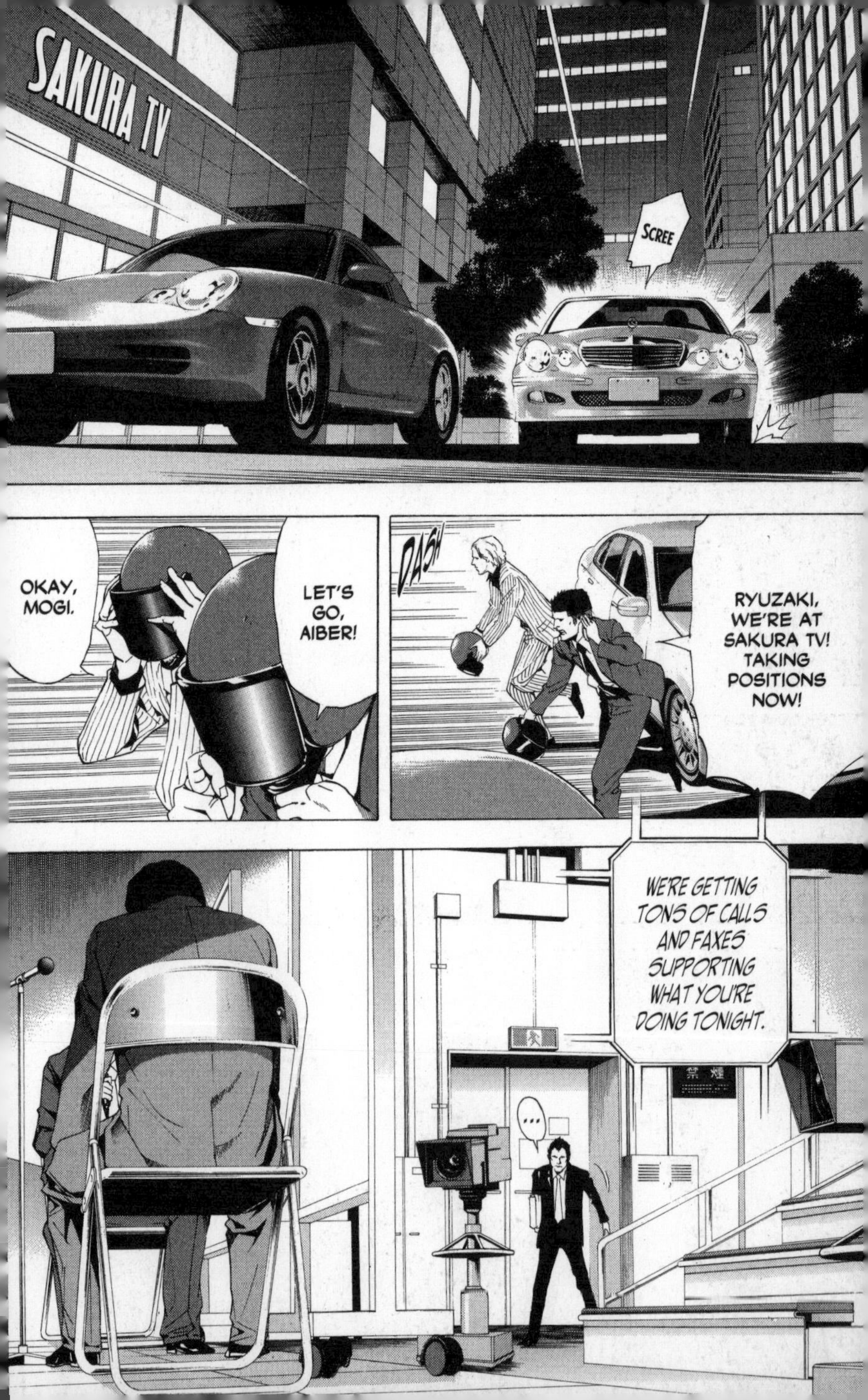
SAKURA TV
SCREE
RYUZAKI, WE'RE AT SAKURA TV! TAKING POSITIONS NOW!
DASH
LET'S GO, AIBER!
OKAY, MOGI.
WE'RE GETTING TONS OF CALLS AND FAXES SUPPORTING WHAT YOU'RE DOING TONIGHT.
...

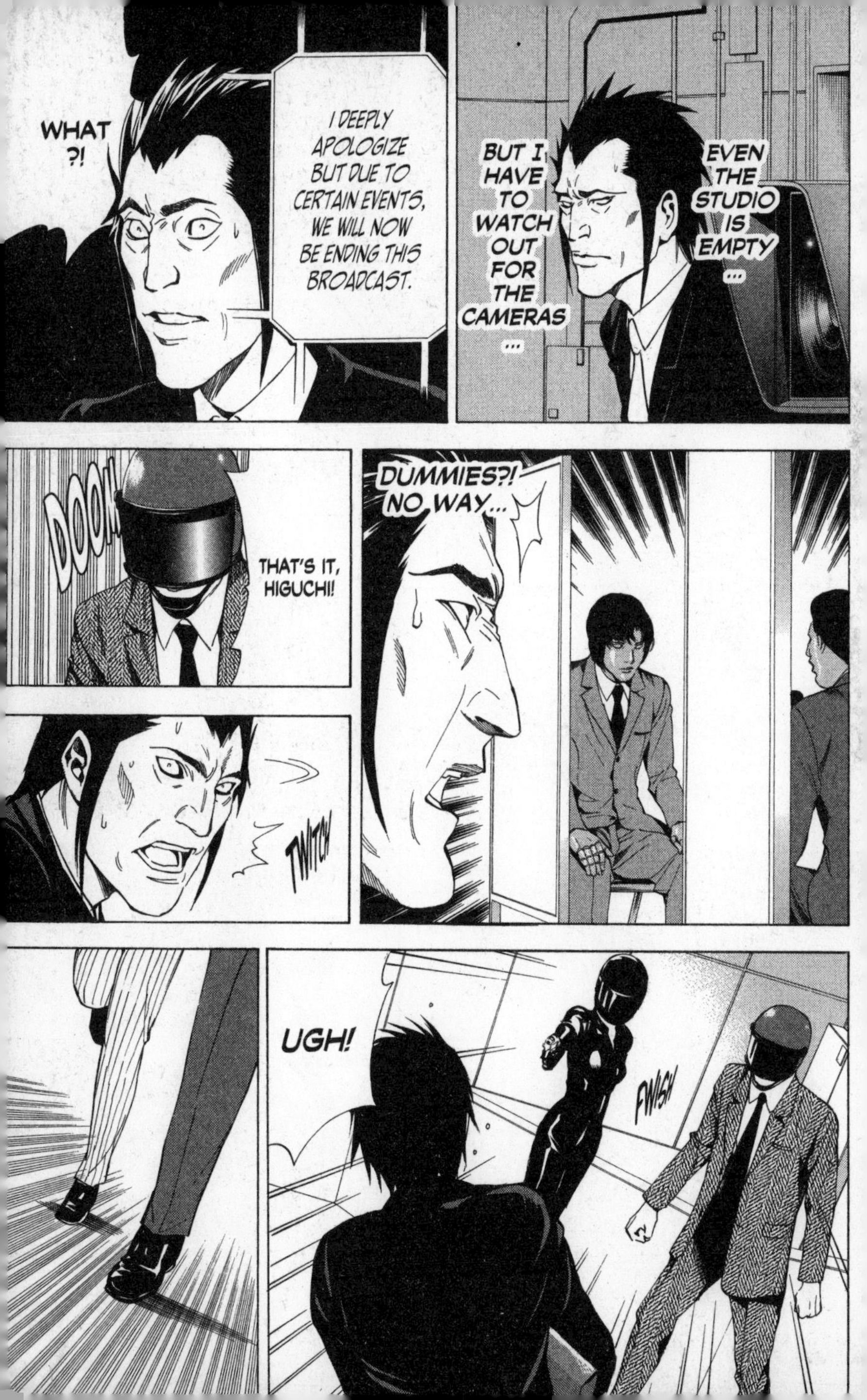
EVEN THE STUDIO IS EMPTY...
BUT I HAVE TO WATCH OUT FOR THE CAMERAS...
I DEEPLY APOLOGIZE BUT DUE TO CERTAIN EVENTS, WE WILL NOW BE ENDING THIS BROADCAST.
WHAT ?!
DUMMIES?! NO WAY...
THAT'S IT, HIGUCHI!
DOOM
TWITCH
FWISH
UGH!

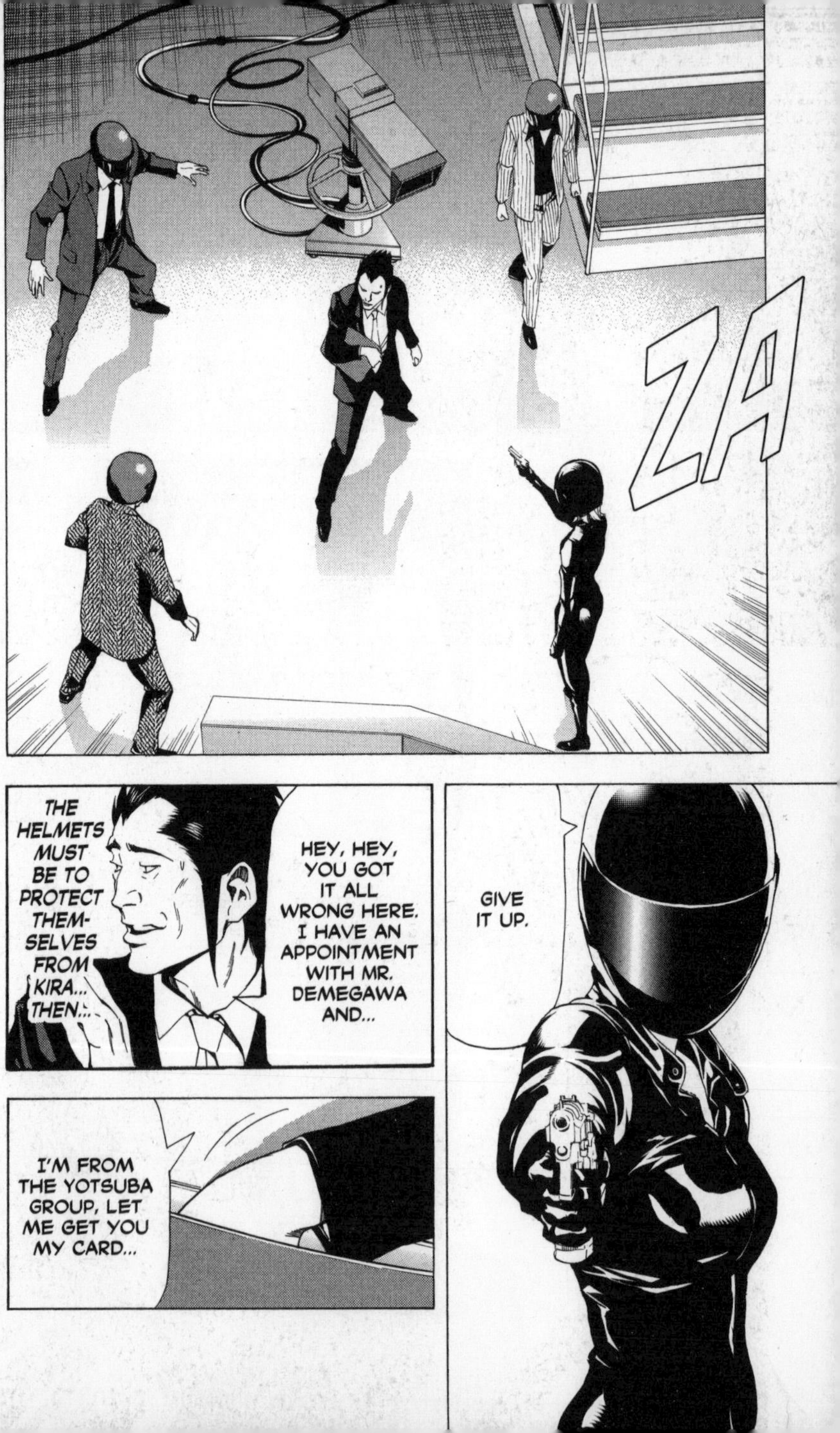
ZA
GIVE IT UP.
HEY, HEY, YOU GOT IT ALL WRONG HERE. I HAVE AN APPOINTMENT WITH MR. DEMEGAWA AND...
THE HELMETS MUST BE TO PROTECT THEM-SELVES FROM KIRA... THEN...
I'M FROM THE YOTSUBA GROUP, LET ME GET YOU MY CARD...

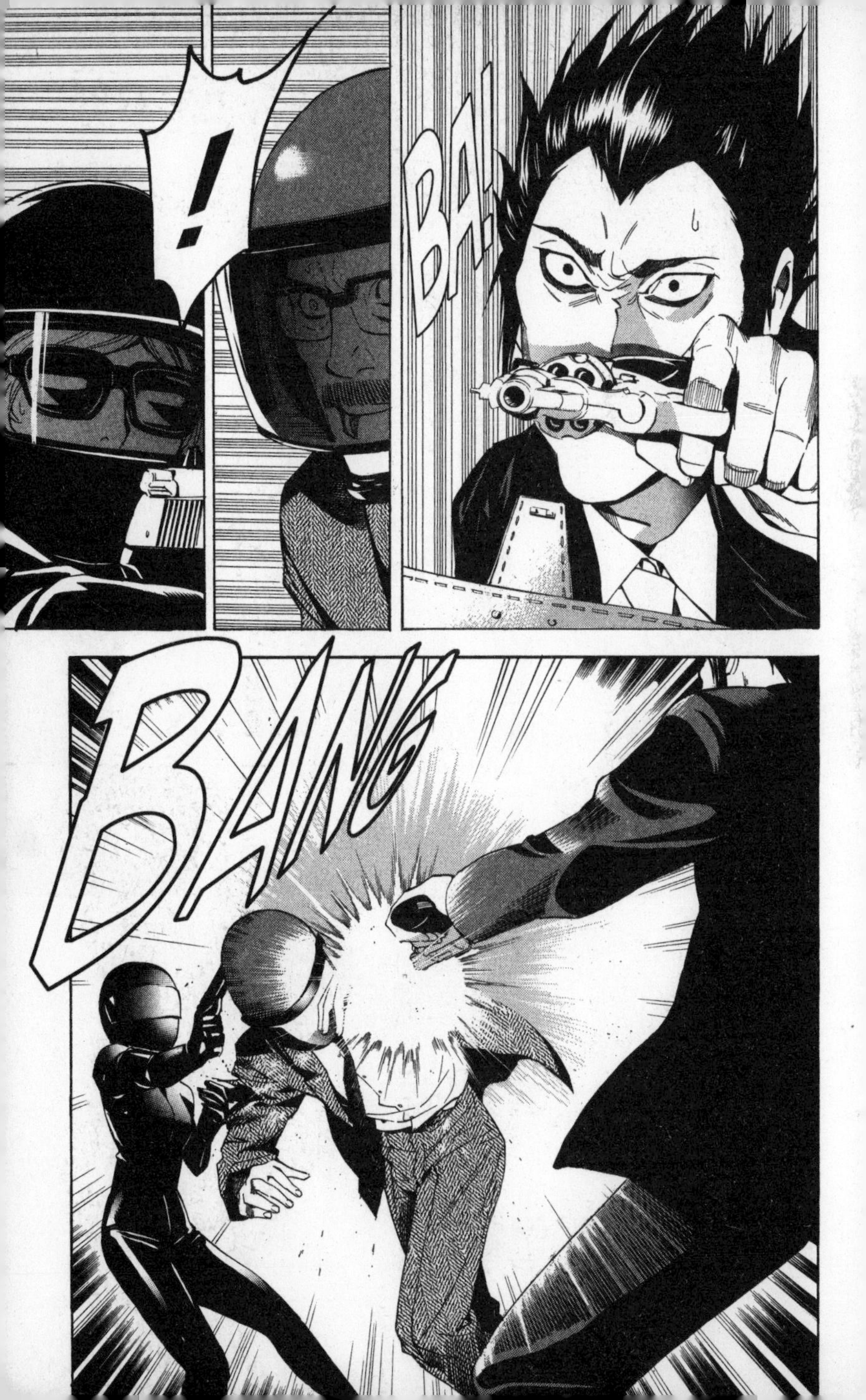
BA!
!
BANG

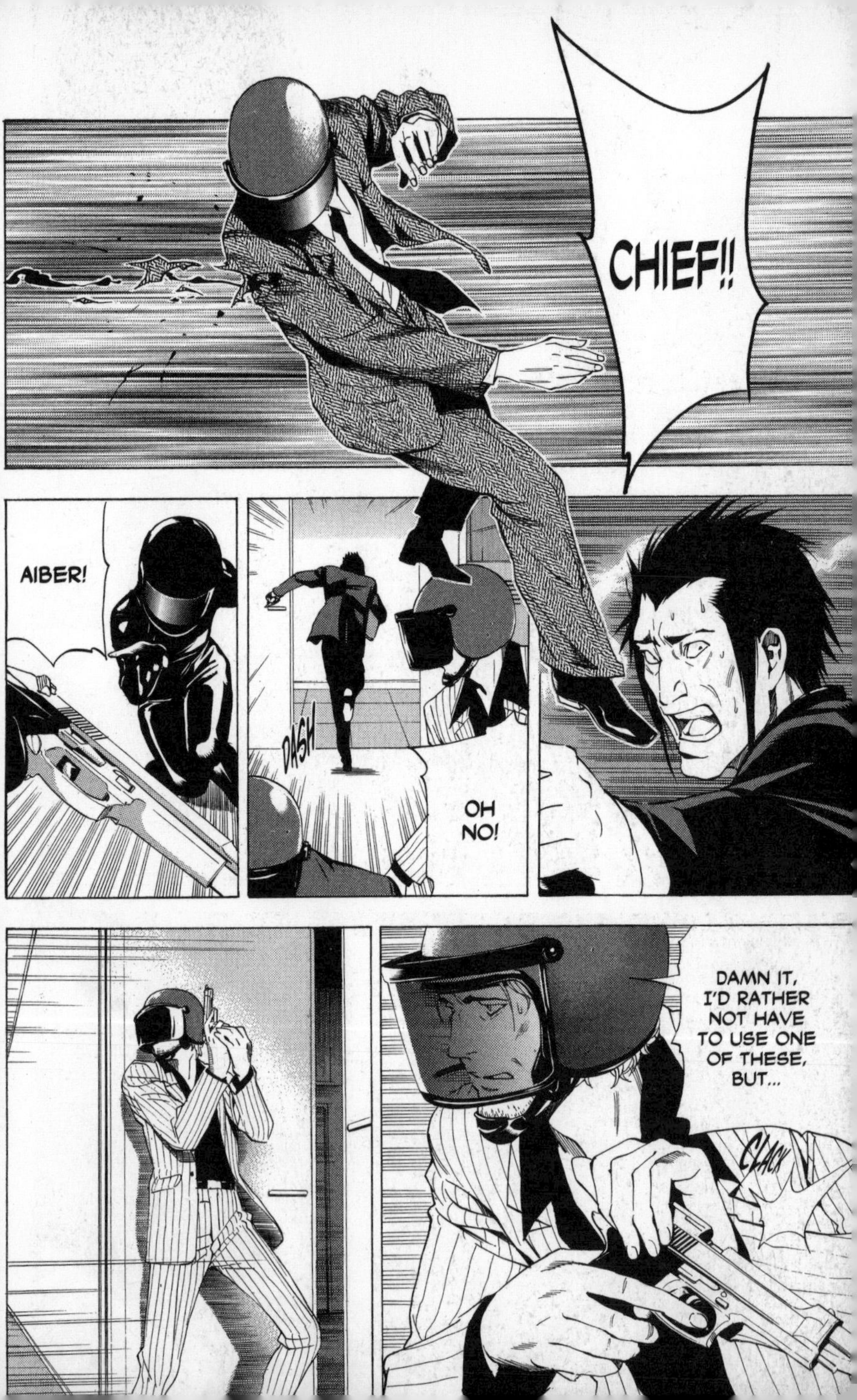
CHIEF!!
DASH
OH NO!
AIBER!
DAMN IT, I'D RATHER NOT HAVE TO USE ONE OF THESE, BUT...
CLACK

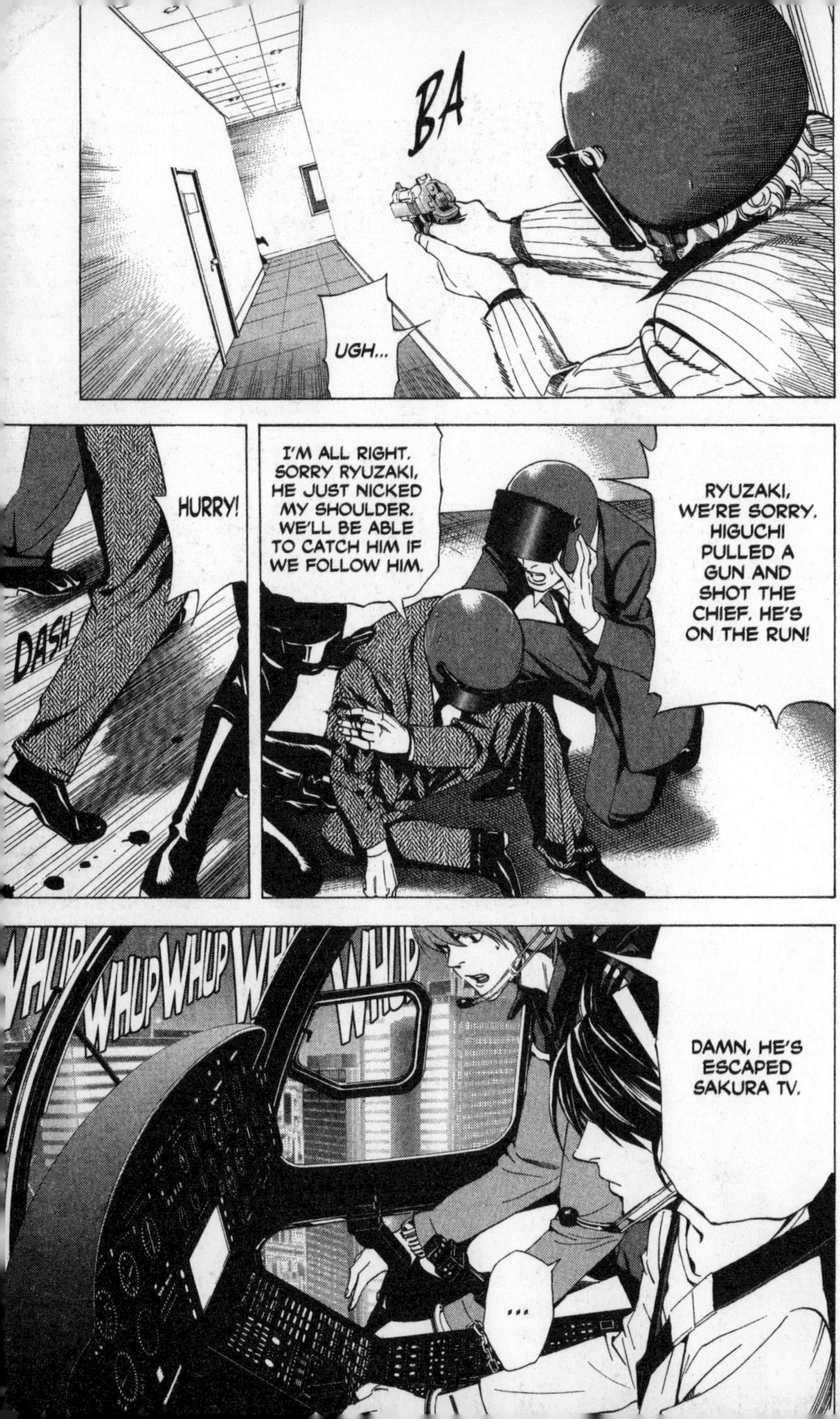
BA
UGH...
RYUZAKI, WE'RE SORRY. HIGUCHI PULLED A GUN AND SHOT THE CHIEF. HE'S ON THE RUN!
I'M ALL RIGHT. SORRY RYUZAKI, HE JUST NICKED MY SHOULDER. WE'LL BE ABLE TO CATCH HIM IF WE FOLLOW HIM.
HURRY!
DASH
WHUP WHUP WHUP WHUP WHUP
DAMN, HE'S ESCAPED SAKURA TV.
...

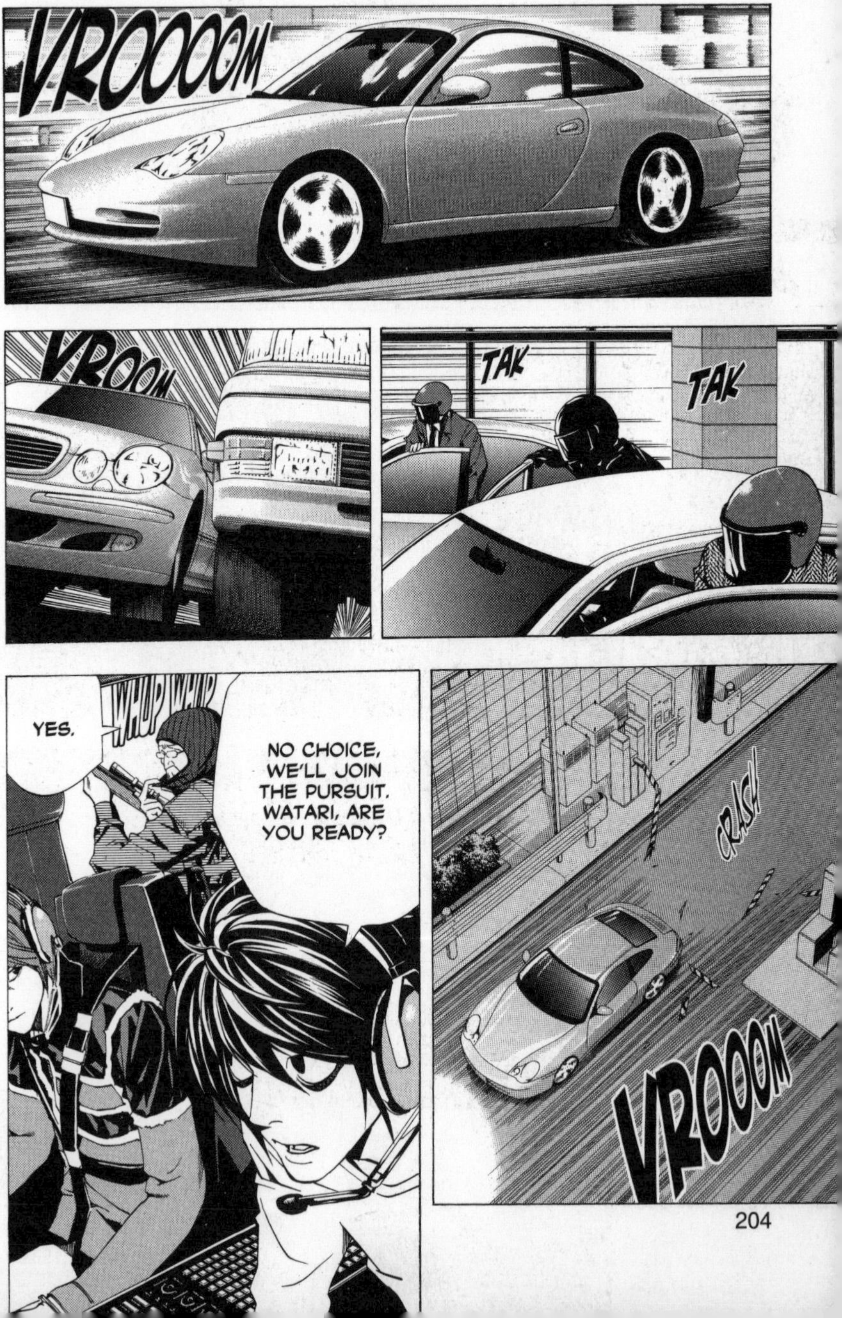
VROOOOM
TAK
TAK
VROOM
CRASH
VROOOM
WHUP WHIP
NO CHOICE, WE'LL JOIN THE PURSUIT. WATARI, ARE YOU READY?
YES.

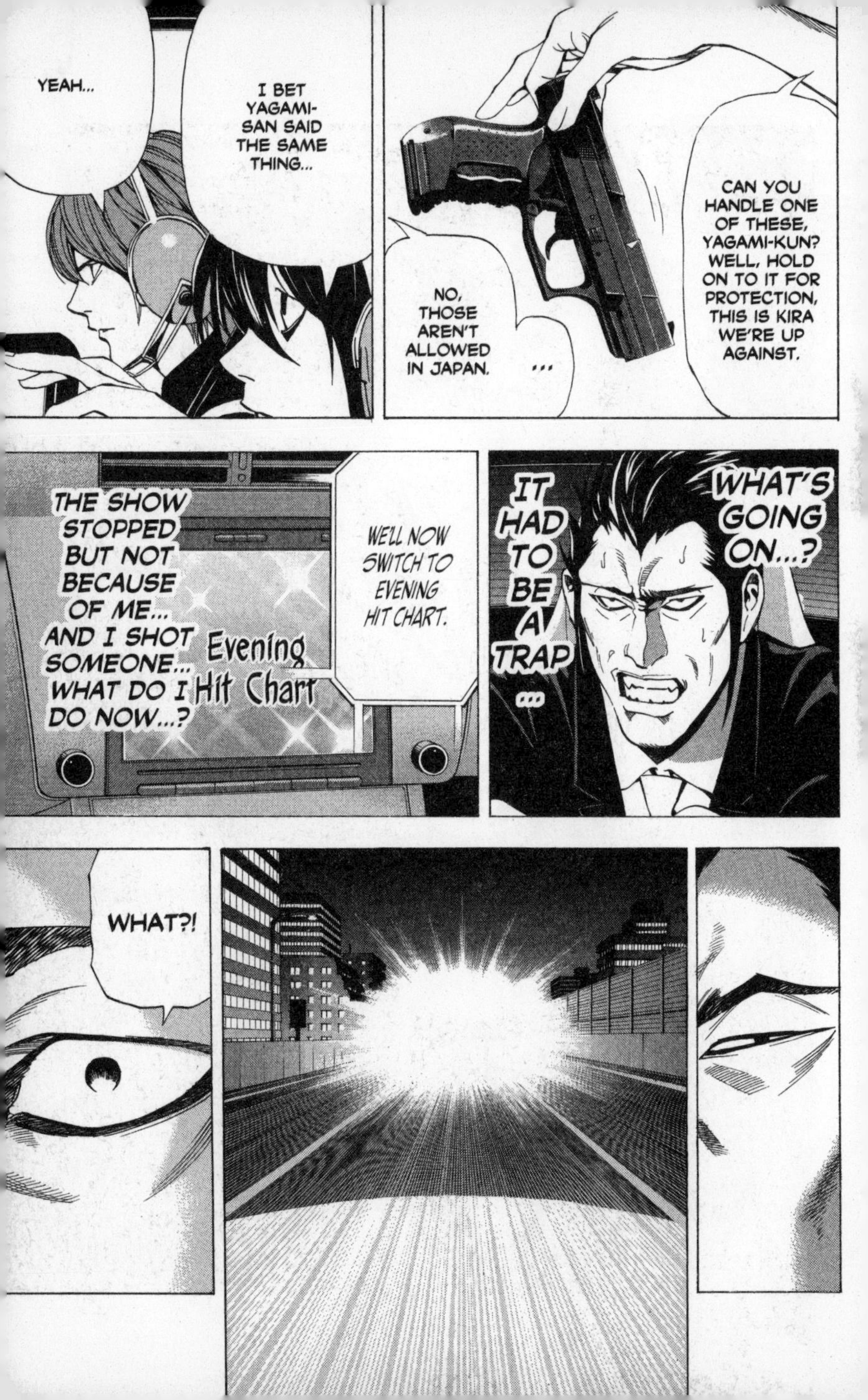
CAN YOU HANDLE ONE OF THESE, YAGAMI-KUN? WELL, HOLD ON TO IT FOR PROTECTION, THIS IS KIRA WE'RE UP AGAINST.
...
NO, THOSE AREN'T ALLOWED IN JAPAN.
I BET YAGAMI-SAN SAID THE SAME THING...
YEAH...
WHAT'S GOING ON...?
IT HAD TO BE A TRAP...
WE'LL NOW SWITCH TO EVENING HIT CHART.
Evening Hit Chart
THE SHOW STOPPED BUT NOT BECAUSE OF ME... AND I SHOT SOMEONE... WHAT DO I DO NOW...?
WHAT?!

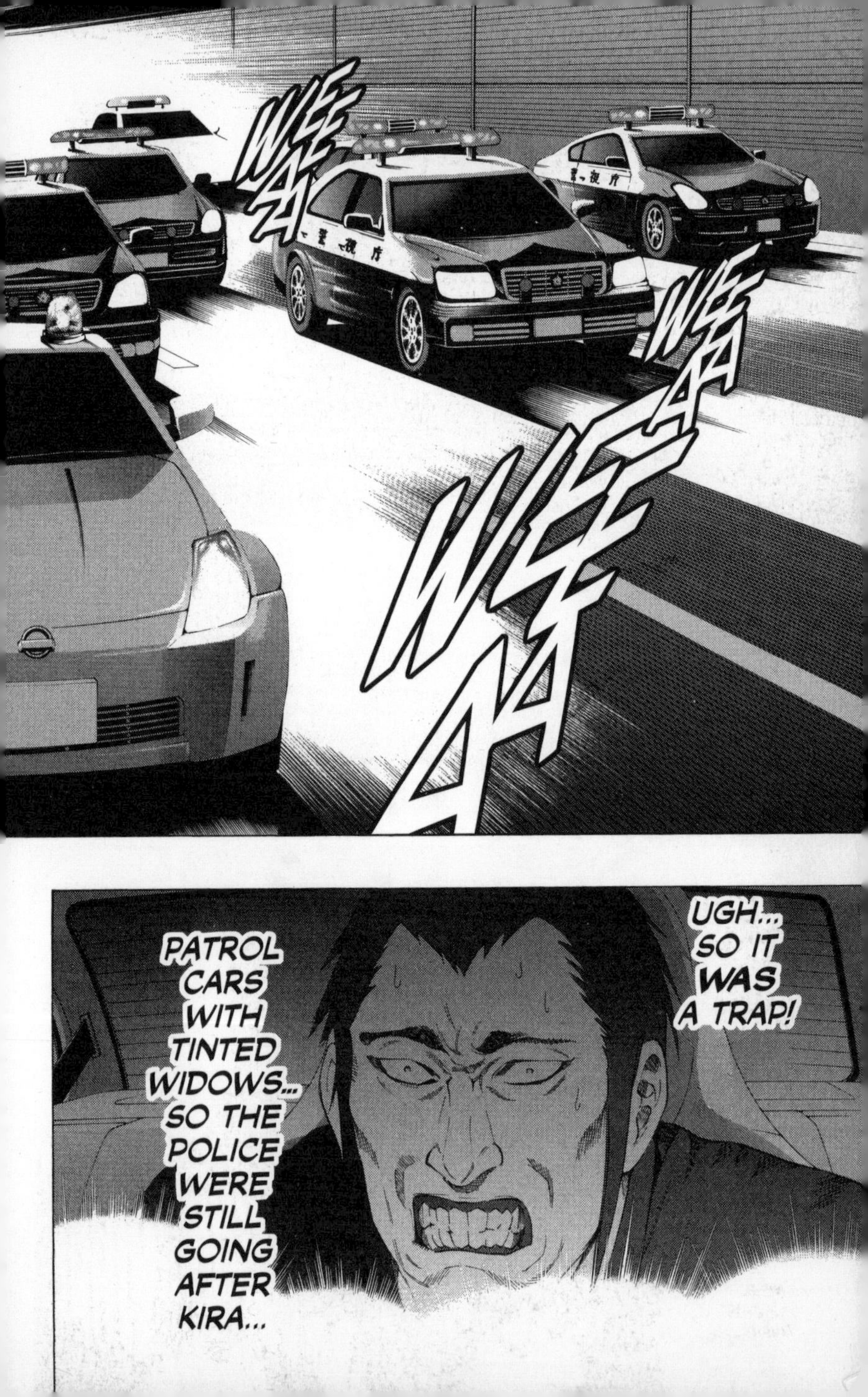
WEEAA
WEEAA
WEEAAA
UGH... SO IT WAS A TRAP!
PATROL CARS WITH TINTED WIDOWS... SO THE POLICE WERE STILL GOING AFTER KIRA...

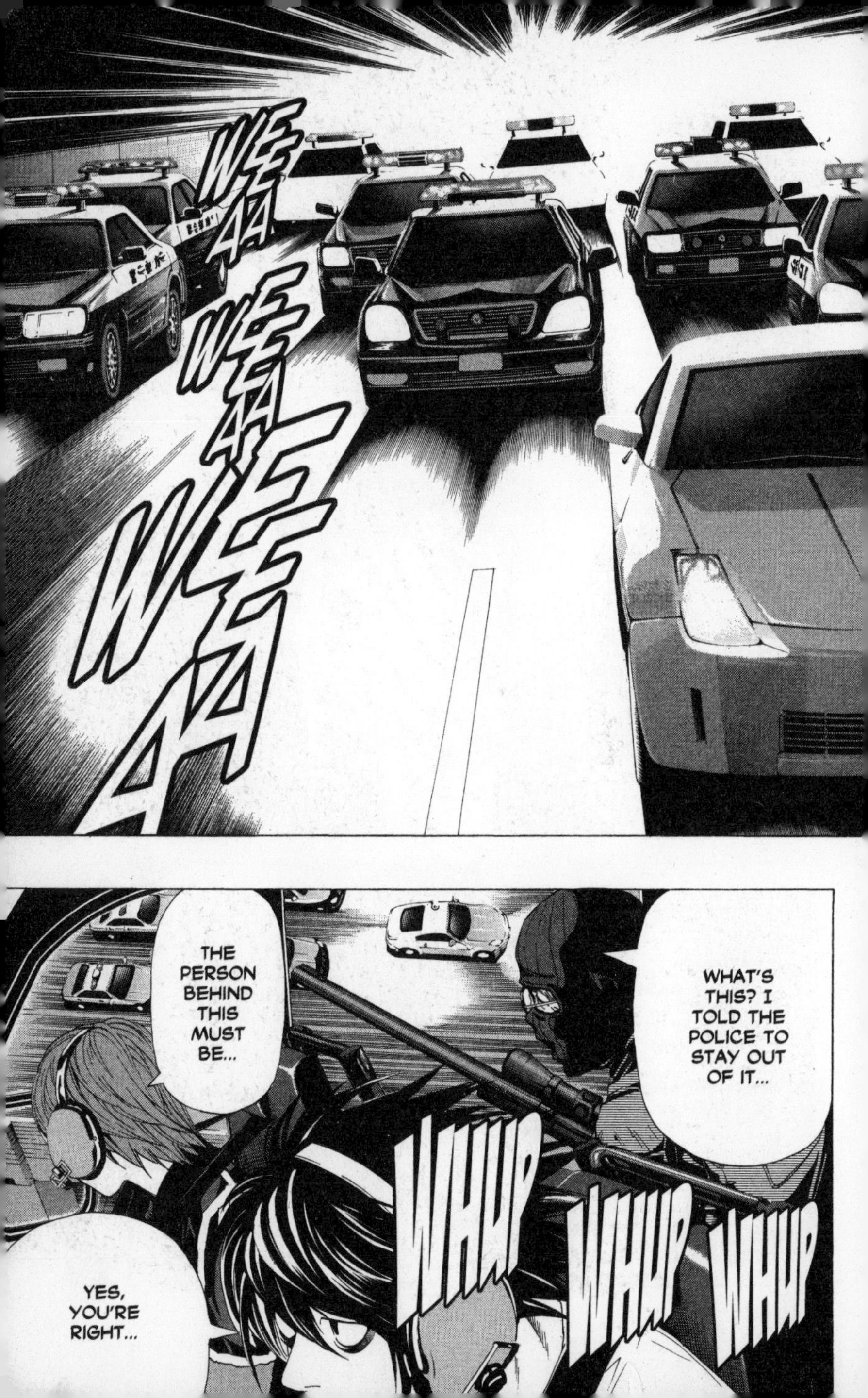
WEE AA
WEE AA
WEE AA
WHAT'S THIS? I TOLD THE POLICE TO STAY OUT OF IT...
THE PERSON BEHIND THIS MUST BE...
YES, YOU'RE RIGHT...
WHUP
WHUP
WHUP

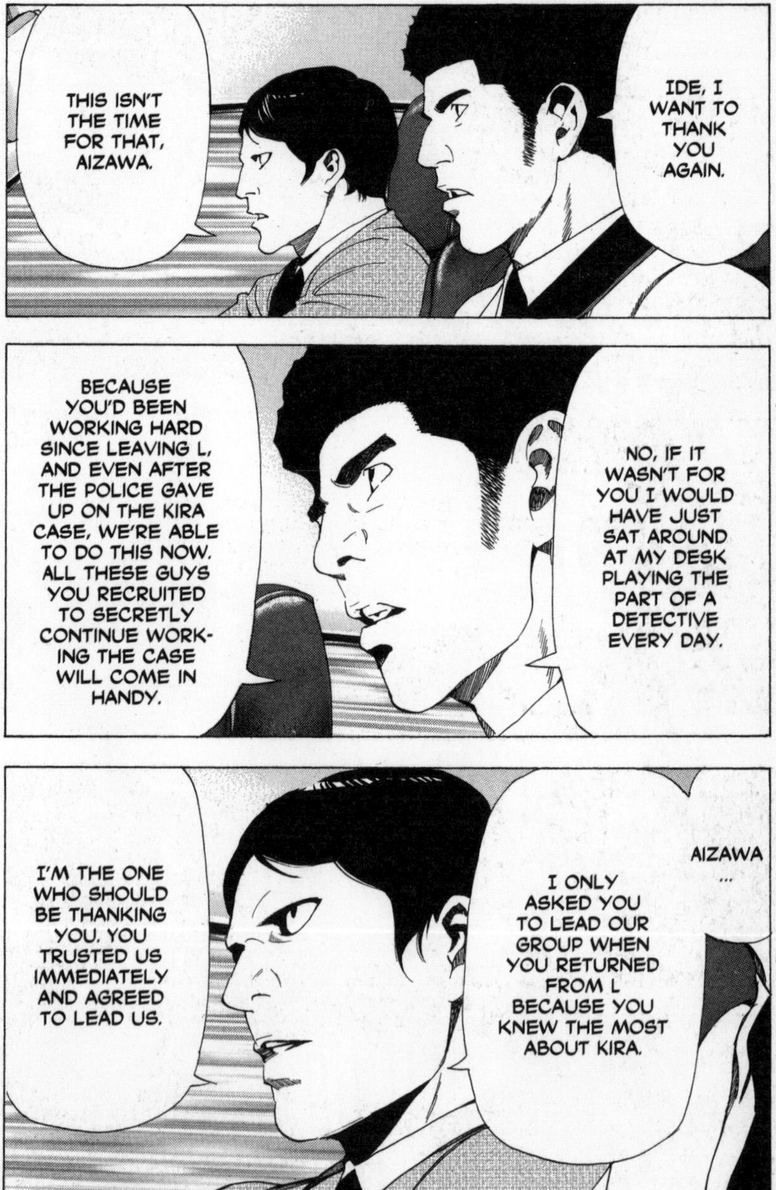
IDE, I WANT TO THANK YOU AGAIN.
THIS ISN'T THE TIME FOR THAT, AIZAWA.
NO, IF IT WASN'T FOR YOU I WOULD HAVE JUST SAT AROUND AT MY DESK PLAYING THE PART OF A DETECTIVE EVERY DAY.
BECAUSE YOU'D BEEN WORKING HARD SINCE LEAVING L, AND EVEN AFTER THE POLICE GAVE UP ON THE KIRA CASE, WE'RE ABLE TO DO THIS NOW. ALL THESE GUYS YOU RECRUITED TO SECRETLY CONTINUE WORK-ING THE CASE WILL COME IN HANDY.
AIZAWA ...
I ONLY ASKED YOU TO LEAD OUR GROUP WHEN YOU RETURNED FROM L BECAUSE YOU KNEW THE MOST ABOUT KIRA.
I'M THE ONE WHO SHOULD BE THANKING YOU. YOU TRUSTED US IMMEDIATELY AND AGREED TO LEAD US.

READ THIS WAY

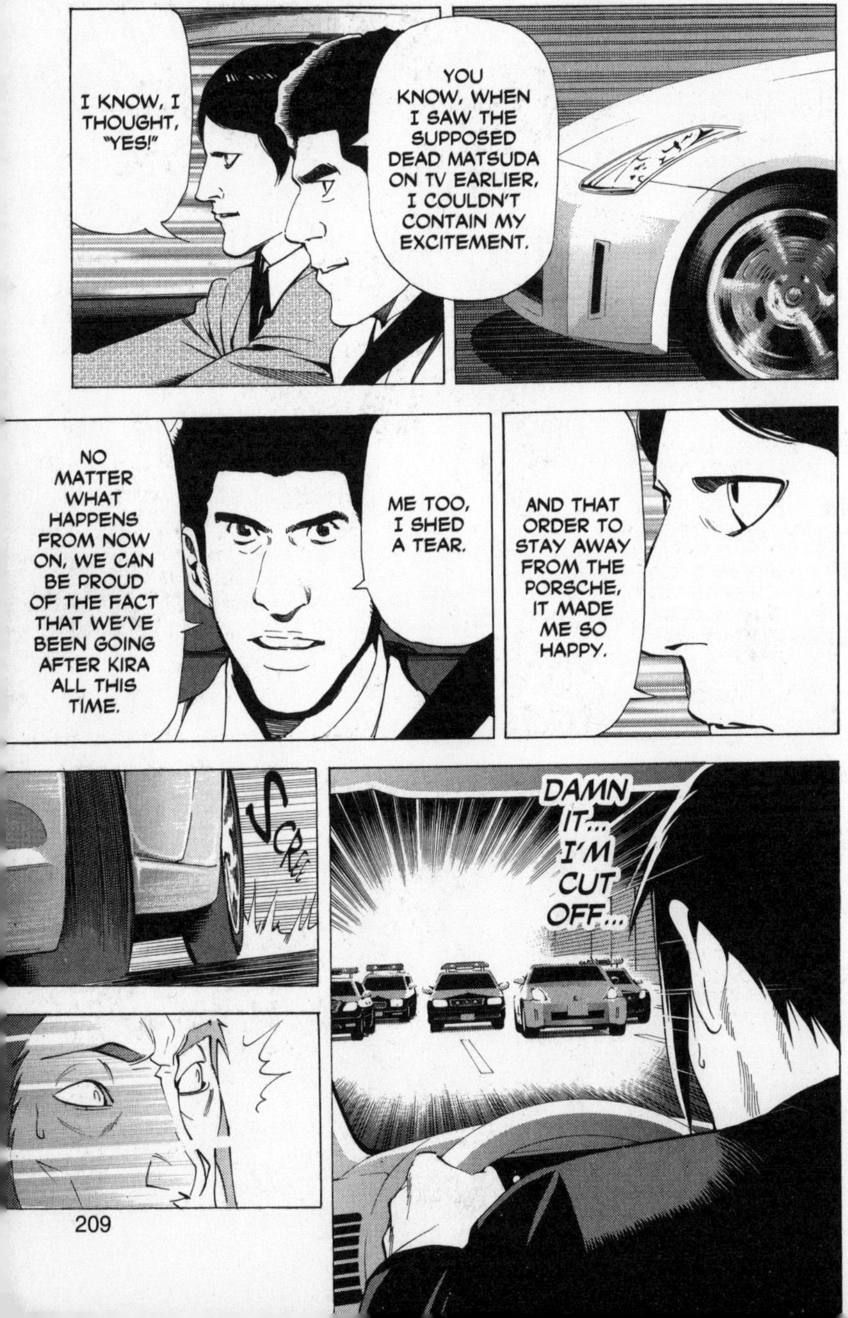

YOU KNOW, WHEN I SAW THE SUPPOSED DEAD MATSUDA ON TV EARLIER, I COULDN'T CONTAIN MY EXCITEMENT.
I KNOW, I THOUGHT, "YES!"
AND THAT ORDER TO STAY AWAY FROM THE PORSCHE, IT MADE ME SO HAPPY.
ME TOO, I SHED A TEAR.
NO MATTER WHAT HAPPENS FROM NOW ON, WE CAN BE PROUD OF THE FACT THAT WE'VE BEEN GOING AFTER KIRA ALL THIS TIME.
DAMN IT... I'M CUT OFF...
SCREE

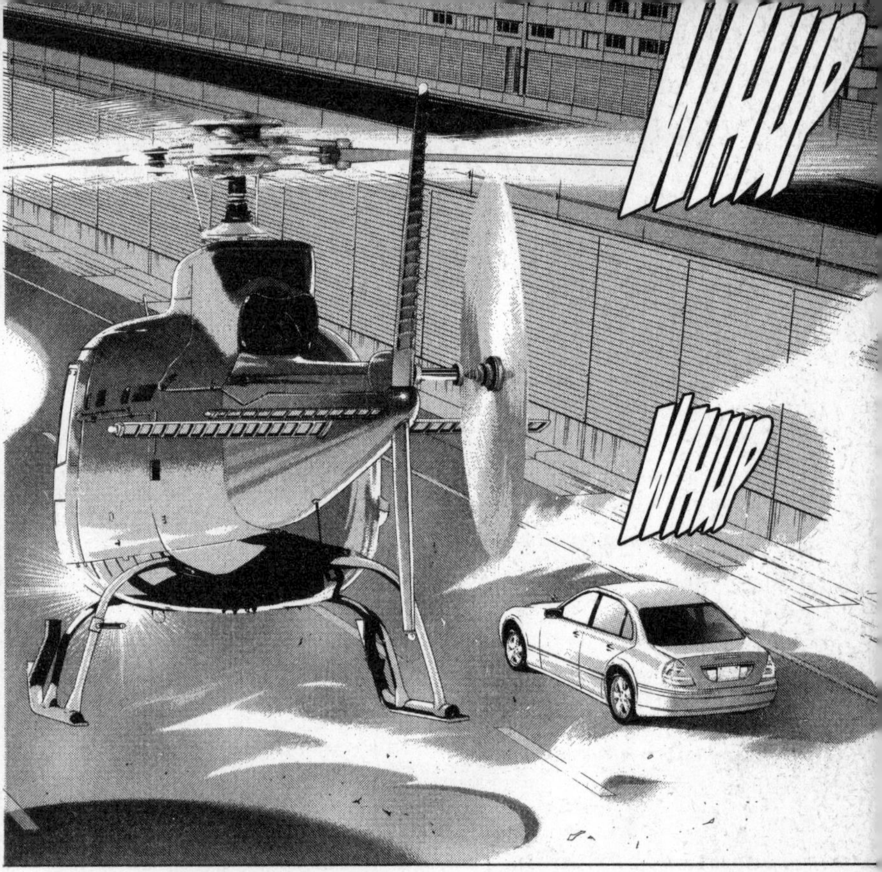
WHUP
WHUP
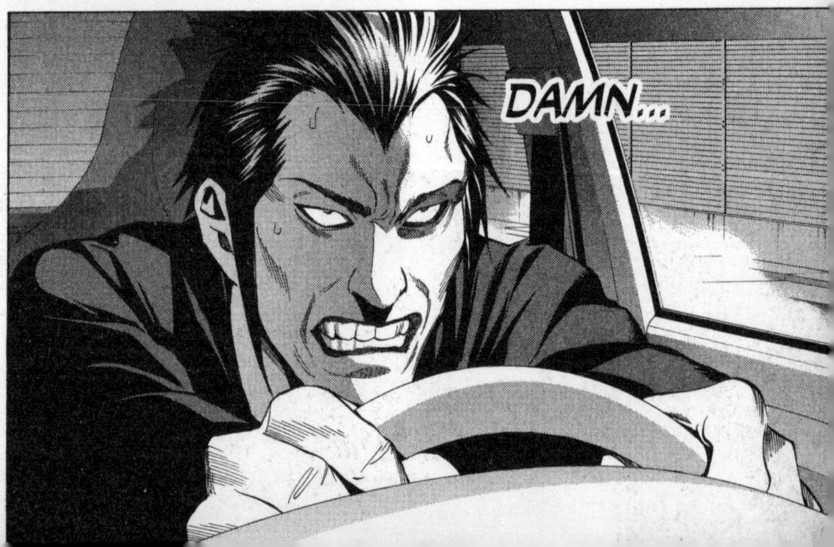
DAMN...

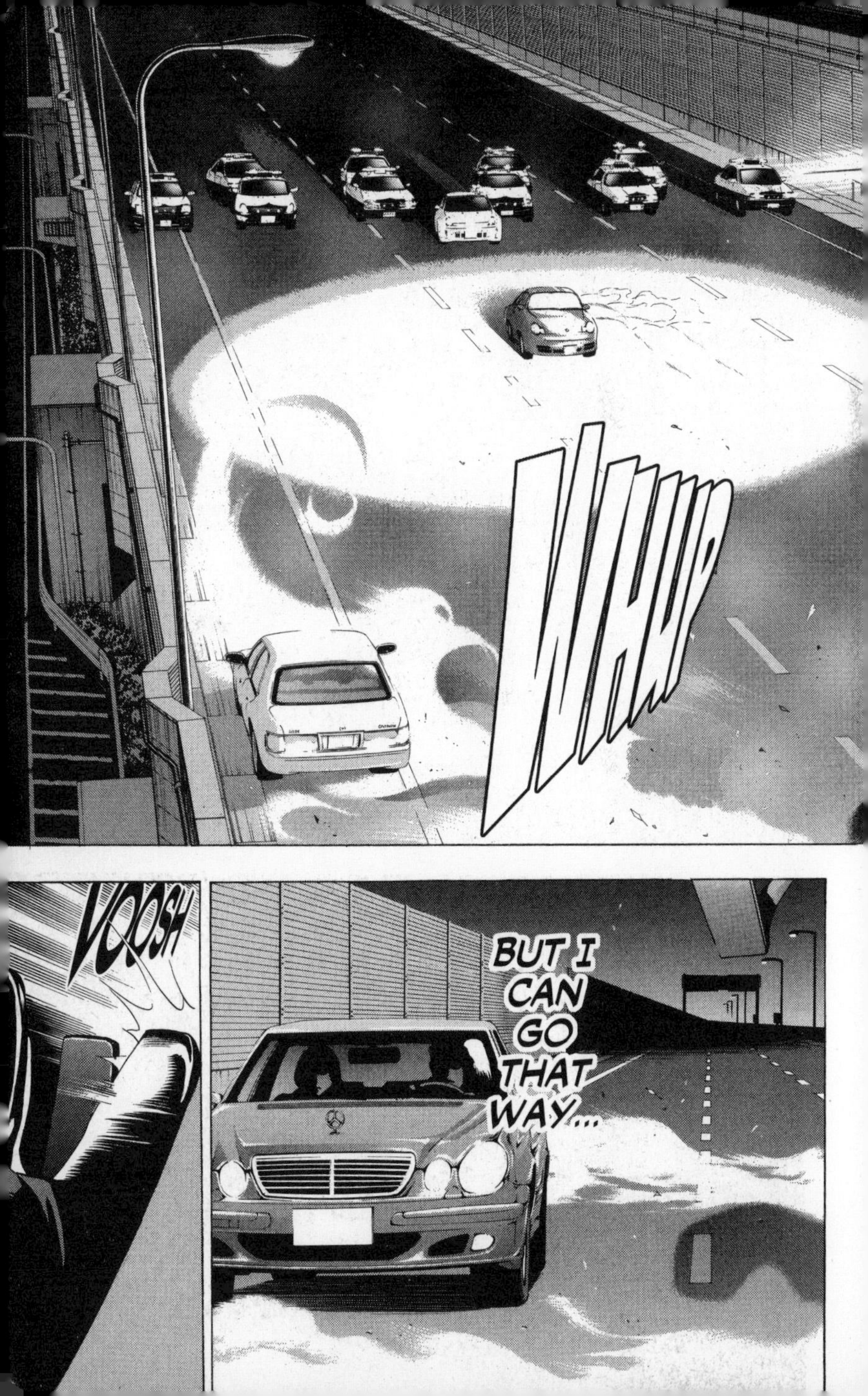
WHUP
BUT I CAN GO THAT WAY...
VOOSH

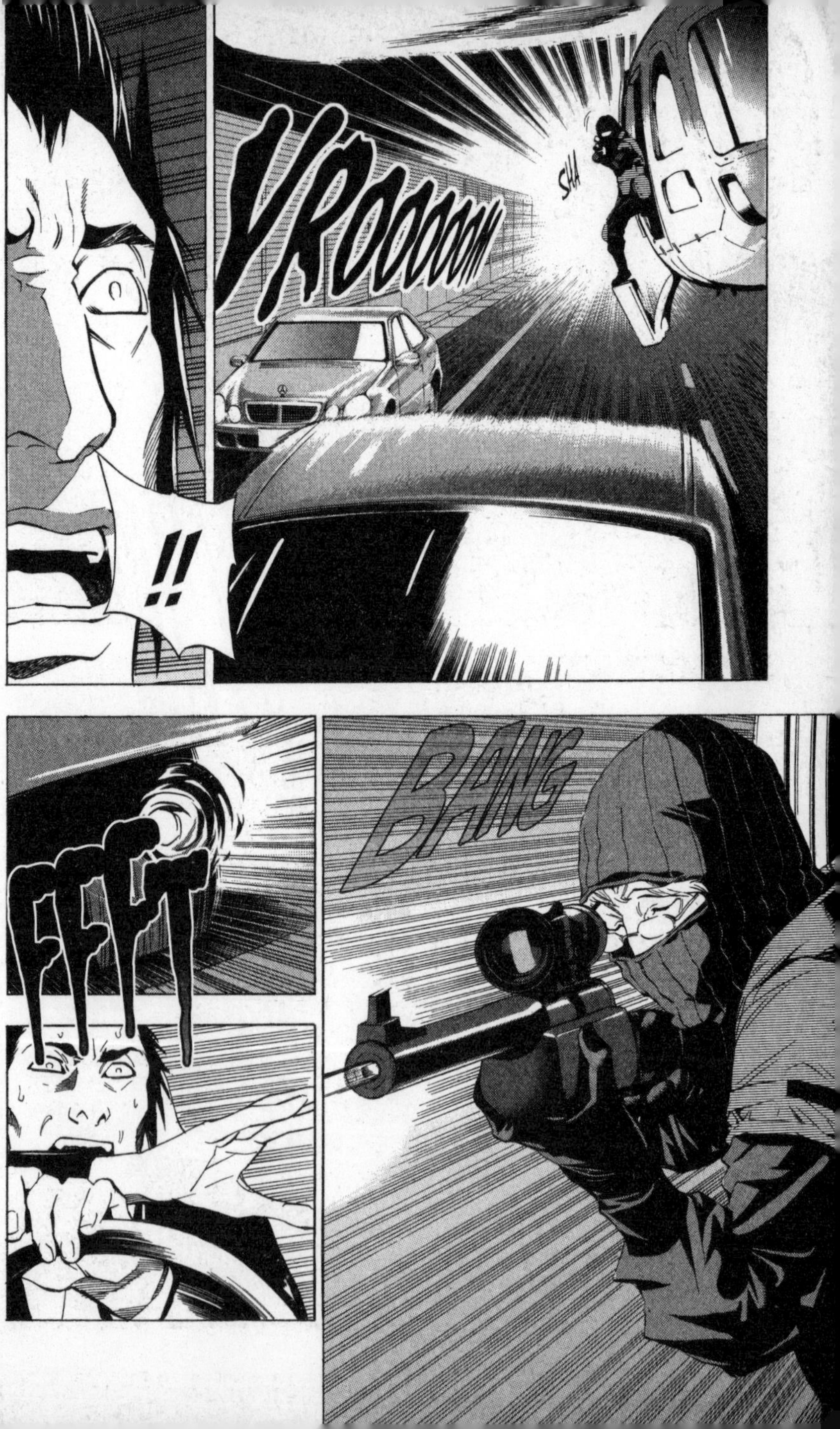
VROOOOOM
SHA
!!
BANG
FFFT

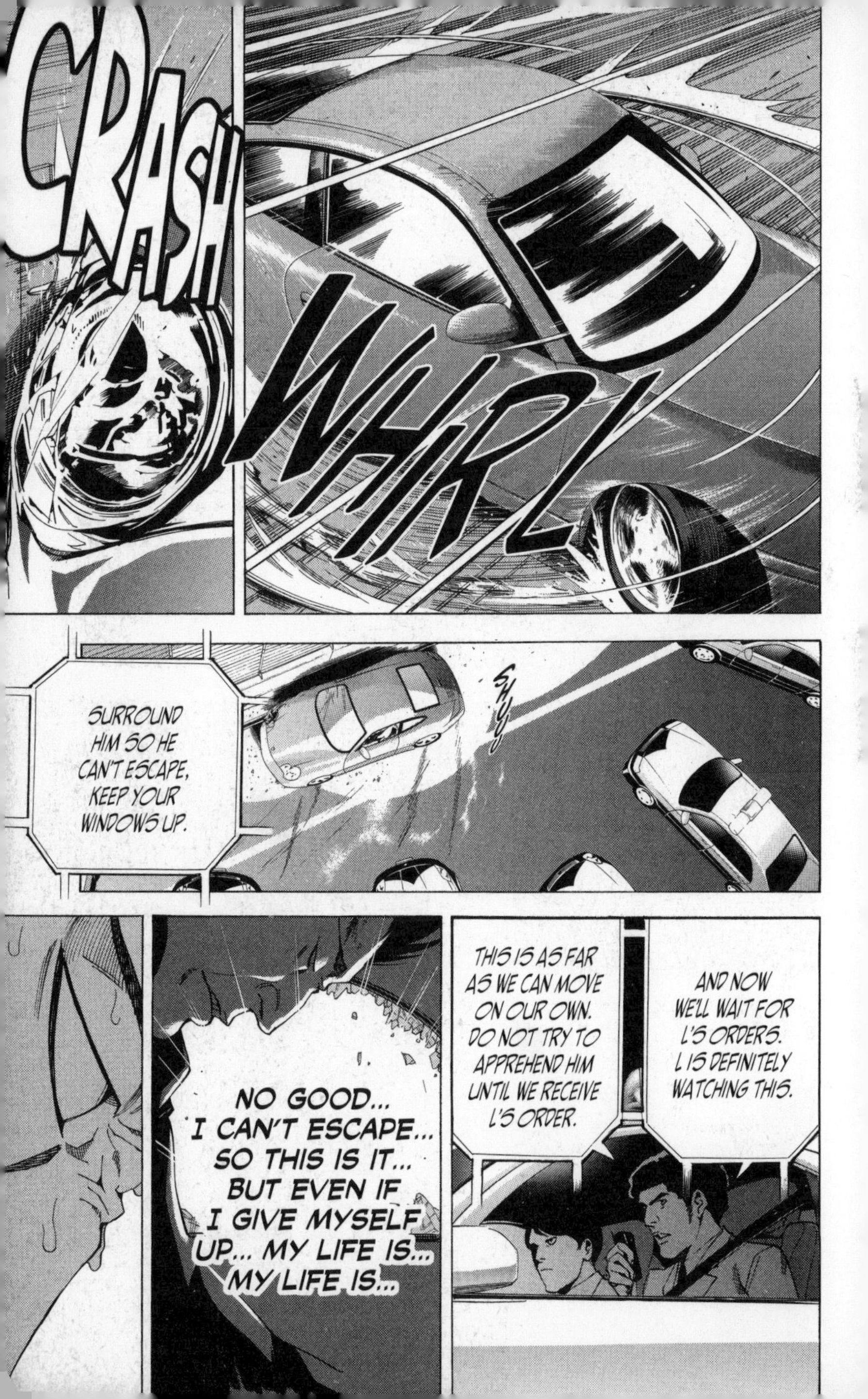
WHIRL
CRASH
SURROUND HIM SO HE CAN'T ESCAPE, KEEP YOUR WINDOWS UP.
SHUUU
AND NOW WE'LL WAIT FOR L'S ORDERS. L IS DEFINITELY WATCHING THIS.
THIS IS AS FAR AS WE CAN MOVE ON OUR OWN. DO NOT TRY TO APPREHEND HIM UNTIL WE RECEIVE L'S ORDER.
NO GOOD... I CAN'T ESCAPE... SO THIS IS IT... BUT EVEN IF I GIVE MYSELF UP... MY LIFE IS... MY LIFE IS...

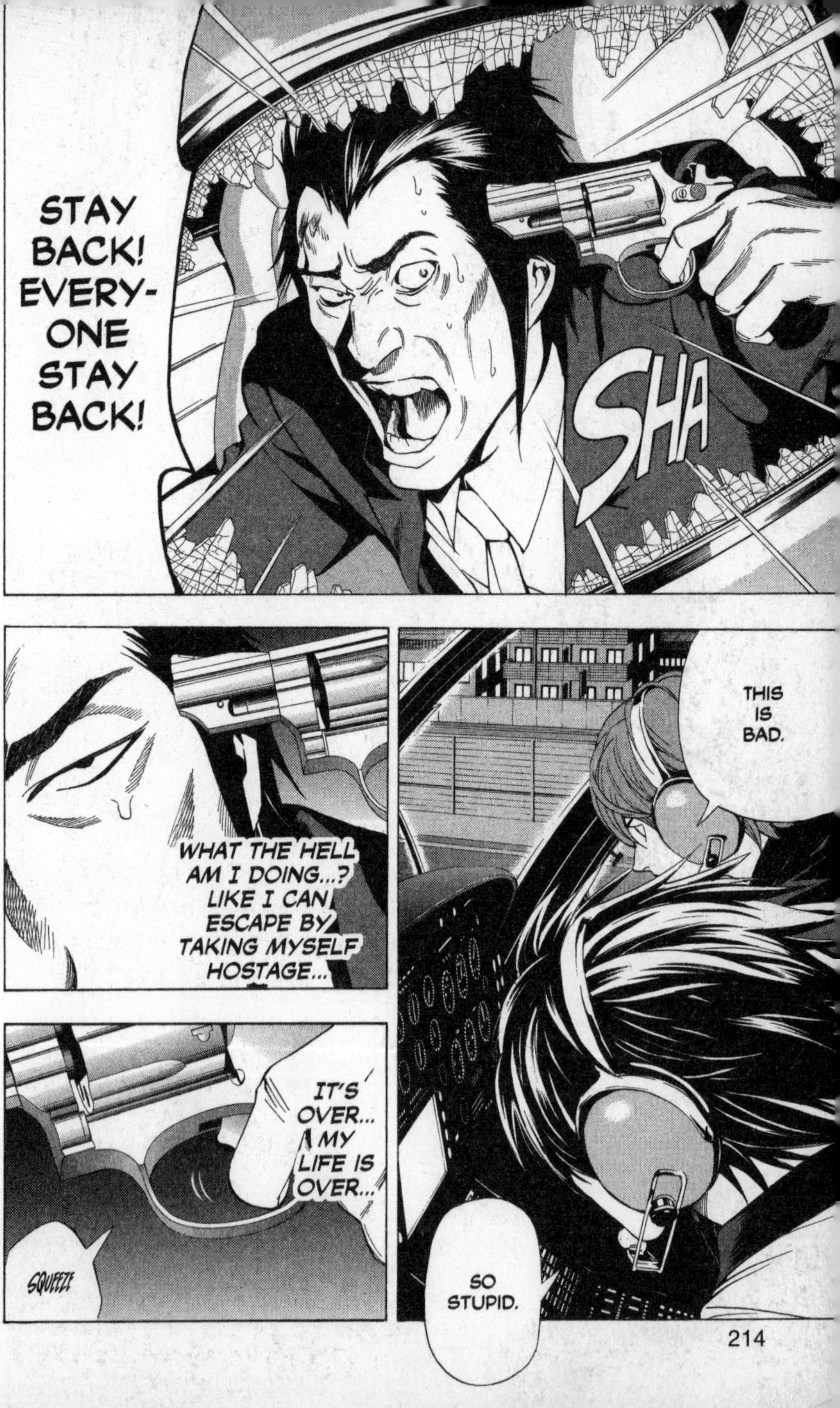
STAY BACK! EVERY-ONE STAY BACK!
SHA
THIS IS BAD.
SO STUPID.
WHAT THE HELL AM I DOING...? LIKE I CAN ESCAPE BY TAKING MYSELF HOSTAGE...
IT'S OVER... MY LIFE IS OVER...
SQUEEZE

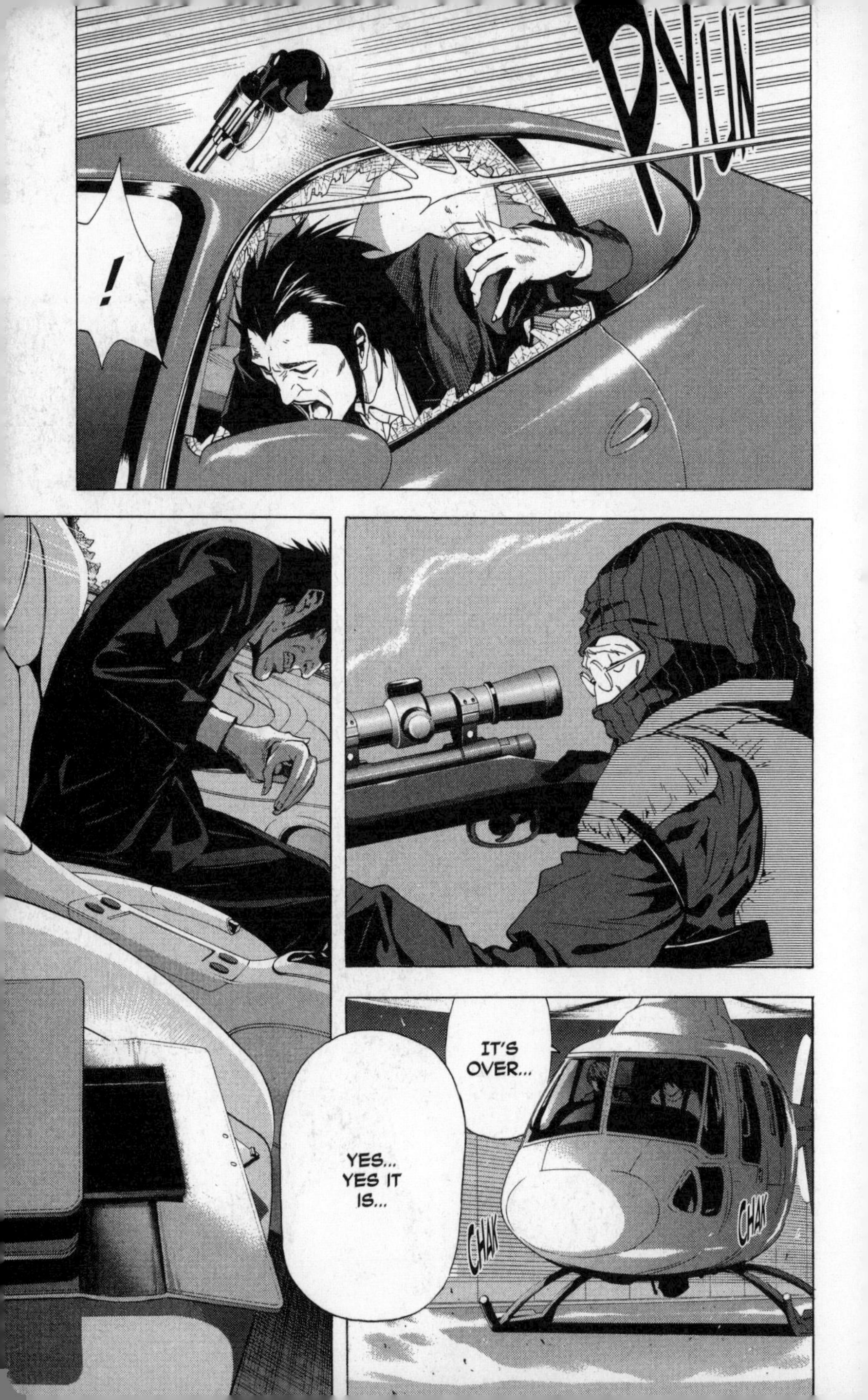
PYUN
!
IT'S OVER...
YES... YES IT IS...
CHAK
CHAK

DEATH NOTE

How to use it

XXXVI

- There are male and female gods of death, but it is neither permitted, nor possible for them to have sexual relations with humans. The gods of death also cannot have sex with each other.

死神(しにがみ)にはオス・メスがあるが、
人間(にんげん)との生殖行為(せいしょくこうい)は許(ゆる)されないし不可能(ふかのう)であり、
死神同士(しにがみどうし)も交尾(こうび)はしない。